Uncertain Empire

Uncertain Empire

American History and the Idea of the Cold War

EDITED BY JOEL ISAAC AND DUNCAN BELL

OXFORD
UNIVERSITY PRESS

Oxford University Press is a department of the University of Oxford.
It furthers the University's objective of excellence in research,
scholarship, and education by publishing worldwide.

Oxford New York
Auckland Cape Town Dar es Salaam Hong Kong Karachi
Kuala Lumpur Madrid Melbourne Mexico City Nairobi
New Delhi Shanghai Taipei Toronto

With offices in
Argentina Austria Brazil Chile Czech Republic France Greece
Guatemala Hungary Italy Japan Poland Portugal Singapore
South Korea Switzerland Thailand Turkey Ukraine Vietnam

Published in the United States of America by Oxford University Press
198 Madison Avenue, New York, NY 10016

www.oup.com

Library of Congress Cataloging-in-Publication Data
Uncertain empire : American history and the idea of the Cold War / edited by Joel Isaac and Duncan Bell.
p. cm.
Includes bibliographical references and index.
ISBN 978-0-19-982612-4 (hardcover : alk. paper)—ISBN 978-0-19-982614-8 (pbk. : alk. paper)
1. Politics and culture—United States—History—20th century.
2. Cold War—Social aspects—United States.
3. Cold War—Historiography. 4. World politics—1945–1989.
5. United States—Intellectual life—20th century.
6. United States—Foreign relations—Soviet Union.
7. Soviet Union—Foreign relations—United States.
I. Isaac, Joel, 1978– II. Bell, Duncan, 1976–
E169.12.U478 2012
973.91—dc23 2012003132

1 3 5 7 9 8 6 4 2

Printed in the United States of America
on acid-free paper

CONTENTS

ACKNOWLEDGMENTS

In its earliest stages, this book project was supported by the Trevelyan Fund of the Faculty of History, University of Cambridge. Planning for the volume was also greatly aided by a conference held at Jesus College, Cambridge, in April 2007. Our thanks to all of the participants in the conference for their contributions. At a critical stage in the development of the manuscript, Eric Foner offered invaluable advice and encouragement. Finally, the editors wish to thank Susan Ferber at OUP for her extensive and unflagging support in bringing the volume to completion.

CONTRIBUTORS

Duncan Bell is Senior Lecturer in Politics and International Studies at the University of Cambridge and a Fellow of Christ's College.

Steven Belletto is Assistant Professor of English at Lafayette College.

Paul S. Boyer was Merle Curti Professor of History Emeritus at the University of Wisconsin-Madison.

Ann Douglas is Parr Professor of Comparative Literature at Columbia University.

Sharon Ghamari-Tabrizi is an independent scholar.

Joel Isaac is Lecturer in the History of Modern Political Thought at the University of Cambridge and a Fellow of Christ's College.

Peter Mandler is Professor of Modern Cultural History at the University of Cambridge and a Fellow of Gonville and Caius College.

Dan Matlin is Lecturer in the History of the United States of America since 1865 at Kings College London.

Philip Mirowski is Carl Koch Professor of Economics and the History and Philosophy of Science at the University of Notre Dame.

Andrew Preston is Senior Lecturer in American History at the University of Cambridge and a Fellow of Clare College.

Anders Stephanson is Andrew and Virginia Rudd Family Foundation Professor of History at Columbia University.

Moshik Temkin is Assistant Professor of Public Policy at the John F. Kennedy School of Government, Harvard University.

John Thompson is Reader Emeritus in American History at the University of Cambridge and a Fellow of St. Catherine's College.

Odd Arne Westad is Professor of International History at the London School of Economics and Political Science.

Uncertain Empire

Introduction

JOEL ISAAC AND DUNCAN BELL

Few concepts in the study of American history are in greater need of clarification than the idea of the Cold War. So ubiquitous has this idea become that it seems a trivial aspect of our understanding of the post–World War II decades. This book shows that the concept of the Cold War is far from trivial and that when we attend to its multiple meanings and historical significance, we can gain new and enriching perspectives on twentieth-century American history.

Before the fall of the Berlin Wall, historians of the United States labored mightily to understand the diplomatic origins and domestic consequences of the geopolitical battle of wills between the United States of America and the Soviet Union; they invoked "the Cold War"—a phrase made famous by the journalist Walter Lippmann—in order to make sense of the fraught and complex "armed peace" that defined modern international relations. Since the collapse of the Soviet bloc, however, the notion of a Cold War has for many ceased being a source of historical puzzlement and has instead been transformed into a rubric that itself explains much about postwar American politics and culture. The explanandum has morphed into the explanans. In recent historical scholarship, the Cold War is frequently conjured up as the name of a political order or worldview that was responsible for key features of post-1945 American history. The term "Cold War" has been transfigured from a noun into an adjective: we are today urged to examine "Cold War science," "Cold War civil rights," and, indeed, "Cold War America" itself. Crucially, the assumptions about the nature of the Cold War that underpin these diverse histories—assumptions about periodization, key themes, and methods of analysis—are themselves rarely interrogated. Historians seldom ask what role the idea of "the Cold War" has come to play in the historiography of the United States. What exactly do we mean when we identify a policy or an idea as a "Cold War" phenomenon? Just how metaphorical or ambiguous is the concept of the Cold War? How ambiguous should it be? Do we all agree on its chronology and does it matter if we do not?

Historical discussions concerning the idea of the Cold War present more than a conceptual problem. Such debates, once begun, ought to have practical implications for scholarship. A further aim of this book is to bring those implications out into the open. One reason why this enterprise seems worth pursuing is that the field of "Cold War history" has never been more varied in its methods and concerns. As the wide range of descriptive uses of the term "Cold War" make clear, historians are now finding manifestations of characteristically "Cold War" mentalities and practices across a considerable expanse of American history: from the history of science and technology to the study of religious institutions and race relations; from the local to the global and transnational; from statecraft to architecture—the list goes on.[1] In contemporary scholarship, the Cold War is therefore no longer confined in its significance to great power summits and military skirmishes; it now ramifies out into the entire domain of postwar American history—politics, culture, technology, and intellectual life. Indeed, the recent transnational turn in the study of American history means that the diversity of Cold War studies cannot even be contained within national boundaries. The peoples of the Southern hemisphere were not just implicated in the American-Soviet battle for the "soul of mankind."[2] Rather, their regional and international histories represent sites of "Cold War" developments equal to, but distinct from, the locking of horns between the White House and the Kremlin. The splintered paradigm of "the global Cold War" now rivals the monolithic vision of "*The* Cold War."[3]

It is clear, then, that what seem at first purely conceptual problems with the idea of the Cold War are also practical ones: how do scholars study the Cold War, and what connections, if any, do the different disciplines or subfields in Cold War studies share? From a variety of perspectives, the contributors to this volume revisit the concept of the Cold War in American history in order to explore its definitions, to test its limits, and to see what claims the experience of the United States has on a moniker now invoked by historians arrayed across a wide spectrum of regional specialisms and disciplinary commitments. Drawing from the resources of diplomatic, cultural, and intellectual history, as well as social theory, comparative literature, and the history of science, our contributors explore the chronological boundaries and thematic uniformity of "the Cold War" in an American context.

"But why," a skeptic might ask, "is this exercise necessary? Surely scholars of the cold war have enough archival research to do without having to interest themselves in 'metahistorical' issues?" On the contrary, we propose that a meditation on conceptual matters of method, definition, and periodization is not just overdue: it can also help further to stimulate and shape the rich archival studies on which the field is built. Cold War historians have often divided up their chosen period under such rubrics as the era of détente, the "second" Cold

War under the leadership of Ronald Reagan, and so on.[4] But little attention has been paid to the intellectual consequences of thinking about all of this as "the Cold War" in the first place. Because of the field's rapid expansion over the last decade, its empirical and methodological boundaries are in flux; the prospects for synthesis, meanwhile, are being widely canvassed.[5] At such a moment, a return to conceptual and methodological fundamentals seems especially apt.

Work on this task must begin more or less from scratch. As Anders Stephanson points out in Chapter 1, the ubiquity of "the Cold War" as an all-purpose rubric in contemporary scholarship has been accompanied by a conspicuous lack of interest in its definition, origins, and explanatory power. This claim is true even of those justly lauded innovations in Cold War history in which new and important dimensions of postwar culture and politics have been uncovered.[6] In many such instances, the *modalities* of the Cold War have been questioned, and periodizations adjusted, but the rubric itself—its meaning and proper application—has not been subject to reevaluation or conceptual analysis. Where historians of the early modern period, for example, have long engaged in spirited polemics about the meaning and application of periodizing schemas like "the Industrial Revolution," "the Enlightenment," and even "the early modern" itself, students of the cold war have not always been committed to thematic reflection on their own favored periodizing concept. Why should this be so and what can we expect from an examination of definitional and conceptual fundamentals?

At first blush, there is a simple explanation for the lack of interest in the genealogy of the idea of the Cold War. For many historians, "the Cold War" is little more than a neutral chronological marker, meant to indicate an epoch in international affairs characterized by superpower rivalry between the United States and Soviet Russia, and an American political culture anchored in a narrow set of ideological categories. On this reckoning, "Cold War" is loaded with no more meaning than periodizing schemas like "the interwar years," which is used, of course, to identify the epoch of 1919–1939. Several considerations, however, prevent us from treating the idea of the Cold War quite so lightly as this.

From a purely linguistic point of view, the notion of a cold war rests on a dense web of metaphorical allusions. Historians such as Charles Maier have shown that even apparently anodyne divisions of the past into decades and centuries—e.g., the 1920s, the eighteenth century—are freighted with moral judgments and with normative commitments to particular views about the nature of historical change.[7] This alone should give scholars pause when faced with the dismissal of conceptual questions about the idea of the Cold War. More importantly, the Cold War shares with such grand periodizing schemas as the Renaissance, the Scientific Revolution, the Enlightenment, and the Industrial Revolution a foundation in rich and tendentious metaphor. One cannot simply slough off the ideological baggage and imaginative possibilities that come packaged with the term, for they are in large part what have given "the Cold War" pertinence and descriptive power—both for historians and for historical actors themselves. In the opening chapter of this volume, Anders Stephanson assesses the connotations and conceptual implications—conscious or otherwise—built in to each term of the formula: to speak of "the" rather than "a" cold war is already a rather definite, and not obviously unproblematic, stance to take toward the historical epoch of the postwar decades. We are being told that "cold war" is a singular episode, an intransitive historical concept. The contrast with "hot" war called up by the adjective "cold" in turn imposes a set of imaginative boundaries—notions of stasis, of the rigidity of totalitarian regimes, of the prospect of an "armed peace." Finally, to describe an era that stopped short of armed conflict between the two principal antagonists as nonetheless characterized by the state of "war," albeit a "cold" one, is to place an evocative if still puzzling paradox at the heart of a supposedly straightforward chronological category.

Whether we like it or not, then, the idea of the Cold War is loaded with conceptual possibilities with which we must grapple. That lesson is underscored by the history of the phrase itself. Like "the Renaissance"—but unlike, to take a parallel example, "the Industrial Revolution"—"the Cold War" was an actors' category, and is thereby entangled in the very history that the label is designed to identify.[8] In another forum, Stephanson has traced the origins of the concept of the Cold War[9]; in Chapter 1, he examines the appropriations of the term by American publicists and policymakers after 1945. What is clear from Stephanson's genealogy is that the historical reference points of the term are as complex and malleable as its linguistic connotations. Whereas the figure who introduced the term into American political discourse, Walter Lippmann, sought to adhere to the 1930s usage of the French phrase *guerre froide*—the undeclared or hidden war so often waged in the interwar years and into the "phoney war" of 1939–40—"the Cold War" passed through diplomat George Kennan's widely disseminated vision of the Soviet Union as an implacably hostile, ideologically immobile, frosty enemy, and into the language of NSC-68 and Dean Acheson's avowedly instrumental investment in the globalist worldview of "the Cold War." This is to say nothing of the subsequent uptake and adaptation of the term by commentators, politicians, and academics, both inside and outside the United States.

Such ambiguity should be thought productive for historical scholarship, not fatal. Consider for a moment the notions of the Renaissance and the Industrial Revolution. Much of the work on the historical periods marked out by these terms has hinged on the pertinence and temporal boundaries of the rubrics in question. Famously, the concept of the Renaissance in historical scholarship has gone through at least two major crises. The first reached a peak in the years before World War II and involved a "revolt of the medievalists" in response to

Jacob Burckhardt's claims about the centrality of the Italian Renaissance in understanding the making of the modern world—a world defined by contrast with a purportedly distinct "medieval," or premodern, Europe.[10] Historians such as Charles Homer Haskins sought to resist the notion of a radical break in Western history during the fifteenth century and relocated many of the novelties attributed to the Renaissance as far back as the twelfth century.[11] Although the term was stabilized in Anglophone scholarship in the 1950s—just when a conviction in the liberal development of Western institutions was becoming a fundamental element of political ideology in the West—the idea of the Renaissance entered a second period of crisis in the age of détente, as historians became increasingly wary of relying on a concept that seemed inherently teleological, honorific, and attached to a master narrative of Western civilization.[12] Likewise, the periodizing model of the Industrial Revolution, rooted primarily in the eighteenth century and in Britain, has been the object of polemical criticism, one product of which has been the introduction of surrogate historiographical concepts of wider and more subtle application.[13] The key point here is that such tarrying with technical matters of periodization produces new maps of the past—new and suggestive redescriptions of what, in many instances, was already known. In Renaissance studies, we see accounts of the reappropriation of the culture of antiquity that blend "early modern" with "medieval" history to create a broad and fecund domain for historians.[14] Meanwhile, in the face of a "revolt of the early modernists," the concept of the Industrial Revolution has given way, at least in part, to the more serviceable concept of what Jan de Vries has called an "industrious revolution," centered around the expansion of household consumption and purchasing power, and beginning in the early (as opposed to the late) seventeenth century.[15] Talk of "the Enlightenment" has now given way to the notion of multiple "Enlightenments"—Scottish, French, Italian, and so on, or "radical" and "moderate" programs.[16] Even studies of the Scientific Revolution today look beyond the seminal contributions of Galileo and Newton to a reconfigured landscape produced by more than a generation of scholarship and debate.[17]

Such controversies have been productive precisely because the participants have understood these historiographical categories to be more than a neutral, taken-for-granted shorthand for particular epochs. They are understood, implicitly or explicitly, to explain and order the historical record. In a similar manner, scholars in Cold War studies should seek to foster their own foundational debates about the idea of "the Cold War"—a notion, as we have seen, at least as allusive and elliptical as the Renaissance or the Enlightenment. It seems reasonable to expect such debates to enrich further the study of postwar American history. As Philip Mirowski puts the matter, with a touch of irony, in Chapter 3, such reevaluation, although driving "believers in a simple correspondence theory of truth to distraction, [is] for practitioners . . . a healthy and necessary process." We must always remain aware of the constitutive, knowledge-producing function of these periodizing schemes, even as they are modified, criticized, and repudiated. Moreover, in so packaging the past through our choice of periodization points and rubrics, we cannot help but draw deep lines of inclusion and exclusion, of identity and difference. One of the contributors to this volume, Ann Douglas, has written elsewhere of how the very notion of a homogenous decade or epoch was invented during the 1920s by Americans eager to sell the post–World War I decade as "the Jazz Age."[18]

For good or ill, scholars in Cold War studies are caught in a conceptual and historiographical web of their own making. Although it might be tempting to abandon the term "the Cold War" and its semantic fuzziness in the hope of finding some more neutral epithet, such a move would be both chimerical and poor strategy. Chimerical because new periodizing schemas will themselves become loaded with thematic and analytical commitments—even the apparently flavorless word "postwar" can, as Tony Judt has shown in the case of modern Europe, have several layers of meaning.[19] It is poor strategy to swear off "the Cold War" because the problem is not that we happen to be entangled in its various meanings, but that we must be sure that we are entangled in the most profitable ways. The act of periodization cannot help but generate new historical meanings and angles of vision. One task of professional scholarship is to make those acts of labeling and periodization as self-conscious as possible. We need to be aware of what has been and can be done with a concept, so as to help us master what might be an effective and supple analytical tool.

With these aims in mind, this book adopts a twofold approach. Part I probes the conceptual dimensions of the idea of the Cold War. This section surveys the different historiographical and methodological uses of the notion of the Cold War in political and intellectual history and in literary studies. What, our contributors ask, can and should we do with the concept of the Cold War? This part of the volume is built around a programmatic essay by Anders Stephanson. Stephanson's essay is best understood as a thought experiment in the fullest sense of the term, for his purpose is to rethink the concept and history of the Cold War from the ground up. He begins in an iconoclastic mood, contesting the apparently self-evident view that the Cold War ended when the Soviet Union did. Being an '89er about the end of the Cold War, for Stephanson, is tantamount to legitimizing Ronald Reagan's tendentious attempt to revive the Cold War during the first term of his administration: periodization is ideology. Stephanson carries his ground-clearing operation further by describing three schools of interpretation in Cold War studies, each of which fails in one way or another to specify adequately what sort of historical phenomenon the Cold War was. Where neo-orthodoxy buys into the Reaganite narrative of the Cold War as a terminal struggle between the American-led democratic West and the Soviet-dominated

East, neorealists in the discipline of International Relations have converted the messy historical unfolding of the Cold War into a theoretical "system." If Stephanson finds both of these options unhelpful for making sense of the Cold War *qua* Cold War, much of his ire is reserved for a loose but large cohort of scholars who subscribe to what he calls "amorphous convention." Placed in the framework we outlined above, amorphous convention may be thought of as the product of the growing diffuseness and ubiquity of the Cold War label in the wake of the global and cultural turns in Cold War studies. Stephanson's principal objection to this broad scholarly church is that it treats the idea of the Cold War more or less unreflectively and without analytical rigor.

These criticisms set the scene for Stephanson's alternative periodization of the Cold War, which rests on a genealogy of the term itself as it entered American political discourse after 1945. In order to combat the "natural" periodization and thematization of the Cold War, Stephanson introduces some linguistic novelties ("coldwar," "thirdworld," and so on) and offers a critique of the turn toward viewing within a "Cold War" framework the postcolonial interventions by the United States and the Soviet Union during the 1960s and beyond. Behind these polemical flourishes stands Stephanson's fullest statement yet of his interpretation of the Cold War. For him, the Cold War was an American project, a work of ideology whose function was not to get the geopolitical state-of-play at any given moment "right," but instead to provide legitimating cover for American globalism at home and abroad. Cold War policy, he observes "proved extraordinarily successful for the promotion of the interests of the United States in the world. 'The Cold War' became a matrix that made unarguable, indeed imperative, a truly globalist role for the United States, a role which it was to play to great advantage for quite some time."

The other essays in Part I offer responses to Stephanson's claims from different historiographical and disciplinary perspectives. Their aim is not so much to vindicate or repudiate Stephanson's thesis about the conceptual and historical structure of the Cold War, as to use it as a platform for sketches of contrasting visions of the idea itself. In Chapter 2, Odd Arne Westad presents a bracing critique of Stephanson's "centering" of the Cold War. Westad rejects on methodological and historical grounds the view that the Cold War was an exclusively American project. Methodologically, he advocates a pluralistic and pragmatic notion of the Cold War, which would treat it as an object—Westad describes it as the "elephant in the room" of most contemporary political conversation—that can fruitfully be investigated on several different levels and from a variety of perspectives. He also questions whether Stephanson's strict periodization of the Cold War according to America's diplomatic stance toward the Soviet Union exhausts the contexts in which the idea of the Cold War actually mattered. As an actor's category, Westad argues, the Cold War was salient not just to Americans, but also to Russian,

Chinese, and "Third World" political elites and social movements—and this was true well into the period in which Stephanson sees a post–Cold War framework emerging in international politics. Westad concludes by proposing the schema of "Cold War conceptualism." This periodizing device would focus on the dispersion and adaption of rival American and Soviet models of development during the second half of the twentieth century. Conceptualism would focus on the battle of these ideas in their global intellectual, cultural, and social context, with an eye on the transmissions and transformations of networks of ideology. Westad wields the concept of the Cold War so as to pluralize the history of the postwar years, rather than "center" it, as Stephanson seeks to do.

In Chapters 3 and 4, Philip Mirowski and Steven Belletto, respectively, consider these issues from rather different vantage points, one exploring the sciences, both natural and social, the other focusing on the realm of cultural, and especially literary, production. Mirowski offers a trenchant defense of the importance of the idea of the Cold War in intellectual history and the history of science. Making common cause with Stephanson, he suggests that the history of the human and natural sciences between World War II and the early 1970s is "a dish best served cold." Only the positing of the Cold War as a thoroughgoing ideological project carried on in the United States, which had in turn a very particular set of chronological boundaries, can explain the shifting foundations of patronage, disciplinization, and research in American science during the postwar decades. Yet Mirowski differs from Stephanson in his periodization. Whereas for Stephanson the Cold War began in the immediate postwar years and effectively ended in the early 1960s, Mirowski argues that, from the perspective of intellectual history, the "Cold War" regime in science and academic life was imposed during World War II and remained the overarching ideological formation until circa 1980. Thereafter it was superseded by a neoliberal system of patronage that fundamentally challenged many of the epistemological and political principles of Cold War-era science. Mirowski also outlines a provisional unifying theme in several major areas of American thought during this period: the "closed world ontologies" drawn from computer science and registered in all manner of philosophical and social-scientific studies from the late 1940s through the 1970s.

Steven Belletto, meanwhile, asks what the concept of the Cold War has done, and might yet do, in literary studies. While finding in the politicized forms of American literature expressions of the ideological project that Stephanson identifies with the Cold War, Belletto also traces a shift away from a "containment" hermeneutic in cultural studies toward "integration models" that highlight the centrifugal pressures placed on the ideological project of the Cold War by the very exercise of globalism in American politics. In this respect, Belletto points toward a middle path between Stephanson's enterprise of centralization and the pluralism of Westad. Both positions can accommodate the increasingly international concerns of American literature as the United States became more deeply engaged in Southeast Asia, Latin America, and Africa.

Taken together, these four chapters allow a more self-conscious, "instrumental" view of the kind of work that the concept of the Cold War can do—and is doing—in the multidisciplinary field of Cold War studies. In bringing together debates about periodization with questions of proper thematization, they help to provide the idea of the Cold War with a richer and more productive set of possibilities. But how might this wider conceptual palette be used in practice? What new perspectives can be found from the latest research on the history of science, technology, religion, music, popular culture, and politics during the Cold War? The essays in Part II address these questions.

The chapters in the second section of the volume cannot, of course, provide anything like a comprehensive response to these pressing historiographical puzzles. Clearly enough, the objects of Cold War studies are now so diverse—encompassing Molotov at one end of the spectrum and *Moby-Dick* at the other—that no single set of essays can be thought to include or unify them all. Nonetheless, the historical investigations in Part II are bound together by two distinct concerns. First, each is in one way or another responsive to the conceptual and methodological issues raised in Part I. Although they are not "case studies" of the models laid out by Stephanson, Westad, Mirowski, and Belletto, they are sensitive to the kind of conceptual work that the idea of the Cold War can do in the writing of American history. Some contributors pick their way through the opposing positions of Stephanson and Westad; others focus more directly on outlining the structures of "Cold War" practices across a range of activities: diplomacy, military training, anthropology, historiography, and so on. These considerations highlight the second common theme. Each of the chapters underscores the contingency, the instrumentality, and the malleability of the idea of the Cold War during the immediate postwar decades. They remind us of the intensive ideological work that had to be undertaken in the United States to make the concept of the Cold War salient and rhetorically effective in postwar American politics, culture, and society. And they show how this jerrybuilt ideological structure was contested, reified, and redeployed from the 1940s through to the 1980s.

We can begin to grasp how these two threads are woven into the essays in Part II by pointing to a thesis shared by Stephanson and Westad. Simply put, the notion that the war-ravaged Soviet Union was, in the immediate postwar years, a rival superpower, bent upon expending vast military and industrial resources to spreading communism across the globe, was a chimera. Westad observes—in a remark quoted by John Thompson in Chapter 5—that "the Soviet Union was never *the other* superpower, the gap that separated the communist regime from the United States in economic achievement, technological innovation, and overall military capability [being] so great that it is impossible to place the two in the same category."[20] This observation about the reality of Soviet power in the late 1940s and early 1950s implies, quite rightly, that the notion of the Cold War—at least in the classical Kennan-Acheson form of a struggle on the part of one superpower (the United States) to contain the expansive power of another (the USSR) across the globe—was a phantasm. But then the question arises of how such overblown estimates of Soviet power could have emerged in the first place, in the face of overwhelming evidence and arguments to the contrary. Considerable ideological work must have been required, because, as Ann Douglas notes, belief in the Cold War was "defined by and predicated on a selective but massive refusal of available information at the top" of American government.

What were the sources of this will to believe in the threat of an all-conquering USSR? The opening three chapters of Part II provide some important answers. John Thompson examines the origins of an axiom of American geopolitical thinking that was to underpin the nation's commitment to the principle of containment during the early years of the Cold War. This was the claim that vital national interests were at stake in the prevention of any one power exercising hegemony over the landmass of Eurasia, and that, as a consequence, US national interests could be seen as global in scope. This formed, and continues to form, a central pillar of the American geopolitical imaginary. The dominance of the USSR over Europe, American political leaders suggested as the Cold War was warming up, would threaten the United States, which could neither compete economically nor defend itself militarily from such a continental behemoth. The flaw in this argument, as Thompson points out, is that America was itself just such a continental behemoth, and that, as several generations of commentators had known very well, the buffer of two oceans and a gargantuan economy made the United States a nearly unconquerable fortress. What made the balance-of-power axiom such an unquestioned feature of American foreign policy during the Cold War was the rhetorical victory of a cohort of internationalist politicians and publicists, who drove home their victory over isolationist thinkers in the wake of Pearl Harbor.

If the balance-of-power axiom gave policymakers and opinion-makers one reason for being preoccupied with the specter of Soviet hegemony in Europe, Ann Douglas explains how the screening out of the reality of Russian military actions immediately before and after the end of World War II allowed American leaders to imagine a "Cold War" between two superpowers. Up to 1947 or so, when the policy of containment crystallized in the Truman Doctrine and the Marshall Aid program, reporting of both the Red Army's role in crushing the Nazi war machine and the state of the Soviet economy, military, and society after war, tended to state the obvious: it was the Eastern front where the fate of

Hitler's war was decided, and the result of this astonishingly fierce and sanguinary effort was the near-collapse of Russian society. The very idea that the United States could have found in the Soviet Union in the immediate postwar years an equal foe, economically or militarily, was from this perspective absurd. In order for the USSR to emerge so rapidly in the American mind as an enemy capable of pulling political strings across the planet, a battle had to be waged on the terrain of memory, and Douglas finds the war over the image of the Soviet Union to be constitutive in making the Cold War an ideological project on the part of the United States. Hence Douglas, like Thompson, helps to flesh out Stephanson's vision of the Cold Was as a work of ideology on the part of the United States.

So, too, from a different angle, does Andrew Preston. A further condition of possibility for believing in the Cold War in the postwar period—for making it a potent rhetorical weapon and efficacious worldview—was the time-honored American concern for religious liberty. Preston reveals the animating force of communist "atheism" and intolerance for religion in stimulating American anti-Communism and resistance to perceived Soviet incursions abroad. He tracks these concerns across activist Christian organizations and the thinking of major policymakers like John Foster Dulles. He also traces the rise and fall of the "axiom" of religious liberty in defining Cold War thinking from the end of World War II to the fall of the Berlin Wall.

The remaining five chapters in Part II show some of the effects, and the discursive and material limits, of this novel ideological framework. One way of testing the strength of the force field generated by the ideological principles sketched above is to see what happened when different ideas, discourses, and practices were passed through it. In distinct ways, the essays by Paul Boyer, Daniel Matlin, Moshik Temkin, Peter Mandler, and Sharon Ghamari-Tabrizi carry out this task. Boyer's study of debates within America's religious communities over the ethics of the policy of deterrence takes up some of the themes present in Preston's discussion, but refracts matters of religious belief through the prism of a quintessentially Cold War concern with nuclear weapons. Whereas Preston suggests that commitments to religious liberty gave the American encounter with the communist world the character of a clash between two civilizational forces, Boyer focuses on how religious leaders attempted to fit classically "Cold War" scenarios of apocalyptic nuclear conflict into existing traditions of religious ethics and prophecy.

Matlin and Temkin, meanwhile, examine the ideological collateral of Cold War thinking. The intensive work it took to believe in the Cold War had ripple effects in other areas of American culture. Matlin looks at how the meanings of American citizenship for African-American intellectuals were transformed by the pervasive moral and political framework of the Cold War. Focusing on the postwar writings of Albert Murray and Ralph Ellison, Matlin charts the internal connections between their partial endorsements of Cold War maxims regarding American liberty and the republic's contest with the communist world on one hand and their promotion of the civil rights agenda at home on the other. In Matlin's study we see in vivid detail the ironies involved in Cold War liberalism and intellectual culture. Temkin describes how the controversy over the Sacco-Vanzetti affair of the 1920s was restimulated within the ideological matrix of the Cold War. Temkin's account displays the novel forms of cultural politics made possible by the principles of the Cold War ideology during the postwar decades. Specifically, the rising generation of conservative intellectuals linked their refutation of liberal "myths" about Sacco and Vanzetti—notably, the near universal consensus that the execution of the two men was a tragic miscarriage of justice—to their attempt to rescue Joseph McCarthy's legacy from the derision of liberals. Temkin shows how talking about Sacco and Vanzetti in postwar America involved contesting the legitimacy of liberal and conservative forms of anti-Communism in political discourse.

The final two chapters continue these historical investigations into the conceptual spaces opened up by the Cold War, but they do so in relation to science and technology. Peter Mandler contests the widespread view that the Cold War was an all-pervasive context for the American social sciences after World War II. Even if the ideological framework was indisputably present for postwar scholars, it was nonetheless something they could, with a considerable degree of self-consciousness, navigate, harness, or avoid. Indeed, Mandler introduces several new vectors into our understanding of Cold War intellectual culture, including generational and professional differences such as those found between the older generation of anthropologists and their students. Mandler's picture once more helps us to disenchant our own concept of the Cold War, by making clear the imaginative and practical possibilities it held for historical agents. In the last essay in the volume, Sharon Ghamari-Tabrizi reconstructs the ideological forces impinging on postwar technology and military planning through a microhistory of the creation and testing of "man-machine systems"—essentially, human-computer interfaces—during the 1950s. She provides us with a revealing glimpse of the forms of life inculcated by the military-technological-scientific complex created to fight the Cold War. Although she eschews at the outset any attempt to speak to the macrohistorical issues canvassed in Part I, her rich analysis of the training systems devised by proponents of the "cyborg sciences" after World War II nonetheless enables us to make better sense of what the Cold War entailed in historical practice. In particular, she outlines the peculiar dimensions of what she calls "Cold War literacy" in the man-machine systems of the American military-industrial-academic complex. The result is a singular and important picture of Cold War culture in process.

The intended cumulative effect of the essays in this volume is one of heightened self-consciousness about the work that the idea of the Cold War does, and ought to do, in the study of American history. No doubt scholars will differ in their views on such matters, as indeed they do in this volume. But it will surely be worthwhile for the expanding field of Cold War studies if we have a stronger sense of the possibilities and limits of our most basic assumptions about the nature of the Cold War. Scholars of the Renaissance, of the Industrial Revolution, and of many other grand historical categories have come to appreciate the merits of such historiographical self-awareness. A similar sensibility in Cold War studies, one may hope, will prove equally productive of debate and scholarship.

Notes

1. The literature on these topics is vast and some of it is surveyed in the following chapters. But for a sample, see the following representative works. On the cultural turn, see Robert Griffith, "The Cultural Turn in Cold War Studies," *Reviews in American History*, 29 (2001), pp. 150–157; Christian G. Appy, *Cold War Constructions: The Political Culture of United States Imperialism, 1945–1966* (Amherst, 2000); Ruth Oldenziel and Karin Zachmann, *Cold War Kitchen: Americanization, Technology, and European Users* (Cambridge, MA, 2009); Ron Robin, *Enclaves of America: The Rhetoric of American Political Architecture Abroad, 1900–1965* (Princeton, 1992); Annabel Jane Wharton, *Building the Cold War: Hilton International Hotels and Modern Architecture* (Chicago, 2004); David Crowley and Jane Pavitt (eds.), *Cold War Modern: Design 1945–1970* (London, 2008); Joanne Sharp, *Condensing the Cold War: Reader's Digest and American Identity* (Minneapolis, 2000). For microhistories, see Jeffrey A. Engel (ed.), *The Local Consequences of the Global Cold War* (Stanford, 2007); Michael Szonyi, *Cold War Island: Quemoy on the Front Line* (Cambridge, 2008); Heonik Kwon, *After the Massacre: Commemoration and Consolation in Ha My and My Lai* (Berkeley, 2006); Paul Steege, *Black Market, Cold War: Everyday Life in Berlin, 1946–1949* (Cambridge, 2007). On the global turn, see footnote 3.
2. Melvyn Leffler, *For the Soul of Mankind: The United States, the Soviet Union, and the Cold War* (New York, 2007); John Lewis Gaddis, *The Cold War: A New History* (London, 2005).
3. Odd Arne Westad, *The Global Cold War: Third World Interventions and the Making of Our Times* (Cambridge, 2005); Rana Mitter, *A Bitter Revolution: China's Struggle with the Modern World* (Oxford, 2004); Matthew Connelly, *A Diplomatic Revolution: Algeria's Fight for Independence and the Origins of the Post-Cold War Era* (Oxford, 2002); Hal Brands, *Latin America's Cold War* (Cambridge, 2010).
4. On the periodization of the cold war, see, e.g., Fred Halliday, *The Making of the Second Cold War* (London, 1983); idem, "The Cold War: Lessons and Legacies," 45 (2010): pp. 1–28; Andrew Preston, this volume.
5. Four methodologically and thematically distinct recent attempts at synthesis are Westad, *Global Cold War*; Gaddis, *Cold War*; Leffler, *For the Soul of Mankind*; Campbell Craig and Fredrik Logevall, *America's Cold War: The Politics of Insecurity* (Cambridge, 2009). The most ambitious attempt at encyclopedic coverage, with some degree of thematic integration, is Melvyn Leffler and Odd Arne Westad (eds.), *The Cambridge History of the Cold War*, 3 vols. (Cambridge, 2010).
6. Klein, *Cold War Orientalism: Asia in the Middlebrow Imagination, 1945–1961* (Berkeley, 2003); Westad, *Global Cold War*.
7. Maier, "Consigning the Twentieth Century to History: Alternative Narratives for the Modern Era," *American Historical Review*, 105/3 (2000), pp. 807–831; Ann Douglas,

"Periodizing the American Century: Modernism, Postmodernism, and Postcolonialism in the Cold War Context," *Modernism/Modernity*, 5/3 (1998), pp. 71–98.

8. On the Renaissance as an actors' category (and a self-promotional label), see Jan de Vries, "The Industrial and the Industrious Revolution," *Journal of Economic History*, 54/2 (1994), p. 253. On the Industrial Revolution as a largely post-hoc epithet, see Tim Blanning, *The Pursuit of Glory: Europe 1648–1815* (London, 2008), pp. 125–127.
9. Stephanson, "Fourteen Notes on the Very Concept of the Cold War" in G. O'Tuathail and S. Dalby (eds.), *Rethinking Geopolitics* (New York, 1999), pp. 62–86.
10. William J. Bouwsma, "The Renaissance and the Drama of Western History," *American Historical Review*, 84/1 (1979), pp. 1–15; Wallace Ferguson, *The Renaissance in Historical Thought: Five Centuries of Historical Interpretation* (Boston, 1948); Jacob Burckhardt, *The Civilization of the Renaissance in Italy*, 2 vols. (New York, 1958). See also Hans Baron, *The Crisis of the Early Italian Renaissance: Civic Humanism and Republican Liberty in an Age of Classicism and Tyranny* (Princeton, 1955).
11. Haskins, *The Renaissance of the Twelfth Century* (1927; New York, 1957). See also Leidulf Melve, "'The Revolt of the Medievalists': Directions in Recent Research on the Medieval Renaissance," *Journal of Medieval History*, 32/3 (2006), pp. 231–252.
12. See Quentin Skinner, "Introduction: The Reality of the Renaissance" in idem, *Visions of Politics*, vol. 2: *Renaissance Virtues* (Cambridge, 2002), pp. 1–9; Bouwsma, "Renaissance."
13. Blanning, *Pursuit of Glory*, pp. 125–141.
14. Skinner, *Visions of Politics*, vol. II.
15. De Vries, *The Industrious Revolution: Consumer Behavior and the Household Economy, 1650 to the Present* (Cambridge, 2008), p. 7 and *passim*; idem, "Industrial." See also C. A. Bayly, *The Birth of the Modern World, 1780–1914: Global Connections and Comparisons* (Oxford, 2004), pp. 51–64.
16. See, inter alia, J. G. A. Pocock, *Barbarism and Religion, vol. 1: The Enlightenments of Edward Gibbon, 1737–1764* (Cambridge, 1999); Jonathan I. Israel, *Radical Enlightenment: Philosophy and the Making of Modernity, 1650–1750* (Oxford, 2001). For a powerful attempt to recenter the idea, see John Robertson, *The Case for the Enlightenment: Scotland and Naples 1680–1760* (Cambridge, 2005).
17. For a summary, see Steven Shapin, *The Scientific Revolution* (Chicago, 1996).
18. Douglas, "Periodizing," p. 72.
19. Tony Judt, *Postwar: A History of Europe Since 1945* (London, 2007); idem, "The Past is Another Country: Myth and Memory in Postwar Europe" in Istvan Deak, Jan T. Gross, and Tony Judt (eds.), *The Politics of Retribution in Europe: World War II and Its Aftermath* (Princeton, 2000), pp. 293–325.
20. Westad, "Introduction: Reviewing the Cold War" in Westad (ed.), *Reviewing the Cold War: Approaches, Interpretations, Theory* (London, 2000), p. 19.

PART ONE

PRISMS

1

Cold War Degree Zero

ANDERS STEPHANSON

Ronald Reagan, it is well to remember, would have denied with indignation in the early 1980s that he was reviving the cold war. In his view, it had never gone away, contrary to the egregious delusions of détente—that shameful era of Western passivity and appeasement that had permitted such vast Soviet advances toward world communist dominance. A good many historians today reflect this general frame, if not the politics or the idea of appeasement. They accept, in short, the notion that the cold war never went away and that it came to last as long as the Soviet Union lasted, as Reagan himself had indeed always insisted it would.

The reason for this agreement is not hard to divine. The Reagan era of drastic coldwar[1] mobilization by the United States was followed by the extinction of the Soviet empire and so the end of an epoch in world politics. Something fundamental did in fact come to an end. The sheer obviousness of this end is overwhelming. By any measure, the expiration of the Soviet Union was a world-historical event. Given the reality of that end, there has to be a period that really and truly corresponds to it, that adequates it, so to speak. As that end game, too, takes place in the wake of Reagan's intense coldwar rhetoric, it is not surprising that the conventional name for the obvious period now laid to rest is "the cold war." The name worked. It still works. Thus we are now in an epoch "after the end of the cold war," the introductory phrase of a million policy articles since the early 1990s, along with that other cliché about "the only superpower." More recent events have put that latter designation into question but the obviousness of "the cold war" remains in full force. Though the period itself is now fading into the distant past, no name of comparable rhetorical power has been invented to describe the ensuing "period." We seem to live perpetually "after the cold war." Ronald Reagan's view of the cold war still, in effect, holds sway. The notion that he was the one who essentially "ended" it with such success is only slightly less common.[2]

With little reflection, serious scholarship left and right has thus fallen into the superficial usage of Reagan's "continuity thesis," which in turn is grounded one way or another in a set of systemic criteria, that there was somehow something inherently "coldwar" about the very difference between the United States and the Soviet Union or solely about the Soviet Union. There, however, the similarities end. Coldwar conventionalism may be said, for analytical purposes, to fall into three ideal types.[3] First, there is what one might call neo-orthodoxy, the position of Reagan's faithful admirers, notably more numerous today than during his own controversial presidency.[4] Their preeminent historian is John Lewis Gaddis.[5] For Reagan's parishioners, nothing much about the cold war is problematic or difficult to grasp. In the spirit of their political authority, they believe that the cold war was a civilizational war that the West, under reinvigorated leadership, won by revealing the naked decrepitude of the perverse empire on the other side. The origins of the "war" have to do, then, with the nasty doings by the intrinsically nefarious Soviet Union, the end of which will therefore also be the end of the "war." Subperiods of the "war" will then be read in terms of a continuing totalitarian threat and the variable adequacy of the Western response.

This, in all its essentials, is also the official US position from 1946–47 into the 1960s. Such a view, centered on "communism" and "totalitarianism," was easier to propound then than now, given, for one thing, the subsequent Sino-Soviet conflict and China's de facto alliance with the United States. Nonetheless, neo-orthodoxy does have a specific account of what made the cold war a cold war, in which regard it compares favorably with the other two conventional tendencies, which evince no very precise idea about that matter and rarely address it. These two positions share the basic, minimalist view of the cold war as a geopolitical period dominated decisively by the United States and the Soviet Union, with the added ingredient (enter the variable chill factor) of "intense rivalry" or "abnormal tension." No normative judgment is necessarily involved. What differentiates the two, however, is the extent of the conceptualization and the importance accorded to the "war" itself.

One—let us call it neorealist—is chiefly interested in "bipolarity" as an overdeterminant system and its functional effects on state actors, with particular reference to the stability of the whole.[6] The domestic character and ideology of the antagonists, then, are largely irrelevant. So are the origins of the structure. No great mystery attaches to them in any case, just two massively powerful continental states of diverging interests bound for conflict after World War II, thus setting the stage for the subsequent stability of duopoly. Exact origins and causes may be left hazy and are at any rate secondary. Notoriously, this position has no convincing account of the end, having disregarded the domestic aspect without which that event is largely incomprehensible, indeed rather a nasty surprise from a conceptual standpoint. "The cold war," more importantly, is not fundamental to the proceedings. It is a semantic convenience (or unavoidable inconvenience).

What matters is the range of possible effects and derivations from the concept of a structure of limited competition. Periodization itself, in fact, is not crucial: the object (since we are chiefly dealing with political scientists) is to produce a timeless, predictive theory wherein the postwar epoch serves as raw material; temporality, historical time, is mainly a disturbance and not a basic concern. The rights and wrongs of that theory, featuring (dubiously) electromagnetic metaphors of "polarity" but actually grounded in economic theories of limited competition, are not relevant for my argument here. What is relevant is the constitutive lack of interest in the cold war as a cold war. Neorealism is really more interested in the structural features that (I will argue) turned the cold war into something else.

The final position—amorphous, historically orientated, and more defined by what it avoids and dislikes—may also be concerned with "bipolarity" and the like but not in any theoretical sense. It emphasizes the existential realities of nastiness and massive threats. Neo-orthodoxy in pure form is wrong, accordingly, because of its politics and lack of detachment. Neorealism, insofar as one acknowledges it, is wrong for the opposite reason: it is too detached. It is also ahistorical and hovering on the brink of amoral model-mongering. For amorphous convention (I am unable to find a fetching name), events of the cold war matter in themselves, so to speak. They are not the metanarrative expressions of some underlying evil empire or functional system. Historical variations within the epoch are thus genuine and profound. "Bipolarity in trouble," for instance, features a unique sequence of events of intrinsic historical interest: China breaks away, Western Europe begins to show signs of independent geopolitics, third-world developments are increasingly hard to control, and so on. The outline and the props are familiar—very familiar—but generally the perspective seems credible enough. As in the case of neorealism, it permits a logical account of the place of the People's Republic of China. Semantically, meanwhile, "the cold war" is more than a terminological convention; it is an expression of something real, if not quite in the essentialist manner of Ronald Reagan (a philosophical realist, if not a political one). It is a term, then, with a great deal of historical resonance and for good reason. People used it. There was tension. Sometimes there was even terror, the terror of being on the brink of nuclear war. The cold war is a pretty good description. It makes sense. It makes obvious sense.[7]

"The cold war" thus serves as shorthand for an amorphous epoch of enormous span, variably defined, if it is at all. The geopolitical polarity is sometimes backdrop, sometimes immediately determinant, but works overall as a frame for investigations of all kinds of events and processes. At its blandest, amorphous convention turns the cold war into little more than an empty container of time, a homogeneous stretch when sundry things happen in sundry places for sundry reasons, nothing much apparently following from it: the cold war here and there and yonder. Even when it is supposed to carry explanatory weight, the actual studies are conceived, in effect, as filling in empirical voids, areas and topics not yet covered. The "cultural" domain, especially, offers a potentially unlimited range of "coldwar studies." Particular histories of substance are possible here, though "the cold war" adds nothing much to them and they in turn add little to it as an object of inquiry. Where amorphous convention makes direct claims about the cold war, where the periodizing device supposedly tells us something significant about the subject at hand, where it is not the backdrop but the stage itself as it were, the cold war still remains no more problematic than in either of the other two accounts. The aim is judicious elaboration and extension, not conceptual challenge. The approach is however not intrinsically vacuous. No one can deny that some kind of epoch comes to an end with the Soviet Union; and amorphous convention does represent a coherent periodization, however minimalist, that can also yield empirical knowledge. Because it is both specific and infinitely capacious, it permits distinctions between its object and other kinds of processes and temporalities. The cold war is not necessarily everything that happens in the cold war. Other histories and periodizations are, in principle, possible.

Beyond the Continuity Thesis

So what is wrong with this view? A great deal, actually. Slipshod periodization aside, it would seem to ignore, in the first instance, the extent to which actors of the 1960s and 1970s thought the cold war had indeed come to an end and acted accordingly. Richard Nixon must have been talking nonsense when, grandly but earnestly, he declared the cold war over in Moscow in 1972, when he envisaged something more traditional by way of great-power rivalry. That Nixon was talking nonsense was of course precisely Reagan's belief; and thus neo-orthodoxy now thinks justified Reagan's deep, not to say visceral, anger at détente and his subsequent restoration of a grand policy that recognized coldwar truth. For the less ideologically inclined, however, the experience of détente as an end and qualitative break is rather a retrospective curiosity, to be registered but of no deeper significance, easily submerged as a mere phase within the fundamental coldwar continuity. Alternatively, it can even be seen as the intensification of the rivalry and "the cold war." The conclusion, whether explicit or not, is in any case identical to that of neo-orthodoxy. The cold war, in fact, continued.

And, indeed, it may be that Reagan and the conventional cohort are right: Nixon was in fact mistaken. Though the appearance of such talk in 1972 can scarcely be ignored as a historical phenomenon, there is no reason to take it at face value either, or for that matter the panoply of actions that manifestly did not conform to coldwar concepts. These acts, then, might have been misconstrued by contemporaries, or perhaps seen as a case of devious recasting of old categories into new form, a performance for the galleries. In short, one might choose, on methodological principle, to treat as immaterial or of very limited pertinence the phenomenological aspects, how events were experienced and defined. While, consequently, it is correct to insist on some kind of account of why participants ceased to think in classical coldwar categories, this does not, obviously, make it incumbent on latter-day amorphous convention to agree with them.

My initial objection is thus of limited scope, the conventional tendency to flatten out what actually happened notwithstanding. The related denigration of the category of the cold war itself is more difficult to ignore. By treating it as self-evident, convention of the detached variety turns the cold war into description and leaves aside its potential as explanatory concept. I realize that the distinction is not absolute: there is no pure "description" or "explanation." Even so, amorphous convention treats "the cold war" more as description of something self-evident than a concept to be produced and used to explain the nature of the period. At most, it is a concept without movement.

One major reason for this is the negligence of how "the cold war" became a term in the first place and its various subsequent meanings. This is certainly improper procedure. How it emerged in the immediate postwar years, the specific references that made up its conceptual ground, how it became a semantic field, are elementary components of any historical inquiry that makes claims about the cold war as a period. The historian (and the odd political scientist) must give a critical, indeed historical, account of the basic terms deployed—subject them to some minimal degree of interrogation. Geopolitical dominance plus intense rivalry here does not equal such an interrogation. The problem is compounded because the term in question is not merely a name we now give to a distinct period ex post facto. It is not an analogue of, say, "the interwar period" for the years 1919 through 1939 that is certainly disputable in making the two World Wars into obvious bookends but surely not as politically and ideologically loaded a term as "the cold war," nor one that carries with it the weight of explanation, nor one that contemporaries actually used since it was hard to imagine oneself (generally) as living between two wars. The cold war, by contrast, seems to tell us something quite powerful about what went on: it was invented by contemporaries and used from the outset, then battled over continuously by politicians and public intellectuals, in due course also by historians in the many polemics about who caused the "war," and then used retroactively when, presumably, the obvious end had occurred. This sedimentation of meanings, this mess of political and scholarly controversies, demands some account if the inquiry is to earn its critical credentials. Yet historians have next to nothing to say about it.

I find this strange. One would think that, regardless of politics, such a strikingly polyvalent term as "the cold war" would occasion excessive fascination rather than drone-like acceptance. Each of the three words that make it up may in fact be put into question. The cold war: was there only one or can there be others? Is it a historical form or type such as for instance "holy war" or "civil war"? If it is, then any systemic interpretation (e.g., democracy/totalitarianism or capitalism/communism) would have some elaboration to do. If it is unique, are all other uses metaphorical analogies and in what sense? The cold war: why this particular metaphor and what does it do? Cold is a relative description on a scale, a continuum, a condition of degree. This is in fact a fundamental reason it works so well. One can account for variations: increasing chill, a warming thaw (though there is a problem with "hotting up"). Moreover, "cold" already has a wide metaphorical register before it becomes a specific one in "the cold war." When one refers to a personal relationship as "cold," the word means unfriendly, hostile, limited in range and expression. A cold person, singularly, is similarly so, the opposite of "warm." The metaphorical register here is grounded in the temperature of water (as is the Celsius scale) and its qualitative "states," as well as in the related, more encompassing domain of weather and climate. Ice, frozen water, embodies several disagreeable features: rigidity, exterior blankness and unresponsiveness, physical threat to the normal state of the human body. Frosty relations are thus bad but not quite as bad as frozen ones, in which nothing moves. If things "warm up" and relations improve, a "thaw" is said to be underway. The rigidity is loosening up, opening up for tactile interaction, a diversity of actions and reactions.

As long as one thinks along these analogical lines of the human body (warm is good) and its environs, and, metaphorically, the relations between them (warm is good), the semantic field seems predictable enough. One might even consider the optimum (warm is good) as some Aristotelian mean between two deviating extremes, hot and cold. There, however, the exercise threatens to go astray because a hot war is infinitely worse than a cold one. This cannot simply be resolved by projecting the referential temperature onto climate and weather, the environs of the human body—a "mild" and temperate one being the best because it permits the widest range of life, a world where people can flourish in a way that is impossible in the arctic or the desert. When pushed further, the climatic sense can then turn the cold into a sign for the outside, to be contrasted with the warmth of the inside. Thus we have entered a world not of frozen immobility and stasis but of action, speed, and dissimulation, the cynical world, in short, immortalized in the novels by John le Carré, the looking glass war of essentially identical antagonists, a space represented directly by the divided city of Berlin on a typically nasty winter day.[8] Berlin may otherwise serve as symbol for the kind of "freeze" that is encapsulated in the very line of rigid demarcation that marks the cold war in its European frame, what Winston Churchill famously referred to as "the iron curtain" (he was recycling an old metaphor originating in the construction of British theatres).[9]

These may seem idle musings on a word ("cold") that happens to be endlessly suggestive. I think not. For the chain of signification had real historical effects. It is not difficult to see, for example, how the notion of a cold war could by transference be associated in the United States directly with the Soviet Union itself and the "totalitarian" system. What is this system imagined to be (not entirely without reason) but a rigid, immobile, and unfriendly one, the very essence of coldness? The identity is obvious—too obvious.

The third and final word, "war," is the trickiest. What kind of war was this? The two sides never went to war with each other. There is no obvious beginning, no single moment of initial aggression, no declaration of war, no crossing of a certain line, and no open military engagement. Is "war" itself then perhaps also a metaphor, not an actual war but an image of something "warlike"? Contemporaries at the outset used it (predominantly) as a category for a new kind of warfare, new but real, as real as "hot war." I myself will argue below that there is an element, an essential element, of truth in this. In particular, it is essential to ask oneself, historically, what kind of "peace" it posited. Soon, in effect, that question came to be bracketed along with the whole issue of metaphor or not. One reason was indeed its potent range of meanings and possible uses: it lent itself to instant metaphorical extension for journalistic purposes. In September 1947 "the cold war" enters public discourse; a month later the term is used in *The New York Times* to describe relations between rival football leagues.

Overall, then, it is a designation of the greatest elasticity and range of use. It can be used relatively to describe variations, degrees of hostility, or the mere impressions of such variable states since there is no objective way of measuring them. Because the condition and the activities it implies are indeed indistinct, almost an absence (of "hot" war), any number of things can appear in it. Recognizing these difficulties, one might of course eliminate the problem by eliminating the term itself, or reducing it to triviality. One might replace it, for instance, with "the postwar epoch" or some such neutral or anodyne designation. In the best of cases, this could then be developed into a genuine concept along the lines of what happened in the 1980s with the analogous category of "postmodernity," where the simple chronological notion of "after" was transformed to the point of explanatory power.[10] Evading the cold war as a proper concept of periodization would turn it into a purely historical object, to be studied by those so inclined as one way among others that contemporaries thought and acted in the world, as a historical conception of a certain condition or series of events. Such an investigation is indeed indispensable but not enough. I am myself opposed to the evasive move. For one thing, the ideological uses of "the cold war" are everywhere in evidence and operation. More fundamentally, it is my contention that the cold war, if treated as a concept, actually tells us something real beyond the archaeological, second-order understanding of contemporary understandings. Its conceptual history is also the history of genuine historical movement. If this is right, then avoidance serves only to obscure that historical movement. It is imperative, in particular, to counteract the tendency to normalize "the end" and reinscribe that normality in the beginning. It is easy, altogether too easy, because of the massively obvious end, to "normalize" the United States, the victorious antagonist, and inversely to turn the pathological Soviet Union into the constitutive factor, the abnormality that actually caused the whole thing. The real, historical conditions of possibility for something called the cold war thus vanish along with the fact that the cold war was a US project.

Such an argument will require a positive account rather than a critique, an alternative that shows that "the cold war" can provide rigorous periodization, which is what historians do or are supposed to be doing.[11] I will attempt a sketch of this kind below. The gist of it may cause unease, even irritation. I shall claim, then, that the cold war was from the outset not only a US term but a US project; that it began as a contingently articulated policy that eventually generated a system, static and dynamic at the same time; that this system was qualitatively transformed in the early 1960s into something else. This is not a moral argument, much less a moralizing one. I am not, in short, inverting neo-orthodoxy by claiming that the United States equals the cold war. The United States from a systemic standpoint did not "need" the cold war.[12] I am proposing, however, that the coldwar frame is "structural" to the extent that it made abundant sense in distinctly American terms for the dominant "internationalists" who articulated the US approach to the world between 1946 and 1950; and that they used it to considerable effect the global purpose of putting the United States into the world once and for all. This, I reiterate, was not a necessity: it did not have to happen that way. Once my account reaches the 1970s, I will shift gear again by turning to a fourth version of the continuity thesis, Odd Arne Westad's ambitious *The Global Cold War: Third World Interventions and the Making of Our Times*. Westad propounds the thesis that the cold war was, or becomes, largely about thirdworld interventionism and that détente signifies its extension and deepening. It is an ambitious attempt to break with amorphous convention that nevertheless ends up reinforcing it because the alternative concept of the cold war is empty.

Emergence and Periodization

I must begin, for archaelogical and conceptual reasons, with a couple of realists, classical realists. Walter Lippmann's symptomatic reading of George F. Kennan's X-Article under the rubric of "the cold war" in the fall of 1947 placed the term into common usage and also offered the beginning of a genuine concept. By reinforcing the media obsession with "containment" as the essence of Kennan's original article, Lippmann's critique condemned Kennan to the fate of having his historical accomplishment perennially summarized in that truly tiresome attribute "architect of containment" and to force that putative architect into half a century of fruitless denials. ("Containment" was not all there was to Kennan's argument and arguably not even its central aspect but let us leave that inexhaustible question aside.[13]) For a month, in fourteen columns no less, the pundit of pundits subjected Kennan to a critical scrutiny that sometimes verged on ridicule. Many things caused his displeasure but above all two. He considered the notion of containing the Soviet Union across the globe a "strategic monstrosity"—a position that would leave the initiative entirely up to Moscow while saddling the United States with the obligation to prop all manner of unsavory and unreliable allies, satellites and clients, all on the sanguine hope that frustration of Soviet initiatives would eventually cause its internal destruction or at any rate a qualitative mellowing. In accordance with the universalist spirit of the Truman Doctrine of March 1947, containment was thus utterly devoid of that basic aspect of any proper strategy, namely, realistic ranking of priorities. Kennan actually agreed but the formulations of his article left him (and the Truman Doctrine) open to the charge.

Lippmann's second complaint, more pertinent in our context, had to do with diplomacy, or more precisely its absence. His point, a correct one, was that Kennan appeared to exclude the normal workings of diplomacy in dealing with the Soviet Union. Lippmann objected specifically to the notion of incommensurability, the notion that somehow the vast chasm, cultural and ideological, between the Soviet Union and the West, the central referent here both for Kennan and Lippmann, rendered agreements impossible in the manner of some thwarted Wittgensteinian language game. Historically there was nothing in difference as such (or lack of "intimacy") between powers that militated against agreements and settlements. In his ideological fixation, moreover, Kennan had forgotten (said Lippmann, a bit unfairly) that the Soviet regime existed in the same geopolitical setting as the old Tsarist empire, a setting that was eminently translatable and meaningful in traditional categories of power. Lippmann's primary example was the presence and place of any given army. An army is either there or it is not. An army is recognizable in any language game, so to speak. Hence, given that the central problem for the West (in 1947) was the presence of the Red Army in central Europe, one might usefully investigate what, if anything, Moscow would be willing to accept by way of bargaining to retract its military line. One would engage in actual diplomacy to adjudicate interests.[14]

Kennan, like Lippmann a realist of sorts, was not on reflection averse to such ideas. His disagreement with Lippmann had to do with the conception of the Soviet Union: Stalin's regime was beyond the realist pale. Kennan's realism was notably bounded by a certain civilizational sense. Interests attach to every form of power but the world is differentiated according to the ways in which these interests are pursued. To be "realistic" vis-à-vis thirdworld nationalism (to name one of Kennan's later horrors) was thus something altogether different from being so in a Western context, a context by the way that for him was not about "democracy" but a certain kind of order and tradition. To be realistic vis-à-vis Moscow was to ignore it or, when that was impossible, vigorously to counteract it. In no way, however, was it a regime with which it was possible to enter into any kind of agreement or deal.[15] Perhaps the closest analogue here is Edmund Burke's conception of revolutionary France and the threat to "Europe," which is to say essentially "Christendom." Containing and eventually crushing the revolution in the name of this civilization of Christian particularities did not assume that the world was unitary or binary, that it represented the quintessence of humankind. So while the French had committed treason against the ruling Christian regime of Europe, the outside of that order was a differentiated, multifaceted series of realities. Meanwhile, the place of Russia within this imagined European community had of course always varied: inside, on probation, after 1721, outside again in 1917.

In 1947, then, Lippmann did not find this Burkean argument persuasive. With piercing clarity, he had diagnosed the undialectical nature of Kennan's diagnosis, that it was really a kind of medical diagnosis of an object under a microscope, the analysis of a virus, an organism, a parasite, a tumor, in short something to be surrounded, contained, suffocated, denied its feeding grounds, forced into submission or, better still, killed off. For Lippmann, this was a serious misreading leading to a potentially disastrous strategy of perimeter defense, a posture singularly ill-fitted for the kind of power that the United States wielded: mobile, specific, firmly Western. The Soviet Union, on its part, wielded power almost exclusively because of its mighty army and on its perimeter. Communist parties elsewhere, however devoted to Moscow, could not become a lasting problem in the absence of that power. Hence it was in the Western interest, indeed paramount for the west, to negotiate with Moscow for the withdrawal of all "alien" armies from Europe (meaning the armies not only of the Soviet Union but also the United States and Britain).[16]

Lippmann was largely right but both he and Kennan turned out to be wrong in the end, displaced as they were by the "meta-realism" of Dean Acheson. By the time Kennan had grasped the truth of Lippmann's objections in the late spring of 1948, his erstwhile position, or what passed for it, had become unshakeable orthodoxy: no real diplomacy with the evil empire, compromise now defined as appeasement. Both Lippmann and Kennan, in fact, found their contributions selectively appropriated for other purposes. The invention of a term and its subsequent uses are, as Nietzsche famously insisted, quite different phenomena.

Lippmann's barrage, published under the rubric of "the cold war," did not explicate the term; in fact, he never once mentioned it in the actual articles. It was present in its absence. In subsequent columns, he did deploy it, sparingly, in the spirit of his earlier pieces to designate, matter-of-fact, a mutual condition, a situation of cold as opposed to hot war that applied to East and West alike and that could be overcome by a more appropriate US policy, viz. a policy of real diplomacy. The term, however, began to appear daily in the press to indicate, quite differently from Lippmann's account, just the current manner of Soviet totalitarian aggression; in which regard a heavily reduced version of Kennan's Soviet Union became axiomatic, condensed into the single proposition that here was a fanatical force committed to the destruction of the West (or "freedom") and impervious to any reasonable or traditional consideration from the outside. From then on, "the cold war" is what the Soviet Union is and does, specifically the strategy it deploys to destroy the Free World since it is (as yet) not strong enough to launch a hot war.

Classical realism, from then on, passes to the margins of the mainstream as it were, ultimately un-American in its assumption that policy must start from the realization that there is no overarching normative order in the world beyond "interests"; and that it is both daft and counterproductive to operate on the belief that the values of the United States apply everywhere. If so, then it is also the case that actors in the field of international relations are for analytical purposes identical, a view that is completely at odds with the notion of a salvational agent such as the United States embroiled in world-historical, global struggle against a mortal enemy. Scattered leftists aside, the only vocal critics of coldwar thinking in the early 1950s are in fact some of the classical realists, outstandingly Kennan himself.[17] Coldwar orthodoxy, meanwhile, became enormously effective. To see how, we need a brief word about the semantic field and contextual politics in which Lippmann's idea was formulated, more precisely how the term might have appeared to him as a proper name for something deeper.

It is largely to do with the understanding of the 1930s. Beginning when the Japanese Kwantung Army created the "incident" at Mukden in 1931 and subsequently invaded Manchuria, the 1930s seems to be about flagrant violations of traditional, legal definitions of war and peace. States, according to the norm, would either be at peace or war with one another, and a war could not properly begin unless openly declared. A string of fascist aggressions (Japan, Italy, and Germany) then made that distinction and notion of propriety nigh-on meaningless. No war is declared. No legal niceties apply. Instead a gradated sequence of possible actions, more or less violent, replaces the old division. This is allowed to go on because traditional powers have more pressing matters to handle, above all the Depression; but the end result is of course World War II, fought not only to extinguish fascist illegality for all time but also to institute a machinery that would not merely establish the status quo ante but make even traditional, legal war virtually illegitimate. Lippmann's critique, then, is articulated when that project, the notion of "one world" of peace and stability, appears to have capsized, not because there are differences between the West and the Soviet Union but because of the way in which those differences are grasped. For Lippmann, it makes sense to call this condition a cold war. He means a condition that is warlike by the old standards in not permitting or exhibiting the normal diplomatic means of peace but at the same time does not involve any overt military engagements.[18] Clearly, too, he finds such a posture to be contrary to the interests of the United States and, more important, the West.[19]

In this last notion, then, Lippmann proved interestingly off the mark. For the "errors" of containment and the underlying misapprehensions about the Soviet regime he had pinpointed proved extraordinarily successful for the promotion of the interests of the United States in the world. "The cold war" became a matrix that made unarguable, indeed imperative, a truly globalist role for the United States, a role it was to play to great advantage for quite some time. In practice, as the policymakers were perfectly aware, the universal struggle for freedom meant quite specific interests in specific places; but the globalist frame was an absolute precondition for that specificity. The whole point of the exercise was in fact not to engage the Soviet Union in the trenches of any war, real or imagined, but to establish Washington's license to act everywhere else. In short, error was productively serving ends of the greatest ambition. It would take Kennan almost a decade of frustration before he realized this, partly courtesy once again of Walter Lippmann (and Raymond Aron). Kennan was dumbfounded.[20]

The basic features of the US matrix are well known and can be summarized quickly: a literal translation of the appeasement lessons of the 1930s, the World War as a result of totalitarian aggression and wanton disregard for traditional standards of peace and war, now in the face of a much more insidious version requiring a huge and global effort on the part of the only power capable of leading the Free World. That "the cold war" passed into general usage was partly, as intimated, because it fit the Soviet Union itself, a very cold place run by a very cold dictator, who, on closer inspection, had turned out to be drastically different from his avuncular wartime image; and partly too because it allowed one to think the intratotalitarian difference between Stalin and Hitler, the difference between using a wide range of cynical, sly, and subversive measures, depending on the circumstances, and the brash, reckless open warfare of the Nazis: Stalin in contrast not only to the open and warm politicians of the west but also to the "hot" dictator Adolf Hitler, hysterically angry and keen on hot wars. The end result however is identity: two totalitarian regimes on a quest for world domination. Moreover, there is now a sense that Stalin's strategy of cold war is more effective, more rational if you will, in this quest than was Hitler's hot war.

The cold war, then, is what the Soviet Union is and does, destruction of the Free World by any means necessary. The matter need not be analyzed any further. Not much by way of analysis did in fact follow, either. What is peculiar in retrospect about the dichotomy (a dichotomy in the true sense of the word) is that it is not in fact Manichean: freedom being the natural state of affairs, the real world is the free world whereas the totalitarian sphere is inherently incapable of independent existence, always taking the parasitic form of an attack on freedom. With this netherworld of world-conquering aggression and subversion, accordingly, there can be no compromise and certainly no traditional diplomacy. Here, then, in all its essentials is the structure Reagan thinks never went away. The axiom is explicit: the cold war, being an effect of the very nature of the Soviet system itself, can only end when that system too has ended, when the Soviet Union has ceased to be the Soviet Union.[21]

What are the auxiliary conceptual effects? Initially this: an exhaustive distinction of such a binary kind renders it incumbent on the keeper of the faith to arrange every phenomenon taxonomically on one side or the other. There can be no place for "neutrality": "you are either for us or against us," to echo a more recent reinvention of the reinvention. (In the early 1960s, Kennedy will respond to Khrushchev's previous innovations in Soviet policy here by visualizing good neutrals, but these are neutrals who, being free, are really objectively not neutral at all but inherently resistant to, and subversive of, the other side.) In short, there can be no distribution of entities along a line of continuity or within clusters based on variable criteria—such as for instance Kennan's alternative (by 1948) to coldwar binarism, the notion of five military-industrial centers of potentially open-ended internal configuration, where the US strategy would be devoted negatively to keeping the Soviets, one of these centers, from seizing control of any of the remaining ones. The rest of the world, then, was essentially of limited or no importance.

Such differentiation, such a principle of nonidentity, is thus illegitimate within the binary coldwar division; but there is another set of divisions, secondary seemingly but crucial, once the overarching divide has been set forth and territorialized. First, there is a certain differentiation on the totalitarian side. Totalitarian space is occupied space, illegitimate, impermanent, and unreal. It is a netherworld of slavery, an unnatural space harboring captive people and peoples whose natural freedom is entirely denied. Thus there is difference, the difference between the dictatorial regime and the people. In practice, however, differentiation is erased precisely because totalitarianism means total domination (which also paradoxically makes it brittle). Reform is inconceivable. Slaves, being slaves, are unlikely meanwhile to liberate themselves. The other order, then, must be abolished in toto for liberation to take place. Hence any deals with the regime are inherently counterproductive, serving only to strengthen the system and to recognize its validity. The immediate reference here is the analogy to the Munich Pact and appeasement. A much deeper, domestic grounding, however, will be found historically in the abolitionism of the 1850s and the ensuing Civil War, a posture expressed with tremendous rhetorical force in NSC-68. The problem with abolitionism, alas, is that while self-evidently true, it is also impossible to implement, either by open war or subversion.[22]

What remains, then, is to bracket the other side while vigorously protecting and fortifying "the free world." This is where a second and decisive differentiation enters the proceedings, having to do with the map of "the free" rather than the totalitarian netherworld. Another line of demarcation is drawn, auxiliary but in fact crucial, namely, the line between the United States and the rest of the Free World. The United States is both part of the Free World and absolutely different from it. For, as guarantor, the United States is invested with unlimited power to act across the board. The (messianic) agent here is thus a precise place and identity, freedom achieved; but the extent and whereabouts of the Free World itself is always up for grabs, under constant construction as it were. Freedom, in short, must everywhere be asserted, inscribed, established, clarified. It must be made legible. In making it legible, one has to posit that it is always already under threat. The Free World, then, is a perpetual and unlimited security problem while the other side of the fence is a nullity that should, all things being equal, be unlocked and "naturalized," totally cleansed of its totalitarian system. While striking a defensive note, then, this posture is in actuality relentlessly offensive. The world, in principle, is a natural whole but perversion happens temporarily to reign in a specific area. History, plainly, is now calling upon the one agent capable of global action to defend existing freedom and eventually root out perversion, the one agent that is not only totally free but also, not accidentally, massively powerful.

It will then be remarked that the Soviet position mirrored the US binary exactly, certainly by the time Andrei Zhdanov had established the two-camp delineation in September 1947. This is not quite true. For there are two crucial and related differences. First, the two-camp theory (democracy/peace versus imperialism/aggression) is grounded in the Stalinist version of the Marxist-Hegelian notion of contradiction, which, unlike the (Augustinian) couplet of good/real/natural versus evil/unreal/unnatural, constitutes a dialectical unity of opposites, always by definition locked in struggle but a struggle of "equals" so to speak. The difference here between a parasite and a real enemy is essential because the latter allows for real deals on the basis of real interests (or interests imagined to be real). That the revolutionary principle is antithetical to this precisely in its refusal to "deal" is ultimately less important than the reality of the unity of opposites and the reality of interests. Long-term transformation here always entails realist recognition of objective interests: the enemy is at once legitimate and not: historically passé, to be superseded and annulled at the most general level but at the same time actually existing in the present, representing interests pursued in accordance with their identifiable nature and so open to calculation of losses and gains. While capitalists as a class are on the verge of becoming historically reactionary, individual capitalists (such as Averell Harriman in the 1920s) may well have interests that coincide with those of the Soviet Union, thus giving rise to mutually profitable and highly realistic relations.

By the time we get to Stalin the Hyperrealist, in any case, "revolution" had undergone drastic reconceptualization. This is the second difference. For the decisive "main contradiction" in Stalinism had been territorialized (i.e., horizontalized) after 1928 such that the line between the Soviet Union and its auxiliaries and the outside now incarnated the old vertical and deterritorialized opposition between capital and labor. Instead of a dual, international set of classes, then, there is now a socialist headquarters in a well-specified place with a well-specified leadership, the survival of which overshadows every other concern. Territorialization is then wedded to the historical vision of capitalism in its last monopoly stage and the inverse notion of rational construction of socialism in one country (and its vicinity); in which case the central object, again, is always by definition the survival and protection of space already gained by the socialist mother/fatherland. Altogether, this is an eminently strategic view, a view featuring a quasi-military conception of space that is itself not a very farfetched reworking of the quasi-military conception of politics found in Lenin (but that is another story). It was also, in fact, an eminently "defensive" conception, one in which there could be no room for any idea of launching a cold war against an enemy that was by all measures infinitely more powerful.

This is why the Soviet response takes the tactical form, not of socialist confrontation, but an appeal to "national independence" supposed to attract sundry bourgeois elements, complemented later by the universal appeal to "peace"—both measures designed to thwart what appears to be in the Stalinist perspective an embryonic, proto-fascist threat from the United States, as embodied in the policy of the cold war (which Stalin always imputed directly to the United States and the United States alone). The notion of "proto-fascist" is significant here. The United States as such is not inherently either fascist or proto-fascist because the Stalinist concept of fascism is (since 1933) at once extraordinarily narrow and arbitrary, locating the phenomenon in the most reactionary part of finance capital, a very small, imaginary class fraction that may be in power but apparently not necessarily so (as evidenced by the highly praised Roosevelt and the wartime alliance). In reality, of course, the index of "fascism" had nothing to do with actual class analysis and everything to do with the degree of perceived hostility toward present Soviet policy. Soviet and auxiliary space is accordingly defined as liberated, democratic, and free, while the imperialist outside is differentiated, to various degrees and at various levels, sometimes but not always under the control of "the most reactionary circles of monopoly capital," thus requiring by way of response an equally differentiated policy designed, above all, negatively to split the forces on the other side so as to prevent "fascization." Degrees, then, are vitally important: fascism full-blown is equal to war, preeminently targeting the rising embodiment of socialist achievement and so forth, while "fascization" is a scale measuring the concrete bourgeois posture toward the Soviet Union and its interests. Spaces and maps can be inscribed correspondingly.[23]

Moscow and Washington, in short, both laid claims on the legacy of 1945, the War that was supposed to have created "One World" but evidently had failed to do so. From the Soviet standpoint, the war had been a class coalition at the state level in the name of antifascism, a massive attempt to root out the sources of fascism. Now, in late 1947, it appeared that residual forces of this kind had not only survived but were indeed flourishing in new guise in the post-Rooseveltian United States. From the US standpoint, the war had been a struggle for freedom everywhere. Owing to appalling mistakes (see Yalta) and dark treachery (see Soviet actions in Eastern Europe and elsewhere), the war effort had turned out in reality to advance hugely the interests of another and potentially much more dangerous version of totalitarianism, the very antithesis of freedom. What followed from these two different conceptions of the one world that, unexpectedly, had turned into two, were two very different strategies: renewed antifascism in the one case, a defensive move amidst retrenchment and continentalism; renewed struggle for global freedom in the other, an offensive move. As it happened, this mirrored the actual power capabilities of the two sides.

The cold war, then, was the manner in which the United States was able in peacetime to enter into the world of international politics on a global scale in the name of conducting a war short of actual war that had allegedly been declared by "International Communism." Domestically, the cold war as an always already assumed structure of aggression imposed by totalitarian Moscow worked magnificently, again, to render virtually impossible any opposition to Washington's license to act everywhere. A Republican Congress reluctant, all things being equal, to go along with governmental largesse in peacetime found itself flummoxed by the coldwar logic. The Truman Administration knew this and instrumentally exaggerated without compunction the worldwide threat. This is why Acheson can be considered a "meta-realist." He saw quite lucidly that the cold war was a way to stamp out once and for all any postwar tendencies to "isolationist" reversal. To deal with the realities of domestic politics one could not be entirely "true" to the realities abroad. In a word, one had to be ideological.[24] From that angle, the concept had the signal virtue of making it impossible to dissent and still remain politically viable. Argument could only be about a cold war more or less vigorously and successfully pursued. Here there was a political price to be paid down the line. If the threat was indeed an immediate matter of life and death on a global scale, then no incumbent could possibly do enough to meet it. One was always, therefore, acting with a certain deficit. Inadequacy, failure, was inherent. Hence of course the Republicans would soon come back with a vengeance after the Truman Administration had "failed" in China and then failed by not winning in Korea. Coldwar ideology, by being unanswerably true, is also ipso facto politically rigid. There is no way of moving beyond orthodoxy.

After the Korean War fizzled out and Stalin died in 1953, a mutually reinforcing "system" was emerging, marked by warlike hostility under ostensible conditions of peace, nonrecognition of the other side's legitimacy coupled with unremitting propaganda, an intense arms race, and the imposition of an increasingly bipolar structure on international politics, and, in qualitatively different ways, suppression of domestic dissidents. The Soviet Union, though sharply opposed to US coldwar hegemony overall, began to recognize too the advantages of physical separation, the potential for recognition of the status quo. The real is rational. Notably, nothing by way of actual, head-on military conflagration takes place: Korea was close and dangerous enough. "The cold war" became not a strategy but a geopolitical system, set in place and dominated by the United States.

The Denouement

Three developments made the US matrix historically unsustainable from the early to mid-1960s. First and most important, nuclear weapons turn out to be very effective ideology killers. The best early indication is the development of nuclear strategy in the United States from the mid-1950s onward, which involved the articulation of various "logics" whose fundamental premise is that the calculation of costs and benefits apply to both sides equally, that there is indeed a positional identity, a sameness, here; and that the "game" is a dialectic of sorts. In short, there is no deep freeze but competition and interaction, a game involving two sides in an identical way with identical premises. This is precisely what coldwar thought denied. The philosophers of escalation are thus not the quintessential cold warriors immortalized by Stanley Kubrick but, unbeknownst to themselves, harbingers of change. More immediately, the heroic "better dead than red" bravura of coldwar culture is hard to maintain amidst the increasing awareness that any postwar world would be devoid of life as we know it. Dwight D. Eisenhower was uncomfortably alive to this (along with, sotto voce, John Foster Dulles); but he was typically incapable of breaking with the existing frame, his great achievement really being the negative one of preventing lunacy. After the Cuban Missile Crisis, however, the issue becomes chillingly concrete and explicit. Nothing is worth the ultimate price of nuclear war, the ultimate hot war, the kind of war that amounts to the very erasure of value itself. The Crisis adds to this intellectual realization the vital, existential experience of the actual abyss and the untruth of the cold war. In the immediate aftermath, the days of October 1962 may have looked like a fabulous coldwar victory but no responsible observer and certainly not Kennedy himself could miss the fundamental lesson that the world no longer made sense in those terms. Instead of hovering on the edge of total destruction, there had to be management, order and predictability, some kind of normality. The Missile Crisis is the cold war degree zero.

Second, the very notion of "international communism" is rendered increasingly phantasmagoric because of the Sino-Soviet split: first an internal fight about "revisionism," then an open cold war bordering on all-out war after the Maoists have decided that "the new Czars" are the new main enemy within imperialism. The Titoist break in 1948 could be integrated into the coldwar frame as a minor anomaly, but the Chinese defection could not. The idea of a territorialized monolith and simple binaries is blasted asunder. The dichotomy is dead. The unavoidable corollary begins to emerge: preserving the coldwar frame is denying oneself the marvelous chance of playing the two communist antagonists off against each other. When none other than Richard Nixon begins to articulate this in 1967, he is saying the unsayable but obvious. Even if some notion of intracommunist quarrels can be maintained within the coldwar orthodox view at the outset, it can certainly not be so once the PRC and the United States move into de facto alliance, to the point where the Maoist regime becomes a fervent supporter of Chilean fascism because it happens overall to serve anti-Soviet interests. The orthodox argument indeed capsizes here: if the Soviet Union was the cold war, how could one with suave ease align with a regime that fulfilled much more accurately the original criteria of what made the Soviet Union the Soviet Union? It makes no sense whatsoever, which is why Ronald Reagan did not like it (yet would maintain the alliance once in power).

The Cuban Missile Crisis and the Sino-Soviet conflict destroy the coldwar matrix. A third event then ratifies this historical rupture. For, if one needed no other proof, the Vietnam debacle was everyday demonstrating in living color the absurdity of coldwar shibboleths, leading indeed by 1968 to something approximating a legitimacy crisis at the very top echelons of the US state apparatus itself. The timing here is subject to debate. Ideology does not change overnight. Lyndon B. Johnson, unlike his mercurial, mobile (and, in a way, more cynical) predecessor, is still operating rudimentarily within Munich memories when he imagines what "Vietnam" is about, not to mention the Dominican Republic in 1965. However, already amidst the great escalation of 1965–66 in Vietnam, he is beginning to sense that the whole endeavor is about face, prestige, and "credibility," as defined by some now defunct categorical frame. Vietnam is not the end of the cold war but the most graphic evidence conceivable that its historical moment has already been over for some time. The decisive change from 1963 onward is recognition: recognition of the other side's legitimacy as a geopolitical actor, if not its domestic system; recognition of the mutual interest in avoiding nuclear war at all costs. It is not recognition of the status quo across the playing field; but it is not, metaphorically or really, a cold war. It becomes, one might say, a rivalry rather than a war where winning and losing is presumably about total destruction of the other's system.

The cold war, then, was a grand policy on the part of the United States and becomes eventually a "system" of sorts, involving both sides. Yet, from another vantage point, it is not systemic at all. Almost all versions of the conventional view are grounded in some kind of systemic conflict. This position can, to reiterate, take two distinct forms: either it locates the cold war as an integral part of the nature of one of the two antagonists (chiefly the Soviet Union), or it locates it in the very difference between the two. Both versions will then have to decide whether the cold war actually began in 1917 with the appearance of the Soviet Union and if Rooseveltian wartime alliances and all the palpable variations in the relation are subordinate phases of the cold war as systemic difference. I think this is altogether mistaken. Neither of the two sides was constituted in such a way as to give rise necessarily to "the cold war," nor was their difference in itself enough to produce one. Neither side needed the cold war for its domestic reproduction. Moreover, there was nothing in the existence of two completely different social and political systems, however antithetical in structure, that in itself would have led to a cold war or the cold war. Though opposed to one another on principle in a wide range of areas, there was no intrinsic reason that the two could not have recognized territorialized demarcation and a more traditional rivalry. Moscow would certainly have gone along with that in 1947; Washington, for specific historical reasons, found it impossible to do so, choosing instead a radically different route. This choice, to be sure, was not a mere whim. Without the systemic differences, the US matrix would have made no sense and so would have been impossible. Yet a choice it remained, a deliberate decision that was not necessary.

Here one wonders, futilely but unavoidably, what would have happened had Roosevelt not died. For the license of the US presidency to create its own foreign realities is extraordinary. Witness the mind-boggling shift in US attitudes that took place with regard to Mao's China in a matter of a year or two in the early 1970s, all against the backdrop of the minutely managed Nixon-Kissinger "opening." Roosevelt, in any case, had a very different view of politics and how one conducts international relations from that which obtained after 1946. He was interested in management, order, and predictability, preconditions for Progressive change.[25] Instead there was a cold war and eventually a structure to go with it, or, to be more precise, two massive, analogous structures, each devoted to outrageous levels of military expenditure and unremitting ideological hostility. Notably, the dissolution of traditional categories of war and peace, the whole notion of a cold war in effect, fitted the United States quite well: the inherent power in the Executive could be deployed in full force, the cumbersome "separation of powers" was overcome, various forms of intervention, if need be, the name of the game, global military installations, all on the old premise that this "war" like any other war in modern US history would take place elsewhere, outside the body politic and its sacred territory. Domestically, meanwhile, it allowed a version of the corporatism of the 1930s to be institutionalized: science, capital, labor, the state, all devoted irrefutably to a single, monumental struggle.

After 1963, this comes to an end when the conservative potential of that duality of structures becomes not only visible but recognized. The military machines, with their domestic deformations, do not go away; on the contrary, their lethality is continuously expanded and much improved. Place and meaning, however, are radically different. Neither side assumes that meaningful "peace," if not bliss, is a matter of the disappearance of the other. Because "the cold war" is not an outright war that can be seen and touched, its transformation is not immediately obvious or easily determined. The problem is readily grasped if we consider present-day Korea, which is at one and the same time a continuing issue of (i) World War II, (ii) the cold war, (iii) great-power conflict, and (iv) above all, local conflict. The historical temporalities of all enter directly into the concrete case. By the same token, it is not necessary to declare the end of the cold war in any definitive manner. It can fade away, recede, cease to be a way of thinking and doing. Indeed, residual coldwar action can take place as I noted in the case of Johnson's Dominican intervention. By the early 1970s, however, the Nixon-Kissinger moves against Salvador Allende in Chile are unmistakably of a different logic and order, based on recognition and geopolitical spheres of influence. That break, that qualitative break, occurs in 1963.

This is the point where convention registers very firmly a diverging opinion. That something does happen to the relationship and so to international politics in 1963 and roughly on the grounds that I have outlined is not generally disputed. What is disputed is that it signifies any end to the cold war. My thesis, indeed, faces the problem of what happens next, how one is to conceptualize and periodize it. There is, initially, the problem of naming. Nothing comparable in rhetorical power to "the cold war" presents itself. "Great-power management"? I think not. Détente? Yes, for a while, but then again that designation leaves the opening to China aside. Détente is not what happens with regard to the PRC. Bipolarity amidst increasing tendencies to multipolarity? Descriptively not without its virtues but unless we want to pursue the neorealist solution, it is not an explanatory concept, in addition to which the whole semantics of polarity is fraught with difficulties, imported as it is from physics. In the end, no single logic dominates or overdetermines the coming era in the same way as did the cold war. Resurrecting a term once peddled by Acheson on Capitol Hill, one might perhaps call it a "cold peace."[26]

Historically, the best way concretely to approach this is through Mario Del Pero's revision of the conventional account and his emphatic insistence that Henry Kissinger's approach (Nixon's being less transparent) is never about the recognition of "multipolarity" but about the attempt to reimpose bipolarity. The conventional account, of course, sees détente as a relaxation of tension, relative cooperation between the two superpowers, and, on the part of the United States, the famed "triangulation" marked by the move on China in 1971. In a larger context, the period is typified by the aforementioned "multipolarity" which begins in the 1960s and now gains recognition: Beijing's break from Moscow, Charles de Gaulle's partial move away from NATO and the United States, Willy Brandt's Ostpolitik, the Czechoslovak Spring in 1968, Japan's and West Germany's rising economic power within the West, the later beginnings of Eurocommunism, and so forth. As Del Pero argues, Kissinger's design is not based on any acceptance of multipolarity and the need to manage it; on the contrary it is about the reassertion of US power in the framework of bipolarity, that is, within the polarity of the real superpowers.[27]

This, in my view, is largely right, with the proviso that Kissinger is only pragmatically interested in bipolarity. His aim, after all, is not bipolarity for its own sake but the reassertion of US power—indeed, all things being equal, the achievement of US hegemony, if not (unrealistically) supremacy. Even so, it is also clear that his "hyperdiplomacy" is not situated within any coldwar frame. In short, the bipolarity in question is not to be confused with any dichotomous division of the world in terms of good and evil, or freedom and totalitarianism. Bipolarity is about a certain power relationship and how one conducts it to the best of one's interests. Kissinger is decidedly indifferent to political coloration. This is why he can find Chou En-Lai so congenial, the most impressive kindred spirit he ever encounters in geopolitics. This is why his idea of the Chilean coup in 1973 as a model for dealing with legitimate Eurocommunist power in Western Europe should not be grasped in coldwar terms. In the privacy of his chamber, Kissinger might well have agreed that the Italian Communist Party would have been the best administrator of local capitalism; but it was simply an irrelevant consideration along with the general principle of Italian democracy. In Chile and Western Europe, policy is a matter of superimposing geopolitical order, reasserting the line. Similarly, Kissinger's sundry actions to subvert and destroy Soviet and Cuban allies in Africa is a matter of making life difficult for the opponent who is getting out of bounds. At no time, however, does Kissinger challenge the right of the Soviets, all things being equal, to control their own sphere.

Kissinger's hyperdiplomacy was thus a recognition of certain realities having to do with the relative loss of US power and an ingenious attempt to recuperate that power by novel means. That the material underpinnings of the cold war had crumbled was one of those realities. It was Kissinger's misfortune, however, that coldwar ideology had not evaporated along with its foundations. It survived superstructurally so to speak, always lurking ideologically in the background should things go wrong. The surviving element of bipolarity itself was similarly open to such potential reinterpretation. Hyperdiplomacy in the name of the balance of power, then, was always going to be a position that lived on borrowed time. By the end of the 1970s, things had gone very wrong indeed, which is why Ronald Reagan, for a period, could reinvent—truly reinvent—the cold war with such success. Yet it is significant that Reagan's cold war remained a policy, that it never became a structure. The policy could never be translated into the kind of international system that characterized the cold war in the 1950s or even lastingly mark the US posture. The very brevity of the exercise demonstrates how weak were its material underpinnings, even with the extraordinary regeneration of the military machine. The brevity, alas, is mostly forgotten now because of the massive, world-historical contingency that actually followed. What is in fact also mostly forgotten is that Reagan's coldwar phase had essentially ended before the Soviet Union ended, before the cold war itself, according to convention, had ended.[28]

Foray Into the Third World

Here, I must confront a common argument for the continuity thesis that also happens in a way to be "true," to have empirical validity, while self-consciously breaking with convention in other ways: the notion that the cold war continues by means of direct intervention and use of proxies in the third world, that it is really about thirdworld interventionism. As the 1970s amply illustrate, client struggles do continue and sometimes intensify in the third world. This is a cogent viewpoint. I will respond by examining Odd Arne Westad's tome on the subject, *The Global Cold War*, which is certainly the most far-reaching attempt from a detached standpoint to think the cold war in the thirdworld frame.[29] Sympathetic as he is to those on the receiving end, Westad is still detached in not setting out to demonstrate interventionism as the natural expression of US imperialism, or for that matter Soviet imperialism. In very much less detached form, the argument could otherwise be traced back as far as Gabriel and Joyce Kolko who dismissed "the cold war" forty years ago as an "egregious" obfuscation of the actual counterrevolution that the United States inflicted on the world and the third world in particular.[30] In Westad's version, interventionism is not the exclusive property of either superpower but a systemic function of the cold war as it developed from the 1960s onward.

Empirically, the novelty is chiefly to do with the Soviet side and its particulars but the periodization is the decisive aspect: the 1970s marks the intensification of the cold war, not the easing or the end of it.[31] Détente and stability in Europe, in short, allow the superpowers to play out the cold war to devastating effect in new thirdworld areas, especially Africa. Where amorphous convention sees a thaw and management, Westad sees huge expansion in space and greater ferocity. He also insists that the confrontations are central because both superpowers, not only the United States, are now capable of projecting power on a global scale and do so. That the frozen fixity of the cold war in its European area of initial confrontation should have generated client warfare (of sorts) in the third world is itself not a new idea. Westad's privileging of thirdworld events, their centrality in the cold war, is however unusual: "the most important aspects of the Cold War were neither military nor strategic, nor Europe-centered but connected to political and social development in the Third World."[32] Consequently, this is in no way a history of "the global cold war." Willy Brandt does not appear in it. Nuclear arsenals are absent. Even the missiles in thirdworld Cuba are referred to only in passing. Europe, refreshingly in a way, is nowhere to be seen except insofar as it has effect on the third world.

The constitutive concept here is not the cold war in any determinate sense but the notion of "the three worlds," more particularly, the United States, the Soviet Union and the third world. Auxiliaries do play a role (above all Cuba); but the essence is superpower confrontation in an area that is largely created by that confrontation itself. The narrative, in its bare essentials, is as follows. In 1945 two major powers with universalist pretensions confronted each other by providing two radically alternative ways of coming to grips with modernity and modernization. The Soviet Union, however, was at the time largely defensive while the United States moved actively to check what it perceived as the advance of international communism. US interventionism in a way created the third world, a differentiated space for battle outside the Eurasian heartland proper. This eventually coincided with decolonization and liberation movements, at first mainly "nativist" and nationalist in orientation but, partly in response to US power, gradually more radical. After Stalin, the Soviet elite woke up to the possibilities here but had few means to mount a real challenge. That challenge came instead from the experiences and revolutions in Vietnam and Cuba (and the solidaric export of the latter revolution). In the 1970s, then, the Soviet Union is caught between two apparent imperatives: to manage through détente the relationship with the United States while at the same time supporting the spreading and increasingly radicalized movements in the third world, above all in Africa. Throughout, thirdworld elites, on their part, had found themselves both courted and repressed by the superpowers, faced with a choice of developmental models and political alliances that might provide opportunities and material support but often too interventionism and unwanted, engineered conflict.

These games are played out through the 1970s with mixed results: the Soviet Union (assisted and pushed by the more enterprising Cubans) scores some apparent victories, in southern Africa for example, but is ultimately dragged down, the disappointment of the Ethiopian "revolution" being only a faint omen of the disaster that would await in Afghanistan. The main cost is not material or even strategic. The Soviet Union could have gone on for a long time in Afghanistan. Yet the Afghan morass and thirdworld moves generally were a decisive part of the growing legitimacy crisis within the elite. Conversely, the United States in the 1980s is able to reconstruct global capitalism and crush revolutionary challenges in Central America. And thus it went, the coldwar victims in the third world mostly forgotten along with their countries and the very idea of the third world itself.

This vivid history of the 1970s and 1980s restores the importance of that conjuncture and the importance of the third world within it. Why, however, we should "forget" nuclear strategy, and why we should accept that "bipolarity" did not weaken, is not obvious. Conflict certainly spread into new areas (whether it intensifies is another matter); but how did client warfare differ qualitatively from the kind of jockeying that went on, say, between Russia and Britain in the arc from Turkey to China in the 19th century? And did the interventionism result from intensified, globalized bipolarity? Westad himself shows with great clarity the degree to which the thrust of Soviet "interventionism" in Africa was directed not at the United States but at the People's Republic of China, a rival power that it openly clashed with militarily in 1969 and feared a great deal. As one of the few western historians outside the ex-Soviet bloc with a command of both Russian and Chinese, Westad knows that conflict better than most but what we get is description, ample description, but nothing but description.

It is easy to see the intention. Westad wants to dislocate or decenter the cold war from its Euro-Western theatre. "Decentering" seems code for rewriting the cold war in the spirit of social history, where the "Euro-centric" comes to stand for rarefied, old-style political history and thirdworld interventionism for the uncovering of a more genuine history from below and beyond, a properly archaeological investigation of the real workings of the cold war, so to speak. My own view is the exact opposite: relentless and rigorous centering. I leave aside the fact that "interventionism in the third world" is hardly what the chief antagonists themselves believed the cold war was about, nor where they spent their preponderant resources: one might argue that they were mistaken about the real. To center the concept and period of the cold war, however, is not to ignore the third world or any other world for that matter. On the contrary, it is only by being insistently specific about the overdeterminant structure that one can see its contradictions and, crucially, how it operated by projection. Thirdworld interventionism would not have happened without the cold war but it should not be conflated with it.

Westad's whole, in that sense, is false. For what is this "cold war" that is being played out to such catastrophic consequence in the third world? Westad has no single concept here. Initially, he thinks, conventionally, that the cold war is just the period when the United States and the Soviet Union dominated international affairs. That dominant relationship became a confrontation because the two happened for various historical reasons ideologically to be universalist and thus necessarily interventionist in orientation; and the confrontation became a cold war because of "the American ideological insistence that a global spread of Communism would, if not checked, result from the postwar extension of Soviet might."[33] So it is perhaps not rival universalism as such but one particular form of it, the US variety, that really generates the cold war. However, there is also the "interventionist" nature of their respective ideologies to consider: they cannot not intervene. And "intervention" amidst the tripartite structure of the world, not the cold war, is Westad's central concern. He is not interested in the cold war as a cold war: he is interested in the ruinous effects of western interventionism and modernization (western here meaning both the United States and the Soviet Union). He is, to coin a phrase, interested in the Clash of Modernizations. Thus, in his concluding remarks, he begins to imagine the cold war as merely the Clausewitzian continuation of colonialism by other means, the latest but not the last form of a process that may have begun, not in 1945, not in 1917, but at Berlin in 1878 when the Europeans divided Africa. Indeed, he says, why not date the beginning to 1415 and the first Portuguese colony?

Indeed, why not? So, at long last, we have arrived at the point where the meaning of the cold war has been reduced to nothing, where all conceptual value has been lost in a historical fog: the cold war as another name for western colonialism as it began in 1415.[34] The difference between Westad's position and the customary continuity thesis, viz. his foregrounding of the triangular in contrast to the simple binary, is in short less radical than it seems. In insisting that the cold war was a condition, a relationship between two equal entities, Westad differs fundamentally, to be sure, from the neo-orthodox idea of the cold war as Soviet aggression against freedom. His triangulation, however, is really the binary confrontation writ large, a confrontation emptied of political meaning. Dislocating the cold war in Westad's fashion makes it disappear. An unconventional account of intense thirdworld conflicts and their increasing geopolitical significance in the 1970s does not in fact require the conventional scaffolding of the cold war in the 1950s. Westad does not need "the cold war" and, after a fashion, he comes to see this: the otherwise absurd reference to 1415, even if half in jest, reveals that his is not a history grounded in any cold war.

None of the above takes care of my own problem with the meaning of that other end, the end of 1989–91. What is it that comes to an end with the end of the Soviet Union, beyond, obviously, the remnants of "bipolarity"? The short answer is the epoch precipitated by the Bolshevik Revolution in 1917. There is one extant way of thinking about the epoch from 1917 onward that shows both systematic precision and explanatory value. I am referring to Francis Fukuyama's once famous thesis, now widely disdained, concerning "the end of history," his quasi-Hegelian notion that the passing of the Soviet Union also signified the end of a certain historical principle or spirit/Geist, leaving liberal, democratic capitalism (reverse the order of the terms as you please) in place as the final legitimate order for the ages to come. The last proposition was a bit of a wager on Fukuyama's part; but if some new negation was to emerge, it was certainly unimaginable at the time. Meanwhile, Perry Anderson's Marxist variation on Fukuyama's theme held out the possibility of such a new oppositional moment but not for the foreseeable future.[35]

This Hegelian motif is of the greatest interest, though it has faded in prominence, perhaps because in desiccated form it has become common wisdom, or because it is no longer meaningful, or both. In any case, I think it may well be right. It allows for different periods and phases within its formal compass, the cold war being one of them. It also allows for other processes, other principles, other temporalities, other "periods" so to speak. It does not treat (or necessarily treat) the entire epoch as a unified, expressive totality. The cold war, however, in the Fukuyama-Anderson frame is never a "problem." It is subsumed under the general contradiction. In principle, this is compatible with my account, with the notion that the cold war has a specific genesis, meaning, function, and place in postwar US policy; but, tendentially, it is easy to miss its salience amidst the grand Hegelian narrative.[36]

I have argued this view of the cold war, the salience and the specificity of the cold war as a US project, in different ways since the 1980s with little or no success. Convention rules OK. The reason for resurrecting the argument in revamped form is the recent eruption of US global power in a unilateralist spirit as expressed above all in the Iraqi operation. Whatever else it did, the presidency of George W. Bush certainly served to concentrate the global mind on the nature, conditions, and possible limits of US power. Hence his presidency also revived the spirit of all those organic intellectuals of US power whose fortunes had dwindled so dramatically in the 1990s, the unheroic era of more and better capitalist globalization along with, in a minor key, humanitarian diplomacy and intermittent war. After the massive shift of 2001, predictably, there were numerous tracts on United States and empire, typically featuring some potted history of what was imagined to have been "the cold war." Once again the period was put to good ideological use. Once again one had to object to the obvious and the self-evident. Once again we were "after the cold war." The ensuing "war on terror/ism" was indeed in some ways a postmodern play on the cold war or what the cold war was supposed to have been about, its pivotal shortcoming being that it had no proper political enemy on which such a war (whether real or metaphorical or both was always unclear) could be waged. We have now entered a new phase, another version of the postmodern, where large concepts and large names are purposely left aside, if not entirely forgotten. It is the heroism of the low-key. Whatever its immediate political virtues, such a pragmatic emphasis on the particular easily renders the cold war historically invisible, invoked if at all as a conventional short-hand for something once useful but now passed. Conventional appropriation or sidestepping is however not always the best way to transcend the Grand American Narrative. The ferocious return of the repressed is not hard to imagine, at which point one had better be prepared.

Notes

1. When used as an attribute, the cold war is rendered "coldwar"; and the noun itself is never capitalized. Here I am following the rule laid down for me in no uncertain terms by the late and lamented Craig Owens, who, among many things, was a stellar editor when he was at Art in America. I have followed the same procedure with "the third world."
2. Melvyn Leffler's latest account, notably, casts a wider net in this regard: the end is a collaborative effort on the part of Mikhail Gorbachev, Ronald Reagan, and George H. W. Bush. The narrative is structured around degrees of "reasonableness" in circumstances that are systematically tense and difficult for both sides after 1947. Leffler, *For the Soul of Mankind: The United States, the Soviet Union and the Cold War* (New York, 2007). Resolution (and so the end) appears once the circumstances and the personalities involved allow reasonableness to be victorious. What needs then to be addressed is that that reasonable end is followed by another end, namely, the end of the Soviet Union. For a remarkable critique of Gorbachev's end game—how he gave away the farm as it were—see Vladimir Zubok, *A Failed Empire: The Soviet Union in the Cold War from Stalin to Gorbachev* (Chapel Hill, 2007).
3. The trinity is necessarily crude and nonexhaustive but, with that proviso, useful for the sake of the argument.
4. Barack Obama's express and typically pragmatic admiration for Reagan is a good index of the now dominant and highly refracted image of a Benign Communicator who revived America as opposed to, say, a far-right ideologue who initiated a massive assault on the working poor.
5. See, conveniently, Gaddis, *The Cold War: A New History* (New York, 2005).
6. This view is represented with characteristic clarity by Kenneth Waltz, *Theory of International Politics* (New York, 1979). "Competition" here is a function of structurally identical positions in a system that is itself not ideological. The cold war qua cold war is virtually absent. Gaddis at mid-career was heavily influenced by this kind of neorealism and wrote some of his best analyses in that mode, roughly the moment between *Strategies of Containment: A Critical Appraisal of American National Security Policy during the Cold War* (Oxford, 1982) and *The Long Peace: Inquiries into the History of the Cold War* (Oxford, 1987). Seeing the cold war as a long peace was a suggestive but limited idea, characteristically single-minded and forcefully expressed. Above all, however, it was badly timed. Gaddis the

neorealist, it should be added, dealt with the cold war as actual history, as was not always the case with the political scientists who inspired him.

7. This ideal type, then, is less than ideal: it has no paradigmatic statement so to speak. It is more of an assumption, an implicit frame, than a clear concept. Much of diplomatic history in the United States operates within its compass.
8. Le Carré "resolves" this identity ultimately by annulling it in some individual and typically quixotic act of heroism that breaks with the systemic altogether. Witness Alec Leamas on the Berlin Wall in the climax of *The Spy Who Came in from the Cold* (1963), a novel whose spirit and appearance are of the greatest interest when it comes to periodization.
9. On Churchill's metaphor (which had a long and not always honorable lineage), see Patrick Wright, *Iron Curtain: From Stage to Cold War* (Oxford, 2007).
10. Jean-Francois Lyotard originated this with *The Postmodern Condition: A Report on Knowledge* (Minneapolis, 1984 [original in French 1979] but for me the best conceptualization remains Fredric Jameson, *Postmodernism, or, The Cultural Logic of Late Capitalism* (Durham, NC, 1991), the original article by the same name appearing in 1984. All in all, Jameson's Althusserian understanding of what it is to produce a concept has been decisive for me.
11. Vulgarly put, historians chop up time and give names to the ensuing entities or periods, offering accounts in the process of origins and causes of expiration. Space is a complicating factor not always recognized.
12. I disagree, therefore, with the many leftwing accounts of the cold war that see the need for capitalist expansion as central. The cold war was a political move, a strategic way of putting the United States into the world in no uncertain ways, of rendering global engagement irrefutable. This is not unrelated to "capitalism" of course but at the same time not reducible to it. An argument could well be made that a better solution for capital in 1947 than the cold war would have been extensive cooperation or at least geopolitical agreement with the Soviet Union; but such a view would also be politically ahistorical.
13. Though only mentioned more or less in passing, "containment" was important in expressing Kennan's notion of a predetermined, unresponsive Moscow. Lippmann spotted this. The idea, however, that containment was a "strategy" is incorrect. It meant nothing more than counteracting in various ways at various points. Kennan would spend the next half-century trying to explain why this was presumably not grasped. The literature on the alleged "meaning" of containment is enormous and still growing. A recent example, typically streamlined and simplified for prescriptive purposes (well intended in themselves) is Ian Shapiro's *Containment: Rebuilding a Strategy Against Global Terror* (Princeton, 2008). Containment functions here chiefly as a fantasized counterpoint to the excesses, real enough, of George W. Bush.
14. Lippmann, *The Cold War: A Study in Foreign Policy* (New York, 1947). The articles appeared from September 2 to October 2 in the *New York Herald Tribune* and the *Washington Post* (and were syndicated elsewhere). "Strategic monstrosity" was used in his column on September 6.
15. The closest analogue, analytically, is in fact FDR's conception of Hitler's Germany: one could do business with unpleasant dictators, even fascist ones such as Mussolini, but not with the Nazi regime, whose gangster nature made all agreement impossible. On the civilizational aspect, see Patrick Thaddeus Jackson's stimulating *Civilizing the Enemy: German Reconstruction and the Invention of the West* (Ann Arbor, 2006). See also John Lamberton Harper, *Visions of Europe: Franklin D. Roosevelt, George F. Kennan and Dean Acheson* (Cambridge, 1994).
16. I have developed the analysis here at greater length in my "Fourteen Notes on the Very Concept of the Cold War" in G. O'Tuathail and S. Dalby (eds.), *Rethinking Geopolitics* (New York, 1999). See also Anders Stephanson, *Kennan and the Art of Foreign Policy* (Cambridge, MA, 1989). 17. Cf. Nicholas Guilhot, (ed.), *The Invention of International Relations Theory: Realism, the Rockefeller Foundation, and the 1954 Conference on Theory* (New York, 2011). Realism was far from a single political position. Reinhold Niebuhr's Christian realism was

eminently compatible with a coldwar posture. Morgenthau's realism, of course, continued to exert a powerful academic influence, not least because he was the author of the standard textbook.

17. Cf. Guilhot, *Invention of International Relations.*
18. Lippmann does not, in my view, think of the term as a metaphor but rather as analogous with what the French writer George Duhamel had referred to in 1939 as La Guerre Blanche, Hitler's blistering bully tactics against the French, a war of terror one might say without the actual violence. Lippmann later claimed indeed that he had picked it up in France in the late 1930s: I have never found it however in the form of "la Guerre Froide." The term was used on a couple of occasions in the spring and summer of 1947 by Bernard Baruch but not in any sustained way. George Orwell used the term in 1945 in a different way to describe, suggestively, a typically dystopian future of superpower domination, internally coherent imperialisms in a system of constant but cold external hostility. The *Chicago Tribune* characterized Truman's "Doctrine" speech in March 1947 as "cold a war speech" as any; and the *India Times* referred in turn to that expression as a "Cold War Speech." It is easy to demonstrate, however, that Lippmann's acidic series inaugurated the public use of the term. By November–December, it was in daily use.
19. Cf. Stephanson, "Fourteen Notes."
20. In his *Memoirs II* (1972), Kennan credits Raymond Aron together with Lippmann with his enlightenment in the late 1950s after the disengagement controversy. It is hard to accept that he remained blind to the "functionality" aspect of the cold war for so long; but it seems plausible, given that he is still, in his famous Reith Lectures of 1957, proposing diplomacy and "disengagement" rather along the lines of Lippmann's critique in September 1947.
21. Cf. Anders Stephanson, "Liberty or Death: the Cold War as US Ideology" in O. A. Westad (ed.), *Reviewing the Cold War: Approaches, Interpretations, Theory* (London, 2000). The model here is of course Augustine's solution to the problem of evil amidst the omnipotence of God: evil is a perversion of good, not a quality of independent existence. Nietzsche's transformation of this is also pertinent: the infection of the strong by the slave mentality, which can only exist parasitically and not in its own right. The political consequence is the essential point. Had the structure been properly Manichean (which is often wrongly assumed), the possibility of a modus vivendi and all manner of deals would have at once been opened up. On the aspect of "unconditional surrender," see NSC-68, the most authoritative US policy statement after Kennan's articulations of 1947–48, which says in April 1950 that "we can expect no lasting abatement of the crisis unless and until a change occurs in the nature of the Soviet system," and that any diplomatic settlement "can only record the progress which the free world will have made in creating a political and economic system in the world so successful that the frustration of the Kremlin's design for world domination will be complete." It is hard to think of a more resolute rejection of the kind of diplomacy and strategy Lippmann had in mind. There can be no agreement unless it is a matter of registering the destruction of the Soviet system. This is an offer one must refuse in Moscow, as indeed was also the intention.
22. This is the notorious problem with "roll-back," the Republican counterpoint to "containment" in the early 1950s. Republican critics were right to say that if "international communism" is all the things that the Truman Administration says it is, then it is inherently immoral by American standards to leave it in place, as "containment" would seem to imply. Logically, then, this system of slavery had to be abolished, or rolled-back, instead of merely contained. Logic then falters: even without the threat of nuclear war, it would have been hard to find a workable roll-back strategy short of outright war, which is to say another world war, at which point one had good reason to flinch. Logic also falters, however, for the same reason that Kennan's contrary position failed as a critique of containment: what the Truman Administration and coldwar thought said about the Soviet Union was only a premise, an enabling condition, for something quite different.

23. The two best analyses of this Soviet complex remain Nicos Poulantzas, *Fascism and Dictatorship: The Third International and the Problem of Fascism* (London, 1974); and Fernando Claudin, *The Communist Movement From Comintern to Cominform* (Harmondsworth, 1975).
24. Thus, in a way, it is an "invention," but the dynamic is certainly not reducible to any functionalist creation of useful myth. Acheson ultimately believed in the essentials of the cold war, the idea of the global threat and the necessity of a commensurate US response. It should be noted that officialdom, as opposed to mass media, used "the cold war" sparingly. Until NSC-68, internal policy documents did not feature it either. One reason was that one did not wish to be seen as warlike, as participants in a war, the implication being identity and similarity perhaps. This is contradicted, however, by NSC-68, which speaks approvingly of fighting the cold war.
25. FDR, representing in many ways the last gasp and generation of the Progressive Era, always insisted on the "worldliness" of the United States, that one had to recognize that "America" was in time and history, part of a larger whole and irrevocably called upon to act in it. His singularly cavalier attitude to the finer points of the Constitution was indicative: there was nothing "sacred" about the United States as a tradition. This is also why he had no trouble in seeing the United States as part of a genuine alliance.
26. *The New York Times*, June 11, 1950, p. 125. Acheson's remark was uttered a couple of weeks before the outbreak of the Korean War.
27. See Mario Del Pero, *The Eccentric Realist: Henry Kissinger and the Shaping of American Foreign Policy* (Ithaca, 2009).
28. Leffler's *For the Soul of Mankind*, it should be said, recognizes this discrepancy.
29. Westad, *The Global Cold War: Third World Interventions and the Making of Our Times* (Cambridge, 2006).
30. Gabriel and Joyce Kolko, *The Limits of Power: The World and the United States Foreign Policy 1945–1954* (New York, 1972), p. 6; see also pp. 2–5, 709–715; and Gabriel Kolko, *The Politics of War: The World and the United States Foreign Policy, 1943–1945* (London, 1969), 3–6, 619–622.
31. Westad's delineation is commendable on specific events and interventions, going all the way back to the Iranian crisis of 1946, where he reminds us that Stalin, far from pushing any communist agenda, typically sold out his political friends for limited and narrow Soviet interests. The treatment of Africa (Congo, Angola, Mozambique, South Africa, Ethiopia, Somalia, and the Horn) is a series of outstanding analyses of local struggles, superpower arrogance, and the ubiquitous revolutionary enthusiasm of the Cubans. Similarly, the ensuing chapters on "the Islamist defiance" and the events of Iran and Afghanistan are superb histories, especially of the fateful Soviet decision-making process on the Afghanistan and the subsequent disaster, all the more poignant a story because Moscow's policymakers were so aware of the dangers involved. It is striking to see, in fact, how often Soviet analysts had a highly realistic view of thirdworld events and allies. Yet policy change was doomed because the given framework did not allow it. Or, as in Afghanistan, letting go was also to let the newly aggressive United States into one's backyard. Westad's treatment of the United States, by contrast, is much weaker than the comparable considerations on the Soviet Union, the PRC, and the third world. He is less interested in the United States and has nothing very probing to say about it.
32. Westad, *Global Cold War*, p. 396.
33. Westad, *Global Cold War*, p. 25.
34. The Iberian reference brings to mind the suggestive idea that the originator of the cold war as a term was the Castilian grandee Don Juan Manuel who, earlier in the fourteenth century, had pondered the nature of the conflict between Islam and Christianity on the peninsula as (so it is said) a kind of cold war. Don Juan Manuel, interestingly concerned with irregularity and ideological incommensurability, is however not talking about a cold war but a "luke-warm" one, a metaphor of rather different implications. See Note Four in Stephanson, "Fourteen Notes."

35. Fukuyama originally proposed the argument in "The End of History?" *The National Interest* 16 (Summer 1989) and expanded it (in more ways than one) in his subsequent book *The End of History and the Last Man* (New York, 1992). Perry Anderson's perceptive critique, dealing extensively with the conceptual history of the whole idea of "the end," appeared in his volume *A Zone of Engagement* (London, 1992).
36. Anderson recognizes that something decisive did happen in 1963, indeed putting an end to the cold war stricto sensu. He insists, however, that the antagonism between the United States and the Soviet Union was systemic, grounded in the conflict between capitalism and communism. Anderson to the author, December 26, 2008. A roughly similar view is espoused by Fredric Jameson in his *The Hegel Variations: On the Phenomenology of Spirit* (London, 2010), wherein he refers to "the Long Cold War" (1917–1989). My objection, to reiterate, is this: once territorialized and stabilized, there is nothing about that conflict that in itself would lead to any cold war, nothing systemic in short that would force either "capitalism" or "communism" to do anything in particular vis-à-vis the other. The two systems side by side are certainly "incompatible" in that neither can work in the same space (though the PRC today shows that capitalism is eminently commensurate with the political dictatorship of the Communist Party; but then again we always knew that capitalism had no inherent political form beyond the legal sanctity of property). Such an incompatibility does not in itself translate into any determinate relationship or foreign policy.

2

Exploring the Histories of the Cold War

A Pluralist Approach

ODD ARNE WESTAD

Sometimes, when listening to conversations about Iraq or Afghanistan or relations with China or other burning issues of the day, I see the elephant in the room. It is a big pachyderm, dressed like Hannibal's beasts of war, with gigantic trunks and elephantastic ears, and with Cold War painted all over it. Its long shadow falls on most things we do or say. But while some try to describe the animal and log its lumbering impact on the world, others are happy to leave it alone: it seems such an antiquated brute, and mentioning it could conjure up past calamities—someone's uncle got trampled, or a distant relative was speared, and surely some people are allergic to elephants. It is better not mentioned.

The few of us who pay no heed to long-standing sensitivities and well-documented allergies and instead attempt to discuss what is standing right next to us, we always wonder about *how* best to describe it. Aware of the risks of acting blindly, most would-be storytellers agree that there *is* such a thing as the elephant (though it can be called by different names). We also—at least most of the time—agree that there are certain characteristics that define it (though there is little agreement as to what the *most important* characteristics are). Some insist that the leg (or part of the tail) they themselves are studying is the one and only elephant. Pluralists—the ones I am celebrating in this chapter—say that the study of all the different parts of the animal is OK. To study its physiology is OK, as is studying its embryology and its ecology, or its mating call. The study of elephant cemeteries is OK. Examining its effects on plants and water is certainly OK. And learning about the consequences for other animals of the elephant's rather dominant behavior is more than OK; it is de rigueur.

While a whole generation has grown accustomed to dangerous denial about how the Cold War affected them, their societies, and their international affairs, the academic study of the conflict has squandered its energy on denying the pluralism that by default should be built into its investigations. Ever since the study of the recent past entered the late twentieth century, there have been insistent attempts at limiting what are legitimate fields of inquiry or defining the term "Cold War" in ways that only fit the narrow research interests of one group or "school" or political tendency. Most of the recent attempts at erecting iron curtains in the study of history have derived from the US culture wars of the 1990s, with Cold War-derived categories of academic Left and Right each cheering themselves back into their corners of the ideological battlefield while ignoring the real tasks they face in explaining the immediate past to their audiences. It has been depressing reading and it has, mostly, been very poor craftsmanship. While the field of international history itself has embarked on one of its most exciting periods in a long while, some senior scholars have attempted to shoehorn the study of the Cold War back into the predetermined shape of US politics. These latter-day attempts at rescuing the "correct" Right or Left discourses from the continuous innovations in interpretation, approach, and method within the broader field have sometimes made Cold War historians the laughing stock of the historical profession. It is time to break free.

Against Hegemony

All hegemonic powers in history have in some way or another attempted to subsume key historical or cultural concepts under their own discourses. The Romans fitted Greek or Jewish histories into their own schools and interpretations. The British reveled in finding that Roman or Indian history integrated remarkably well into Whig or Tory interpretations.[1] Nineteenth and twentieth-century North African or Caribbean historians found that their histories were perfect fodder for the mills of Parisian intellectuals, whether in the cafes on the Left Bank or in the offices on the Right. All the world could be taken as examples of why one view (or the other) of Roman, British, or French history were correct, and others idiotic, faulty, or knavish. Stepping outside these discourses at best betrayed one's provincialism or at worst one's hidden allegiance to the other party of the metropole. For nothing existed beyond what the center offered; just like Edward Said's Orientalists produced "a Western style for dominating, restructuring, and having authority over the Orient," these histories mined evidence in order to fit it into what was known and therefore authoritative.[2]

The writing of Cold War history in the United States has, since its initiation in the 1950s, been at least as bipolar as the conflict itself. The political Right—a distinct majority stretching from political liberals to moderates to conservatives—have insisted on the Cold War being a battle between American freedom and its domestic and international opponents. While roundly condemning Soviet policy, it has always been more preoccupied with beating domestic critics over the head with accusations of pro-Soviet (and therefore anti-American) viewpoints than ever investigating the claims that Stalin and his collaborators started the Cold War (in order to do the latter they would have to have had a research strategy that involved learning Russian, for instance). I have written a great deal about the deficiencies of the Cold War histories by the US Right: some of them are arrogantly self-centered and self-referential, they are usually hegemonic in execution and intent, and—for those written after the Cold War ended and a broad access to non-American historical materials opened up—they are mostly historiographically redundant, new wine into old bottles (and the wine does indeed run out).[3]

There is also the American Left, on which I have had much less to say in the past, both because it has been less relevant for Cold War studies overall given its limited historiographical influence and because it has clashed less with my own views (indeed, significant parts of my investigations of the Cold War as a global conflict have been inspired by contrary, left-wing voices within US academia). As a general rule, the Left has been much more open not just to critical analyses of US foreign policy (that is a given), but also to debating new paradigms, research methods, and research orientations within the field of US international history. While some of the Right (but in no way all) has been writing triumphalist court-history, the Left for obvious reasons has not joined in the euphoria about how the Cold War ended (though few—to their credit—have seen much to deplore in the demise of the Eastern European dictatorships).[4]

But, for all its chastising of US foreign policy, part of the American Left—represented in this volume by Anders Stephanson—has been as relentlessly US-centered in its approach to international affairs as the Right has been. While the Right, present in Stephanson's critique through John Lewis Gaddis, sees the rise of US global predominance as a cause for celebration, the Stephansonian Left sees it as the root of all evil.[5] I do not use the latter expression as a cliché: for parts of the US (or in Stephanson's case US-based) Left most devilishness in the postwar world was in some form or another caused by an immoral use of US power. From Korea to Vietnam to the Iraq-Iran War, the root cause of conflict was the policy of the United States. Instead of studying how US interventions interacted with local elites to create the specific conditions for war or repression, the focus is invariably on the United States itself. Stephanson does not support the "decentering" of study of the Cold War that some of us have been calling for; on the contrary, he calls for "the exact opposite: relentless and rigorous centering . . . it is only by being insistently specific about the overdeterminant structure that one can see its contradictions and, crucially, how it operated by projection."[6]

Anders Stephanson is a historian for whom I have great respect and I have learnt much from his work (though I must confess that I have sometimes struggled to understand parts of it). I think, however, that his campaign for centering the Cold War exclusively on the United States is wrong-headed, and that it leads in a wrong direction in terms of how we want to approach the study of the conflict. By attempting to limit our investigations of the Cold War to the exploration of a particular US strategy for world dominance, Stephanson is breaking away from the trails blazed by radical US historians who have shown the value of studying American power in its local contexts, such as Marilyn Young and Lloyd Gardner (to use just two examples of historians of the war in Vietnam), or—for that matter—William Appleman Williams, whose call for the study of "economic theory and practice, abstract ideas, past and future politics, anticipations of Utopia, messianic idealism, social-psychological imperatives, historical consciousness, and military strategy" assumes that the only way US foreign policy can be understood is through its encounters with a real world that is massively different from itself.[7]

I have little doubt that the historiographical trends that came out of the United States during the Cold War are now at the end of their utility as overall approaches to international history. The field has become much too diverse, methodologically and interpretatively, for the old constraints to hold. What is emerging is a new ability to draw on international and comparative scholarship in social and intellectual history and in the social sciences, which sets the United States as one country among many and therefore systematically relativizes American claims to subsume the historical experience of others.[8] Instead of categorizing all views and actions according to division lines in American politics, a growing strain in the post–Cold War literature sees other rationalities, other political or social agendas, or other intentions at work. While never denying the dominant role of the most super of superpowers, they write about the Cold War as part of international and transnational history, as a complex and rapidly globalizing ideological confrontation, with lots of unintended consequences, misunderstandings, and rapid role-changes. The zoology of the Cold War pachyderm is an expanding one, and attempts to limit it are bound to fail.

Against Reductionism

At the core of the reductionist argument that Stephanson puts forward is the belief that the term "Cold War" should only be used for US foreign policy (and possibly only for US policy toward the Soviet Union, though that remains unclear) for a brief period between the end of World War II and the Cuban Missile Crisis. It was the US suspension of "normal" diplomacy in dealing with the Soviets during this period that set it apart; it was the focus on destroying Soviet socialism rather than dealing with it diplomatically that constituted a Cold War. After 1962–/63 the American government decided that the Cold War was too dangerous and returned to regular Westphalian forms of interaction. The "Cold War" therefore has little to do with the postcolonial wars of the 1960s and 1970s, or even with the liberation of Eastern Europe or the collapse of the Soviet system. "The cold war . . . was a grand policy on the part of the United States," Stephanson holds—nothing more, and nothing less.[9]

What makes this argument dangerous is not primarily the "relentless centering" that is built into it—though that, as I have argued above, is bad enough—but the specific form of reductionism that makes others foils against which US policy can be seen. By removing the Third World Left from the conflict that they thought they were part of and by telling them that they were not fighting U.S. interventions as allies of the Soviet Union or on behalf of their socialist ideals, Stephanson presents a world-view of the late Cold War in which the significance of developments outside Europe have been reduced to near zero.

The chronological "centering" also fails. For what exactly is it that sets the 1947–48 to 1962–63 period apart from later decades? It cannot be the absence of negotiations; Geneva I & II, the Austrian State Treaty, and the Laos agreement of 1961–62 show that even during the first part of the Cold War the United States would agree to talks when they felt it was in their interest to do so. It cannot be the high level of militarization; military expenditures continued to rise on the two sides. It cannot be enforcement within the blocs, unless Stephanson has failed to notice the Soviet invasion of Czechoslovakia and US meddling in Italy, Greece, Cyprus, Portugal, and Turkey in the 1960s and 1970s. It cannot be indirect wars; Vietnam (and later the Horn, southern Africa, Afghanistan) were at least as bloody as the war in Korea. Having the Cold War end around 1963 is meaningless, unless one wants to see the détente era as absence of Cold War in strictly US terms (and the problem then is to explain foreign policy under Carter and Reagan).[10]

An important corollary of the Stephanson approach is that the "other side"—be it Stalin or Chinese leader Mao Zedong—must play the realist (or "conventionalist") role against US leaders' attack on Westphalia. This is, to put it mildly, not the impression Russian or Chinese sources give us. Although I agree with Stephanson (and he has done some truly excellent work on this) that ideology probably played even more of a role on the US than on the Soviet side during the Cold War, portraying Stalin as a "hyper-realist" makes no sense. As historians who have worked on Stalin's materials have shown, he too was a prisoner of his worldview, his concepts, and his ideas. The Soviet leader was, as I have argued earlier, *primed* for misunderstanding the postwar world.[11] But Stephanson's problem is that he needs Stalin to play the straight man against the ideological hyperphobias of American leaders, because it is only through such a postulation that the concept of the Cold War as *exclusively* an American project can be rescued.

Closer to my own present preoccupations, the idea (widely held, especially in North America) that the Chinese Maoists' post-1972 cooperation with the United States marked an end to their revolutionary aspirations is also very faulty. Being convinced that his regime was in mortal danger, Mao Zedong sought to exploit one imperialist power against another and more dangerous one (in this case the Soviet Union). To the end of his days, the Chairman remained puzzled as to why US President Richard Nixon and his national security adviser Henry Kissinger would help revolutionary China survive (lack of brains was his favored explanation). But Mao had no doubt as to how he would employ his regime's new lease on life: he wanted to expand and deepen the processes of revolutionary change that he had begun with the Cultural Revolution during the previous decade. What prevented the Chairman from so doing were not his parleys with Kissinger in Beijing. It was that the grim reaper got him too soon for his horrendous plans to be realized.[12]

I appreciate Stephanson's search for a clearer definition of what *Cold War* means in a conceptual sense for his own work (see more on conceptual approaches below), but cannot accept the principle that only one definition can be meaningful for the field as a whole. Historians *always* contest each others' definitions—it is part of what this profession is about. What is the War of the Roses? The Qing Empire? The French Revolution? Contending with the definitions of others gives historians a sense of accomplishment, but it can also help them clarify and refine their own terms, and in that sense, at least, have a positive impact. Taking possession of a key term, as Christopher Hill did with the English Revolution, and wrestling with ingrained opinion (and political establishments) over control of it, is of course particularly worthwhile.[13] Problems only occur when a historian becomes convinced that there is only one possible definition that ipso facto has meaning to everyone, and that all other definitions are muddled, incorrect, or politically suspicious. In that direction lie broken dialogues and fragmented fields of study.

A Pluralist Approach

Against the reductionist wing of American Cold War studies, I would simply set the pluralism that is developing within the broader study of twentieth-century international history today. The first of the two trends that are emerging is one that in an informed and conscious manner works with social and intellectual history (and, at least in part, with the social sciences) to create a much bigger canvas for studying the Cold War than we hitherto have had. While I sometimes find that part of this work is moving us a bit too far away from political history (for instance, in a relegation of US Cold War policies to the sidelines even in cases when they form a crucial part of the interpretation of events), I welcome the new vistas that open up before us: the confrontation between capitalism and socialism as seen by housewives in Berlin, or students in Beijing, or mine-workers in South Africa adds much that is new to the picture.[14]

The other trend is the internationalization of the field, which adds scholarly breadth in terms of interpretation to massive amounts of new evidence. Let me be concrete here, so that this does not sound just like an often-repeated mantra: I have spent some time researching the Cold War in Southern Africa. Without the cohort of younger African scholars who are just now moving into the field (working on everything under the [African] sun from the training of the ANC army in the Crimea to the covert operations of the *apartheid* regime in the United States to the presentation of the Soviet Union during Communist Party recruitment drives in Soweto) my understanding of the global Cold War would have been so much poorer. And without access to archives in Pretoria, Cape Town, and Fort Hare, our chances of grasping the views of the people whose voices they represent would be so much slimmer.

What then about the issue of US predominance? While the concentration on US actions may sometimes be overblown, is it not right to point out (and act upon) the assumption that the Cold War is a subset of a much larger story, which is the US rise to global supremacy in the twentieth century? Why bother with other angles if the only angle that counts in the end is that of the United States? If the Cold War was an American war for preeminence, is a "relentless and rigorous centering" (as opposed to the decentering I have called for) not the best way to proceed in terms of research? If the Cold War belongs in the United States, are attempts at writing global histories of the conflict both useless and irrelevant?

It seems to me a rather straightforward proposition that the Cold War is, at the same time, part of both US history and of global history. There is no doubt that studying the Cold War in and through the study of American domestic economy, politics, culture, and social development is a very worthwhile enterprise, which may in some cases lead to significant breakthroughs for our broader understanding of the conflict. In parts of the more Realist-oriented scholarship, both among historians and political scientists, it is often the US domestic perspective that is conspicuously lacking, to the detriment of our overall grasp of the interaction between the domestic and the international. In some of the cases that I have been eager to explore, the US position within the global system is such that it is hard to see much of a distinction between the internal and the external. But be that as it may, it would still be very wrong to mistake this particularly important part for the whole. Reducing the history of the Cold War to be a section of the history of the United States is neither methodologically meaningful nor historiographically liberating.

I have often speculated about what people in other fields of research (for instance art historians) would make of the "schools of interpretation" that some historians still believe exist in Cold War studies. A couple of my art historian friends helped me to come up with the new school of *Cold War conceptualism*, an entirely tongue-in-cheek designation for people like myself who, in terms of definitions, find it useful to think that the Cold War was the spread of US and Soviet-centered concepts of development, which fuelled a global war of ideas for much of the twentieth century. Just like conceptualist artists believe in links between art-forms, conceptualist Cold War historians believe that social, intellectual, or cultural histories form part of the larger picture that needs to be drawn. While conceptualist art often questions the content of familiar objects (Marcel Duchamp's hat-rack or Damien Hirst's cow), Cold War conceptualists question the content of familiar concepts and ideas. In art, conceptualism often turns the gaze from (known) causes over onto their rumbustious effects. In history, conceptualists are sometimes more preoccupied with the tail end (spatially or chronologically) of transmissions, movements, or events than with their origins.[15]

All of which brings me back to the elephant. Beginning with the tail is one way of describing the animal. But it is only one among many that may make sense to seasoned observers at some point during their observations. At times it may be useful to go for another one, starting with the trunk, for instance. The only form of observation that does not make any sense is the belief that the part of the body you are seeing now must necessarily be the only one that exists. The possible cost of reductionism when operating in close proximity to one of the big beasts in the forests of historical international systems is not a delight to contemplate.

Notes

1. The classic cases are Edward Gibbon, *The History of the Decline and Fall of the Roman Empire* (6 vols.; London, 1776–1789) and Montstuart Elphinstone, *The History of India* (2 vols.; London, 1841).
2. Said, *Orientalism* (London, 1978), p. 6.
3. See for instance my *The Global Cold War: Third World Interventions and the Origins of Our Times* (Cambridge, 2005), pp. 396–407.
4. Ellen Schrecker (ed.), *Cold War Triumphalism: The Misuse of History after the Fall of Communism* (New York, 2004).
5. The best example here is in fact not Gaddis writing on the Cold War, but Robert Kagan explaining its deep origins in *Dangerous Nation: America's Place in the World, from its Earliest Days to the Dawn of the 20th Century* (New York, 2006), a perfect counterpiece to Stephanson's own *Manifest Destiny: American Expansion and the Empire of Right* (New York, 1996).
6. Stephanson, in this volume.

7. See Lloyd Gardner, *Pay Any Price: Lyndon Johnson and the Wars for Vietnam* (Chicago, 1995); Marilyn Young, *The Vietnam Wars, 1945–1990* (New York, 1991); Williams, *The Tragedy of American Diplomacy* (Cleveland, OH, 1959), p. 94. For a very insightful and succinct overview of the US global role from a Left perspective, see Bruce Cumings, "The American Way of Going to War: Mexico (1846) to Iraq (2003)," *Orbis*, 51/2 (2007), pp. 195–215.
8. See Thomas Bender, *A Nation among Nations: America's Place in World History* (New York, 2006) and Charles Maier, *Among Empires: American Ascendancy and Its Predecessors* (Cambridge, MA, 2006). See also Erez Manela's excellent piece "A Pox on Your Narrative: Writing Disease Control into Cold War History," *Diplomatic History* 34 (2010): 299–323.
9. Stephanson, in this volume.
10. Fred Halliday found his solution to this problem already in the early 1980s with his *The Making of the Second Cold War* (London, 1993).
11. For Stalin and the Soviet Union, see my "Secrets of the Second World: The Russian Archives and the Reinterpretation of Cold War History," *Diplomatic History*, 21/2 (1997), pp. 259–271.
12. There is still no good exploration of this period in Chinese international history in English; in Chinese An Jianshe (ed.), *Zhou Enlai de zuihou suiyue, 1966–1976* [*Zhou Enlai's Last Years, 1966–1976*] (Beijing, 1995) does a good job (though some of the source-base is still lacking). See also, from a more critical perspective, Gao Wenqian, *Wannian Zhou Enlai* [*Zhou Enlai's Later Years*] (Hong Kong, 2003; the English edition of 2007 is less satisfactory).
13. For an appreciation of Hill's attempts at turning established definitions upside down, see Geoff Eley and William Hunt (eds.), *Reviving the English Revolution: Reflections and Elaborations on the Work of Christopher Hill* (London, 1988).
14. For a good example, see Matthew Connelly, *Fatal Misconception: The Struggle to Control World Population* (Cambridge, MA, 2008); see also my discussion of these trends in "The Cold War and the International History of the Twentieth Century" in Melvyn Leffler and O. A. Westad (eds.), *The Cambridge History of the Cold War*, vol. 1 (Cambridge, 2010).
15. Conceptualism is of course only one constellation in a universe of possible and ever-changing interpretations. It does, however, have the potential for incorporating others—Anders Stephanson's work could, for instance, be said to be intra-conceptualist, as it deals with concepts within a predefined essence.

3

A History Best Served Cold

PHILIP MIROWSKI

It was inevitable that historians would eventually reconsider and reevaluate the concept of a "Cold War" as organizing principle. The "Enlightenment," the "Industrial Revolution," the Belle Epoque, "the 60s," . . . these are the units within which historians ply their trade, in an endless blue rondo of postulation, acceptance, critique, rejection, ritornello. While this spectacle drives believers in a simple correspondence theory of truth to distraction, for practitioners, it is a healthy and necessary process. It is axiomatic that such categories, be they coined by the actors (Cold War, Knowledge Society) or else attributed retrospectively (Industrial Revolution), change their meaning and significance dramatically with the passage of time. As Anders Stephanson explains, when it comes to the Cold War, much of this revisionism has been happening in political history, pitting the triumphalist neocons versus the neorealists and the amorphous culturalists.[1] He reminds us of what we have forgotten, namely, that when Walter Lippmann popularized the term in 1947, it was intended to imply a mutual condition of suspended animation for both East and West, an unsatisfactory stasis, rather than the containment of an essentially implacable Soviet aggressor. That seems both useful and valuable in freeing us from certain ingrained reservoir dogmas. Yet, for reasons of both training and interest, I am here less concerned with political than intellectual history, especially the role Cold War periodization plays in contemporary intellectual history.

Professor Stephanson is concerned to warn of the uses of revisionism in politics; I am more concerned to issue a caution for recent uses in the history of the social sciences. One finds this development, for instance, in the work of historians like David Engerman, economists like Roger Backhouse, and science studies scholars like Charles Thorpe.[2] It has become characteristic of the "performativity" literature in the science studies community, fascinated as it is with "constructivism" and the postwar success of the economics profession. Perhaps the most sophisticated version of this revisionist strand is found in the work of historian Joel Isaac.[3] He and others who have written in this volume, such as Odd Arne Westad, have suggested that we are living through a "Cold War moment" in the history of the social sciences, and perhaps have already experienced something similar for the history of the natural sciences. In an earlier critical survey, Isaac approaches much of this work with a skeptical eye, complaining "Every discipline, it seems, has its Cold War dirty laundry to air."[4] The stereotypic pattern he discerns in intellectual history projects a well-worn narrative line: the American state (and particularly the military) entered in a big way into the funding and management of science and the university from World War II onward; this in turn promoted some distinctive transdisciplinary tendencies across the board, such as a fascination with scientism, positivism, mathematization and formal statistical estimation, big dualisms (positive/normative, theory/empiricism, emic/etic, formalist/substantivist, rational/moral, and so on), and a tendency to rationalize American power politics. Since many of the historians involved in these fields themselves adopted a critical stance toward those developments, Isaac complains that these Cold War intellectual histories tend to be promoters of disguised *Methodenstreiten* prosecuted by other means. Whereas the protagonists thought they were elaborating grand themes in the postwar flowering of social thought, historians portrayed them as mere shills of the state, or sock puppets for structural forces, providing screens for the real business of Foucauldian power/knowledge.

In later work, Isaac surveys these historiographic developments and suggests that there is a different, more modern approach to writing Cold War history, associated with some recent trends in science studies. He detects a shift in emphasis from disembodied ideas colliding with each other in hyperspace to a stress on a practice-based understanding of disciplines and their theories, itself a consequence of the general "constructivist" orientation of science studies since the 1980s. Abstract exhortations to pay closer attention to practices are themselves relatively praiseworthy; the nub of the matter comes when Isaac identifies the subset of science studies he finds exemplary. He glosses this approach as dealing in "forms of life" or "subcultures," where theories are less a reflection of background conditions than themselves something that entrepreneurial academics creatively use to mold and alter surrounding reality. He cites the philosopher Ian Hacking on "looping effects," which signifies the process of intellectual creations defining and reifying categories of existence for their subjects, and then layers upon it potential reinterpretation by the people so subjugated in revising the categories themselves.[5] Yet the champions of "performativity" are Bruno Latour and Michel Callon of the Paris School of "actor/network theory," wherein it is asserted that economists use their theories to recast reality in order to better approximate their own prior conceptions and that the "economy is embedded not in society but in economics." Performativity has been frequently used by sociologists to berate earlier critics of economics, who had complained of the unrealism of its assumptions and the mandarin abstractions of its models. Isaac seems to want to do something similar with earlier Cold War historians. Where they saw dour conformity, he instead sees diversity; where they saw quislings, he sees exemplary epistemic agents. In Westad (this volume) this is associated with the notion of a "pluralist" approach to Cold War history. The attraction of this different sort of intellectual history is not only that it apparently nudges the pointer on the trembling dial of agency v. structure a bit back in the direction of agency (a reliably Anglo preoccupation), but also that it lends itself to according various disciplinary formations a greater modicum of intellectual legitimacy than might have otherwise been the case in the prior sock puppet portrayal. It restores the tropes of freedom and intentionality to historical literatures that had grown gray and dour with determinism. However, judging by counts of citations, in practice there seems to have been more examples of this sort of history written for the natural sciences; for the social sciences, it exists far more as a programmatic promise than in paradigmatic successful realizations.

But this raises the question once again: What is so very "Cold" about Cold War intellectual history? Are we really living through a "Cold War moment" in historiography? In the "subculture" or performativity approach, as the various intellectual disciplines go about constructing their worlds and their versions of agency, we confront a "many worlds" problem: what, if anything, is held in common by the free creations of such Nietzschean overmen? With each discipline engineering not one, but many worlds, and each local subculture beavering away on its own proprietary concepts, it becomes much more difficult to discern any profound commonalities among intellectual trends that coexist in time and space. Peter Galison's work on "trading zones" suggests that identity is not preserved when theories and tools cross disciplinary boundaries. Indeed, the "Cold War" itself threatens to dissolve into a thousand local peccadilloes of key figures on a thousand plateaus responding in relative isolation to disembodied disciplinary imperatives of their actual and imagined interlocutors. Attention thus turns to locally fragmented "practices" and ill-defined "trading zones," wherein one gets the quasi-libertarian impression that almost anything could have happened.

In this short note, I would like to suggest that revision of the very notion of the "Cold War" in intellectual history, as in political history, is a healthy and inexorable process, but that the "subculture performativity" variant may not be the elixir for intellectual historians. Its problems are partly shared by the field of science studies, where the inspiration for the Performativity turn originated.[6] While one can sympathize with the complaint that intellectuals were frequently treated as "sociological dopes" in the first wave of Cold War historiography and that in many instances narratives were structured around the naïve premise that "the military paid for it and therefore it was flawed," contemporary revisionism risks almost completely losing sight of what made the Cold War landscape so palpably frosty for all its participants. Perhaps seconding Anders Stephanson, but in the arena of intellectual history, I would also like to buck current trends in the redefinition of the Cold War, but here in the interests of restoring our appreciation for the ways in which it pervaded most scientific thought in that era. I also wish to suggest the current revisionists "evince no very precise idea" about what made the cold war a Cold War. By contrast, in my experience most contemporary scientific disciplines, natural or social, have opposed and still strenuously resist any suggestion that the structure of their inquiry and the content of their preferred theories was affected in any way whatsoever by the Cold War.[7] For them, it was simply all about how the Soviet regime corrupted science, full stop. When outside historians have raised commensurate issues about Western science, they have been greeted with stony silence precisely in that regard. The "performativity" narrative thus ends up merely reinforcing a tendency amongst both natural and social scientists to flatly reject the possibility that there would be transdisciplinary forces that have informed and shaped their own disciplines: Latour is notorious for his mantra that, "There is no such thing as society." Hence I argue that the performativity narrative not only encourages misrepresentation of the Cold War in substantive ways, but does so for many of the same reasons the neoconservative version has come to dominate political history: it perturbs contemporary complacency to the minimum amount possible.[8]

To pursue that argument, I want to briefly consider three aspects of intellectual life that were clearly shaped by Cold War forces and should be taken into account in any revisionist movements in intellectual history: the constitution of the appropriate time frame for Cold War historiography; the problem of the identity and coherence of disciplines both within and without the university and new knowledge production institutions; and Cold War metaphysics. I will simply presume, due to space constraints, that my comments apply indiscriminately to both the social and natural sciences.

Cold War Time Frames

Anders Stephanson points out that the neoconservative narrative has located the temporal limits of the Cold War at the Fall of the Wall, so as to support the (misleading) impression that its demise can be credited to the policies of Ronald Reagan; he suggests that contemporaries might have wanted to place the terminus somewhat earlier. This distinction matters because historians should take that indeterminacy into account. I would like to suggest something similar for the purposes of intellectual history. If the Cold War was less narrowly concerned with the behavior of the Soviet Union, and more concertedly about how intellectual life was organized in the United States, then the origins of the Cold War should be situated firmly within the boundaries of World War II, due to the unprecedented incursion of military funding and organization into knowledge production.[9] The story is well-known how the push to convert this system of science subsidy to a civilian basis immediately at the end of the war failed, and that the result was a university-military-industrial complex that lasted for decades. The Sputnik scare merely reinforced the already accepted principle that a stable and dispersed research base was a necessary prerequisite for national security and therefore not just a few strategic areas of research, but rather whole universities should be subsidized and nourished. This was the period of the belief in the possibility of technological planning.[10] Teaching and research functions at universities were welded together as a consequence of the funding process, with lavish inducements to provide all manner of disciplines with graduate students to participate in the research process. Later, subsidies would be extended to foreign nationals, as part of a push to inculcate third-world elites with respect for Western research. Academic freedom in the context of tenure was taken seriously, even when it was violated during periodic Red Scares; freedom of inquiry was tolerated because it served as explicit instantiation of the superiority of Western political and social organization over Soviet totalitarianism. Even if the scholars in question did not themselves have to get security clearances or take money from the Office of Naval Research or the Defense Advanced Research Projects Agency, they were not insulated from the myriad ways in which the Cold War had transformed academic life from its prewar status. The Cold War mode of knowledge production was so pervasive that, for a short while, it was literally invisible.

However, it was never clear that the military had relished acting the role of science manager in charge; the campus revolts of the 1960s made their presence even less tenable; and, inevitably, political demands for accountability and relevance in research rendered the task too much to bear. Hence, the military began a phased withdrawal from the science management in the 1970s; and many have argued that by 1980 the United States had embarked upon an entirely new regime of knowledge production. In one area after another—intellectual property, replacement of student subsidies by loans, cutting back on public education, scaling back on grant overheads, shutting down the Office of Technology Assessment, fostering "entrepreneurial technology transfer," replacing tenured faculty with temp labor—the Cold War system was dismantled. Technological planning was replaced by "knowledge management," which was an entirely different animal altogether. This regime was predicated upon the privatization and globalization of knowledge, in conjunction with the offshore outsourcing of manufacturing from much of the developed world. If the Cold War was about building national citadels of knowledge fortification, the new regime was about spawning little dispersed and flexible knowledge startup firms across the globe, fungible and just-in-time, largely disengaged from previous nationalist and cultural rationales. Some universities notoriously sought to emulate their corporate mentors and open "branches" or "subsidiaries" in far-flung climes, such as Abu Dhabi or Shanghai.[11] Hence one might reasonably assert that, for the purposes of periodization of intellectual history, the Cold War had effectively ended circa 1980.

Moving the watershed back sooner might also inform some generalizations that have arisen concerning the changing political centers of gravity of the sciences versus the humanities, sometimes discussed under the rubric of the "two cultures controversy."[12] Although such generalizations need qualification, it can be said to a first approximation that conservative thought was primarily located in the humanities in the 1950s, whereas the sciences frequently viewed themselves as allied with the planning and modernization agendas of the Left. After the long Sixties, a strange reversal took place, with natural scientists becoming notably more conservative and fearful of democratizing impulses, whereas the humanities came to regard themselves as the vanguard voice of the Left. Whatever the veracity of such self-conceptions, the advent of the new regime of privatized science was ushered in by prior profound changes in the political identifications of the intellectual disciplinary landscape. Such role reversals cannot simply be attributed to the Fall of the Wall, but clearly have an intimate relationship to the fate of the Cold War.

As far as I am aware, there is no contemporary intellectual tradition that has managed to successfully hold itself aloof from these profound changes in the funding and management of knowledge. The ongoing reconstruction of the university has breached any ivory tower refuge. While this story has been mostly told so far as an American tale, reconstruction of intellectual life had spread to most developed economies by the new millennium, transforming universities from political institutions to knowledge businesses.[13] This rise of the multinational knowledge consortium would have made no sense during the Cold War. Intellectual historians ignore these vast structural transformations at their own peril.

The Problem of Disciplinarity, and the Incompatibility of the University and Think Tank

There endures a fair amount of confusion about the impact of the Cold War upon the disciplinary structure of intellectual inquiry. On the one hand, it has become commonplace to suggest that "the most important developments in the postwar social sciences are transversal phenomena, criss-crossing and helping to (re)constitute various disciplines."[14] Yet, on the other, it has not escaped notice that the Cold War was the very high point of the disciplinary organization of the sciences, notable now precisely because the demands for flexibility in research careers has begun to erode the supervisory capacity of disciplinary imperatives in the modern university.[15] So which one was it during the Cold War: a landscape of impenetrable silos or a sylvan glade of polymorphous cross-pollination?

This contradiction signals that there persist some critical flaws in our understanding of the ecology of disciplines in contemporary intellectual history. The sociological literature on the related topic of "professionalism" has been less helpful in this regard than one might have had cause to expect.[16] The reason may be that the vast bulk of intellectual history, contrary to some impressions, takes as its unspoken point of departure a disciplinary platform and a conceptual map drawn from the perspective of some disciplinary perch within the intellectual landscape. If ideas are to be plumbed in any depth and sophistication, there abides an ideal reader with specialized training lurking somewhere in the background. Authors who produce grand synoptic syntheses from a great height for general audiences have been frequently indicted for rank dilettantism, whether justified or not.[17] Hence historians can rarely rise above the disciplinary framework within which most intellectual labor has been conducted in their lifetimes. This has borne serious consequences for our understanding of the development of disciplinarity over the course of the twentieth century, and particularly during the Cold War.

The crucial distinction that needs to be made is that between the institutional/professional structures of the "discipline" and the image of a proprietary disciplinary package of ideas-cum-practices. The distinction is trivial, yet often overlooked. The "performativity" account also falls down at this point. I deal with the former aspect here, and the latter in the next section. As far as the institutional structure goes, it is again well-known that the various academic disciplines professionalized in the later nineteenth century, with some further fields fissioning off in the early twentieth century. Yet these structures were still extraordinarily weak by the 1930s, with figures moving between disciplines with relative impunity, and credential barriers relatively loose. The German model of disciplinary hierarchies had only just been introduced into American academia, with lukewarm success. The real change came with the advent of the Cold War.

It has only intermittently been noticed that the institutional side of academic disciplines was immensely fortified during the Cold War era. The immediate impetus came from the need of the new military science managers to have a reliable system of quality control and trans-university comparability that had been lacking up until then in the notoriously mongrel system of American colleges and universities. Indeed, one of the fiercest battles in the immediate postwar era was over how to jettison the head of wartime Office of Scientific Research and Development Vannevar Bush's belief that he personally knew all the "best men" in science and therefore should be exempt from all accountability and replace it with some meritocratic bureaucracy for doling out government largesse. The constitution of advisory panels, the imposition of peer review standards, the subsidy of national meetings, and the fortification of elite societies like the National Academies were all Cold War phenomena, all part of the rationalization of the organization of science along preconceived disciplinary lines. Through NATO and other alliances, much of this system also spread to Europe.[18] How are we to reconcile the evident strengthening of academic disciplinary structures with the equally pertinent observation that the military was open to innovation of special-purpose transdisciplinary units, with free-standing think tanks like RAND, quasi-independent units like MIT's Lincoln Labs (later spun off as MITRE), and government labs like Los Alamos, Lawrence Livermore UCRL, Oak Ridge, and Fermilab, all of which sought to foster interdisciplinary research? The key would be that different organizational forms might require different levels of "discipline." If the science managers were going to contract out research to the universities, the lack of direct managerial control would have to be compensated by interposing a layer of professional disciplinary subordination. By contrast, the science managers realized that the intended end-products of research rarely conformed to disciplinary imperatives, and therefore direct supervision (which included security clearances and formal presentations to patrons) could allow for more latitude in intellectual transgression of subject boundaries in other units outside of academia.[19] Hence, from the vantage point of the universities, disciplinarity became the arbiter of certified knowledge and the hallmark of serious intellectual endeavor, while for knowledge areas too novel to claim such legitimacy, from artificial intelligence to molecular biology to computer science to operations research, or sheltered "gray" research, special transdisciplinary incubators were set up outside the ivy walls, to hasten development. Hence the rise of the Cold War university was paralleled by the rise of the Cold War think tank complex.

What is most notable about the Cold War was the way that the two formats almost never succeeded when one was forcibly grafted onto the other. In an experimental mode, think tank-style interdisciplinary units were set up within universities by the new funders, only to fail miserably. One can point to (among others) Harvard's Department of Social Relations, MIT's Lincoln Labs and Human Resources Research Lab, Chicago's Committee of Mathematical Biology, and Michigan's Mental Health Research Institute and Institute for Social Research. One might here also include Ford's Center for Advanced Study in the Behavioral Sciences, only weakly tied to Stanford, which never amounted to more than a motley collection of well-connected scholars enjoying the California sunshine. Even

Carnegie Mellon's Graduate School of Industrial Administration, sometimes praised because it did set the tone for postwar business schools throughout the nation, actually was an intellectual failure, with the economists and experimental psychologists in full revolt, exiling Herbert Simon from their midst as the chief interdisciplinary polymath in charge.[20]

It was not only government functionaries who learned this lesson of the need to outsource interdisciplinarity in the Cold War. Powerful interest groups who were dissatisfied with the state of existing disciplines and of learning in the university tended to mimic this pattern. Perhaps the most important for later developments was the institution of the Mont Pèlerin Society, founded as a private closed interdisciplinary discussion group in 1947 in order to counter the governmental monopoly on knowledge production within universities in the immediate postwar era. The MPS rapidly formed the core of an entirely alternate universe of knowledge production, extending from right-wing foundations to dedicated political think tanks and beyond.[21] The MPS existed because no academic discipline alone was itself capable of revising the whole of liberal thought to better respond to the twin disasters of the Great Depression and World War II. Lippmann, fabricator of the moniker of "'Cold War,' was also the original source of inspiration for bringing together many of the subsequent MPS members in a precursor dubbed the "Colloque Walter Lippmann."[22] Although the MPS was undeniably a Cold War phenomenon, in the sense its members were first and foremost animated by a desire to oppose socialism in all its guises, it eventually provided the wherewithal to theorize the justifications for the new regime of knowledge management that superceded the Cold War system. It was the MPS network that eventually produced the distinctive body of thought now designated as "neoliberalism," probably the most consequential innovation for intellectual life in the entire period, one that became the white hot center of the program of the eventual commercialization of the entirety of knowledge production.

The Metaphysics of Closed Worlds

The Cold War may not have just influenced individual thought collectives; it may also have promoted a more pervasive ontology across the board. I take the concept of "closed worlds" from Paul Edwards,[23] which is a nice elaboration of the metaphysical idea in the context of the rise of the computer-related disciplines. Edwards borrowed a technical term from artificial intelligence—a "closed world assumption" applied to a database means if an atomic sentence is not found in the database, then its default value is false—and noted that it betokens a much bigger ontology, one where anything not known to be true is effectively presumed false. While Edwards compared "closed world" ontologies in computer-related disciplines and Cold War politics, I should like to venture further out on a limb, and suggest that closed world ontologies were one transcendental common denominator that held together much of Cold War thought.

What is it about a set of propositions-cum-practices that mark it as characteristic of a particular era? Many historians would disparage the notion altogether—we know that diversity, complexity, and even self-contradiction can be found in just one individual's intellectual trajectory—the attribution of earmarks across whole disciplines smacks of EarMarxism. (The hand mill gives you the feudal lord; the steam mill, the joint-stock company; the electric grinder, McDonald's . . .) The mere fact of military funding or disciplinary reorganization covered in the previous section does not automatically dictate content in physics, or economics, or philosophy. But military patronage in the context of a larger atmosphere of looming apocalypse and implacable ideological rivalry might have conceivably operated to produce family resemblances in traditions chosen to represent orthodoxy during the postwar years.

Let me propose one application of this principle. Isaac starts off by indicating that there was a pronounced tendency in Cold War science studies to portray the scientific community as inhabiting closed worlds sufficient unto themselves: Carnap's linguistic frameworks, Neurath's holism, Quine's conceptual schemes, Kuhn's paradigms, Lakatos's research programs, Polanyi's monastic communities, Fleck's thought collectives. . . . The list just goes on and on.[24] Each stressed the difficulty of in-group interaction with "outsiders" due to problems of incommensurability, lack of socialization, specialized expertise, and so forth. Conveniently, such doctrines could readily be recruited by the military paymasters to justify keeping the democratic populace out of science policy—to pay for their activities without demanding a say in the agenda or accountability[25]—and indeed they were. But it went far beyond the simple rationalization of Cold War science policy. The conviction that there was a unique and stable "scientific method" was deployed to demarcate true knowledge from mere opinion. The belief that one might tame the unknown through the rational planning of technological innovation was the ultimate in attempts to treat everything unknown as potentially knowable, and therefore, less disruptive.[26] In a sense, the assertion of quasi-transcendental grand conceptual schemes impervious to outside comprehension was one major hallmark of the "closed world" ontology, where every eventuality has been covered, every threat countered, and every unknown accounted for. In this manner, the Closed World was the master narrative of the Cold War sciences. It is noteworthy that this only becomes apparent when the Cold War went into remission.

Isaac identifies four characteristic Cold War complexes in the social sciences: the "system" or cyborg sciences, rational choice models, behavioral science, and modernization theory.[27] Now, one might parse all of these histories in a number of ways: for instance, it is not clear that behavioral science or modernization theory ever attained a strong analytical core (or even really survived the Cold War); or conversely, that the cyborg sciences eventually blended into neoclassical rational choice theory.[28] But for current purposes the specifics aren't important. The main point to be made is that each trafficked in closed world ontologies, which turned out to be a major source of their persuasive power. The same case could be made for certain dominant traditions within the classical academic traditions. For example, I have argued that the Nash equilibrium in game theory is the very epitome of the closed world ontology, and that, without the Cold War, it is difficult to discern why anyone would come to believe that it was the sign of a healthy rationality. S. M. Amadae has argued that rational choice theory was a way to restrict the reach of politics through reference to economic metaphors.[29] The stochastic presumptions of behavioral psychology and decision theory depended explicitly upon closed world ontologies. Artificial intelligence found the closed world so indispensable that it coined the term.[30] "Creativity" itself—seemingly the antithesis of closure—was supposedly confined to a fixed set of psychological "traits" in order to distinguish it from the "authoritarian personality."[31] In a fascinating article, Ann Johnson[32] documents how the closed world approach of computational chemistry during the Cold War has given way in the last few decades to the much looser configuration of computational nanotechnology, an exceptionally mongrel form of applied research. Even Cold War physics, the kingpin of postwar sciences, privileged Grand Unification Theories as the ultimate expression of explanatory ambitions. Models had to be closed and determinate, even when they incorporated stochastic components. Risk was something to be tamed and neutered. Closed world ontologies were ubiquitous in Cold War thought.

Getting Warmer . . .

If one accepts this set of propositions, then the significance of the "Cold War moment" in intellectual history takes on an entirely different hue. One reason why historians—but not disciplinary practitioners—could experience the shock of recognition of Cold War concepts in the 1990s is that they now live in an environment where closed world ontologies have gone out of fashion. Indeed, the very imperatives of the globalized privatization of knowledge have tended to erode the once-functional distinction between universities and think tanks, which I have argued was central to Cold War research protocols. The proliferation of science parks, hybrid public-private research centers, and the like have made mockery of the closed world pretensions of impenetrable yet coherent disciplinary specialties.

As Isaac reports, science studies scholars like Bruno Latour, Ian Hacking, and Peter Galison ridicule the quasi-transcendental artifacts of Kuhn and Lakatos and Polanyi, and indeed, partake in neoliberal dogmas that there is no such thing as society, or any coherent whole, or integrated framework of concepts and practices. Instead there is only fragmented contingency, opportunism, fluid local stabilizations, and primarily, satisfaction of the short-term contract for the paymaster. The latter is often glossed as "performativity,"[33] the short-term imposition of archipelagos of order. The popular natural sciences incubated at the Santa Fe Institute (a gathering of Los Alamos refugees) and elsewhere are sciences of "emergence," chaos, and evolution.

Latour has proposed that "democracy" be recast in the new regime as a "Parliament of Things," where humans and objects work out temporary reconciliations—no more ripping Cold War tales of speaking truth to power. The new open world ontology nicely dovetails with the commercialization of knowledge, since the marketplace of ideas is deemed to always know more than any human being: boundaries are always pitched beyond our ken. Technological change cannot be planned; the best you can do is manage knowledge within the confines of the New Information Economy. It becomes possible to treat "Big Science" in service of the state as a Cold War oddity (as Galison[34] does), lacking any particular quiddity, since for the most part, it has vanished.

I hope it is becoming apparent that there was indeed something that deserves the designation "Cold War thought" in intellectual history, but that the reason we can perceive it so is that we now operate in a regime that funds and organizes knowledge production along dramatically different lines. But when historians attempt to impose such science studies descriptions as "performativity," trading zones, technoscience and the like on the period between 1945 and 1980, they are seeking to paint their portraits with a palette that is almost exclusively the product of the current regime of globalized privatized science.

Notes

1. This volume.
2. David Engerman. "Social Science in the Cold War," *Isis*, 101 (2010): 393–400; Philippe Fontaine and Roger Backhouse, *The History of the Social Sciences since 1945* (Cambridge, 2010); Charles Thorpe, "Political Theory in Science and Technology Studies," in *Handbook of Science and Technology Studies*, 3rd ed. (Cambridge, 2008), pp. 63–82.
3. Isaac, "Tangled Loops: Theory, History and the Human Sciences in Modern America," *Modern Intellectual History* 6 (2009): pp. 144–173. See also idem, "Introduction: The Human Sciences and Cold War America," *Journal of the History of the Behavioral Sciences* 47 (2011): pp. 225–231.
4. Isaac, "The Human Sciences in Cold War America," *The Historical Journal* 6 (2007): pp. 397–424, at 398.
5. Ian Hacking, *Historical Ontology* (Cambridge, MA, 2002).

6. I discuss the role of science studies in the modern regime of science funding and organization in greater detail in Philip Mirowski and Esther-Mirjam Sent, "The Commercialization of Science and the Response of STS" in *Handbook of Science, Technology and Society Studies*, ed. Ed Hackett, Olga Amsterdamska, and Michael Lynch (Cambridge, MA, 2007), pp. 635–689; and Mirowski, *ScienceMart™* (Cambridge, 2011). A more detailed critique of Latour and Callon can be found in Philip Mirowski and Edward Nik-Khah, "Markets Made Flesh: Callon, Performativity and the FCC Spectrum Auctions" in *Do Economists Make Markets? On the Performativity of Economics*, ed. Donald MacKenzie, Fabien Muniesa & Lucia Siu (Princeton, 2007). One possible example of Cold War science studies gone wonky is Ruth Oldenziel & Karen Zachman (eds.), *Cold War Kitchen: Americanization, Technology, and European Users* (Cambridge, MA, 2009).
7. Compare the reaction of psychologists to the work of Ellen Herman, or philosophers of science to the work of George Reisch, or solid-state physicists to that of Paul Forman. There are a few rare counterexamples, for instance, Jerome Kagan, "Historical Selection," *Review of General Psychology*, 13 (2009), pp. 77–88; Don Howard, "Better Red than Dead—Putting an End to the Social Irrelevance of Postwar Philosophy of Science," *Science and Education*, 18 (2009), pp. 199–220. But these individuals stand out in their commitment to the importance of history in their respective disciplines.
8. In some correspondence with Dr. Isaac, we have explored the question whether the performativity approach *necessarily* plays into the hands of reactionary forces. I doubt that issue could be effectively settled in this venue. We might however begin with the observation of Sheldon Wolin, that "the demotion of science . . . means that the ideal of a disinterested arbiter, of a forum wherein partisan claims might be tested "objectively," is as much a relic of the past as the ideal of an independent judiciary." Wolin, *Democracy Incorporated: Managed Democracy and the Specter of Inverted Totalitarianism* (Princeton, 2008), p. 127.
9. Mirowski and Sent "Commercialization of Science."
10. Jeremy Klein, "Technology Management as a Cold War Construct" (2003) http://www.mngt.waikato.ac.nz/ejrot/cmsconference/2003/proceedings/thecoldwar/klein.pdf;.
11. Elisabeth Redden, "Outsourcing Teaching Overseas," *Inside Higher Education*, July 24, 2009.
12. Guy Ortolano, *The Two Cultures Controversy* (Cambridge, 2009); John Guillory, "The Sokal Affair and the History of Criticism," *Critical Inquiry*, 28 (2002), pp. 470–508.
13. Maureen McKelvey and Magnus Holmen (eds.), *Learning to Compete in European Universities* (Cheltenham, 2009).
14. Duncan Bell, "Writing the World: Disciplinary History and Beyond," *International Affairs*, 85 (2009), pp. 3–22, at p. 12.
15. Michael Gibbons, et al., *The New Production of Knowledge* (Thousand Oaks, 1994).
16. Julia Evetts, "The Sociological Analysis of Professionalism," *International Sociology*, 18 (2003), pp. 395–415.
17. One thinks here of Michel Foucault or Immanuel Wallerstein, for instance. Authors who attempt to transcend this trap by resorting to equally transcendental theses, such as Dorothy Ross, *The Origins of American Social Science* (Cambridge, 1991), with her insistence upon a transdisciplinary "American exceptionalism" that uniformly infused all American social sciences, often just end up satisfying no one.
18. John Krige, *American Hegemony and the Postwar Reconstruction of Science in Europe* (Cambridge, 2006).
19. Hunter Crowther-Heyck, "Herbert Simon and the GSIA: Building an Interdisciplinary Community," *Journal of the History of the Behavioral Sciences* 42 (2006), p. 313, captures this distinction, suggesting, "support for interdisciplinary work came from a network of powerful new patrons, most notably the Ford Foundation and the military. . . . They deliberately defined their goals in terms of solving problems, not building new disciplines."
20. Crowther-Heyck, "Herbert Simon and the GSIA," pp. 311–334; Esther-Mirjam Sent, "Sent Simulating Simon Simulating Scientists," *Studies in History and Philosophy of Science*, 32 (2001), pp. 479–500.

21. Philip Mirowski and Dieter Plehwe (eds.), *The Road from Mont Pèlerin: The Making of the Neoliberal Thought Collective* (Cambridge, MA, 2009); Angus Burgin, "The Return of Laissez Faire" (Harvard University PhD thesis, 2009); Philip Mirowski, *Never Let a Dire Crisis Go to Waste* (London, forthcoming).
22. See the discussion by Francois Denord in Mirowski and Plehwe, *Road from Mont Pèlerin*. As a sidelight, just as Lippmann's connotation of the Cold War was ignored and debased in later discussion, so too were his meditations on liberalism ultimately dispensed with by the Mont Pèlerin participants. A catalyst cannot exert control over his reaction products.
23. Edwards, *The Closed World* (Cambridge, MA, 1996).
24. Isaac, "Tangled Loops," p. 402.
25. Michael Dennis, "Historiography of Science: an American Perspective" in *Science in the Twentieth Century*, ed. John Krige and Dominique Pestre (Amsterdam, 1997).
26. Klein, "Technology Management."
27. Isaac, "Tangled Loops," p. 410.
28. Mirowski, *Machine Dreams: Economics Becomes a Cyborg Science* (Cambridge, 2002).
29. Amadae, *Rationalizing Capitalist Democracy: The Cold War Origins of Rational Choice Liberalism* (Chicago, 2003).
30. Edwards, *Closed World*.
31. Jamie Cohen-Cole, "The Creative American: Cold War Salons, Social Science, and the Cure for Modernity," *Isis*, 100 (2009), pp. 219–262.
32. Johnson, "Modeling Molecules: Computational Nanotechnology as Knowledge Community," *Perspectives on Science*, 17 (2009), pp. 144–173.
33. Mirowski and Nik-Khah, "Markets Made Flesh."
34. Peter Galison and Bruce Hevly (eds.), *Big Science: The Growth of Large-Scale Research* (Stanford, 1992).

4

Inventing Other Realities

What the Cold War Means for Literary Studies

STEVEN BELLETTO

When I tell people that I write on American literature of the Cold War, they often think of transparently anti-McCarthyite works like Arthur Miller's *The Crucible* (1953) or of works that reflect the absurdities and fears of the Atomic Age (the *Dr. Strangelove* school of political critique). For most people, in other words, Cold War literature means work that explicitly thematizes Cold War politics. This tends to be true even for those especially familiar with the era; consider, for instance, *Cold War: An Illustrated History*, the glossy coffee table companion to CNN's television series. The editors give more than two pages to literature, focusing on Russian anti-Soviet works like Boris Pasternak's *Doctor Zhivago* (1957) and Alexander Solzhenitsyn's *One Day in the Life of Ivan Denisovich* (1962); thrillers with political backdrops like John le Carré's *The Spy Who Came in from the Cold* (1963) and Ian Fleming's Bond novels; and "paranoid fantasies" like Richard Condon's *The Manchurian Candidate* (1959). The relationship between aesthetics and politics is summed up in two evocative sentences: "Blood and terror in the East, fear and loathing in the West. The Cold War was an uneasy time for writers."[1] This cartoon version of the Cold War—two grim, implacable rivals caught in their own ideological constrictions while doggedly opposing everything the other stands for—is easy to digest, appealing perhaps to those browsing the clearance racks at Barnes & Noble, as I was when I came across the book. But, from a literary studies perspective, the problem with such conceptions is that whole syllabi of interesting and consequential work is thereby pushed out of this particular frame, understood as written *during* the Cold War but not, somehow, as *of* the Cold War. Some scholars have tried to address this problem by offering various models for thinking about Cold War literature; from about the mid-1980s, the dominant model was containment—which focused on the domestic echoes of American foreign policy—but in recent years, there has been more interest in models that understand domestic culture, literature included, in a global frame.

I. What Reality Really Is

Those working in the field of Cold War literature tend to think of the relationship between the Cold War and aesthetic production in terms of language and are interested in the various claims that language makes on reality. For historians, the lack of definitive bookends for the Cold War may emphasize the term's fuzziness; it has become, as Anders Stephanson remarks in Chapter 1, "shorthand for an amorphous epoch of enormous span, variably defined, if it is at all." When Stephanson parses the metaphorical resonances of the term "Frosty relations are thus bad but not quite as bad as frozen ones," he does so to pinpoint what is characteristic about a particular historical and political epoch, with the aim of ultimately claiming, as he writes, that "the Cold War was from the outset a US project... [that] was qualitatively transformed in the early 1960s into something else." Rather than speculating about what does or does not seem just in Stephanson's argument, I would like to take his chapter as an occasion to think about what "the Cold War" means for literary studies. For me, the term's amorphous, metaphorical quality is tremendously suggestive, but for a different reason: it signals a war of words, a rhetorical game during which ideological systems claimed not only moral supremacy but indeed the better purchase on "objective reality."[2] Because the nature of the Cold War required that rhetorical brinksmanship accompany nuclear proliferation, these competing ideologies became increasingly obvious to average Americans *as* ideologies.[3] This in turn meant that language itself became politicized in unusual ways, since ideologies—articulated through language and image—shaped what could count as reality. Those inclined could, for example, pick up a popular analysis of life in the USSR like the best-selling *The Future Is Ours, Comrade* (1960) and read all about "Soviet reality"—a fog of rhetoric so thick that it obscured "objective reality" itself.[4]

But this does not mean that contemporary literary critics assume that the United States, in contrast to the Soviet Union, was then (or is now) free of ideology. Far from it. In fact, it is scarcely an exaggeration to say that one of the principal interests of literary and American studies after World War II has been describing various kinds of ideologies and theorizing their constitution and meaning. As Thomas Schaub has written, for example, "the postwar derogation of ideology [found in American literary criticism]—condemned as a simplification of social and political reality—was itself an ideology that served to reinforce the dominant Cold War polarities which privileged American democracy, imagined as a fruitful tension of conflicting groups in contrast with the monolithic repressiveness of the Soviet Union."[5] Although Stephanson worries that when writing about the Cold War "it is by slippage easy to 'normalize' the United States, the victorious antagonist, while constituting the pathological Soviet Union as the basic factor", it should be clear from Schaub's emphasis on American ideology as "imagined" in specific ways that literary critics at least have been reluctant to normalize the United States. It has rather been a question of identifying the language at work in a text (whether political, literary, or otherwise) and then exploring how the rhetoric associated with the Cold War affected one's evaluation—or production—of such language.

Schaub quotes, for instance, from Richard Chase, a prominent postwar literary critic, who wrote that "if one had read and understood Melville one could not vote for Henry Wallace [1948 Progressive Party candidate for US president known for his political naivety] . . . because Melville presents his reader with a vision of life so complexly true that it exposes the ideas of Henry Wallace as hopelessly childish and superficial."[6] In this view, as Schaub points out, it is not so much the political content of a Melville novel that interests Chase, but rather how the novel represents a "mode of knowing," a reminder of "what reality really is."[7] Chase's enthusiasm for Melville's view of reality over Wallace's can in fact be read as ironically emblematic of consensus culture's reach. Glossing Wallace's unorthodox campaign stances such as mending relations with the Soviet Union, Lynn Hinds and Theodore Windt write that "Henry Wallace spoke from outside the developing rhetorical reality of the Cold War. In practically every respect, his view of the world and the policies he advocated clashed directly with those of the Truman administration and the growing consensus among Americans."[8] Beyond Chase's apparent alignment of Melville's reality with Truman's, Schaub argues more broadly that "the novel's relationship to social history—to 'reality'—was the central preoccupation of the critics who wrote about narrative fiction in the years after World War II" and that this preoccupation was shaped by the Cold War precisely because its rhetoric could confuse ideology with reality.[9]

From a literary studies perspective, then, the Cold War is less about specific dates and policy decisions and more about a privileged mode of knowing that shaped the way reality was understood and analyzed.[10] Literary and cultural critics have thus taken an interest in the Cold War insofar as it offers a frame for tracing the circulation of dominant narratives with the hope of understanding how American culture constituted itself. Such an approach has led to a rich variety of work exploring a dynamic—rather than simply causal—relationship between political norms and aesthetic production. In writing about how the Cold War affected the American literary canon, for example, Donald Pease has suggested that Melville's *Moby-Dick* was elevated to canonical status at mid-century partly for the ways it was perceived to embody the rhetorical situation of the Cold

War. According to Pease, postwar literary critics began to see *Moby-Dick*'s intellectual, digressive narrator, Ishmael, in opposition to Ahab, the maniacal captain of the whaling vessel *Pequod*: "they set Ishmael's subversive narrative energies against a totalitarian will at work in Ahab's policy. . . . [The] canonical reading appropriated *Moby-Dick* to a modern scene of cultural persuasion analogous to the one at work in Melville's age. This modern scene of persuasion is the global scenario popularly designated as the Cold War."[11] Pease is arguing, in other words, that *Moby-Dick* became a canonical American novel when it was understood as privileging Ishmael over Ahab because Ishmael could be read as a symbol of the free world struggling against totalitarian aggression.[12]

Pease's analysis has been influential for literary critics because it views the Cold War as requiring the dominance or suppression of large cultural narratives, narratives that in turn affected other, seemingly apolitical aspects of life. In this way, the Cold War encourages literary critics to understand aesthetic objects as being "political," even if these objects do not thematize politics in the conventional sense. Thus while *Moby-Dick* is obviously not about the United States and the Soviet Union, it became relevant during the Cold War because it seemed to illustrate the logic underpinning contemporary rhetorical reality. The pervasiveness of politicized language in the Cold War has therefore confirmed for literary critics that all language is political (or, as the late David Foster Wallace put it in a subtitle to an essay about lexicography, "Why 'Politics and the English Language' is Redundant").

II. How Containment Made the Personal Political

One consequential result of the Cold War politicization of language was that these large cultural narratives became yoked to people's personal lives. In this regard, Elaine Tyler May's social history, *Homeward Bound* (1988), is often cited as a foundational demonstration that the personal was political. According to May, containment, that watchword of the early Cold War, had a corollary in what she calls "domestic containment": "More than merely a metaphor for the Cold War on the homefront, containment aptly describes the way in which public policy, personal behavior, and even political values were focused on the home."[13] Although May does not discuss literature at any length, her work has been provocative for literary scholars writing on the Cold War because it suggested a framework for negotiating connections between the political and the private specific to the period.

In 1995, Alan Nadel's *Containment Culture* began with the basic premise that the political could be manifest in countless ways in many cultural arenas; his subtitle, which refers to "American Narratives"—not American novels or American fiction—suggests that Cold War American culture can be profitably understood by attending to the interplay of narratives. Nadel's work has been likewise influential not because he was the first literary critic to claim that containment is a metaphor that travels, but because his work so ably demonstrated the range and pervasiveness of Cold War rhetoric in a variety of places, from the film *The Ten Commandments* (1956) to Joan Didion's novel *Democracy* (1984). Nadel demonstrates the subtle links between cultural narratives—the stories cultures tell about themselves—and personal lives; as he writes: "the American cold war is a particularly useful example of the power of large cultural narratives to unify, codify, and contain—perhaps *intimidate* is the best word—the personal narratives of its population."[14] There are two things of note in this sentence: first, that Nadel specifies he is discussing the *American* Cold War; he, like May, is interested in the domestic reverberations of Cold War politics (he begins with a close reading of "The Sources of Soviet Conduct"); second, that the effects of these large cultural narratives are mainly negative. The latter idea especially characterizes the way that literary critics tend to view the Cold War—as a large-scale political phenomenon that quashed individual difference and dissent by branding as subversive those who did not fit comfortably into Gray Flannel Suits.

This perspective on the Cold War as sanctioning large cultural narratives that bullied individual Americans comes in part from a leftist critique of American norms, and the conformity such norms encourage. Much of what is designated as contemporary "critical theory" in fact descends in spirit if not in direct lineage from the Frankfurt School, shorthand for a group of largely neo-Marxist philosophers, sociologists, and literary critics associated with the Institute for Social Research at the University of Frankfurt, many of whom left Europe for the United States in the 1930s. In their most well-known analyses of 1940s American culture, Max Horkheimer and Theodor Adorno compared US popular culture with authoritarian political regimes: "Culture today is infecting everything with sameness. Film, radio, and magazines form a system. Each branch of culture is unanimous within itself and all are unanimous together. Even the aesthetic manifestations of political opposites proclaim the same inflexible rhythm. The decorative administrative and exhibition buildings of industry differ little between authoritarian and other countries."[15] In this view, the "culture industry" promotes an ideology of consensus that appears to offer a range of free choices, but that actually dictates individual taste and offers false models of self-expression. And with the advent of the Cold War, there was even more pressure placed on the notion of American freedom, an idea starkly expressed by a home-grown critic of the American Way of Life, Carl Solomon, a leftist editor and poet who volunteered for shock treatment at the Columbia Psychiatric Institute in 1949—and the man to whom Allen Ginsberg dedicated "Howl"—"Only in America and from America came the slogan: Freedom. The slogan freedom meant white supremacy and the suppression of every movement for human hope on the face of the planet. So the cold war began."[16] Solomon's inversion of what freedom normally signifies is typical of cultural critique during the Cold War: there is a difference between appearances, slogans, and the way things really are, so that, as Horkheimer and Adorno argue, even Donald Duck seems innocuous enough but really takes "beatings so that the spectators can accustom themselves to theirs."[17] If emblems like American freedom and long-suffering Donald Duck can be read negatively, it suggests the potential work to be done understanding the complexities of ideology during a period largely defined by ideology.

Nadel, for instance, sees the contradictions inherent in the concept of Cold War freedom (along the lines of Solomon's sense) as leading to the development of a postmodern sensibility. His formulation has in fact proven lasting for many critics interested in Cold War literature, so it is worth pausing over what he does with his principal definition. When Nadel writes about containment, he is not thinking mainly about the theories underlying American foreign policy, but rather about a "privileged American narrative" that helps explain postwar culture. "The story of containment," he writes, "had derived its logic from the rigid major premise that the world was divided into two monolithic camps, one dedicated to promoting the inextricable combination of capitalism, democracy, and (Judeo-Christian) religion, and one seeking to destroy that ideological amalgamation by any means. By the mid-1960s, the problems with the logic of containment—its blindness, its contradictions, and its duplicities—had started to be manifest in a public discourse displaying many traits that would later be associated with 'postmodernism.'"[18] Although this definition of containment certainly plays on Kennan's sense, what is significant about it for literary studies is its problems; Nadel tells the story of containment to show how its blindness and contradictions led to the emergence of postmodernism, which would underscore the real-world importance of ideology by conceptualizing even reality itself as contingent.

With such a model in place, when Nadel wants to demonstrate the relationship of McCarthyism to literature, he does not discuss a work like Irwin Shaw's *The Troubled Air* (1951), whose plot concerns the curtailing of free speech during a hunt for communists at a radio station, but J. D. Salinger's *The Catcher in the Rye* (1951), whose plot concerns the wanderings and ramblings of a teenage boy. At first blush, Holden Caulfield has little to do with McCarthyism, but by attending to his rhetoric, Nadel shows that what he calls Holden's "testimony" "reveals an organization of power that deeply reflects the tensions of post-World War II America from which the novel emerged."[19] Nadel points out that Holden emphasizes the veracity of what he is saying to the point of obsession, a fact which for Nadel implicates Holden in a culture likewise obsessed with truth telling ("are you now or have you ever been . . . ?"). In Nadel's reading, *The Catcher in the Rye* is political because, even though it may not offer sustained meditations on communism or atom bombs, Holden's narrative strategies mirror the rhetorical logic of the Cold War. Tellingly, these strategies cannot be sustained: "Holden voices many of the domestic themes of containment and also demonstrates the impossibility of articulating those themes while speaking veracious speech . . . [he] internalizes the mechanisms of surveillance—social, sexual, political, economic, and theological—that comprise the privileged domestic security devices of containment. Converting his rhetoric into mental breakdown, he becomes both the articulation of 'unspeakable' hypocrisy and its critic."[20] Nadel argues that Holden's hunt for phonies, and his subsequent break from dominant American culture, represents a kind of cultural schizophrenia encouraged by the untenable logic of the Cold War (a more obvious example that Nadel does not discuss is *Dr. Strangelove*, which demonstrates, ad absurdum, the irrational rationality of nuclear brinksmanship rooted in theories of deterrence).

This sort of work on literature and the Cold War, which pays special attention to the ways that rhetoric functions and how large cultural narratives affect smaller ones, has been a mainstay of Cold War literary studies for about the last fifteen years. The containment model has been so useful for explaining the relationship between aesthetics or home life and politics that there has been a critical tendency to assume that attention to containment is the best or only way to have the notion of "Cold War literature" make sense. There was recently, to cite but one example, a twenty-four-page essay in the leading American literature journal explaining how a twenty-two-line Elizabeth Bishop poem from 1950 appears on first read to be apolitical but is actually a sophisticated engagement with the domestic norms of containment.[21] So pervasive has been the containment model that some people have reacted against it as limiting the ways that literature scholars can understand the Cold War. Consider, for instance, the position laid out in 2002 by Andrew Hoberek, who has been especially vocal in this regard: "While the Cold War culture framework has revolutionized the way we talk about the 50s . . . its dominance as a critical paradigm has produced a certain blindness as well. At its worst, it has become a routinized reading generator: take a 50s text that hasn't been discussed yet, explain how it reflects an ambivalent liberalism hostile to political extremes (or designates some group as subversive, or denigrates the radical legacy of the 30s), and publish."[22]

III. From Containment to the Global Community

Cold War literary studies is thus in a particularly generative moment as a new generation of scholars attempt to conceptualize the period without only falling back on the containment model. One way that people have begun to do so is to think about US domestic culture in a global frame, not just in opposition to perceptions and projections about the Soviet Union. Some of this current thinking may in fact reconcile Stephanson's sense of the Cold War as a US ideological project with his rebuke of, as he puts it, "the notion that the Cold War continues by means of direct intervention and use of proxies in the third world, that it is really about third world interventionism." In other words, literary scholars remain committed to understanding the complexities of US ideologies and cultural narratives, but they have begun to do so by thinking about domestic culture in terms of the global scenario, a conceptualization that has affinities with Odd Arne Westad's picture in *The Global Cold War*. In fact, those interested in American literature in a global context have followed the lead of histories like Mary Dudziak's *Cold War Civil Rights*, which argues that postwar domestic race relations must be understood in light of Cold War global politics. As she writes, "civil rights reform was *in part* a product of the Cold War. . . . In addressing civil rights reform from 1946 through the mid-1960s, the federal government engaged in a sustained effort to tell a particular story about race and American democracy: a story of progress, a story of the triumph of good over evil, a story of US moral superiority."[23] Just as Dudziak is interested, from a legal history perspective, in the "story" the federal government told about itself to its own citizens and to the world, some literary critics have taken the Cold War to imply a similarly global frame.

Picking up on the work of Dudziak, Penny Von Eschen, and others, Christina Klein's *Cold War Orientalism* demonstrates how popular imagination was affected by the United States' changing relationship with Asia. Klein offers what she calls the "integration model" as a complement to containment; by looking at the ways Asia was coming to be seen in popular American culture, she develops an argument that figures the United States as "a member of a [global] community bound together through emotional bonds" rather than as the "armed defender of the world."[24] For Klein, middlebrow works like *The King and I* (1956) and *Flower Drum Song* (1957) "produced a sentimental culture of integration that coexisted with and counterbalanced the culture of containment."[25] Her work is significant for those working in the field of cold war literature because she demonstrates, and powerfully so, that the relationships between aesthetics and politics during the Cold War cannot be entirely explained by the containment model.[26]

From a definitional standpoint, Klein's work is also important because it represents a willingness in literary studies to envision the Cold War on a global scale, a willingness that informs a growing body of work.[27] In a 2005 book that links the culturally pervasive figure of the rebel to a sense of the Cold War as a "three-world imaginary" rather than a two-world binary, for example, Leerom Medovoi has argued that the rebel became significant in domestic US culture partly because of the many third-world countries that were likewise rebelling against the old colonial powers: "the third world designated a region in which newly sovereign 'national characters' were emerging from their former 'dependence' upon colonial masters."[28] Putting a character like Holden Caulfield to quite a different use than Nadel, Medovoi claims that "In all of its complexity, the teenager of postwar US culture represented nothing less than a figure of psychopolitical sovereignty, a Cold War instantiation of [psychologist Erik] Erikson's 'freeborn American son' as defined against his antithesis, the compliant youth of totalitarian society."[29] With this framework, Medovoi offers analyses of numerous aesthetic objects that normally would not be considered political—rock songs, the film *Rebel Without a Cause*, key texts of the Beat Generation—without claiming that they are merely bridling against containment. Medovoi claims, in fact, that "the much-touted 'Cold War consensus' never actually existed. . . . postwar American culture was deeply troubled by ideological tensions between the norms of Fordist suburbia and the America idealized by the three worlds imaginary."[30] By assuming a global frame, Medovoi simultaneously theorizes and criticizes how reality was prescribed and defined by various Cold War sensibilities, thereby challenging the view that a culture of consensus did indeed reign.

In my own work, I have tried to acknowledge the global dimensions of the Cold War while still focusing on the narratives circulating in domestic US culture. There are some intersections among literary studies, intellectual history, and cultural studies in what I term the "game theory narrative"—a "cultural narrative that told the story of game theory's potential to prevent nuclear exchange by conceptualizing the cold war as a game, and by playing this game according to specific rational strategies."[31] By attending to the difference between what mathematicians, economists, and other professionals thought of as game theory, and the way that game theory was popularized in the print media, I traced instances of the game theory narrative through various aspects of Cold War culture, from Philip K. Dick's science fiction novel *Solar Lottery* (1955)—which imagines a future political system rooted in a popular understanding of game theory—to the films *Dr. Strangelove* and *Fail-Safe,* to Richard Powers's late Cold War novel *Prisoner's Dilemma* (1988). Reading the game theory narrative in light of the global Cold War, I suggested that it conceptualized "the global conflict involving the fates of many nations as a two-person game of the highest stakes. If the stakes were indeed the hearts and minds of third world countries, then one consequence of the game theory narrative was that these countries were viewed largely in terms of how they related to the game being played."[32] As is the case with Medovoi's sense that "consensus culture" is an inadequate description of postwar America, I found that looking at the game theory narrative *as* a narrative (rather than as a method for dealing with physical laws of the universe, as it was often understood) makes visible the idea that it was imperfect metaphor for explaining the nature of the Cold War, and as such its later creative appropriations were almost always negative.

IV. The Cold War and Postmodernism

If from a literary studies point of view the Cold War marked a time when cracks in consensus culture began to appear, then Stephanson is especially canny when, thinking through the potential of the Cold War as a "genuine concept," he compares it unfavorably to "what happened in the 1980s with the analogous category of 'postmodernity.'" After all, postmodernism names, among other things, an attention to cultural ironies in the interest of reconceptualizing what "the real" means. As Jean-François Lyotard, one of the most influential philosophers of the postmodern, has put it, "Modernity, in whatever age it appears, cannot exist without a shattering of belief and without discovery of the 'lack of reality' of reality, together with the invention of other realities."[33] Lyotard is known for theorizing what he calls a legitimation crisis, the problem that occurs when differing narratives or ideologies claim authority—how are we to know which are legitimate? When Lyotard thus speaks about the "invention of other realities," he is recognizing that even the most objective-seeming aspects of reality are themselves products of ideology, and therefore subject to a crisis of legitimation. As Stephanson's evocation of postmodernism perhaps suggests, for many literary critics and continental philosophers, the emergence of postmodernism—and the critique of reality it implies—is intimately bound up in the rhetorical situation of the Cold War, which encouraged people to conflate ideologies with reality.[34]

Although it was not until the 1970s and 1980s that postmodernism had its most widespread cultural expression, some people who think about literary postmodernism, myself included, locate its roots in the 1950s and 1960s, when US domestic culture was dominated by narratives that prescribed reality in particular (and particularly limiting) ways. One consequence of Nadel's view of containment is that its inherently contradictory binary logic was identified and challenged in innovative literary work that would later be associated with postmodernism. One of the hallmarks of postmodernism is, in fact, an experimental sensibility that, to borrow Lyotard's phrase once again, undertakes the "invention of other realities." Read in light of the Cold War, literary postmodernism does not retreat from politics into its own metafictional navel gazing (as those dismissive of postmodernism tend to assume), but rather demonstrates that what was being called reality by those in power was merely one way to view reality.[35] Given such a context, it becomes clearer how the Cold War put pressure on narrative as such. Marcel Cornis-Pope, for one, see a politics inherent in innovative literary fiction because it arose from what he calls "the polarized ethos of the latter half of the twentieth century that held cultures hostage to a confrontation between rival ideologies abroad and a clash between champions of uniformity and disruptive others at home."[36]

I tend to think of the Cold War as a rhetorical field that helps us recognize how the use of language may be understood as political—that is, as challenging, expanding, accommodating, or otherwise engaging the dominant cultural narratives in circulation. In an essay about Jack Kerouac, for example, I looked at what he was doing with representation and reality and compared it to what was happening in professional historiography.[37] As Peter Novick and Richard Pells have shown, one effect of the Cold War on historiography was the encouragement of objectivity.[38] This idea is illustrated in J. G. Randall's 1952 presidential address to the American Historical Association, in which he says that history, "if not strictly 'scientific,' must be authentic. . . . Objective truth must be and is the goal of the scientist."[39] Another historian, writing in 1950 on contemporary historiographic practice, argued that "The acceptance of subjective realism . . . will make history especially vulnerable to the renewed activities of pressure groups who would dictate, respectively, the 'value theory' that they would have historians employ . . . [relativist historians] have transformed history into an instrument of propaganda and surrendered it in advance to whatever power group gains control of the Capitol."[40] This historian, citing explicitly the "pressure groups" made visible by the Cold War, wants to fix subjective reality in an objective way in order to be apolitical. Lyotard would say that he is not free from politics, but rather that he is being political in a different way.

In his book *Visions of Cody* (written in 1952–53) Kerouac likewise begins with a desire to record life "exactly like it happened"—and to this end even includes 128 pages of transcriptions from taped conversations, with the idea that his dispassionate transcribing would amount to an objective, "complete record."[41] What Kerouac ultimately realizes, however, is that the moment he narrates the transcriptions—even to include a miniscule adjective—the representation of the event gets further away from the event; the signifier, to use the Saussurian parlance, is always distinct from the signified, which disrupts Kerouac's sense of a coherent, unmediated reality. *Visions of Cody* then proceeds from the conclusion that radical subjectivity is a better route to historical truth, an idea that has more affinities with Hayden White's later theories of postmodern history than it does with Kerouac's contemporaries. Reading Kerouac as being of the Cold War thus suggests the politics inherent in any narrative attempting to represent reality, whether an ostensibly objective history or an obviously subjective work of fiction.

Stephanson's claim that the Cold War "began as a contingently articulated policy which eventually generated a system, static and dynamic at the same time" is in fact an apt description of what the Cold War has meant for literary studies. When I think of the Cold War as viewed through the lens of literature, I think of both stasis and dynamism; of leftist author Hettie Jones writing in a letter to a friend in October, 1962, "Hello out there where the bombs may not go . . . Can't say much because my hand is shaking"; of an African American experience redefined so that the right and left seem to echo each other ("We're *Communists*!" cries a party leader in Richard Wright's novel *The Outsider* (1953), "And being a Communist is not easy. It means negating yourself, blotting out your personal life and listening only to the voice of the Party. The Party wants you to *obey*!"); of Norman Mailer's thought that the best way to describe his experience with the March on the Pentagon was in a book subtitled "History as a Novel/The Novel as History."[42] In such works, a special pressure is placed on language, whether Jones's literal inability to communicate because of the Cuban Missile Crisis, or Wright's insight that both communists and capitalists engage in rhetorical violence, or Mailer's sense that conventional generic forms are inadequate for describing the strange logic governing American politics. As these examples imply, those with a literary sensibility tend to imagine "the Cold War" as a monolith encouraging a static view of reality that ought to be opposed and reacted against by those presumably on the side of creativity and individual freedoms. At the same time, this framework has also generated critical dynamism precisely because it has ruptured and given way to numerous models that assume the Cold War elevated language in political ways, but that emphasize differing aspects of this elevation. Although contemporary literary-minded theories about the Cold War may not yield a neat picture of an epoch, they do succeed in demonstrating, analyzing—and perhaps reproaching—the ways in which rhetoric and narratives have been understood as reality, certainly some of the most urgent work that can be performed by either literature or criticism.

Notes

1. Jeremy Isaacs and Taylor Downing, *Cold War: An Illustrated History* (Boston, 1998), p. 269.
2. For a discussion of the Cold War as a "rhetorical state of mind," see Lynn Boyd Hinds and Theodore Otto Windt, *The Cold War as Rhetoric: The Beginnings, 1945–1950* (New York, 1991), p. 5. My sense of the Cold War has certain affinities with Hinds's and Windt's, especially in the way they see rhetoric as affecting what counts as reality: "in the postwar period a single all-encompassing reality about the international world arose that, when it took hold, admitted no exceptions to its basic premises. Soon it was transferred to domestic political life. It was the Cold War reality and it was an ideological reality" (p. 23).
3. I am using the term "ideology" in the sense that contemporary literary critics tend to use it, which is different from the way that it was used in the early Cold War period. The latter is the sense that Hinds and Windt invoke when they write: "ideologies strive for universality, a representation or refraction of a complete political world into an internally consistent and

cohesive whole . . . ideologies divide the world they rhetorically represent into a bipolar world of protagonists and antagonists, of theses and antitheses, of good and evil. . . . those who embrace ideologies consent that human motives are ideologically determined and cannot be known" (pp. 23–24). This understanding has obviously negative implications, and as such an American policymaker during the Cold War could claim that America had no ideology whereas the Soviet Union did—this is sense of ideology that Daniel Bell proclaimed the end of in 1960 (the jacket copy for his *The End of Ideology* (Glencoe, IL, 1960) claims that the book is "written from a perspective that is anti-ideological but not conservative"). The sense of ideology I use in this essay is more in keeping with the definition found in the glossary I assign to students in my introduction to the English major course: "A set of beliefs underlying the customs, habits, and practices common to a given social group. To members of that group, the beliefs seem obviously true, natural, and even universally applicable." Ross Murfin and Supryia Ray, *The Bedford Glossary of Critical and Literary Terms*, 2nd ed. (Boston, 2003), p. 206. Of course, no discussion of ideology in this context would be complete without attention to the category of power and to the question of the subject's relationship to the state. For an influential argument about ideology, individuals, and the state, see Louis Althusser, "Ideology and Ideological State Apparatuses: Notes Toward an Investigation." *Lenin and Philosophy and Other Essays*, trans. Ben Brewster (New York, 1971). 85–126.

4. Joseph Novak, *The Future Is Ours, Comrade* (New York, 1960). This book was written under a pseudonym by Jerzy Kosinski, who later went on to write such novels as *The Painted Bird* (1965) and *Being There* (1971).
5. Thomas Schaub, *American Fiction in the Cold War* (Madison, 1991), p. 23.
6. Quoted by Schaub, *American Fiction in the Cold War*, p. 23.
7. Hinds and Windt, *The Cold War as Rhetoric*, p. 212.
8. Ibid.
9. Schaub, *American Fiction in the Cold War*, p. 25.
10. In this sense, the Cold War has become for literary critics, along with terms like modernism, postmodernism, and postcolonialism, a powerful way to periodize the twentieth century. For more on the distinctions and continuities among these terms, see Ann Douglas, "Periodizing the American Century: Modernism, Postmodernism, and Postcolonialism in the Cold War Context," *Modernism/Modernity*, 5/3 (1998), pp. 71–98. As I hope this essay indicates, much has changed in literary studies since Douglas wrote "the 'Cold War' is familiar to both historians and literary critics. Only historians, however, make it central to their periodizing attempts, and it is precisely there that cultural critics have the most to learn" (p. 73). See, for example, Adam Piette, *The Literary Cold War, 1945 to Vietnam* (Edinburgh, 2009).
11. Donald Pease, *Visionary Compacts: American Renaissance Writings in Cultural Context* (Madison, 1987), p. 243.
12. For a critique of Pease, see William Spanos, *The Errant Art of Moby-Dick: The Canon, The Cold War, and the Struggle for American Studies* (Durham, NC, 1995), pp. 31–36.
13. Elaine Tyler May, *Homeward Bound: American Families in the Cold War Era* (New York, 1988), p. 14.
14. Alan Nadel, *Containment Culture: American Narratives, Postmodernism, and the Atomic Age* (Durham, NC, 1995), p. 4.
15. Max Horkheimer and Theodor Adorno, *Dialectic of Enlightenment*, ed. Gunzelin Schmid Noerr, trans. Edmund Jephcott (Stanford, 2002), p. 94.
16. Carl Solomon, "I Was a Communist Youth," in *The Floating Bear: A Newsletter*, ed. Diane di Prima and LeRoi Jones (La Jolla, 1973), p. 129. For a discussion of this passage in the context of a more widespread engagement with the leftist politics on the part of postwar writers, see Ben Lee, "*Howl and Other Poems*: Is There Old Left in These New Beats?" *American Literature*, 76 (June 2004), pp. 367–389.
17. Horkheimer and Adorno, *Dialectic*, p. 110.

18. Nadel, *Containment Culture*, pp. 2–3.
19. Ibid., p. 73.
20. Ibid., pp. 71–74.
21. See Steven Gould Axelrod, "Elizabeth Bishop and Containment Policy," *American Literature*, 75/4 (2003), pp. 843–867.
22. Andrew Hoberek, "Cold War Culture to Fifties Culture," *Minnesota Review*, 55–57 (2002), p. 146.
23. Mary L. Dudziak, *Cold War Civil Rights: Race and the Image of American Democracy* (Princeton: Princeton University Press, 2000), pp. 12–13.
24. Christina Klein, *Cold War Orientalism: Asia in the Middlebrow Imagination* (Berkeley, 2003), p. 54.
25. Klein, *Cold War Orientalism*, p. 5.
26. In her introduction, Klein emphasizes a dynamic relationship between aesthetics and politics: "the texts that I explore do not exist in a cause-and-effect relationship with the Cold War foreign policies pursued by Washington: they did not simply reflect those policies, nor did they determine them. Rather, they serve as a cultural space in which the ideologies undergirding those policies could be, at various moments, articulated, endorsed, questioned, softened, and mystified" (pp. 8–9).
27. See, for example, Uta Poiger, *Jazz, Rock, and Rebels: Cold War Politics and American Culture in a Divided Germany* (Berkeley, 2000); Ross Hammond (ed.), *Cold War Literature: Writing the Global Conflict* (London, 2005); Leerom Medovoi, *Rebels: Youth and the Cold War Origins of Identity* (Durham, 2005); Rebecca M. Schreiber, *Cold War Exiles in Mexico: U.S. Dissidents and the Culture of Critical Resistance* (Minneapolis, 2008); and Ann Sherif, *Japan's Cold War: Media, Literature, and the Law* (New York, 2009).
28. Medovoi, *Rebels*, p. 11.
29. Ibid., p. 30.
30. Ibid., p. 22.
31. Steven Belletto, "The Game Theory Narrative and the Myth of the National Security State," *American Quarterly* 61/2 (June 2009), p. 333. An expanded version of this essay appears in my book *No Accident, Comrade: Chance and Design in Cold War American Narratives* (Oxford, forthcoming).
32. Belletto, "Game Theory Narrative," pp. 352–353.
33. Jean-François Lyotard, *The Postmodern Condition: A Report on Knowledge*, trans. Geoff Bennington and Brian Massumi (Minneapolis, 1989), p. 77.
34. See also Jean Baudrillard, "The Precession of Simulacra," in *Simulations*, trans. Paul Foss, Paul Patton, and Philip Beitchman (Paris, 1983).
35. This idea is of course well known to Stephanson and the *Social Text* collective; see Andrew Ross (ed.), *Universal Abandon? The Politics of Postmodernism* (Minneapolis, 1989). See also Linda Hutcheon, *The Politics of Postmodernism*, 2nd ed. (London, 2002).
36. Marcel Cornis-Pope, *Narrative Innovation and Cultural Rewriting in the Cold War Era and After* (Basingstoke, 2001), p. xi.
37. See Steven Belletto, "Kerouac His Own Historian: *Visions of Cody* and the Politics of Historiography," *Clio*, 37 (2008), pp. 193–218.
38. See Peter Novick, *That Noble Dream: The "Objectivity Question" and the American Historical Profession* (Cambridge, 1988); and Richard Pells, *The Liberal Mind in a Conservative Age: American Intellectuals in the 1940s and 1950s* (New York, 1985), pp. 148–162.
39. J. G. Randall, "Historianship," *The American Historical Review*, 58 (January 1953), p. 251.
40. Chester McArthur Destler, "Some Observations on Contemporary Historical Theory," *The American Historical Review*, 55 (April 1950), pp. 507–526.
41. Jack Kerouac, *Visions of Cody* (New York: Penguin, 1993), 99.
42. Hettie Jones, *How I Became Hettie Jones* (New York, 1996), p. 200; Richard Wright, *The Outsider* (New York, 1953), p. 168; Norman Mailer, *Armies of the Night: History as a Novel/The Novel as History* (New York, 1968).

PART TWO

VISTAS

5

The Geopolitical Vision

The Myth of an Outmatched USA

JOHN A. THOMPSON

It is surely the case, as Odd Arne Westad emphasizes in chapter 2, that the Cold War is a part of global history as well as of United States history. Given this, and the diversity of the perspectives and goals of those who became involved in it, the pluralist approach to studying the Cold War that Westad recommends is appropriate. Yet Anders Stephanson is right to remind us in his own contribution to this volume that the term originated in the United States as a description—originally negative but soon also positive—of the approach to world politics that came to shape American policy during the Truman administration. Here I wish to explore the nature and origins of a foundational element in that approach—a conception of the position of the United States in the world that portrayed this most powerful state as being in potentially mortal danger. Doing so brings out the extent to which axioms that were basic to the justification of US defense and foreign policies had their origins not in the actions of the Soviet Union but in the long-running internal debate over whether the United States really needed to play a role in international politics commensurate with the scale of its power and resources. As Stephanson points out, the Cold War resolved this debate by "putting the United States into the world once and for all." Recovering the influence of this internal debate upon the rationale for US policy highlights the importance of "the domestic perspective" that, as Westad notes, is neglected by "Realist oriented" scholars—who, in this case, generally take the axioms in question to be indeed axiomatic.

Geopolitics and America's Cold War

The American commitment to the Cold War was propelled by fear. Throughout its course, and particularly when the commitment came under pressure, the nation's leaders and much public commentary insisted that nothing less than the survival of the republic was at stake. Thus, President Harry S. Truman declared that American servicemen in the Korean War were fighting to protect "our right to govern ourselves as a free nation."[1] "How many times—in my lifetime and in yours—have the American people gathered, as they do now, to hear their President tell them of conflict and tell them of danger?" asked Lyndon Johnson shortly after the major deployment of American troops to Vietnam. "Each time they have answered. They have answered with all the effort that the security and the freedom of this Nation required."[2] On the face of it, such existential anxiety seems surprising given that the United States was always much more powerful than its adversaries. As Odd Arne Westad has observed, "the Soviet Union was never *the other* superpower, the gap that separated the communist regime from the United States in economic achievement, technological innovation, and overall military capability was so great that it is impossible to place the two in the same category."[3] Why should the world's one superpower have felt so threatened by a weaker adversary?

In part, this imbalance between the level of fear and the scale of the threat may be explained through ideology. As Anders Stephanson has shown, the struggle with international communism fits into a pattern of thought with deep roots in American history in which freedom was always precarious because it aroused such mortal hostility from the forces of tyranny and slavery. The Kremlin was thus endowed with the same sinister, encompassing power as had earlier been George III, the Pope, and the South's "slave power."[4] But the fear also rested on a quite different, and more recent, tradition of thought. This was the idea that, in the realm of power politics, America's physical security as a nation-state depended upon there being a favorable balance of power in Europe or Eurasia because otherwise a hegemonic power bent on world domination might amass resources sufficient to out-match the United States in war. There was a danger that the Soviet Union, or the Communist bloc, might achieve substantial control of the resources of the Old World. In this way, the threat to the existence of the republic was perceived to be not merely ideological but also geopolitical.

Many commentators and scholars have seen this geopolitical concern as the basic explanation for US policy in the Cold War. According to the political scientists Barry R. Posen and Stephen W. Van Evera, for example,

> the United States was motivated to contain Soviet expansion after World War II largely by the same concern that had earlier drawn it into war: the need to preserve the political division of industrial Eurasia. . . . American policymakers recognized that any state controlling the entire Eurasian landmass would command more industrial power than the United States. Such a state, they feared, could distill more military power from its national economy and thus could threaten the United

> States, even across the Atlantic. These policymakers accordingly concluded that the United States should strive to contain any state that threatened to gain hegemony in Eurasia, as the Soviet Union appeared to do in 1946–1947. Similar considerations had impelled the United States to check German expansionism in 1917 and in 1941 and had earlier drawn Britain to contain the expansion of Napoleonic France and Czarist Russia.[5]

Leading Cold War historians like John Lewis Gaddis and Melvyn P. Leffler also see this conception of the nation's security requirements as central to American policymaking.[6]

This explanation for US policy implicitly rests on realist assumptions that considerations of power and security are both primary in shaping states' behavior and essentially objective in character. These features of realism have been among the targets of constructivist criticism in recent years.[7] It is not necessary to endorse the epistemological skepticism of the more radical versions of this approach in order to recognize that perceptions of threat are socially constructed.[8] On the contrary, even if all such perceptions are to some extent underdetermined by reality, it is still helpful to be able to discriminate how far this is true in any particular case. In the case of American anxiety about the danger of the nation being overwhelmed by a hostile power controlling all the resources of the Old World, the extent of underdetermination by reality would seem to be extreme, to put it mildly. It is, therefore, all the more interesting to examine the process by which this hypothetical danger acquired such axiomatic status that it was able to serve as a central rationale for the policy of global containment. Tracing the history of the idea shows that it was first advanced in the early twentieth century by some of those who sought to have the United States play a more active role in world politics. It was developed and energetically promoted in the 1930s by opponents of the policy of neutrality. However, it was only after the United States abandoned neutrality following the fall of France that the proposition that the nation's security depended upon the European balance of power entered the reasoning of military planners. The official redefinition of American strategic interests was thus a product of a policy change, rather than the cause of it.

Fault Lines in the Geopolitical Vision

Those who emphasize geopolitical anxiety as the explanation for America's containment strategy can undeniably find supporting evidence in the documents produced by policymakers. In NSC 20/4, approved by Truman as an authoritative statement of United States policy on November 24, 1948, it was flatly stated that "Soviet domination of the potential power of Eurasia, whether achieved by armed aggression or by political and subversive means, would be strategically and politically unacceptable to the United States."[9] Two months earlier, in a lecture to the National War College, George F. Kennan, director of the State Department's Policy Planning Staff, had stressed how vital it was to America's own safety to prevent Germany and Central Europe, Great Britain and Japan coming under the control of the Kremlin because in these locations there existed "the requisite conditions of climate, of industrial strength, of population and of tradition which would enable people there to develop and launch the type of amphibious power which would have to be launched if our national security were seriously affected."[10]

It is of some significance, however, that in pinpointing "the five centers of industrial and military power in the world which are important to us from the standpoint of national security," Kennan was actually seeking to limit the scope of America's commitments. Between 1947 and 1948, his concern was to avoid a major effort to preserve Chiang Kai-shek's regime in China.[11] When, two decades later, Kennan publicly called for the de-escalation of America's involvement in Vietnam, he again began by emphasizing that "Vietnam is not a region of major military, industrial importance."[12] In the 1980s Kennan's analysis was endorsed and developed by critics of the Reagan administration's wide-ranging interventionism and those anxious to avoid the dangers of military "overstretch" as they made the case for "why the Third World doesn't matter." Arguing that America's economic interests in the Third World were, with the exception of oil, minor and in any case not dependent upon political commitments, such critics emphasized that "by the principal and best measure of strategic importance—industrial power—the entire Third World ranks very low."[13]

If United States policy had really been driven by concern with the material balance of power, one would expect it to reflect such assessments of different areas' comparative importance in this regard. Yet none of these Kennan-esque critiques had any significant influence in policymaking circles. With the exception of the early years of the Carter administration, in the immediate aftermath of Vietnam, anticommunist interventionism in the third world was a constant feature of American foreign policy throughout the Cold War.[14] The regnant version of containment remained that outlined in NSC-68 of April 1950. According to this, "any substantial further extension of the area under the domination of the Kremlin would raise the possibility that no coalition adequate to confront the Kremlin with greater strength could be assembled" and "in the context of the present polarization of power a defeat of free institutions anywhere is a defeat everywhere."[15] In various specific contexts, versions of "the domino theory" were developed to justify this universalist interpretation of America's security requirements. No matter how strategically insignificant a particular country was, its loss to communism was seen as likely to lead to a ripple effect that would have serious consequences for the global balance of power.

The vulnerability of such rather formulaic scenarios to skeptical appraisal is one reason for doubting that United States actions can in fact be explained by hard-headed geopolitical calculations. Revealingly, one of the chief counterarguments to the calls by "hyper-realists" for the United States to cease intervening in the third world was that "the domestic political environment will ensure that their views will never be fully accepted."[16] This salutary warning against an overly rationalistic explanation of American policymaking can, however, be taken further by pointing to the questionability of the basic premise that the security of the United States depended upon the balance of power in Eurasia.

Two main arguments were regularly adduced in support of the proposition, one looking to the past, the other to a possible future. The first was that a concern with the European balance had in fact been a constant element in American statesmanship, determining the nation's course of action. In the postwar years, policymakers like George Marshall took it for granted that this was why the United States "had waged two world wars."[17] This view became standard not only in public commentary but also in the works of historians and political scientists.[18] The tradition was sometimes perceived to be one that went back to the earliest days of the republic. "Hamilton, Jay and Madison fully understood that American security lay in no one sovereign's gaining the upper hand in Europe," William T. R. Fox insisted in 1948.[19] According to the historian Gordon Craig, it was not only Federalists who had been concerned with the European balance of power but also that apparently archetypal isolationist, Thomas Jefferson. Craig cited letters in which Jefferson had expressed misgivings about a Bonaparte-controlled Europe and speculated that his embargo policy might have reflected "the suspicion that the French Empire was potentially a greater threat to American liberties than Great Britain and that, despite their present differences, Britain and the United States were tacit partners against the possibility of a domination of the Western world by Napoleon."[20] Jefferson's fear of "the whole force of Europe wielded by a single hand," Arthur Schlesinger confidently wrote a little later, defines "the national interest that explains American intervention in the twentieth century's two world wars as well as the subsequent Cold War."[21]

The other, more direct, argument for seeing the maintenance of a balance of power in Eurasia as a requirement for American security involved positing a situation in which a single hostile power had gained control of the whole continent and would thereby outmatch the United States in potential or actual military strength. In an influential paper of April 1947, the joint chiefs of staff pointed out that

> the area of United States defense commitments includes, roughly, the lands and waters from Alaska to the Philippines and Australia in the Pacific and from Greenland to Brazil and Patagonia in the Atlantic. This area contains 40 percent of the land surface of the earth but only 25 percent of the population. The Old World (Europe, Asia and Africa) contains only 60 percent of the land surface of the earth but 75 percent of the population. The potential military strength of the Old World in terms of manpower and in terms of war-making capacity is enormously greater than that of our area of defense commitments, in which the United States is the only arsenal nation.[22]

"If Western Europe were to fall to Soviet Russia it would double the Soviet supply of coal and triple the Soviet supply of steel," Truman told Congress. "And Soviet command of the manpower of the free nations of Europe and Asia would confront us with military forces which we could never hope to equal."[23] Four decades later, the political scientist Stephen Walt made essentially the same argument, while observing that developments in the meantime had strengthened it: "At the beginning of the Cold War, the loss of Western Europe would have been serious but not disastrous; the United States controlled nearly 40 percent of gross world product in 1949 and Western Europe was just beginning its postwar recovery," but by 1989 "Soviet control over Western Europe would provide the Soviet Union with an advantage of more than 2.5:1 in population and gross national product, to say nothing of tangible military assets."[24]

The widespread acceptance of these arguments is remarkable because neither would seem well-placed to withstand skeptical scrutiny. There is little historical evidence to support the theory that American statesmen have had a perennial concern with the maintenance of the European balance of power. On the face of it, the War of 1812 with Great Britain is hard to reconcile with the idea that Washington policymakers were exercised by the danger of a Napoleonic hegemony. In any case, as Robert W. Tucker and David C. Hendrickson have shown in their thorough dissection of Jefferson's thinking on these matters:

> insofar as Jefferson saw the balance of power as an objective of American statecraft (as opposed to simply an existing constellation of forces to be manipulated), he saw it as a function of the balance of sea and land power. It is misleading to see in his thought a concern for the balance of power as such. He tended rather to look favorably on France's triumphs in Europe. These victories presented no immediate danger to the United States; they were over monarchies with which (save for the Tsar) he had little sympathy; and they were useful in restraining England and would induce the British, he thought, to respect American "rights."

Tucker and Hendrickson observe that Napoleon's "victory over Great Britain never appeared more likely than in late 1807" when Jefferson adopted an embargo policy that in effect constituted a reinforcement of Napoleon's attempt to bring Britain to terms through his Continental System.[25] For the remainder of the nineteenth century, American policymakers clearly followed the same path as Jefferson in prioritizing the advancement of immediate American interests over any concern with the outcome of European conflicts. Their republican disdain for the power politics of Europe rested on an implicit confidence that no vital American interests were involved.

It could be said, of course, that after the defeat of Napoleon it was not until the twentieth century that a serious danger of a hegemonic power dominating the Old World reemerged. Again, however, the common assertion that it was fear of this eventuality that explains America's entry into the two World Wars is a distortion of the historical record. As Robert Osgood demonstrated very thoroughly long ago, few Americans at the time of World War I believed that American security depended upon the balance of power in Europe, and this idea played little part in the process through which the United States came to enter the conflict.[26] Although in retrospect it is easy to assume that the unacceptability of the German submarine campaign in 1917 reflected a fear that it would be successful in forcing Britain to its knees, there is no evidence that this was the case. In fact, even supporters of intervention assumed that the German campaign was a desperate move and that the British navy would soon get on top of it.[27] (It was only after the United States entered the war that American officials were shocked to discover how serious the threat was.) Even had more Americans envisaged the possibility of a crushing German victory, it is not clear that many of them would have seen this as posing a threat to America's own security. It is true that both of Wilson's chief advisers, Colonel Edward M. House and Secretary of State Robert Lansing, at times argued that this would have been the case, but Wilson himself responded to House that the war was exhausting all the European belligerents, and he seems never to have doubted that the United States possessed more than enough strength to defend itself unaided against any possible attack.[28] Certainly, as Osgood again pointed out, this was common ground between both sides in the "preparedness" debate of 1914–16, and both war planning and the nature of America's armed forces were premised on the assumption that their mission was to defend North America rather than to project power across the ocean.[29] Even in World War II the behavior of the United States was not that of a state that saw the preservation of the European balance as a truly vital security interest. This time the danger of a German victory was clear—and clearly perceived by informed Americans. Following the fall of France in June 1940, Britain might have been forced to terms at any point in the next year and a half, leaving Hitler as undisputed master of the continent. Although the United States provided increasing aid during this period, it failed to respond to Churchill's fervent pleas that it enter the war as a full-scale belligerent until it was forced to do so by the contingent and unpredicted attack at Pearl Harbor—and it could well be argued that by December 1941, with the German offensive in Russia bogged down, the main danger had passed.[30]

The questionable nature of the history cited to support it did not, of course, bear directly on the validity of the argument that the United States would face great danger in the future should a hostile power succeed in mustering the combined resources of the Eurasian continent against it. Yet this proposition, too, was vulnerable to skeptical appraisal. The projected scenario involved several rather implausible assumptions. In the first place, the issue of why any state should wish to embark upon the extremely hazardous and costly enterprise of attacking North America was not really addressed. It was only covered by the attribution to America's enemies of an ambition to master the entire globe. "Twice within this generation," according to Truman's version of history, "we have had to take up arms against nations, whose leaders, misled by the hope of easy conquest, sought to dominate the world."[31] Hitler's fantasies, especially in his "Second Book," may serve as some sort of justification for this claim, but it is surely a bizarre description of the goals of Wilhelmine Germany. Truman also made frequent references in his speeches to "the Soviet rulers' . . . plans to take over the world" and their "dream of world conquest."[32] The same megalomaniac ambition was attributed to the Kremlin in internal government documents. NSC 7 of March 1948 emphasized the need "to thwart the communist design of world conquest," and NSC 20/4 in November 1948 amplified the point by asserting that "communist ideology and Soviet behavior clearly demonstrate that the ultimate objective of the leaders of the USSR is the domination of the world." So there was nothing startlingly new about the claim in NSC-68 of April 1950 that "the Soviet Union, unlike previous aspirants to hegemony, is animated by a new fanatic faith, antithetical to our own, and seeks to impose its absolute authority over the rest of the world."[33] In retrospect, such assessments, resting as they did upon a conflation of visionary ideological aspirations with geopolitical ambition, seem superficial as well as mistaken.[34] At the time, Russian specialists like Kennan and Charles Bohlen offered more nuanced appraisals, stressing the cautious and risk-averse character of Soviet policy, but the threat of "world domination" nevertheless became the accepted premise of American strategic thinking.[35]

For Dean Acheson, whose influence was paramount at the time, the precise nature of Moscow's current intentions was less significant than its capacities for aggression.[36] Some realist political scientists see this approach as both natural and rational for leaders of great powers. "Great powers balance against capabilities, not intentions," John Mearsheimer writes. "Intentions are ultimately unknowable, so states worried about their survival must make worst-case assumptions about their rivals' intentions. Capabilities, however, not only can be measured but also determine whether or not a rival state is a serious threat."[37] Yet Mearsheimer also argues that "it is virtually impossible for any state to achieve global hegemony," and from the perspective of capabilities, too, it is hard to justify the expressed fears for America's own security. In the first place, the comparisons between the aggregate resources of the Old and New Worlds made no allowance for the advantageous defensive position of the North American continent or for what Mearsheimer calls "the stopping power of water." For this reason, Mearsheimer argues, "even if Moscow had been able to dominate Europe, Northeast Asia, and the Persian Gulf, which it never came close to doing, it still would have been unable to conquer the Western Hemisphere and become a true global hegemon."[38] Secondly, the comparative assessments of global resources were themselves generally very loosely made. This applies, for example, to Kennan's much cited identification of the "five centers of industrial and military power in the world which are important to us from the standpoint of national security."[39] In taking no account of the relative productive capacity and potential of these "centers," Kennan obscured the scale of America's industrial production (which, in the postwar period, was greater than that of all the others combined), as well as the military advantages provided by its technological superiority.

Moreover, all such assessments assumed a protracted conventional war on the model of World War II. This might well seem more than a little unreal in the nuclear age. How could any aggressor have expected after 1945 to attack North America without risking nuclear retaliation? All it needed to deter any such attempt was a credible second-strike capacity. That this itself requires access to resources beyond the Western Hemisphere has sometimes been argued—but not very convincingly. Thus Truman emphasized the need to import uranium and other critical raw materials, without making reference to the ample strategic reserves.[40] Similarly, Walt's later suggestion that the task of maintaining a secure second-strike capacity would be "daunting" if a rival had command of larger productive resources seemed to rest on an exaggerated notion of what would be required.[41] So, too, did Truman's argument that an America without allies "would have to raise huge armed forces to try to protect our shores against all comers" and "become a garrison state."[42] Indeed, it could well be thought that there was more to be said for the contrary view that in the nuclear age America's alliance commitments detracted from the nation's security rather than enhanced it—by increasing the risk of a confrontation that could escalate with catastrophic consequences. "Why," Robert W. Tucker asked in 1972, "should we persist in commitments whose sacrifice would not risk our physical survival but whose retention does?"[43]

The Rise of an Axiom

When a proposition that falls so far short of being self-evident is so widely accepted, it calls for explanation. In seeking one, it is helpful to examine the contexts in which the proposition was first adumbrated and later came to be accepted as the basis of the nation's strategic planning. The idea was introduced into public debate in the early twentieth century at the time when there was considerable sentiment in elite American circles that the growth of the nation's power had brought with it a responsibility to adopt a wider role in world politics, generally in tacit if not formal association with Great Britain. In 1913, for example, the diplomat David L. Einstein argued that the security of the United States had always depended upon the European balance of power and that therefore "it would hardly be wise statesmanship to remain passive if England should by any series of disasters be crushed" in a war with Germany.[44] Virtually ignored at the time, this argument was taken up by some partisans of the Allied cause after 1914. Among these was Robert Lansing who during the period of American neutrality recorded his belief that the German government sought "world domination" and that "if that oligarchy triumphs over the liberal governments of Great Britain and France, it will then turn upon us as its next obstacle to imperial rule over the world; and that it is safer and wiser and surer for us to be one of many enemies than to be in the future alone against a victorious Germany." But Lansing recognized that these views were accepted neither by "the American people" nor by the president; the private memoranda in which they were expressed did not see the light of day until Lansing published his *War Memoirs* in 1935. Indeed, when it came to the crunch in 1917, Lansing himself made the case for war more on ideological than strategic grounds.[45]

Belligerency naturally led to a general belief that the defeat of the Kaiser's government was a necessary national goal but there is little evidence that it gave rise to a wider acceptance of the broader proposition that America's future security depended on maintaining a balance of power in Europe. In the contentious debates over the peace treaty, there were conflicting views over whether Germany should be treated harshly or leniently but these arguments were conducted more in moral than in strategic terms. Both the League of Nations Covenant and the security treaty with France that Wilson agreed to in Paris would have involved an obligation implicitly to maintain the European balance but the unpopularity of this commitment was a major reason why both were rejected. The unilateralist character of American diplomacy in the 1920s and 1930s rested upon an assumption that the country's basic security was not dependent on the outcome of overseas conflicts. As the historian Maurice Matloff explains, the armed forces took their mission to be "continental defence and protection of possessions in the Pacific." On the extent of the latter interest and the best means of defending it, the army and the navy tended to disagree, but "the keynote of all colour planning as late as 1939 was the strategic concept . . . of defending, against any foreign threat, the continental United States and its interests by the United States alone."[46] That this concept was a viable one was generally accepted. Thus, the respected military analyst Hanson W. Baldwin, writing in *Foreign Affairs* in April 1939, concluded that, with the increases in America's armed forces currently being approved by Congress, "any invasion of our borders in force, even by a combination of Powers, becomes virtually impossible in the foreseeable future."[47]

By 1939, however, this assumption and the related strategy of continental defense was under challenge, not least from President Franklin D. Roosevelt himself. Following the Munich crisis, FDR sought to open the way for the United States to provide material aid (including aircraft) to France and Britain in the hope that this would stiffen their resistance to "the totalitarian powers."[48] To this end, he called in his Annual Message in January 1939 for the repeal of the arms embargo that was part of the neutrality legislation. In doing so, the president stressed the values at stake in Europe: "There comes a time in the affairs of men when they must prepare to defend, not their homes alone, but the tenets of faith and humanity on which their churches, their governments and their very civilization are founded. The defense of religion, of democracy, and of good faith among nations is all the same fight."[49] However, he also made the case in strategic terms, particularly in a White House meeting with the Senate Military Affairs Committee, when he argued that "the first line of defense in the United States" was "the continued independent existence of a very large group of nations" in Europe.[50] In subsequent press conferences, FDR sought to sharpen the sense of threat by suggesting that if the Axis Powers won in Europe they would be able to gain footholds in Latin America and bomb the United States itself.[51]

In employing strategic arguments against isolationism, Roosevelt was following a path already trodden by some publicists. In 1937 Livingston Hartley, a former State Department official, had written a book in which he urged his countrymen to "throw the full weight of the United States, at present so decisive, into the European balance in order to halt the Third Reich and place an insurmountable barrier in the path of German hegemony over Europe or German victory over the British Empire." Like Roosevelt, however, Hartley linked the Far Eastern and European crises to posit a single, global threat; it was the configuration of power in Eurasia as a whole, not simply Europe, that mattered.[52] After providing statistics on the relative populations, coal, steel, and electricity production of the United States, Europe, and Asia, Hartley argued that nothing less than the survival of the nation depended upon the balance of power in Europe and Asia: "If the United States were ever faced on both the Atlantic and the Pacific by a combination of Germany and Japan that together controlled virtually the whole of the Eastern Hemisphere, its end would be certain."[53] Less extravagantly,

Walter Lippmann argued for the repeal of the arms embargo on the grounds that "if Great Britain and France fall before the menace which confronts them in Europe and are no longer able to hold the western coast of Europe and Africa . . . we shall have become for the first time in our history insecure and vulnerable."[54]

In the context of the time, those who sought to have the United States help Britain and France to resist Hitler had a strong incentive to argue that the nation's most basic interest of homeland security was at stake. There was overwhelming evidence in the 1930s—poll data, scholarly and journalistic writing, the debates and votes on the Neutrality legislation—that the great majority of Americans had come to view US participation in World War I as a mistake, and that Wilson's justification of it as a crusade for democracy and world peace had been thoroughly discredited.[55] In 1938 the British writer Sidney Rogerson warned his readers that "it will need a definite threat to America, a threat, moreover, which will have to be brought home by propaganda to every citizen, before the republic will again take arms in an external quarrel."[56] As the historian Felix Gilbert recalled, "it was considered highly desirable to emphasize that, if the United States would enter the war, this would not happen for Wilsonian idealistic reasons, but for reasons of *Realpolitik*, i.e. reasons of national security."[57] In other words, advocates of intervention should not follow Wilson in arguing that with America's great power came a new responsibility to help maintain world order. Rather, they should argue that the traditional and generally agreed objective of homeland security now demanded a much wider set of strategic commitments.

However, there is little to suggest that such arguments made much impact before the fall of France. In *The New York Times*, Hanson Baldwin mocked Hartley's alarmist scenarios "with one 'if' or 'might' or 'probable' leading to another, until the final picture is lost in the dim mists of a future pregnant with fantastic imaginings."[58] Roosevelt failed to secure the repeal of the arms embargo in the summer of 1939, and when the measure passed in the autumn it does not seem to have been due to anxieties over America's own security. In the debate, no senator took issue with Senator Henry Cabot Lodge Jr.'s assertion that "even if Germany were victorious and desired to conquer the United States, she could never do so."[59] In May 1940, the new army chief of staff, General George C. Marshall, assured a Senate Committee that the limited range of all existing bombers meant that air attacks on American cities "would not be practicable unless we permitted the establishment of air bases in close proximity to the United States."[60]

Hitler's stunning victories in the spring and summer of 1940 had a dramatic effect upon both American opinion and US policy but assessments of America's security requirements were not affected as much or as directly as is often suggested.[61] It is true that the fall of France quickly produced a strong consensus in favor of building up the nation's defenses. Congress massively increased defense appropriations and passed by large majorities the first peacetime draft in the nation's history. But the Act confined the service of those drafted to American possessions and the Western Hemisphere. This was in accordance with the views of the service chiefs. The military's prioritizing of hemispheric, or even continental, defense was only reinforced by developments in Europe. This was partly the product of pessimism about the European situation but it also reflected a confidence that the United States could defend its homeland unaided if it mobilized its resources properly. In January 1941, an assessment by the Joint Planning Committee prepared for the Joint Board (the predecessor of the Joint Chiefs of Staff) stated flatly that "the United States can safeguard the North American continent and probably the western hemisphere, whether allied with Britain or not."[62]

Nevertheless, the fall of France did bring about a profound change in the character of US policy in that it led to an increasing commitment to assisting the Allied cause even at the risk of war. This began with the destroyers-for-bases deal in September 1940 and by early 1941 included secret Anglo-American staff conversations as well as Lend-Lease. It was as a consequence of this commitment that the nation's security goals were redefined and expanded, a process led by the head of the service that had always taken a relatively positive view of the projection of America's power beyond the Western Hemisphere. In his famous "Plan Dog" memorandum of November 1940, Admiral Harold R. Stark wrote that "a very strong pillar of the defense structure of the Americas has, for many years, been the balance of power existing in Europe. The collapse of Great Britain or the destruction or surrender of the British Fleet will destroy this balance and will free European military power for possible encroachment in this hemisphere."[63] However, this strategic reassessment was more the consequence of the change in American policy than the cause of it. As the historian Mark Stoler writes, "the planners were forced to come to grips with . . . a White House-directed policy, supported by the public, of aid to and collaboration with London."[64] That the military continued to view this as a secondary priority is shown by their reluctance to allow much of America's expanding munitions production (particularly the new B-17 bombers) to be sent to the Allies.[65] Military planners also pointed out that the defeat of Germany would in practice require entry into the war and the full-scale mobilization of American power.[66]

Roosevelt clearly did not feel that the American people were ready to sustain such a major effort. The policy of aiding the Allies never had the same depth or breadth of public support as did that of strengthening the nation's own defenses. The effort to develop such support led to an energetic campaign to discredit the premises of "isolationism." The proposition that American security depended upon the balance of power in Europe or Eurasia played a major role in that campaign. It was presented in a variety of forums—popular, elite, and academic. In newspapers, journals, and books, a number of writers argued that American statesmen had in fact always recognized that the nation's safety depended upon the European balance of power and British maritime supremacy.[67] It was now that the security explanation for US entry into World War I was developed. Walter Lippmann deployed the authority of his own role at the time in support of this thesis. "America entered the World War because Germany's declaration of unlimited submarine warfare threatened to blockade and starve the Allies and to destroy British sea power," he wrote as France was falling. "I venture to say this categorically and on the basis of direct personal knowledge of what determined President Wilson's decision."[68] Attributing to Americans in early 1917 a knowledge (including that of coming events) that they did not have, Edward M. Earle wrote that

> the very success which attended the submarine campaign, threatening as it did to starve Britain into submission, compelled the American people for the first time since the Battle of the Marne to face what they had not seriously contemplated: the defeat of the Allies. And simultaneously, mutinies in the French army, virtual withdrawal of Russia from the war, and the exhaustion of Allied credits in the United States created a critical situation which presaged a German victory. In the minds of the members of Wilson's cabinet, as well as in the opinion of large sections of the public, such an eventuality would have been a catastrophe of major proportions to the United States.[69]

At the popular level, it was the president himself who led the way in describing the dire consequences for American security if the Allies were defeated. "If Great Britain goes down, the Axis powers will control the continents of Europe, Asia, Africa, Australasia, and the high seas—and they will be in a position to bring enormous military and naval resources against this hemisphere," he warned nationwide radio audiences.

> If the world outside of the Americas falls under Axis domination, the shipbuilding facilities which the Axis powers would then possess in all of Europe, in the British Isles, and in the Far East would be much greater than all the shipbuilding facilities and potentialities of all of the Americas—not only greater, but two or three times greater—enough to win. Even if the United States threw all its resources into such a situation, seeking to double and even redouble the size of our Navy, the Axis powers, in control of the rest of the world, would have the manpower and the physical resources to outbuild us several times over.[70]

This view of America's potential vulnerability was challenged during the course of the "great debate" of 1940–41 by advocates of "hemisphere defense" like Hanson Baldwin as well as by Charles Lindbergh and the writers and speakers for America First.[71] This was the context in which Nicholas John Spykman, professor of International Relations at Yale, wrote *America's Strategy in World Politics*, by far the most thorough and well-argued presentation of the case for the vital importance to America's own security of the balance of power in the Old World. Repudiating argument "by precedent and appeal to the authority of the Founding Fathers," Spykman adopted a geopolitical approach analyzing the power of the world's states in terms of their geographical position and resources base. Strikingly, however, he did not endorse the specter of military conquest. The loss of southern South America would not make the United States militarily indefensible as the Amazonian forest constituted "an enormous buffer zone" against attack by land or by air. "The North American Continental Zone could undoubtedly be held against the invader," he concluded. "Here all the advantages are on the side of the defense: proximity to war industries, well-prepared bases, and a truly continental system of communications that permits quick concentration of forces in any section." What was at stake was not survival as such:

> Our power position in the world, which has always depended on the existence of a balance in Europe and Asia, is now threatened by a combination between unified hemispheres across the seas. The outcome of the Second World War will determine whether the United States is to remain a great power with a voice in the affairs of the Old World, or merely become a buffer state between the mighty empires of Germany and Japan.[72]

Although Spykman's book was clearly written as a contribution to the "great debate," it did not appear until after Pearl Harbor. However, that by no means rendered it irrelevant because opponents of isolationism, anxious to avert a repeat of the reaction after World War I, continued their campaign vigorously during the war years. Recognizing that confidence in the viability of a "Fortress America" strategy had been basic to the isolationist position, they seized on the surprise attack as a demonstration of its impracticality. The "terrible lesson," Roosevelt told the nation, was that "there is no such thing as impregnable defense against powerful aggressors who sneak up in the dark and strike without warning."[73] Following Spykman's lead, there was much interest during the war years in geopolitical thinking, with Karl Haushofer sometimes cast as Hitler's evil genius and Halford Mackinder as a benign one. Mackinder's *Democratic Ideals and Reality*, originally published in 1919, was reissued in 1942 with an introduction by Earle.[74] In a related development, cartographers like George Renner and Richard Edes Harrison led an assault on the Mercator projection, described by the author of one geographical treatise as making the Atlantic and the Pacific a sort of "Maginot Line" that created in Americans a "psychological isolationism." New maps showed the proximity of North America to Europe and Asia over the North Pole, which one writer described as "in the age of air power, close to the pivot of world strategy."[75]

No one made a bigger contribution to this wartime campaign against isolationism than Walter Lippmann, whose *U.S Foreign Policy: Shield of the Republic* (1943) sold half a million copies, was condensed in *Reader's Digest,* and was even reduced to seven pages of cartoon strips by the *Ladies' Home Journal.*[76] In this highly influential work, Lippmann lucidly and confidently expounded what was becoming the regnant narrative of American foreign policy. The security the nation had enjoyed during its "illusory isolation" in the nineteenth century had in practice depended upon British maritime supremacy and the balance of power in Europe. Lippmann reiterated his thesis that the United States entered World War I to prevent a German victory that would have destroyed these conditions of American security but went further than before in claiming that this was "recognized intuitively" by "a majority of the people." Somewhat inconsistently, he argued that "because this simple and self-evident American interest was not candidly made explicit, the nation never understood clearly why it had entered the war"—which explained the rejection of the League of Nations and subsequent reversion to unilateralism. Employing a geopolitical analysis to discredit the strategic premises of isolationism, he made the case that "the potential military strength of the Old World is enormously greater than that of the New World" in terms very similar to those used a few years later in the JCS paper.[77] However, in arguing for the strategic imperative of concern with the security of Western Europe, Lippmann was strikingly inconsistent in his treatment of the potentialities of air power. On the one hand, the United States could be subject to transatlantic attack: "The American regions cannot be defended by waiting to repel an attack by a formidable enemy. . . . American security . . . has always, as Monroe, Jefferson, and Madison saw so clearly, extended to the coast line of Europe, Africa, and Asia. In the new age of air power it extends beyond the coast line to the lands where there are airdromes from which the planes can take off." On the other hand, American planes apparently had less range: "For military purposes, it is just theoretically conceivable that planes could be built which took off in the United States, attacked in Europe or Asia, and returned to the United States without coming to the ground. But such flights would be of no military importance against well-defended objectives across the oceans." Consequently, the United States could not hope to deploy its air power effectively "without the use of advanced air bases across the oceans."[78]

This contradiction was revealing. For the need of the United States for allies and overseas commitments was much more obvious if the purpose was power projection rather than simple self-defense. More basically, the rationale for a concern with the balance of power in the Old World was more evident if the national interest was conceived as involving more than securing physical safety against foreign attack. That there was this broader conception of the national interest is implicit in most of the texts reviewed here and it is explicit in the more rigorous strategic analyses, such as Spykman's.[79] Admiral Stark observed, in the covering note to his famous memorandum, that if Britain fell, "the problem confronting us would be very great; and while we might not *lose everywhere*, we might, possibly, not *win anywhere*."[80] It would, indeed, have been very difficult for the United States to liberate Europe from Nazi domination without friendly bases in Britain and Africa, as military planners in 1941 argued.[81] In other words, what was at stake was not so much the safety of North America as America's ability to shape world affairs. "If any one power dominates Asia, Europe and Africa," a General Staff officer wrote in his diary in 1941, "our country will ultimately become a second class power even if we gain South America and the whole of North America."[82] The concern with the power position of the United States was more than a matter of sheer national pride, although that was important. It also involved the nation's ability to defend and promote the values that Roosevelt so eloquently proclaimed in 1939 (and, of course, on other occasions).[83]

In the early Cold War, too, the official documents that stressed that America's own security depended on the balance of power in Eurasia also made it clear that United States policy and strategy had wider concerns and more ambitious goals than simple self-defense. Envisaging "an ideological war," the joint chiefs of staff pointed out in 1947 that "unless we can retain allies on the eastern side of the Atlantic strong enough, in the event of an ideological war, to hold the Soviets away from the eastern shores of the Atlantic, the shortest and most direct avenue of attack against our enemies will almost certainly be denied to us." In the following year, National Security Council memoranda declared "the defeat of the forces of Soviet-directed world communism" to be a "vital" objective, and to this end outlined measures to achieve "the retraction of Russian power and influence."[84]

Why Geopolitics? Explaining the Durability of an Axiom

The proposition that America's safety was dependent upon the balance of power in Europe (or later Eurasia) did not, then, achieve its axiomatic status on the basis of evidence and irrefutable logic. Rather its general acceptance in official and public discourse was the outcome of a long-term process in which the argument was developed by people who sought to persuade their countrymen that the United States should play a wider and more active role in world politics. The argument was promoted particularly energetically in the years preceding and during World War II. It was challenged, in a manner that many Americans seem to have found persuasive, in the months before Pearl Harbor, but resistance to it faded as the "isolationist" option lost political support after the United States had become fully involved in the war.[85] Although the geopolitical argument became a rationale for the Cold War, it was not a product of the fight against communism but of the fight against isolationism. Lippmann, for example, raised the specter of a possibly outmatched US at a time when he hoped that a postwar understanding with the Soviet Union could be worked out; his concern was to develop support for an active national commitment to a future world order.[86] If the argument predated the Cold War, it also outlasted it. "The domination by a single power of either of Eurasia's two principal spheres—Europe or Asia—remains a good definition of strategic danger for America, Cold War or no Cold War," Henry Kissinger wrote in 1994. "For such a grouping would have the capacity to outstrip America economically and, in the end, militarily."[87]

The persistence of this argument across a century in which both the configurations of world politics and techniques of warfare have changed dramatically is a further reason for seeking its origins in the domestic context of American foreign policy debate rather than in objective strategic necessities. At a very basic level, it is clear that Americans have over the years been torn between two conflicting sentiments. One has been a consciousness of the nation's great potential power in international affairs, a desire to maintain this and to use it to right perceived wrongs abroad and generally to create a world order congenial to American values and interests. But the other has been a belief that the employment of military force, with all the human costs that this inevitably involves, can only be justified on the grounds of self-defense. This sentiment was particularly strong in the 1930s and 1940s when the geopolitical argument we have been examining was really developed. "Nothing can persuade the peoples of the earth that any governing power has any right or need to inflict the consequences of war on its own or any other people save in the cause of self-evident home defense," Roosevelt declared in 1939.[88] And in the United Nations Charter, "the inherent right of individual or collective self-defense if an armed attack occurs" (Article 51) is the only qualification of the commitment by member states to "settle their international disputes by peaceful means" (Article 2(3)). A consequence of this tension has been what Henry Luce, in his famous essay, called "deceit and self-deceit" over the concept of defense.[89] A related phenomenon is the discrepancy, noted by writers with different perspectives, between the views of US foreign policy held by the American public and by people in other countries. "Americans have cherished an image of themselves as by nature inward-looking and aloof, only sporadically venturing forth unto the world, usually in response to external attack or perceived threats," writes Robert Kagan. "This self-image survives, despite . . . an ever-deepening involvement in world affairs, and despite innumerable wars, interventions, and prolonged occupations in foreign lands."[90] The geopolitical specter has helped to square this circle, but in doing so it has also demonstrated that strategic assessments may be as much the product of a process of "social construction" as any other aspect of "the national interest."

Notes

1. Truman, Annual Message to the Congress, January 8, 1951. *Public Papers of the Presidents: Harry S. Truman [PPS: HST] 1951* (Washington, DC, 1965), p. 4.
2. Johnson, Annual Message to the Congress, January 12, 1966. *Public Papers of the President: Lyndon B. Johnson, 1966* (Washington, DC, 1967), vol. 1, p. 9.
3. Westad, "Introduction: Reviewing the Cold War" in Westad (ed.), *Reviewing the Cold War: Approaches, Interpretations, Theory* (London, 2000), p. 19.
4. Stephanson, "Liberty or Death: The Cold War as US Ideology" in Westad (ed.), *Reviewing the Cold War*, pp. 81–100.
5. Posen and Van Evera go on to state that "the logic behind containment would have required American opposition to Soviet expansion even if the Soviet Union had abandoned communism for democracy." Posen and Van Evera, "Reagan Administration Defense Policy: Departure from Containment" in Kenneth A. Oye, Robert J. Lieber and Donald Rothschild (eds.), *Eagle Resurgent? The Reagan Era in American Foreign Policy* (Boston, 1987), pp. 77–78.
6. John Lewis Gaddis, *The Long Peace: Inquiries into the History of the Cold War* (Oxford, 1987), pp. 21–22; Melvyn P. Leffler, *A Preponderance of Power: National Security, the Truman Administration, and the Cold War* (Stanford, 1992), pp. 10–13, 191.
7. For a concise and lucid summary, see Ian Hurd, "Constructivism" in Christian Reus-Smit and Duncan Snidal (eds.), *The Oxford Handbook of International Relations* (Oxford, 2008), pp. 298–316.
8. For a characterization and critique of the epistemology of "radical" constructivism (often called postmodernism), see Alexander Wendt, *Social Theory of International Politics* (Cambridge, 1999), pp. 54–57.
9. NSC 20/4 "U.S. Objectives with Respect to the USSR to Counter Soviet Threats to U.S. Security," *Foreign Relations of the United States [FRUS], 1948* (Washington, DC, 1976), vol. 1, part 2, pp. 663–669, quotation on p. 667.
10. National War College lecture, "Contemporary Problems of Foreign Policy," September 17, 1948, cited in John Lewis Gaddis, *Strategies of Containment: A Critical Appraisal of Postwar American National Security Policy* (Oxford, 1982), p. 30. See also George F. Kennan, *Realities of American Foreign Policy* (Princeton, 1954), pp. 63–65; *Memoirs 1925–1950* (Boston, 1967), p. 359.
11. Wilson D. Miscamble, *George F. Kennan and the Making of American Foreign Policy 1947–1950* (Princeton, 1992), pp. 220–223.
12. Testimony of George F. Kennan to the Senate Foreign Relations Committee, February 10, 1966, *The Vietnam Hearings*, intro. J. William Fulbright (New York, 1966), p. 108.
13. Stephen M. Walt, "The Case for Finite Containment: Analyzing U.S. Grand Strategy," *International Security*, 14 (1989), pp. 19–21; Posen and Van Evera, "Reagan Administration Defense Policy: Departure from Containment," pp. 93–98. See also Robert H. Johnson, "Exaggerating America's Stake in Third World Conflicts," *International Security*, 10 (1984/85), pp. 32–68.

14. For an overview, see Odd Arne Westad, *The Global Cold War: Third World Interventions and the Making of Our Times* (Cambridge, 2005).
15. NSC-68 "United States Objectives and Programs for National Security," April 14, 1950, in Thomas H. Etzold and John Lewis Gaddis (ed.), *Containment: Documents on American Policy and Strategy, 1945–1950* (New York, 1978), pp. 386, 389. The clearest (perhaps over-clear) analysis of the difference between Kennan's version of containment and that of NSC 68 remains Gaddis, *Strategies of Containment*, especially Chapters 2 and 4.
16. Steven R. David, "Why the Third World Matters," *International Security*, 14 (1989), p. 60.
17. Leffler, *A Preponderance of Power*, p. 191.
18. For example, Arthur A. Stein, "Domestic Constraints, Extended Deterrence, and the Incoherence of Grand Strategy: The United States, 1938–1950" in Richard Rosecrance and Arthur A. Stein (eds.), *The Domestic Bases of Grand Strategy* (Ithaca, 1993), p. 97; Gaddis, *The Long Peace*, p. 25.
19. Fox, "American Foreign Policy and the Western European Rimland," *Proceedings of the American Academy of Political Science*, 22 (January 1948), p. 74.
20. Craig, "The United States and the European Balance," *Foreign Affairs*, 55 (October 1976), pp. 189–190.
21. Schlesinger, "Foreign Policy and the American Character" in *The Cycles of American History* (London, 1987), p. 53.
22. JCS 1769/1 "United States Assistance to Other Countries from the Standpoint of National Security," April 29, 1947. *FRUS. 1947*, vol. 1 (Washington, DC, 1973), pp. 734–750, quotation on p. 739.
23. Truman, Annual Message to Congress, January 8, 1951. *PPS: HST 1951*, p. 8.
24. Walt, "The Case for Finite Containment," p. 18.
25. Tucker and Hendrickson, *Empire of Liberty: The Statecraft of Thomas Jefferson* (Oxford, 1990), pp. 214–219, 226–227.
26. Osgood, *Ideals and Self-Interest in America's Foreign Relations: The Great Transformation of the Twentieth Century* (Chicago, 1953), chapters VI–XI.
27. For example, the editors of *The New Republic* and Senator Henry Cabot Lodge. See *New Republic*, 10 (February 17, 1917), p. 57; Arthur S. Link, *Wilson: Campaigns for Progressivism and Peace, 1916–1917* (Princeton, 1965), pp. 302–303, and more generally, Osgood, *Ideals and Self-Interest*, pp. 253–254.
28. E. M. House diary, November 4, 1914; Wilson speeches in New York, November 4, 1915, in St Louis, February 3, 1916. *The Papers of Woodrow Wilson* [*PWW*], edited by Arthur S. Link et al (Princeton, 1966–94), vol. 31, p. 265; vol. 35, p. 171, vol. 36, p. 120.
29. Osgood, *Ideals and Self-Interest*, pp. 209–211, 221–222; John A. S. Grenville and George B. Young, *Politics, Strategy and American Diplomacy: Studies in Foreign Policy* (New Haven, 1967), pp. 334–335; or J. A. S. Grenville, "Diplomacy and War Plans in the United States, 1880–1917" in Paul M. Kennedy (ed.), *The War Plans of the Great Powers, 1880–1914* (London, 1979), pp. 35–37.
30. On this point, see Bruce M. Russett, *No Clear and Present Danger: A Skeptical View Of U.S. Entry into World War II* (New York, 1972), pp. 25–28.
31. Truman, Special Message to the Congress, November 17, 1947. *PPP:HST 1947* (Washington, DC, 1963), p. 494.
32. Truman, Annual Message to the Congress, January 8, 1951; Radio and Television Address to the American People on the Mutual Security Program, March 6, 1952; *PPP:HST 1951*, p. 10; *1952–52* (Washington, DC, 1966), p. 191.
33. NSC 7, March 30, 1948, NSC 20/4, November 23, 1948, NSC 68, April 14, 1950. Etzold and Gaddis, *Containment*, pp. 167, 204, 385.
34. After the end of the Cold War, the Soviet diplomat Georgi M. Kornienko observed that "the fundamental conceptual flaw of NSC-68, to my mind, consists in the fact that its authors—consciously or not—equated the Soviet government's declared confidence in the victory of communism around the world with an imaginary aspiration of the Soviet

Union as a state 'to establish its absolute power over the rest of the world.' The thesis that the Soviet Union was striving for world domination is often repeated in the text as something perfectly self-evident without the slightest attempts to base it either theoretically or factually." Ernest R. May (ed.), *American Cold War Strategy: Interpreting NSC 68* (London, 1993), pp. 125–126.

35. For Bohlen's doubts about this aspect of NCS 68, see Charles Bohlen to Paul Nitze, April 5, 1950. *FRUS, 1950* (Washington, DC, 1977), vol. I, p. 222.
36. Paul Y. Hammond, "NSC 68: Prologue to Rearmament" in Warner R. Schilling, Paul Y. Hammond and Glenn H. Snyder (eds.), *Strategy, Politics, and Defense Budgets* (New York, 1962), p. 309.
37. Mearsheimer, *The Tragedy of Great Power Politics* (New York, 2001), p. 45.
38. Ibid., pp. 41, 138.
39. See above, footnote 10.
40. Truman, Annual Message to the Congress, January 8, 1951; Special Message to Congress on the Mutual Security Program, March 6, 1952. *PPP:HST 1951*, p. 8; *1952–53*, p. 180.
41. Walt, "The Case for Finite Containment," p. 29.
42. Truman, Radio and Television Address to the American People on the Mutual Security Program, March 6, 1952; Special Message to the Congress on the Mutual Security Program, March 6, 1952. *PPP:HST 1952–53*, pp. 192, 189. Leffler attaches great explanatory importance to this aspect of policymakers' conception of national security—the desire to maintain the "core values" of a free society. See *A Preponderance of Power*, especially pp. 497–498; "National Security" in Michael J. Hogan and Thomas G. Paterson (eds.), *Explaining the History of American Foreign Relations* (Cambridge, 1991), pp. 204–205, 207–208.
43. Tucker, *A New Isolationism: Threat or Promise?* (New York, 1972), pp. 46–47.
44. Einstein, "The United States and Anglo-American Rivalry," *National Review*, LX (January 1913), pp. 736–750. For the presentation of this thesis in the writings of other publicists, such as H. H. Powers and A. T. Mahan in the pre–World War I era, see Osgood, *Ideals and Self-Interest*, pp. 65–66, 99.
45. Lansing, *War Memoirs of Robert Lansing* (Indianapolis, 1935), pp. 19–21, 102–104; Lansing Memorandum of Cabinet Meeting, March 20, 1917. *PWW*, vol. 41, pp. 440–441; Osgood, *Ideals and Self-Interest*, pp. 163–168.
46. Matloff, "The American Approach to War, 1919–1945" in Michael Howard (ed.), *The Theory and Practice of War: Essays presented to Captain B.H. Liddell Hart* (London, 1965), pp. 215–218.
47. Baldwin, "Our New Long Shadow," *Foreign Affairs*, 17 (April 1939), p. 476.
48. Barbara Rearden Farnham, *Roosevelt and the Munich Crisis: A Study of Political Decision-Making* (Princeton, 1997), pp. 152–156, 174–184; John Morton Blum, *From the Morgenthau Diaries: Years of Urgency 1938–1941* (Boston, 1965), pp. 48, 65. FDR used the phrase "the totalitarian powers" at a Press Conference, April 20, 1939. *Complete Press Conferences of Franklin D. Roosevelt* [*CPC*] (New York, 1972), vol. 13, p. 307.
49. Roosevelt, Annual Message to the Congress, January 4, 1939. Samuel I. Rosenman (ed.), *Public Papers and Addresses of Franklin D. Roosevelt* [*PPA*], vol. 8, *1939* (New York, 1941), p. 2.
50. Transcript, "Conference with the Senate Military Affairs Committee," January 31, 1939, in Wayne S. Cole, *Roosevelt and the Isolationists 1935–45* (Lincoln, NE, 1983), pp. 305–306.
51. Roosevelt Press Conferences, April 20, 1939, June 23, 1939. *CPC*, vol. 13, pp. 307–313, 462–464.
52. On the centrality and significance of a global perspective in Roosevelt's approach, see David Reynolds, *From Munich to Pearl Harbor: Roosevelt's America and the Origins of the Second World War* (Chicago, 2001), pp. 4–5, 10–11, 53–54, 106–107, 148, 169, 179–183.
53. Hartley, *Is America Afraid? A New Foreign Policy for the United States* (New York, 1937), pp. 140–141, 73–75, 133.
54. Lippmann, "The Doors of America," *New York Herald Tribune*, January 12, 1939.

55. Robert A. Divine, *The Illusion of Neutrality* (Chicago, 1962), pp. 74–79; Manfred Jonas, *Isolationism in America, 1935–1941* (Ithaca, 1966), pp. 1, 26–31; Warren I. Cohen, *The American Revisionists: The Lessons of Intervention in World War I* (Chicago, 1967), chapters 6–7.
56. Rogerson, *Propaganda in the Next War* (London, 1938), p. 148.
57. Quoted in Daniel Yergin, *Shattered Peace: The Origins of the Cold War and the National Security State* (Boston, 1977), p. 194.
58. Review of Livingston Hartley, *Our Maginot Line: The Defense of the Americas*, *New York Times Book Review*, April 9, 1939, p. 19.
59. *Congressional Record*, 76th Congress, 2nd session, vol. 85, part 1, p. 250; Osgood, *Ideals and Self-Interest*, pp. 405–407.
60. Mark Skinner Watson, *United States Army in World War II: The War Department. Chief of Staff: Prewar Plans and Preparations* (Washington, DC, 1950), pp. 150–151.
61. For a fuller development of this argument, see John A. Thompson, "Conceptions of National Security and American Entry into World War II," *Diplomacy and Statecraft*, 16 (2005), pp. 671–697.
62. Maurice Matloff and Edwin M. Snell, *Planning for Coalition Warfare* (Washington, DC, 1953), pp. 12–13; Mark Stoler, *Allies and Adversaries: The Joint Chiefs of Staff, the Grand Alliance, and U.S. Strategy in World War II* (Chapel Hill, 2000), p. 25; Instructions for ABC staff conversations, January 21, 1941. Steven R. Ross (ed.), *American War Plans, 1919–1941* (New York, 1992), vol. 3, *Plans to Meet the Axis Threat, 1939–40*, p. 309.
63. H. R. Stark, Memorandum for the Secretary, November 12, 1940. Ross, *American War Plans*, vol. 3, p. 243.
64. Stoler, *Allies and Adversaries*, p. 28 (also p. 39).
65. David Reynolds, *The Creation of the Anglo-American Alliance, 1937–1941: A Study in Competitive Co-operation* (London, 1981), pp. 109–113.
66. In his memorandum, Stark plainly stated that victory would require a successful land offensive which Britain lacked the capacity to make and that "the United States, in addition to sending naval assistance, would also need to send large air and land forces to Europe or Africa, or both, and to participate strongly in this land offensive." In the "Victory Program" of September 1941, Army Planners estimated that no less than 215 American divisions would be required for success. "Joint Board Estimate of United States Over-all Production Requirements," September 11, 1941. Ross, *American War Plans*, vol. 3, p. 241; vol. 5, *Plans for Global War: Rainbow 5 and the Victory Program*, p. 201.
67. In addition to the works cited below, see, for example, Forrest Davis, *The Atlantic System: The Story of Anglo-American Control of the Seas* (New York, 1941); Francis Perkins Miller, "The Atlantic Area," *Foreign Affairs* 19 (July 1941), pp. 726–728; and Alfred Vagts, "The United States and the Balance of Power," *Journal of Politics*, 3 (November 1941), pp. 401–449.
68. Lippmann, "The Generation That Was Duped," *New York Herald Tribune*, June 15, 1940. In support of this assertion Lippmann cited an editorial from the *New Republic* in February 1917 (without disclosing that he himself had written it) on the "profound web of interest which joins together the western world" and the consequent need to fight to preserve "the safety of the Atlantic highway." Lippmann developed this argument in "The Atlantic and America," *Life*, April 7, 1941, pp. 84–88, 90–92.
69. Earle, "National Security and Foreign Policy," *The Yale Review*, 29, March 1940, pp. 444–460, quotation on pp. 451–452; "The Threat to National Security," *The Yale Review*, 30, March 1941, pp. 454–480. Before the United States entered the war, the Wilson administration, let alone the American public, did not in fact have any awareness or foreknowledge of any of the developments Earle lists.
70. Roosevelt, Fireside Chats, December 29, 1940, September 11, 1941. *PPA*, vol. 9, p. 635, vol. 10, p. 388.
71. Hanson Baldwin, *United We Stand: Defense of the Western Hemisphere* (New York, 1941), especially pp. 74–82.

72. Spykman, *America's Strategy in World Politics: The United States and the Balance of Power* (New York, 1942), pp. 7, 465, 455–456, 392–395, 404–406, 443, 195, *passim*. For a thorough assessment of the validity of Spykman's analysis that concludes it was too pessimistic, see Robert J. Art, "The United States, the Balance of Power and World War II: Was Spykman Right?" *Security Studies*, 14 (July–September 2005), pp. 365–406.
73. Roosevelt, Fireside Chat, December 9, 1941. *PPA*, 10 *1941*, pp. 528–529. As Senator Arthur Vandenberg immediately observed, it would have been possible for a different lesson to be drawn: "The interventionist says today—as the President virtually did in his address today—'See! This proves we were right and that this war was *sure* to involve us.' The non-interventionist says (and I say)—'See! We have insisted from the beginning that this course would lead to war and it has done exactly that.'" Diary entry, December 11, 1941. Arthur H. Vandenberg, Jr. (ed.), *The Private Papers of Senator Vandenberg* (Boston, 1952), p. 19.
74. Robert Strausz-Hupé, *Geopolitics: The Struggle for Space and Power* (New York, 1942); Hans W. Weigart, *Generals and Geographers: The Twilight of Geopolitics* (Oxford, 1942); Halford J. Mackinder, *Democratic Ideals and Reality* (London, 1942); Robert Strausz-Hupé, *The Balance of Tomorrow: Power and Foreign Policy in the United States* (New York, 1945). Employing Mackinder's categories, Frederick Sherwood Dunn, director of the Yale Institute of International Studies, wrote that "the most important single fact in the American security situation is the question of who controls the rimlands of Europe and Asia. Should these get into the hands of a single power or combination of powers hostile to the United States, the resulting encirclement would put us in a position of grave peril, regardless of the size of our army and navy." "An Introductory Statement" in Nicholas J. Spykman, *The Geography of the Peace* (New York, 1944), p. x.
75. Susan Schulten, *The Geographical Imagination in America, 1880–1950* (Chicago, 2001), pp. 2–3, 138–145, 214–236; Weigert, *Generals and Geographers*, p. 195. See also Alan Hendrikson, "The Map as an 'Idea': The Role of Cartographic Imagery During the Second World War," *American Cartographer*, 2 (April 1975), pp. 19–53. Harrison's maps were used to illustrate *General Marshall's Report: The Winning of the War in Europe and the Pacific* (New York, 1945).
76. Ronald Steel, *Walter Lippmann and the American Century* (London, 1981), p. 406.
77. "The area of American defensive commitment is not quite 40 percent of the land surface of the earth. But it contains a little less than 25 percent of the population of the earth. The Old World contains 75 percent of mankind living on 60 percent of the land of this globe. Thus it is evident that the potential military strength of the Old World is enormously greater than that of the New World. When we look more closely at the facts of power the disparity is even greater. The only arsenal of the New World is in North America.... The Old World, on the other hand, comprises the military states of Britain, Russia, Germany, France, Japan, Italy, and China—all of them arsenals or potential arsenals and each of them with a population used to war and the carrying of arms." Lippmann, *U.S. Foreign Policy: Shield of the Republic* (Boston, 1943), pp. 30–39, 109–110. Compare the passage from JCS 1769/1 quoted above (footnote 22).
78. Lippmann, *U.S. Foreign Policy*, pp. 94–95, 120–121.
79. See above (footnote 72).
80. Stark, Memorandum for the Secretary, November 12, 1940. Ross, *American War Plans*, vol. 3, p. 225.
81. Ross, *American War Plans*, vol. 5, pp. 171, 192.
82. Diary of Colonel Paul Robinett, September 12, 1941, quoted in Stoler, *Allies and Adversaries*, p. 50.
83. See above, footnote 49.
84. JCS 1769/1, April 29, 1947. *FRUS, 1947*, vol. 1, p. 739; NSC 7, March 30, 1948. *FRUS, 1948*, vol. 1, Part 2, p. 548; NSC 20/1, August 18, 1948. Etzold and Gaddis, *Containment*, pp. 176–187.
85. On the debate in 1940–41 and its impact on public opinion, see Thompson, "Conceptions of National Security," pp. 682–687.

86. For Lippmann's wartime assessments of the postwar Soviet-American relationship, see *U.S. Foreign Policy*, pp. 146–154; *U.S. War Aims*, pp. 131–154.
87. Kissinger, *Diplomacy* (New York, 1994), p. 813.
88. Message to A. Hitler (and B. Mussolini), April 14, 1939. *PPA*, vol. 8 *1939*, pp. 202–203.
89. After declaring "we are *in* the war," Luce asked "how did we get in? We got in on the basis of defense. Even that very word, defense, has been full of deceit and self-deceit. To the average American the plain meaning of the word defense is defense of American territory. Is our national policy today limited to the defense of the American homeland by whatever means may seem wise? It is not. . . . If the entire rest of the world came under the domination of evil tyrants, it is quite possible to imagine that this country could make itself such a tough nut to crack that not all the tyrants in the world would care to come against us. No man can say that that picture of America as an impregnable armed camp is false. No man can honestly say that as a pure matter of defense—defense of our homeland—it is necessary to get into or be in this war." Luce, "The American Century," *Life*, vol. 10 (February 17, 1941), pp. 61–62.
90. Kagan, *Dangerous Nation: America and the World 1600–1898* (New York, 2006), p. 5. See also Richard Crockatt, *America Embattled: September 11, Anti-Americanism and the Global Order* (London, 2003), p. 8.

6

War Envy and Amnesia

American Cold War Rewrites of Russia's War

ANN DOUGLAS

The Denial of the Eastern Front: Movies and Historians

General Georgi Zhukov, the star of a cadre of formidable Russian commanders in World War II, was a lifelong admirer of Overlord, the amphibious feat that launched the Western Allies' long delayed second front in France on June 6, 1944. The strong rapport he and Dwight Eisenhower, Overlord's architect, had instantly established while administering Berlin together after the war was the most promising manifestation of the continued spirit of cooperation to which both the United States and the Soviet Union were then pledged. Lucius Clay, who succeeded Eisenhower as military governor in Berlin in early 1946, always believed their friendship proved that "we could have avoided the worst of what followed; . . . Soviet behavior grew out of events rather than being predetermined." "I still look upon the hours I spent in friendly discussion with you," Eisenhower wrote Zhukov in March 1946, "as among the most pleasant and profitable I have ever experienced."[1] The friendship didn't, and couldn't, last, though neither man ever forgot it. After the war, a jealous and paranoid Stalin refused to let Zhukov travel to the United States, despite Eisenhower's reiterated invitations. Both men were wholehearted partisans of their respective capitalist and communist worldviews; both hardened their stance in the early 1950s. But, as Zhukov's *Memoirs* make clear, the United States' distorted and self-glorifying depictions of its role in World War II's European Theater were a contributing factor as well. The United States had adopted a "Germany first" policy but, Zhukov knew, this was not the war they had won.

Zhukov had noted, as had all the Soviets stationed in Berlin, that the United States had reserved its highest military honors at war's end for the British commanders, awarding the Russians only second-tier commendations, a double insult since the Soviets had already given Eisenhower and Britain's Bernard Montgomery the Order of Victory, the USSR's top award. As the postwar decade unfolded, Zhukov fumed privately about the United States' ever more explicit contention that it had, in Zhukov's words, "all but saved" Russia from Hitler's Wehrmacht. When he saw Darryl Zanuck's *The Longest Day* (1962), a box office sensation that presented the landing in Normandy as the turning point, the peak of heroism and self-sacrifice in World War II, Zhukov had had enough. Russia's Operation Bagration, in good part designed and executed by Zhukov, launched in Belarus sixteen days after D-Day, had been the real show-stopper of June. Within a few weeks the Soviets had destroyed the entire German Army Group Centre, while the Western Allies were still mired in a struggle for a narrow bridgehead in France. Hitler did not underestimate the importance of the Normandy landing; he still kept the bulk of the Wehrmacht fighting the Red Army in the East. Yet there is no mention of any Soviet operation in *The Longest Day*, no suggestion that the German troops the Americans met in France had already been bled by three years of exhausting combat on the Eastern Front, where Germany suffered more than 80 percent of its casualties and the Soviets fought alone. "There has to be a limit somewhere!" Zhukov exclaimed.[2] But there wasn't, and isn't.

Zhukov understood the United States' real and enormous, if primarily industrial and economic, contributions to the European war; in the Pacific theater, the Americans were indisputably the principal agents of Axis defeat. But because Japan and Germany, unlike the Allies, never successfully coordinated their wars, Germany had to be beaten on its own, and on the ground, where its greatest strength lay, and the USSR was the one who did it. Why, Zhukov wondered, weren't the Americans content with their legitimate, and large, share of the glory? Why did they need to steal Russia's credit too? The sleight-of-hand by which the United States buried the Soviet Union's role in the war against Hitler deserves close investigation; the geopolitical, diplomatic, and cultural history of the Cold War can't be separated from the military history of the war that preceded it.

A number of scholars have suggested that the United States "deliberately underplayed," in David Glantz's words, Soviet Russia's "decisive impact" on World War II because of the Cold War.[3] If Stalin was no better than Hitler, if the USSR was all along, as Cold War wisdom had it, Nazi Germany's totalitarian twin and the West's mortal foe, the wartime alliance constituted a betrayal of Western ideals with tragic and global consequences. The historical facts of the matter—that by summer 1941, with the rest of Europe occupied by or allied with the Third Reich, Stalin's USSR represented the West's last, best chance of stopping Hitler's Wehrmacht; that Russia, defying all expectations, provided its allies, at astonishingly low cost to them, with an epochal victory for which the Soviets themselves paid dearly—didn't fit the postwar narrative. But the United States' willed amnesia about Russia's impact on the war and the war's impact on Russia wasn't, I believe, simply a symptom or byproduct of the Cold War. It was also one of that war's constitutive goals, preconditions, and motives, both geopolitical and psychological; "war envy," as I call it, predated and partly determined the Cold War. The Cold War was, in Anders Stephanson's phrase, a US project, a project defined by and predicated on a selective but massive refusal of available information at the top.[4] The known and knowable became the unknowable, a site of intense conjecture and projection; the unknowable, always more malleable than fact, permitted the formation of new narratives, which in turn found or fictionalized their own sources of substantiation and proof. The Cold War was, among other things, a war about memory, and the recasting and rewriting of World War II was at the heart of the struggle.

A growing reluctance to acknowledge the Soviet war record was hardly unique to the United States in the postwar period. Churchill's famed oratory notwithstanding, much of the UK's wartime performance, particularly on the ground, was dismal; France had more or less consented to its own occupation, collaborating in the evils of the Nazi regime; and Germany, whose war crimes set new standards in horror, had been brutally and humiliatingly defeated by the USSR. All of them, now dependent to varying degrees on US economic aid and military protection, had their own reasons for investing in the American storyline. The United States nonetheless held, and retains, the title of denier-in-chief, and it was willing and able to back its message with all the resources of the world's only global media empire. As Zhukov had discovered, the American attitude toward historical accuracy has never been too far removed from the producer Jerry Wald's contemptuous dismissal of a scriptwriter working on a 1945 Warner Brothers picture about the US army in Burma, who dared to remind him that there were no Americans fighting there: "So what?. . . . put in some British liaison officers and stop worrying."[5]

The United States has been slow to recognize or assimilate the reevaluation of the Eastern Front, including Stalin's wartime leadership and the Nazi-Soviet war more broadly, flourishing abroad today in a range of fields from military to diplomatic and geopolitical history. The leaders of the new World War II history, with the notable exception of David Glantz, whether focused primarily on Russia or Germany, are not American but German, like Jürgen Förster, Hannes Herr, Christian Streit, Alfred Streim, Wolfram Wette, and Götz Aly, or from the U.K., like John Erickson, Richard Overy, Max Hastings, Evan Mawdsley, Richard Evans, Geoffrey Roberts, and Adam Tooze. Although Mark Mazower at

Columbia and Omer Bartov at Brown include the USSR in their studies of World War II, they are recruits, born and trained elsewhere, then wooed to the United States. Misleading language, startling omissions, and outright misinformation still crop up routinely in American scholarly discussions of the Eastern Front. In *A War To Be Won* (2000), Williamson Murray and Allan R. Millett state that Germany and the USSR killed about the same number of each other's civilians, approximately 1.5 to 2 million apiece. Casualty estimates for World War II notoriously vary, but this seems wildly off the mark. Most historians agree that about 2 million German civilians died, more of them from US/UK bombing than from the Red Army's counterinvasion and occupation; the Soviet Union's civilian deaths are usually set at somewhere between 16 and 18 million. There can be, in any case, no equivalence between Nazi and Soviet war crimes, between unprovoked, unprecedented aggression in deliberate defiance of international law and the excesses of retaliation, no matter how awful. Murray and Millett also omit the USSR from their list of the nations that suffered large losses because of "strategic bombing," yet some 500,000 Soviets died under German bombs, over ten times as many as the total number of British citizens killed in the London Blitz.[6]

American historians have not been indifferent to all Hitler's victims, however. It is rather that, until recently, they have concentrated almost exclusively on the Jews killed in the Holocaust. In *The Unmasterable Past* (1988), Harvard historian Charles Maier explained that Hitler's Final Solution, and apparently the Final Solution alone, made Nazi Germany more morally reprehensible than Stalin's USSR. Had there been no Holocaust, Maier writes, "the *furor teutonicus* might have raged in the conquered regions of Russia. . . . But the great extermination centers in Poland . . . would not have been established." Maier omits the fact that most of the death camps were originally built by and for Soviet prisoners of war; according to several witnesses, the POW camps, where monthly death totals climbed as high as 85 percent in the first half year of the war, were if anything worse than the Jewish concentration camps. "Furor teutonicus" also seems too playful, too arch a term for the mass murder the Nazis perpetrated in the east. Almost two of every three prisoners of war (at least 3.3 million of them) and up to one in every seven Soviet citizens *in toto* were starved, exposed, worked, shot, or (in the case of some 600 to 1,500 POWs) gassed to death, most of them in the first eighteen months of the war, an almost unbelievably accelerated pace of slaughter.[7]

The American historians who have made significant contributions to the study of the Nazi invasion of the USSR have usually viewed it, to borrow the title of Christopher Browning's 2004 masterwork, as part of "The Origins of the Final Solution," a kind of warm-up and prelude to the Holocaust, making the murder of Europe's Jews, if only by implication, the Eastern war's ultimate aim.

When the Princeton historian Arno Mayer (born in Luxembourg) reversed this order in his clarion call-to-intellectual-arms, *Why Did the Heavens Not Darken?* (1988), arguing that the "Judeocide," as Mayer terms it, was in fact a "graft" on Barbarossa, he found a more sympathetic reception abroad than at home. To argue that Barbarossa would have occurred without the Judeocide while the Judeocide's timing and form depended on developments in Barbarossa, that Barbarossa was preplanned in a way that the Judeocide was not—one plausible explanation of why the peak of the murder of the Soviet POWs between June 1941 and February 1942 came before the peak period of the Holocaust in 1942—has not been an acceptable position in the United States. Although Soviet Jews, with the USSR's Communist officials, received the worst treatment from the start, the Nazis' plan to starve to death 30, 60, even "zig [countless, umpteen] Millionen Menschen" in the Soviet Union in order to gain *Lebensraum* for German expansion and the *Ausrottung* (eradication) of Bolshevism, as it was formulated on May 2, 1941, seven weeks before Barbarossa began and a good half year before the Final Solution became official, if secret, policy, clearly targeted a population far larger than the USSR's roughly five million Jews.[8]

Few Americans know that the USSR saved more than five million Jews in the course of the war, or the bulk of Europe's Jewish survivors, although rescuing Jews was never for Stalin (or for that matter, for Roosevelt or Churchill) a priority. Five million dwarfs the 104,000 to 250,000 Jews the United States rescued (largely by manipulation of its immigration quotas) and offers evidence of just who actually defeated the Germans.[9] Whichever of the Allies took back the territory the Wehrmacht controlled would shut down the killing fields; the ghastly honor of liberating the death camps went to the Red Army, not the American or British troops. Although by the 1990s 97 percent of Americans could identify the Holocaust as a genocide perpetrated against Jews and a majority considered it "the worst tragedy in history," a sizable minority of them didn't know when or how it happened or, apparently, who did it. Most recent high school graduates believe the United States and Germany fought together in World War II against Russia.[10]

What signs there are to date of a new direction in World War II studies in the United States are not entirely encouraging. In his blockbuster book *Bloodlands* (2010), Timothy Snyder, an American-born historian of Poland at Yale, foregrounds the gentile as well as the Jewish Eastern European civilians who died between 1933 and 1945, fourteen million in all by his count, in what Snyder calls "Molotov-Ribbentrop Europe," the territories occupied in tandem or successively by Hitler and Stalin's dueling regimes and most directly affected by the Nazi-Soviet Pact of 1939. Gentile Eastern Europeans, Snyder points out, were equally despised and at risk under both dictators; Jews were not. Jews, at least, comparatively-speaking, had an ally, however inadvertent. Snyder is not writing a history of World War II, yet his lack of interest in military history still seems surprising: German aggression and Russian retaliation were redefining the European map for most of his chosen period. Although Snyder is not concerned with the American role in the European war or in the Cold War that followed it, *Bloodlands* still bears traces of the American Cold War narrative; it is at once a pathbreaking work of historiography and a throwback. There is, apparently, more than one way to skin the Cold War cat. A master of plausible deniability, Snyder is not above sophistry, and he exhibits his own form of war envy. How else to explain his speculation that the USSR might not have been able to withstand the German attack had Poland, Hungary, and Romania allied themselves with Hitler?[11] In plain fact, nearly 700,000 Romanians and almost a million Hungarians died fighting with the Wehrmacht, and Germany crushed Poland's gallant resistance in a matter of weeks. Again and again, Snyder belittles and discredits, if not exactly the USSR, its leading republic, Russia, and its post–Cold War successor state, promoting the Soviet Union's then subordinate republics, satellites, and territories at Russia's expense. Who needs to worry about the USSR's wartime role, if there never really was a Soviet Union at all?

Snyder accuses Russia, past and present, of "martyrological imperialism," "implicitly claiming territory by explicitly claiming bodies."[12] The bulk of the Soviet civilians who died in the war, he emphasizes, whether Jewish or gentile, were ethnic Ukranians, Belarusians, Balts, and Poles, not Russians. This would not hold true, however, of the Red Army soldiers who were killed in the Bloodlands, which may be one reason Snyder omits them (along with several civilian groups like slave laborers and bombing victims) from consideration. Although roughly half of its soldiers were Russians, the Red Army was the only ethnically integrated force in World War II; every Soviet republic was represented in the 62nd Army that fought at Stalingrad in 1942 and 1943, the war's most pivotal, bloody, and legendary battle. Soviet military training included, as Snyder has acknowledged, prohibitions against racism, anti-Semitism, and nationalism; indeed, the USSR had been virtually the only major power to outlaw eugenics in the 1930s, a movement for selective breeding then very popular in the US as well as Nazi Germany. Patriotism was strongest among the Russian soldiers, but millions of men and women from the national ethnic groups whose civilian victims Snyder spotlights were fighting and dying in the Red Army. Soviet Jews, though they were only the seventh largest ethnic group in the USSR, won one quarter of the Soviet Union's war honors.[13]

Snyder's implicit charge, that Russia's World War II was really a civil war pitting Stalin against his own subject peoples, is as old as the Cold War itself, and as inadequate now as it was then. Of course there were intensely anti-Soviet and nationalist parties in the western Soviet territories the Wehrmacht occupied, groups Hitler unwisely never tried to enlist on Germany's side. Snyder is nonetheless reading present-day Eastern Europeans' sometimes strident self-identifications back into a moment and a war where such markers were less clear. To the end of his life, the great Russian novelist Vasily Grossman, a Ukrainian Jew who lost most of his family in the Holocaust, always stood when he proudly led his children in singing the Red Army songs he had learnt in covering the Eastern front. "Arise, the huge country!" he sang, his daughter remembered, his face "solemn and stern." Despite his bitter disillusion with the postwar Soviet regime, Grossman never ceased to believe that the Soviet soldiers had sacrificed themselves to save the world from fascism. "In this war," Grossman wrote, no matter how sinful his life, the "Russian soldier puts on a white shirt . . . [and] dies a saint."[14]

To downsize the Russian republic's military contribution and its suffering, Snyder is forced to bend geography as well as cherry-pick the data. His assertion that "the war on Soviet territory was fought and won chiefly in Soviet Belarus and Soviet Ukraine rather than in Soviet Russia" is belied by his own admission that there were "important exceptions": not only Stalingrad, but the battle of Moscow in December 1941, a surprise Soviet victory increasingly viewed today as the war's real turning point, and the siege of Leningrad between September 1941 and January 1943; the Germans starved one third of the city's population to death yet could not extract a surrender. But, one might ask, what of Smolensk in July 1941, a Soviet defeat but the first unmistakable sign that the Russians would fight to the end and beyond? And Kursk two years later, the largest tank battle in history and a costly triumph that ushered in the war's final phase? Snyder's maps situate both locales, plus Leningrad for good measure, within the Bloodlands, though all three were (and remain) Russian and outside the Pact's purview.[15]

As for "martyrological imperialism," it has never been a winning strategy for Russia, particularly not among the US media and political elite, not even during World War II. In a February 5, 1945, cover story on Stalin, *Time* magazine, after remarking the "surge of Allied gratitude and respect" for the USSR's wartime performance, took up the question of the USSR's recent request for a $6 billion loan from the United States. In exchange for what? asks *Time*. "The graves of her heroic dead? If so, . . . no deal, since bargains are made for the future not for the past." Snyder has a weakness for straw men. "Why," he asks the European scholar Dovid Katz, who has faulted what he sees as Snyder's pandering to Eastern European "anti-Russianism," "should Stalin's strategic actions be exempt from moral interrogation?"[16] Who, precisely, anywhere, has given Stalin such a pass? Debunking Soviet Russia's wartime achievement is strictly a coals-to-Newcastle operation on this side of the Atlantic. An "imperialism of . . . victims" does, however, nicely describe *Bloodlands* itself and the wider Eastern-European-First school to which Snyder belongs, a school given its start in part by the US's Cold

War prayers (and cash) for the "captive nations" and its equation of human rights with anti-Communism, now the cornerstone of Eastern Europe's mythology of its self-liberation in 1989. Although he seldom uses the word "totalitarianism," Snyder's stress on Hitler and Stalin as collaborators, wittingly or otherwise, his substitution of two genocidal mass murders for one, only underscores the American Cold War's most basic contention: that German fascism and Soviet communism were, in ideology and practice, if not one and the same, inseparable.

Even as he subtly undercuts it, Snyder repeatedly acknowledges the unique status of the Holocaust. He extenuates and minimizes, but never denies, gentile Eastern Europeans' complicity in it. Snyder is looking for admission, if only as a guest member, to the club; he never doubts its legitimacy or prestige. If he had, the response to *Bloodlands* in the United States would probably not have been, unlike its European reception, almost uniformly laudatory, even rhapsodic.[17] Let me be clear. There are no conceivable circumstances under which the study of the Final Solution could or should not have emerged as a primary task for historians of World War II. Indeed, I object to Snyder's expanded victimology because, despite his protestations, I believe it to be detrimental to our understanding of the Holocaust—indisputably the Reich's greatest crime—as well as Russophobic. It is too soon to know whether Snyder's paradigm will become a template for historians outside his own school, but whether the focus is on two crimes against humanity or one, neither can substitute for, neither can be fully explained apart from, the actual military war in which Russia, not the United States or the UK, beat Germany, saving the world from a fate far worse than Soviet communism. Therein lies the story to which the American Cold War was in part the sequel.

American Gender Anxieties and Political Strategies

Whatever postwar recalibrations in storyline they made in the interests of German denial and the need to pander to their new American sponsors, as the war was actually being fought, German commanders and soldiers were again and again shocked and impressed by the tenacity and courage, the "unbelievable toughness," of their Red Army foes. The Russians might be subhuman animals, one German soldier wrote home, but "these dogs fight like lions." A baffled General Günther Blumentritt reported from outside Moscow in 1941 that the Russians "seemed quite unaware that as a fighting force they had almost ceased to exist," a response for which nothing in the Wehrmacht's recent romp through Central and Western Europe, with its "poor fighting material," in Hitler's scornful words, had prepared them. The Germans would dismiss the American soldier too, despite his lavish materiel, as "nothing like the Russian." Denouncing the cowardice of Field Marshall Friedrich Paulus, who had surrendered, against Hitler's orders, to the Russians at Stalingrad on January 31, 1943, Hitler bitterly compared him with the scores of Soviet commanders and commissars trapped in similarly dire circumstances who "closed ranks, formed a hedgehog, and shot themselves with their last bullet." "Whine[rs]," in the German ranks, Hitler snapped on another occasion, should consider "the Russian . . . at Leningrad."[18]

To the end, Hitler derided Roosevelt and Churchill as the weak-minded if dangerously dishonorable agents of world Jewry. Who would have remembered Churchill, he once inquired, were it not for him? Though he badly underestimated the USSR's military and industrial strength at the start, Hitler respected the "tremendous" Stalin, that "incomparable and imperturbable blackmailer," from first to last, and not only because Stalin too was willing to shed blood on a genocidal scale. A good part of what made them simpatico was their shared fondness for citing Western imperial and industrial precedent for their blackest crimes, painting the West's proclaimed ideals as mere decoy operations no shrewd and ambitious rival could afford to credit. Hitler, himself a gate-crashing parvenu in the Aryan establishment, understood, as the rest of the West did not, that Stalin was the West's pupil as well as its nemesis. Even remarking that Stalin, "a clerk" who had chosen to remain a clerk, "owes nothing to rhetoric," Hitler's tone was more admiring than derisory. Hitler always seized the oratorical spotlight; Stalin waited in the dark for the right cue.[19]

In World War I, the only member of the Entente the Germans were able conclusively to beat was Russia. In World War II, the USSR became the sole European power the Wehrmacht was *not* able to conquer or hold at bay. Russia's allies rode to victory on its shoulders, an achievement for which Stalin and the tight patterns of party organization and administration he had forced on his vast country deserve some of the credit. Western historians, following Churchill's duplicitous lead, still gloat over Stalin's folly in trusting Hitler's word, a mistake that left his country defenseless before the attack of June 22, 1941, but Hitler himself only briefly, if ever, shared this view. "Stalin has without doubt," he told Joseph Goebbels in August 1942, "reorganized a state of 170 million people and prepared it for a massive armed conflict."[20] If he was hideously unready for the blitzkrieg Hitler unleashed, Stalin, and Stalin alone among Allied leaders, had been girding his nation for a decade and more for precisely the kind of protracted war that Germany could not win. Although his mistakes did not end on June 22, Stalin might have won Hitler's war; Hitler could only have lost Stalin's. Reckless, ideologically propelled foreign ventures were anathema to Stalin. There would have been no equivalent to Barbarossa had he headed the Reich. Zhukov, as outspoken and stubborn as he was talented, wouldn't have lasted a year in Hitler's high command; Stalin had learned to listen and on occasion defer to his generals. It is possible to evaluate Stalin's wartime role as commander and statesman without taking into account his undeniable psychopathology; with Hitler, the reverse is true. While we focus on Stalin as "the murderer . . . he was," Lucius Clay observed in his last TV interview in May 1976, we forget that "he saved his country," a remark no one has ever made of Hitler.[21]

After the war, US military and intelligence experts often blamed the Soviet army's staggering casualties not on the Wehrmacht or the delay of the Western Front, but on Stalin, and even the Red Army soldiers themselves. The average Soviet soldier, they concluded, derived his stoicism from his "Mongol blood" and "Asiatic" indifference to the value of individual life. Impervious to season, terrain, or hunger, according to an Army manual of 1950, "primitive and unassuming . . . [if] innately brave," the Russian cannot think or act outside "the herd." Don't worry about *them*, such reports seemed to say; unlike our soldiers, they don't feel a thing!—a dismissal that smacked unpleasantly of the imperial West's habit of valuing some lives and not others, many others, conveniently transferring its own lack of concern for native life to the natives themselves. As the war was actually being fought, however, as US movie screens filled with unwonted images of Soviet peasants and burning Ukrainian villages, Americans believed what their war correspondents told them. "These men were not fighting animals," Walter Kerr wrote in *The Russian Army* (1944). "They wanted to live. They wanted to go home to their families. But they were not afraid to die." In wartime polls, Americans consistently gave sky-high ratings to the Red Army and the Russian people themselves.[22] The American feat of amnesia in which the USSR and US wartime roles were in part exchanged has never been complete. A rewriting of history, all of it recent and much of it in the public domain, of this magnitude inevitably left traces behind, hints of the gender as well as geopolitical anxieties the actual military record aroused, a fear, as Eisenhower described it in 1952, that the Russians were "fourteen feet high," the toughest of the tough guys on the international block. The grotesquely overblown estimates of Soviet military strength characteristic of the US Cold War were, among other things, backhanded homages to the wartime history the United States was suppressing.[23]

Every US World War II strategist and commander knew that more Soviet deaths meant fewer American lives lost. Between 1941 and 1943, as the tide of war turned in the USSR's favor, military officials cut their estimates of how many divisions would be required to defeat Germany from 215 to 90. American casualties, approximately 300,000 in battle (including the Pacific theater) and another 100,000 from war-related causes, were the smallest of any combatant's. Soviet deaths at Stalingrad alone, in contrast, significantly exceeded the number of Americans who died in the entire war. "Stalingrad," Eleanor Roosevelt said simply, "makes me ashamed." Overall, roughly one American died to every 172 Soviets, a troubling as well as an enviable outcome. Weren't real men supposed to protect others and die if necessary to do so, not be protected themselves as women and children, or at least the more fortunate among them, were? "Why are [the Americans] sitting at home? Must we all die?" an anguished Russian peasant woman with a baby in her arms asked a visiting American journalist in the summer of 1942. When a US representative at the Paris Peace Conference in October 1946, arguing against German reparations for Russia, remarked that the United States could claim $20 billion for its own war costs if it chose, the mercilessly incisive Vyacheslav Molotov, Stalin's foreign commissar, responded by reading aloud from the *World Almanac*. By its own account, the income the United States gained during the war was equal to its total income in 1938; its population had shot up too, reversing the trend everywhere else.[24] Regardless of whoever actually won the war, the United States had already won the peace, but this story, one less about "The Greatest Generation," as Tom Brokaw has christened the United States' World War II soldiers, than about the Richest Generation, was not quite the story Americans wanted to tell.

The US's central and highly successful strategy in the Cold War was to force the Soviets to spend disproportionately on defense, ensuring that Stalin and his successors would renege on their repeated promises to expand the production of consumer goods, all the "small things," in Stalin's words back in 1935, "that make life pleasant." The Americans were replacing a war they had not won with one they could not lose. The Cold War was to be waged not by arms but by an arms race, conducted, as Ilya Ehrenburg, perhaps Russia's most influential wartime reporter, concluded on a 1946 visit to Washington, not against "Soviet tanks" but against "Soviet saucepans."[25] Yet here too there was a disturbing subtext, a Catch-22 that bedeviled American presidents from Truman to Nixon and beyond. The greater the US's abundance, the higher its standard of living compared to the USSR's, the more "replete" it was with "goods and services," as John F. Kennedy put the problem in a 1960 campaign speech, the easier it might be for the country to forget the "tough" virtues it needed to win the Cold War. At one moment during Richard Nixon's visit to Moscow in August 1959 for the famous Kitchen Debate, Khrushchev, a former miner from a dirt-poor family of Ukrainian miners, contemptuously asked the vice president, "What do you know of work? You never worked." The question troubled Eisenhower when he heard of it; he made plans to show Khrushchev the hardscrabble, rough Kansas milieu from which he himself sprang on the Russian premier's upcoming trip to the United States.[26]

Claiming that America, not the Soviet Union, defeated Hitler also addressed concerns more concrete, and political, than the US's anxieties about its masculine image. Only if America had been, in the words of policy planner George Kennan, "chosen by the Almighty to be the agent" of Hitler's destruction, only if US aid alone had "saved Russia from ignominious defeat," as David Lawrence flatly asserted in *United States News* on February 8, 1946, could Franklin Roosevelt be cast as a naïve and self-infatuated appeaser hoodwinked by Stalin and unwilling to wield his actual bargaining power, a misrepresentation that gave legitimacy and momentum to the longstanding right-wing effort to discredit and dismantle FDR's policies at home and abroad. The vain, irascible, and talented William Bullitt, FDR's first and soon bitterly disillusioned ambassador to Russia, lamented in "How We Won the War and Lost the Peace," a two-part article published in *Life* in the summer of 1948, that had FDR only exacted pledges from Stalin to "respect the eastern boundaries of Europe" and keep his hands off China in exchange for US aid, Stalin "*would have been obliged to accept our terms*"—a falsification of history on several levels. Blackmailing Stalin into submission was not an option. As Molotov later bluntly summarized the Allied ledger, "We did more for them."[27]

Although few Americans realized it at the time, a misapprehension FDR, on most counts the USSR's best wartime booster, did little to correct, Russia made at least 90 percent of its own war materiel. Lend-Lease, while absolutely vital to Russia's great counteroffensive in the last two years of the war, including Kursk and Bagration, came too late for Smolensk, too late even for the battle of Moscow; up to 85 percent of Lend-Lease arrived after the German surrender at Stalingrad in early 1943.[28] Little wonder that Henry Stimson, FDR's secretary of war, backed by George Marshall and Eisenhower, pushed FDR to reject Churchill's "pinprick" operations in the Mediterranean and open the Second Front in Western Europe instead. Stalin would not be "fooled," Stimson said, nor would he be likely to let a people who had consigned the "heavy fighting" to Russia "share much of the postwar world with him."[29] The joint chiefs of staff, assessing in the summer of 1944 the consequences of what they considered the most "epochal" shift in global power since the fall of Rome, predicted that, with the British empire's decline now irrevocable, the Soviets' postwar dominance in Europe would be unchallengeable "east . . . of the Rhine and the Adriatic," putting not just Eastern Europe but possibly Turkey, Greece, and the Straits of Dardanelles, precisely the prizes formally recaptured by the Truman Doctrine in 1947, into the Soviet sphere. The JCS also advised American caution in handling Russia at Yalta and Potsdam; even the US and UK's forces combined were, in their estimate, no match for the Red Army.[30] By the time of the February 1945 Yalta Conference and what Bullitt saw as FDR's capitulation to Stalin, the Red Army was well on its way to occupying most of Eastern Europe. It would not serve American interests, FDR believed, to make demands the US had no means of enforcing. The atom bomb, which joined the US arsenal only in July 1945, decided Japan's postwar fate, but it could not change Eastern Europe's. That FDR understood the concept of the fruits of war and Soviet Russia's title to them does not mean, however, that he included Russian hegemony outside its traditional sphere of influence or if unmodified, within it, among the Soviets' legitimate spoils, or that he put no price on US postwar support.

The masculine sport of over-assertive insecurity that disfigured much World War II and Cold War discourse was alien to Roosevelt. It is difficult to imagine FDR boasting, as a member of Arthur "Bomber" Harris's staff did in November 1943, barely three months after the Soviet victory at Kursk, that British bombing was "doing more toward shortening the war than any other offensive, including the Russians." It is downright impossible to imagine FDR asserting again and again that he wasn't "afraid of the Russians," or vowing to speak "in words of one syllable" to Molotov, as Truman did in his first weeks in office. Roosevelt relied on his gift for improvisation and his uncanny geographically grounded geopolitical instincts; his Soviet policy was based not on mano-a-mano ego combat but on an organic grasp of the complex interplay between Russia's strengths and weaknesses. If he was mistaken about some of the players, and he was, starting with Stalin (no hope of a "Christian gentleman" there) and including himself (no paragon of anti-imperialism, he), he had the knack of getting the mix, the balance right. The U.S.S.R.'s new power was real, and Roosevelt was prepared to work with it. He was not prepared to exaggerate it.[31]

FDR understood, as Hitler had, that Stalin, despite his crimes, was a cautious and shrewd international player; it wasn't folly to think the USSR might respond to something approaching fair treatment from the West. But he also remembered the utter wreckage left by Russia's invaders, which he had seen for himself in the Crimea, the backward state of its potent but painfully undiversified economy, and most of all the inhuman rigidities inherent in a dictatorship like Stalin's. Roosevelt's belief that, when it came to the big questions, the postwar world order would be, and for the benefit of all, should be, at bottom unipolar was as sturdy as his faith in his own personal superiority. But to treat those who, however great their achievements, could not be in the foreseeable future fully accredited rivals as if they were equals, wasn't to his mind appeasement but Christian ethics, good manners, and very smart geopolitics—an insight integral to what Henry Stimson described in 1946 as Roosevelt's "vision over the broader vista of events."[32] Distrustful of all absolutes, FDR knew that some devils are preferable to others; he never doubted which dictator was the supreme threat to everything the United States stood for.[33] By temperament and principle, Roosevelt was immune to the US's addiction to threat inflation, its strategic and psychological need to be endangered, a legacy neither his opponents or his titular heirs found compatible with the Cold War they were now waging or the World War II narrative in which they wished to frame it.

Nothing in FDR's example was more enraging to his critics or more inconvenient to those putatively committed to carrying on his policies than the shockingly self-confident nonchalance with which he had dismissed the threat of communism, an ideology whose credentials had now been burnished by the Soviets' wartime performance. Communism and socialism's American opponents have seldom been content simply to prefer and support democratic capitalism. They are happy only when they have proved, to their own satisfaction at least, that seventy years of "real existing Socialism," in Tony Judt's excited summation, "contributed nothing to the sum of human welfare. Nothing." The Soviet Union would do, and by World War II had already done, a great deal to justify such condemnations, but the "Nothing" is still important. By this absolutist logic, there can be no exceptions whatever—nothing to complicate the picture of what *The New York Times* calls "the unique evil of Communism." Communism doesn't *go* wrong in this view; it essentially, biologically, *is* wrong, and so, therefore, must be all its works. Soviet Russia's war at the very least threatened to claim exception-status. Denouncing American communists before Congress on October 28, 1945, FBI Director J. Edgar Hoover, the vicar of red scares, felt obliged to explain that he was in no way "detract[ing] from the heroic fight Russia waged against the invading Nazi hordes to emerge as one of the great powers of the world." CPUSA's "antics" should not blind Americans to Russia's "right to any form of government she desires."[34] Could communism be vilified as it deserved if the USSR's war record was allowed to stand?

"[I am] a revolutionary against the revolution," Hitler proclaimed in the 1924 speech that made his national reputation. For him, the communist and Jewish threats were intertwined as "Judeo-Bolshevism"; he was nonetheless well aware that in his anticommunism, not his anti-Semitism, lay his most potent recruitment strategy at home and abroad.[35] This was the part of Hitler's mission, suitably repackaged and stripped of its genocidal language, though not of its murderous consequences, the US proved ready, just as Hitler had predicted, to forward. Several influential Americans actually anticipated the German military command's postwar claims that there had been no Russian victories, just "Lost [German] Victories," in the title of Erich von Manstein's popular 1955 memoir. Hitler, and Hitler alone, had lost the war against the Bolshevik menace his generals could and should have won. The liberal economist John Kenneth Galbraith explained in a *Fortune* December 1945 article that the Germans, like the Americans at Pearl Harbor, had been "caught napping" at Stalingrad, a startling statement given that Germany, unlike the US, the attacker not the attacked, had spent almost half a year on a single battle, suffering the greatest defeat in its history and sacrificing the bulk of its Sixth Army while it slumbered. Galbraith's primary source seems to have been the man he calls "the now famous Albert Speer."[36] If a totalitarian state had to be given credit, better, it seemed, Hitler's fascist Germany than Stalin's communist Russia. Americans today, like Europeans, recognize and repudiate the naked pathology of Hitler's anti-Semitism; the irrational and pathological element in his anti-Marxism can escape those who to one degree or another share it.

In addition to the decimation of its population, a loss not made up until 1956, Soviet war damage included the destruction of more than 1,700 towns, 70,000 villages, and one-third of its industrial capital. Far from being good news, however, the weaknesses of its adversary posed as great a difficulty to the US and its post-FDR narrative of World War II as did Soviet valor or the wartime efficacy of its communist state. The USSR's devastation had to be forgotten if the US was to rehabilitate and rearm Germany, deny the USSR the postwar credit and reparations promised by FDR, and, most important, claim that it was now engaged in an all-encompassing struggle against a congenitally aggressive and expansionist totalitarian behemoth. Unless the Cold War represented a symmetrical conflict, a duel, in the fond words of Whittaker Chambers's biographer Sam Tanenhaus, between two "lethally well-matched colossi," the US could not credibly present itself as the mortally endangered champion of the "Free World," selling its own postwar global expansion as the necessary check to the Soviets' global ambitions. The US's insistence on viewing the Korean War as an affair of Soviet puppets, like its failure to foresee Tito's rebellion or the Sino-Soviet split, was built into the logic of the Cold War. To admit that the Communist bloc wasn't a monolith would have been to acknowledge the myriad and multiplying problems limiting Soviet control in its sphere of influence and the radical advantage the almost infinitely wealthier capitalist West, which was bound together by a global system, no matter how fractious and fratricidal, of some five hundred years' duration, held over its upstart communist rival. "One only has to visit Russia to realize how much of its policy is affected by dire need," Lucius Clay, who then favored some reparations for the Soviets, pointed out at the last meeting of the Council of Foreign Ministers held in Moscow in March 1947. By then "visit[ing] Russia" was not an acceptable idea even when one was, in fact, visiting Russia. By mutual agreement with George Marshall, the head of the American delegation, Clay withdrew from the conference.[37]

In Moscow on May 26, 1945, Stalin, conceding the Americans' right to play a role even in Poland, told Harry Hopkins that the United States had "more reason to be a World Power than any other state." Stalin was at all times, in the words of Walter Kravitsky, a defector from the Soviet Military Intelligence (GRU), "guided . . . by the rule that one must come to terms with a superior power." And with Russia, there was always a superior power. As Kennan acknowledged in the "Long Telegram" (1946), the document that inaugurated the US's Cold War, Russia had "never known a friendly neighbor," and the peoples and nations that assaulted it, from the Mongols to the French and the Germans, were usually superior to it in military strength or economic development or both. In the modern era, its army ventured into Western Europe only twice, in the Napoleonic Wars and in World War II, each time pursuing an enemy that had attacked Russia first. In a letter of April 1948 he never sent, Kennan wrote to Walter Lippmann, his best critic, "The Russians do not want to invade anyone. It is not in their tradition."[38] The contents of the Russian and American archives opened after the end of the Cold War have forced historians of the domestic Cold War to recalibrate their arguments, if not their conclusions, but to date there is no foreign policy equivalent to Venona's long list of Soviet spies and agents, no document suggesting Stalin had plans to take over Western Europe or directly challenge the United States in its sphere.

Policymakers and the Problematics of Cold War Logic: Noir Nations

Several peculiar paradoxes about the USSR were tacitly established by the United States' Cold War narrative: that Russia had been too weak to beat Hitler by itself yet was now, a few years later, capable of overrunning Western Europe and attacking North America, and eager to do so; that the USSR, though denied German reparations and American credit or loans, could nonetheless mushroom into a superpower on its own steam, while Western Europe, all of it far wealthier and, save Germany, far less damaged by the war than the Soviet Union, needed a five-year Marshall Plan to recover; that Soviet communism was a kind of viral infection set loose in the global body, able to jump hosts regardless of local circumstances, traditions, or national ambitions, a notion closer to the popular new sci-fi movies of the day than to history. These, like other contradictions inherent in Cold War logic, had to be accepted and promulgated more or less on faith by presidents, policymakers, and politicians all the while convinced of their own status as objective practitioners of hard-headed if lofty-minded realism.

The geopolitical and political issues of US national security that American Cold War leaders and policymakers addressed were real and weighty in themselves as well as better suited to the light of day than the work of building, in James Carroll's phrase, a "fantasy Kremlin," but the first activity can't be separated from the second.[39] No one should underestimate the lengths to which a power elite with few challengers save fact will go to give the world, and themselves, reason to believe their own pronouncements, half-truths, and outright lies. It is a dereliction of duty for historians to leave unexplored, as Odd Arne Westad does, the proposition that Cold War leaders pretty much meant what they said; although it is legitimate to "question whether they were honest to themselves," in Westad's words, "that line of argument does not take us very far."

Nor is it intellectually respectable for historians to plea-bargain for American administrations they themselves acknowledge to be operating irrationally on the grounds that, as Thomas Maddux puts it, they "believed [their own statements] however incorrectly." This is simply a variant of the well-worn "intent" ploy, the alibi under whose various formulations the West has exercised its fiat of definition to justify its crimes as "collateral damage" since Spain and Portugal began to plunder the Americas in the fifteenth century. When the consequences are predictable, and even predicted, yet the action is taken, and repeated, and repeated yet again, the results *are* the intentions. As D. H. Lawrence, speaking of both the American literary tradition and the American psyche in 1923, advised, "trust the tale," not the teller.[40]

No one could claim that Russia, Churchill's famous riddle wrapped in a mystery inside an enigma, was easy for outsiders to read or that Stalin did not make his own sizable contribution to the Cold War. As his behavior with Lenin and Hitler attests, he had a proven, even fatal penchant for testing and undermining the alliances he needed and valued most. Truman invited him to visit the US; Stalin, whose relationship to Soviet soil was much like Dracula's to the Transylvanian earth in his coffin, refused. What Soviet leaders took to be Western intimidation worked no better. The arms race that followed the United States' development of nuclear weapons, though it helped bankrupt the Soviet Union, also provided an arena in which Russia, in all other areas not a competitor, could inflate its credentials far past their merits or due date. But the stubborn imperviousness and cultivated opacity of the Stalinist regime did not mean that Stalin sought or welcomed a USSR-US confrontation; and it certainly did not mean that no accurate information about the Soviet Union was available. If the US never had the kind of veto power over Soviet behavior that Bullitt took as the premise of his critique of FDR, it still had several possible sources of leverage, provided the right hand was on the lever.

At war's end, unlike the US, now by any reasonable standard the world's only superpower, outside its own hemisphere at least, a global object of gratitude and admiration, and fully equipped and programmed for further expansion, the USSR faced the daunting challenge of maintaining its wartime gains; its new territorial acquisitions taxed both its relatively slim economic resources and its limited powers of attraction. Suspicious of outsiders, autocratic, a laggard in the ranks of material progress, under Tsar and Bolshevik (and post-Soviet) alike, Russia's soft power has never been commensurate with its geopolitical standing or its cultural achievement. If it was to manage its newly inflated sphere of influence by methods more effective in the long run than unadorned force, what the USSR needed at war's end, along with US loans and German reparations, was some facsimile of outside approval, an extension of the credit it had earned as the liberator of Europe, a legitimation only its allies, and the US above all, could bestow. There is evidence that Stalin was willing to make concessions to obtain it, that he initially understood what was at stake, though eventually he stepped full-square into the trap anyway.

In the speech he gave on May 5, 1941, six-and-a-half weeks before Hitler launched Barbarossa, Stalin reminded his audience that Hitler's initial strength in the war in Europe lay in his "progressive" role as the declared liberator of the countries chafing under "the yoke of Versailles." Now, however, Stalin continued, Germany was fighting "under the flag of subjugation, the subordination of other peoples"; as a conqueror, Germany was leaving in its rear "hostile territory and masses."[41] Stalin was warning Hitler that if Hitler broke the Nazi-Soviet Pact and attacked the USSR, he, not Hitler, would have the "progressive" role, and the PR advantage. "Be worthy of this great mission!" Stalin told the Soviet people on November 7, 1941, in his most memorable wartime speech, nerving them for the struggle to free themselves, Europe, and the world from the Fascist menace.[42] Some degree of legitimation was precisely the bait FDR was determined to use to bring Soviet behavior closer to what he saw as the workable if imperfect norms of international practice. As his interviews with Forrest Davis in 1943 and 1944 reveal, Roosevelt always kept in mind a fall-back position, a hard-line plan B based on his knowledge of the US's economic, political, and overall military superiority, but he proposed to implement it only if Soviet recalcitrance left him no other option.[43] The Red Army's war crimes in postwar Germany, particularly its notorious mass rapes, sullied the Soviet record; it still mattered that FDR's plan B became the Truman administration's plan A.

The striking decline in top-level Soviet-US diplomatic engagement under Truman, running athwart FDR precedent and popular opinion, which favored diplomacy even with the USSR, criticized at the time publicly by Walter Lippmann and privately by Henry Stimson, served as a space-clearing gesture, a willful refusal of knowledge permitting the exchange of one image of Russia for another. Such a transubstantiation of conjecture into fact sometimes necessitated skating on thin ice far beyond evidence's reach. Truman liked to cite the so-called "Testament of Peter the Great" as authority for his assertion that the Russians were guided first to last by "fixed ideas" about world conquest. Although he was told in 1948 that the document was a notorious eighteenth-century Franco-Polish forgery, he continued to invoke it in private.[44] The authors of the alarmist but vague Clifford-Elsey report, presented to the president on September 24, 1946, found it, in their words, "difficult to adduce direct evidence" of Russian transgressions. The Truman Doctrine speech of March 5, 1947, never named the Soviet Union at all, an omission to which Lippmann, who understood the license it conferred, strenuously objected; as one of its authors confessed, they had found no "overt action in the immediate past by the U.S.S.R." to explain the speech's "All-out" tone.[45]

In a telling round of insiders' commentary during the summer of 1951 on NSC-68, the classified paper that militarized US Cold War policy, Charles Bohlen, dissenting from its overblown estimates of the USSR's aggressive motivation and capacity, pointed out that those who had written it, unlike Bohlen himself, had "no actual experience of the Soviet problem." NSC-68 was "speculation," not fact. Even NSC-68's authors, after all, had conceded that the Soviets had committed no "technical breach of the peace" despite their patently "aggressive foreign policy." Bohlen, FDR's translator at Tehran and Yalta and Truman's at Potsdam, was with Kennan the State Department's leading Russian expert, with years of service in Moscow under his belt—which was presumably why his advice had been solicited in the first place. But Paul Nitze, Secretary of State Dean Acheson's right-hand man and the mastermind of NSC-68, whose knowledge of Russia came largely from anti-Bolshevik White Russian sources, dismissed Bohlen's comments on the grounds that they were "not supported by any information I have." For Nitze, information was what he already knew, and preferred, not something he needed to acquire more of to reckon with the world as it actually is. Yet, though Bohlen had objected to the mismatch between NSC-68's "argumentation" and its "conclusions," he was guilty of the same thing himself, prefacing his sometimes stinging critique with an abject acceptance of the document's basic contention: the USSR, in Bohlen's words, represented "an international conspiracy . . . relentlessly and unappeasably hostile to the United States." Lippmann had already diagnosed a "real case of schizophrenia" in the State Department. "When they state the realities," he wrote, "they come to one set of conclusions; when they consult their political ideas, they come to an opposite set."[46]

The top echelon of the Truman administration was now operating on the assumption, one anathema to FDR on any front, that they already knew how the Soviet Union would behave, no consultation or corroboration needed. Once the terms of future interpretation were established, usually by hints, dark insinuations, occasional accusations whose sources were difficult if not impossible to verify, and ringing declarations about "freedom-loving peoples" threatened by "totalitarian regimes"; once policymakers could be sure that the public was trained to read Soviet Russia in the correct way, automatically disposing of any countervailing information as subversive, deceptive, or irrelevant; once the actual Soviet Union, the principal national victor and victim in the war against Hitler, had been distanced by time and displaced, consigned to oblivion in the US and to the province of more or less known but unmentionable fact as far as US influence extended abroad; once, in short, the historical "Russia," the term FDR preferred for the USSR whenever sense permitted it, had ceded to the forbidding "Kremlin," NSC-68's title of choice, the curtain could go up again on a totalitarian Soviet state solely preoccupied, according to NSC-68, with "impos[ing] its authority over the rest of the world."[47]

The Cold War American refusal of information about Soviet Russia stands as a classic example of Hannah Arendt's definition of ideology: an explanation in which an assumption masquerades as a conclusion. This is not a conspiracy theory. Policymakers were not engaged in a "naked grasp for power," as James Peck would have it, nor did they plot to precipitate and maintain a Cold War. No one needs to be a conspirator to lie to himself and others when the established order of rewards and verities favors the falsehood. In the "X-Article" (1947), Kennan quoted a passage from Gibbon: "a wise man may deceive himself. . . . a good man may deceive others, . . . the conscience may slumber in a mixed and middle state between self-illusion and voluntary fraud."[48] Kennan purported to be discussing the Soviets' self-interested exploitation of Marxist doctrine but, as Kennan himself later recognized, American Cold War portraits of Russia were sometimes self-portraits in disguise. Although lies can demand serious upkeep, deception is often an improvisational not a premeditated act. Ideology is by definition a work still in progress. Systems of thought have their own impetus—they don't necessarily require their agents' conscious cooperation or their consent to every article of the creed in question. That reluctance to recognize or admit any save noble purposes often held good for policymakers in private as well as public is not surprising; belief is the mark of an ideology's efficacy, not its truth.

But the possibility that sometimes, somewhere, some of the Cold War's American players knew the potentially disastrous consequences of actions they would never in good faith cease to justify, can't be ruled out either. Kennan, who articulated and promoted the Truman administration's hard-line policy with Russia, changed his mind, though he was never quite willing to say so. The chilling implications of his 1946 injunction, "*Do not be afraid to use heavy weapons for what seem . . . to be minor matters*" were precisely the ones he spent the second half of his career contesting. On a darker note, Frank Wisner, the head of the CIA's Office of Policy Coordination, itself a Kennan brainchild, spent the last decade of his life in the throes of what can only be called Cold War paranoid dementia, complete with specters of the "black op" Nazi agents hired by the CIA on his watch. He shot himself in 1965.[49] The seldom mentioned Cold War casualty count of up to 25 million, with most of the deaths occurring in the Third World and more of them lost in US-instigated wars or under US-backed regimes than Soviet ones, suggests that there is a Black Book of Capitalism—Marx wrote the first chapter in *Das Kapital*—as surely as there is a "Black Book of Communism."[50] Of course, protecting and expanding capitalism's domain was not the only or perhaps the primary purpose of the US Cold War. But neither can fidelity to Marxist-Leninist doctrine adequately explain all the USSR's brutal policies, though its misdeeds are routinely laid at communism's door.

The denial of Russia's role in World War II was the foundational fiction, the place where the dishonesty that characterized the US's Cold War top to bottom found part of its origins and raison d'être, the moment when America's own "black legend," to appropriate Martin Malia's term for Russia's long-standing noir image in the world's eyes, took off.[51] Noir cinema and pulp thrillers, genres associated with the United States ever since, became the rage in the same years the National Security State was officially assembled, and a taste for detective stories and chiaroscuro effects characterized a number of Cold War figures from Dean Acheson and John Foster Dulles to JFK and Nixon. But no one employed noir metaphors as extensively and skillfully as Kennan, the only genuinely gifted writer in the group. Kennan's views of Russia cannot be disentangled from the portentous and sinister language in which he clothed them. Even in his early, most inflammatory papers and articles, Kennan voiced reservations and qualifications, hints of his later more tempered stance; his style always trumped them. Shadows were among Kennan's great subjects, the "long shadows" cast by the Kremlin in particular, and he gives us a clue why in a passage from Thoreau he quoted in the April 1951 issue of *Foreign Affairs*: "There is no ill which may not be dissipated, like the dark, if you let in a strong light upon it . . . [But] if the light we use is but a paltry and narrow taper, *most objects will cast a shadow wider than themselves*." The effect to which Kennan is alluding here, the creation of deep, high-contrast shadows by the use of sharply restricted and angled lighting, obscuring the wider scene or set in order to over-enunciate a few charged details within it, is noir cinema's version of threat inflation and information deprivation. John Alton, perhaps noir's finest cinematographer, called it "criminal lighting."[52]

Stalin, to whom Kennan devoted several of his most brilliantly etched portraits, might awaken the noir imagination latent in the most staid observer. Next to him, Kennan remarked, the "wildest murder mystery seems banal." But Stalin himself, whose nocturnal habits, armored limos, bodyguards, and "tough guy" (a bit of American slang Stalin knew) persona were regularly chronicled by a far from disapproving American wartime press, understood exactly, as his Western peers did not, the role he was playing. During an August 1942 meeting with Churchill, after dazzling the prime minister with his mastery of military strategy, Stalin remarked that Molotov had taken a detour on his recent trip to Washington to go to Chicago, to see "where the other gangsters live."[53] Molotov had done no such thing, but Stalin had made his point. Weren't they all, behind the smoked glass, partners in crime?

Notes

1. Jean Edward Smith, *Lucius D. Clay: An American Life* (New York, 1990), p. 262; Stephen Ambrose, *Eisenhower, 1890–1952* (New York, 1983), pp. 429, 448.
2. Otto Preston Chaney, *Zhukov*, rev. ed. (Norman, 1996), pp. 334–337; Zhukov, *The Memoirs of Marshal Zhukov* (New York, 1971), pp. 682–684. The same objection can be raised against Steven Spielberg's *Saving Private Ryan* (1998).
3. Benjamin Schwartz, "A Job for Rewrite," *The New York Times* (February 21, 2004), B7, B9.
4. Stephanson, "The United States' Cold War" in Silvio Pons and Federico Romero (eds.), *Reinterpreting the End of the Cold War: Issues, Interpretations, Periodizations* (London, 2004).
5. I. C. Jarvie, "Fanning the Flames: Anti-American Reaction to 'Operation Burma,'" *Historical Journal of Film, Radio, and Television*, 1/2 (1981), p. 121.
6. Murray and Millett, *A War To Be Won: Fighting the Second World War, 1937–45* (Cambridge, MA, 2000), p. 555. But see Evan Mawdsley, *Thunder in the East: The Nazi-Soviet War 1941–1945* (London, 2005), p. 405; Richard Overy, *Russia's War: A History of the Soviet War Effort* (New York, 1997), p. 89.
7. Maier, *The Unmasterable Past: History, Holocaust, and German National Identity* (Cambridge, MA, 1988), p. 75. For Nazi claims that the POW camps were as bad as the Jewish ones, see Robert Jay Lifton, *The Nazi Doctors: Medical Killing and the Psychology of Genocide* (New York, 1986), p. 199. On gassings and death rates, see Christian Streit, "Soviet Prisoners of War in the Hands of the Wehrmacht" in Hannes Heer and Klaus Naumann (eds.), *War of Extermination: The German Military in World War II, 1941–1944* (Oxford, 2000), p. 81; Streit, "Ostkrieg, Antibolschewismus und 'Endlösung'," *Geschichte und Gesellschaft*, 17 (1991), pp. 241–255. For estimates of Soviet casualties, see John Erickson, "Soviet War Losses: Calculations and Controversies" in *Barbarossa: The Axis and the Allies* (Edinburgh, 1994), pp. 255–277; and Boris Sokolov, "How to Calculate Human Losses During the Second World War," *Journal of Slavic Military Studies*, 22:3 (2009): 437–458.
8. Mayer, *Why Did the Heavens Not Darken? The Final Solution in History* (New York, 1988), p. 270; for "Zig Millionen Menschen," see Omer Bartov, *The Eastern Front, 1941–45: German Troops and the Barbarisation of Warfare* (Basingstoke, 1985), p. 188 n.19.
9. Peter Novick, *The Holocaust in American Life* (New York, 1999), pp. 47–54, 293n.19, gives the higher estimate; Howard Sachar, *A History of the Jews in America* (New York, 1992), p. 495, the lower. See Adam Tooze, *The Wages of Destruction: The Making and Breaking of the Nazi Economy* (New York, 2007), p. 486, for the 5 million number.
10. David Gates, "War and Remembrance," *Newsweek* (September 24, 2007), p. 55.
11. See Snyder, *Bloodlands: Europe Between Hitler and Stalin* (New York, 2010) p. x; he concludes with the postwar expulsion of Germans from Eastern Europe and Stalin's aborted campaign against Soviet Jews. See also Snyder, "Nazis, Soviets, Poles, Jews," in *NYRB* (12/3/09), p. 53. Few of the revisionist World War II historians I have cited here are in Snyder's *Bloodlands* bibliography.
12. Snyder, *Bloodlands*, p. 406. See also Snyder, "Holocaust: The Ignored Reality," *NYRB* (7/16/09), p. 16.
13. See Michael K. Jones, *Stalingrad* (Philadelphia, 2007), p. xiv; Amir Weiner, "When Memory Counts: War, Genocide, and Postwar Soviet Jewry," in *Crimes of War: Guilt and Denial in the Twentieth Century*, ed. Omer Bartov, Atina Grossman, Mary Nolan (New York, 2002), p. 311, n.3. For patriotism among Russian and non-Russian Soviet soldiers, see Roger R. Reese, *Why Stalin's Soldiers Fought: The Red Army's Military Effectiveness in World War II* (Lawrence: University of Kansas, 2011), 307, 312.
14. *A Writer At War: Vasily Grossman with the Red Army, 1941–1945*, ed. and trans. Anthony Beevor & Luba Vinogradova (New York, 2005), p. 348. See also Omer Bartov, "Bloody Redemption: The Difficult Memory of Life and Death in the Red Army," *Times Literary Supplement* (January 27 2006), p.3-4. Snyder ignores this aspect of Grossman's legacy to focus on the parallels he drew between the Soviet and Nazi regimes.

15. See *Bloodlands*, pp. 335, 384–385; see also Snyder, "Nazis, Soviets, Poles, Jews," p. 53. Snyder includes the contemporary Russian Federation's "Western rim" in the *Bloodlands*.
16. "Russia: Historic Force," *Time* (February 5, 1945), p. 38. See Snyder, "The Fatal Fact of the Nazi-Soviet Pact" published online at guardian.co.uk on 5 October 2010.
17. For an example of an enthusiastic and intensely Russophobic American review, see Anne Applebaum, "The Worst of the Madness," *NYRB* 11/11/10: 8–12; for a European critic, see Richard J. Evans, "Who Remembers the Poles?" *LRB* 32:21 (11/4/10): 21–22.
18. Richard J. Evans, *The Third Reich at War* (New York, 2008), pp. 198–199; Anthony Beevor, *Stalingrad: The Fateful Siege: 1942–1943* (New York, 1999), pp. 206, 391; Chaney, *Zhukov*, pp. 201–202; Albert Speer, *Inside the Third Reich*, trans. Richard and Clara Winston (New York, 1970), p. 306. Max Hastings, *Armageddon: The Battle for Germany, 1944–1945* (New York, 2004), p. 69. Hastings, pp. 232–233, 341, also records the low opinion several US officers held of their own troops' performance.
19. *The Testament of Adolf Hitler: The Hitler-Bormann Documents*, trans. R. H. Stevens (London, 1961), p. 109; *Hitler's Secret Conversations 1941–1944*, trans. Norman Cameron (New York, 1953), pp. xx, 7.
20. Quoted in Geoffrey Roberts, *Stalin's Wars: From World War to Cold War* (New Haven, 2006), p. 373. Gabriel Gorodetsky, *Grand Delusion: Stalin and the German Invasion of Russia* (New Haven, 1999) has decisively refuted Churchill.
21. Smith, *Lucius D. Clay*, p. 278. Clay's opinion seems to me more intellectually sophisticated as well as more historically accurate than Norman Naimark's insistence in *Stalin's Genocides* (Princeton, 2010), p. 37, that Hitler and Stalin alike "destroyed their countries."
22. See Catherine Merridale, *Ivan's War: Life and Death in the Red Army 1939–1945* (New York, 2006), pp. 12–13; Walter Kerr, *The Russian Army: Its Men, Its Leaders, and Its Battles* (Washington, DC, 1944), p. 3. According to a *Fortune* survey of "U.S. Opinion on Russia," as late as September 1945, only 1.4 percent of Americans had anything unfavorable to say about the Russian people, and two-thirds especially praised Russia's military (pp. 237–238).
23. Ambrose, *Eisenhower*, p. 534. For a top Russian diplomat's later reaction to the US's "deliberately false and risible" estimates, see Georgi M. Kornienko, "Commentary" in Ernest R. May (ed.), *American Cold War Strategy: Interpreting NSC 68* (Boston, 1993), pp. 127–128.
24. David Kennedy, *Freedom from Fear: The American People in Depression and War 1929–1945* (New York, 1999), p. 631. Even in the Asian war, American losses, while heavier than in Europe, were small next to the Japanese totals. At Okinawa, Japan lost 110,000 of 120,000 men, the United States 12,000 of 250,000; see John Keegan, *The Second World War* (New York, 1990), pp. 568–573. See Doris Kearns Goodwin, *No Ordinary Time: Franklin and Eleanor Roosevelt: The Home Front in World War II* (New York, 1994), p. 403. See Ilya Ehrenburg, *The War, 1941–1945*, trans. Tatiana Shebunina (New York, 1964), p. 84, for the Russian peasant woman; Molotov, *Problems of Foreign Policy: Speeches and Statements April 1945–November 1948* (Moscow, 1949), pp. 212–213.
25. Ehrenburg, *Postwar Years: 1945–1956*, trans. Tatiana Shebunina (Cleveland, 1967), p. 81; Stalin, "Address Delivered in the Kremlin Palace" (May 4, 1935) in *Problems of Leninism* (Moscow, 1976), p. 269. For American historians replacing World War II with the Cold War, see Warren Kimball, "The Incredible Shrinking War," *Diplomatic History* 25:3 (Summer 2001), pp.347–365.
26. Kennedy quoted in Stephen Whitfield, *The Culture of the Cold War* (Baltimore, 1991), p. 76; Stephen Ambrose, *Nixon: The Education of a Politician 1913–1962* (New York, 1987), p. 529.
27. Kennan, *Memoirs 1925–1950* (New York, 1967), p. 429; Bullitt in *Life* (August 30, 1948), p. 91 [emphasis mine]; *Molotov Remembers: Inside Kremlin Politics: Conversations with Felix Chuev* (Chicago, 1993), p. 72.
28. Mawdsley, *Thunder in the East*, pp. 191–193, 455–456, n.9, gives a balanced view of Lend-Lease's role and a survey of scholarship.
29. David F. Schmitz, *Henry L. Stimson: The First Wise Man* (Wilmington, DE, 2001), pp. 161–162.

30. Eric Larrabee, *Commander-in-Chief: Franklin Delano Roosevelt, His Lieutenants, and Their War* (New York, 1988), p. 499; Eduard Mark, "Review," in Wilson D. Miscamble Roundtable (September 10, 2007) at http://www.h-net.org/~diplo/roundtables/PDF/FromTrumantoRoosevelt-Roundtable.pdf.
31. Alexandra Richie, *Faust's Metropolis: A History of Berlin* (New York, 1998), p. 536; Harry S. Truman, *Year of Decision* (New York, 1955), pp. 70–72; *Off the Record: The Private Papers of Harry S. Truman*, ed. Robert H. Ferrell (New York, 1980), p. 349; Robert Dallek, *Franklin D. Roosevelt and American Foreign Policy 1932–1945* (New York, 1979), p. 521.
32. Henry L. Stimson and McGeorge Bundy, *On Active Service in Peace and War* (New York, 1948), p. 665.
33. See Warren Kimball, *The Juggler: Franklin Roosevelt as Wartime Statesman* (Princeton, 1991), p.199.
34. See Stefan Collini, "The Reminder-General," *Nation* (June 9, 2008), p. 18 for Judt; "J. Edgar Hoover Alerts the Nation" in Albert Fried (ed.), *McCarthyism: The Great American Red Scare: A Documentary History* (New York, 1997), pp. 17–18.
35. Alan Bullock, *Hitler and Stalin: Parallel Lives* (New York, 1993), p. 134. See Lorna Waddington, *Hitler's Crusade: Bolshevism and the Myth of the International Jewish Conspiracy* (London, 2007).
36. Galbraith, "Germany Was Badly Run," pp. 74–75. For the US's postwar romance with the German military, see Ronald Smelser and Edward J. Davies II, *The Myth of the Eastern Front* (New York, 2008), pp. 90–119.
37. Tanenhaus, "From Whitaker Chambers to George W. Bush," *New Republic* (July 2, 2007), p. 14; for Clay in Moscow, see Daniel Yergin, *Shattered Peace: The Origins of the Cold War* (1977; rpt., New York, 1990), p. 298.
38. Robert E. Sherwood, *Roosevelt and Hopkins: An Intimate History*, rev. ed. (New York, 1950), p. 860; Kravitsky, *In Stalin's Secret Service* (1939; rpt. New York, 2000), p. 3; Kennan, *Memoirs*, p. 550; Walter Isaacson and Evan Thomas, *The Wise Men: Six Friends and the World They Made* (New York, 1986), p. 446.
39. James Carroll, *House of War: The Pentagon and the Disastrous Rise of American Power* (Boston, 2006), p. 135.
40. Westad, "Author's Response," Maddux, "Introduction," and Jerald A. Combs, "Review," in "Global Cold War Roundtable" (October 9, 2007) at http://www.h-net.org/~diplo/roundtables/PDF/GlobalColdWar-Roundtable.pdf; D. H. Lawrence, *Studies in Classic American Literature* (1923; rpt. New York, 1973), p. 2.
41. Stalin's May 5, 1941, speech is reassembled from several contemporary accounts and analyzed in Jürgen Förster and Evan Mawdsley, "Hitler and Stalin in Perspective: Secret Speeches on the Eve of Barbarossa," *War in History*, 11/1 (2004), pp. 61–103.
42. See Alexander Werth, *Russia at War, 1941–1945* (1964, rpt, New York, 1984), p. 249.
43. See Davis, "Roosevelt's World Blueprint," *The Saturday Evening Post* (April 10, 1943), p. 110.
44. For the pro-diplomacy views of the public, see Gabriel A. Almond, *The American People and Foreign Policy* (1950; rpt., New York, 1960), p. 98; Athan G. Theoharis, "The Rhetoric of Politics" in Barton J. Bernstein (ed.), *Politics and Policies of the Truman Administration* (Chicago, 1970), p. 209. See Ronald Steel, *Walter Lippmann and the American Century* (Boston, 1980), p. 439; Stimson and Bundy, *On Active Service*, p. 648; and J. Garry Clifford, "President Truman and Peter the Great's Will," *Diplomatic History*, 4 (1980), p. 379.
45. See Melvyn Leffler, *A Preponderance of Power: National Security, the Truman Administration, and the Cold War* (Stanford, 1992), p. 133, for the Clifford-Elsey report; Lynn Boyd Hinds and Theodore Otto Windt, Jr., *The Cold War as Rhetoric* (New York, 1991), 143, for the Truman Doctrine.
46. For the NSC-68 memos see *Foreign Relations of the United States* 1951, vol. 1 (Washington D.C., 1951), pp. 163–175; see also Steel, *Walter Lippmann*, pp. 447–448.; May (ed.), *American Cold War Strategy: Interpreting NSC 68*, p. 31.

47. May (ed.), *American Cold War Strategy: Interpreting NSC 68*, p. 25.
48. Peck, *Washington's China: The National Security World, the Cold War, and the Origins of Globalism* (Boston, 2006), p. 23; Kennan, *American Diplomacy* (Chicago, 1985), p. 109.
49. Kennan, *Memoirs*, p. 563; for Wisner's suicide, see Evan Thomas, *The Very Best Men: Four Who Dared: The Early Years of the CIA* (New York, 1995), pp. 318–321.
50. Odd Arne Westad's monumental *The Global Cold War: Third World Interventions and the Making of Our Times* (Cambridge, 2005) provides a chilling account of both "Black Books." James A. Lucas, "Deaths in Other Nations Since WWII Due to U.S. Interventions" (April 24, 2007) at http://www.countercurrents.org/lucas240407.htm, counts up to 30 million deaths due to US actions and policies alone, although he includes the post–Cold War period too.
51. Martin Malia, *Russia Under Western Eyes: From the Bronze Horsemen to Lenin's Tomb* (Cambridge, MA, 1999), p. 84.
52. Kennan, *Memoirs*, pp. 350–351; Kennan, *American Diplomacy*, p. 154 [my emphasis]; John Alton, *Painting With Light* (1949; rpt. Berkeley, 1995), p. 51.
53. Kennan, *Russia and the West under Lenin and Stalin* (New York, 1960), p. 241; "Man of the Year," *Time* (January 4, 1943), pp. 21–22; Simon Sebag Montefiore, *Stalin: The Court of the Red Tsar* (New York, 2003), pp. 419, 423–4.

7

The Spirit of Democracy

Religious Liberty and American Anti-Communism during the Cold War

ANDREW PRESTON

The Cold War and the Question of Religious Liberty

Scholars have divided the Cold War into three distinct phases. The first, which lasted from shortly after the end of World War II until 1963, was the era of the First Cold War, in which Soviet-American tensions were consistently high and the stakes clearly defined; some historians, such as Anders Stephanson in this volume, argue that this period marked *the* Cold War. The second period, stemming from the relaxation of tensions following the Cuban Missile Crisis, was a period of superpower détente, embodied by summit diplomacy and arms control, that lasted, at the latest, until the Soviet invasion of Afghanistan in 1979 and the election of Ronald Reagan in 1980. The collapse of détente, and the accompanying increase in tensions, led to the Second Cold War, which reached a peak in 1983 and culminated, five years later, in the end of the Cold War itself. By tracing the ebb and flow of the Soviet-American rivalry and its ideological foundations—specifically, in the case of this chapter, America's promotion and protection of religious liberty—these three phrases best capture the nature of the Cold War itself.[1]

This is not to say, as Stephanson does, that the Cold War was exclusively an American construction. In his chapter, Odd Arne Westad is surely correct to argue for a pluralist (i.e., internationalist) approach to the study of the Cold War. Yet we must also beware of being ahistorical in our quest for diversity: even if the United States was but "a nation among nations" in the Cold War world, it was always one of the most important nations and often *the* most important nation.[2] In contrast to Westad's pluralist approach, the Americanist view—similar but certainly not identical to Stephanson's interpretation—insists upon a tight focus on the United States.[3] However, it is not impossible to balance Westad's search for pluralist interpretations with the Americanist emphasis on the United States. Both approaches simply need to acknowledge each other, as Westad himself points out, and avoid portraying their own version of Cold War history as exclusive or dogmatic. Thus a focus on the United States, as in this chapter on religion, should not be taken as a view of the Cold War in its entirety. But America was a major factor in causing and prolonging the Cold War, and thus an examination of its ideological underpinnings is inherently necessary. The ebb and flow of American religious conceptions of geopolitics does not explain the Cold War writ large; but it does help, in part, to explain one of its primary components, American behavior and motivations.

Few conflicts have been as intrinsically ideological as the Cold War. For four decades, the United States and the Soviet Union were at neither peace nor war. They cooperated on almost nothing, contested almost everything, and yet never did so by force of arms, at least not directly. While the Cold War had its share of military conflict, its most decisive battles were political and psychological. According to Harry Truman, the first president to turn a Soviet-American strategic rivalry into a holy war, the Cold War was "a struggle, above all else, for the minds of men." Or, in the words of its last US president, echoed by one of its leading historians, the Cold War was a battle "for the soul of mankind."[4]

Yet for Americans, the intensely ideological nature of the Cold War was nothing new. In form and substance, it differed little from the ideological underpinnings of the two world wars, particularly Franklin Roosevelt's political campaign to mobilize popular opinion against Nazi Germany. Indeed, the Cold War's roots go even deeper. Since at least the nation's founding, the promotion of national ideals—particularly political liberty in the form of representative democracy—had been as central to US foreign policy as the pursuit of supposedly clear-headed national interests. In fact, Americans have almost always viewed the pursuit of ideals as synonymous with pursuit of the national interest. The belief that Americans cannot live as Americans—that is, as a free people—in a world of tyranny is one of the oldest traditions in the history of American foreign relations. But the American conception of freedom was not simply the aggregation of discrete rights. Democracy was important, but it could not survive in isolation. Other freedoms, be they economic, cultural, or social, were deemed just as important as voting rights: for one to exist, all had to be present. Liberty, in other words, was indivisible.[5]

Like most aspects of US foreign policy, the promotion of religious freedom as an essential ingredient of political freedom was rooted in domestic political ideology. These powerful domestic sources have shaped US foreign policy by giving it an unusually dogmatic and often emotive ideological force. Such values did not always determine the direction or purpose of foreign policy, but they almost always determined their character. Cold War presidents' views on political economy and social justice, for example, affected how foreign policy would be implemented: NATO operated along the same federalist principles that governed American democracy; Dwight Eisenhower distrusted, even feared, an interventionist foreign policy because it would inevitably lead to higher federal taxes, perhaps even a "garrison state"; and Lyndon Johnson's war in Vietnam assumed many of the progressive objectives of his Great Society programs.[6] Johnson put it best in 1966 when he boasted, without apparent irony in the midst of race riots at home and the Indochinese quagmire abroad, that "the best way to judge America's foreign policy is to look at our domestic policy."[7] Despite the twin insurgencies that crippled his presidency, LBJ had a point: foreign policy began at home, often in ways that made foreign and domestic sources of diplomacy indistinguishable.

And so it was with religious liberty. Americans believed that promoting and protecting political freedom abroad also required the promotion and protection of religious freedom because the US Constitution itself is grounded in the same principle. The First Amendment in the Bill of Rights begins with two basic but important statements on religion that enshrine the separation of church and state—the "establishment clause" prohibiting the federal government from founding an official church and the "free exercise" clause protecting individual religious freedom—because James Madison, among others, believed that state regulation of religion was not only unjust and undemocratic, but also had the potential to stoke sectarian conflict and tear apart the new republic's polity and undermine its political freedom.[8] To American officials from Madison on, moreover, religious faith served as a foundational freedom, a vital component of democracy, because they saw in it the source of individual conscience and collective morality.[9] Even relatively nonreligious commentators, such as Zbigniew Brzezinski, a Columbia University professor who later became Jimmy Carter's national security adviser, argued that one of the hallmarks of a totalitarian society was its repression of religious freedom because it was one of the few institutions in society that competed with the state for the people's loyalties.[10]

While the Cold War did not mark an ideological departure within the American diplomatic tradition, its unprecedented duration, global breadth, and sheer intensity exaggerated and cemented these existing trends. Not coincidentally, the Cold War not only marked one of America's most ideological struggles, but also triggered two important shifts in American religion. The first was an astounding resurgence of faith. Both the 1950s and the 1970s witnessed a tremendous surge in piety: in the 1950s, overall church attendance and membership soared, while the 1970s ushered in an intensification and radicalization of religion.[11] The second shift was perhaps a logical consequence of the first: the Cold War witnessed an especially strong fusion of religious faith, mainstream politics, and public policy. But politics had an effect on religion, too. The emergence of a strong, centralized federal government in the New Deal, World War II, and the Cold War inadvertently transferred many of the social functions of the church, such as the provision of social welfare services, to the state. Denominational identities, once so strong as to be inviolable even in the face of the broadly popular ecumenical movement, weakened as a result. American religion became politicized, as religious Americans—particularly Protestants, among whom religious pluralism was strongest and thus for whom denominational identity had been most pronounced—began to define themselves, and their religion, along political rather than liturgical lines. Christian conservatives, in other words, now defined themselves as "conservative" according to political views on race and economics instead of on doctrinal matters such as baptism and predestination, as they had in the past.[12] In the Cold War, then, politics became faith-based and faith became politically based.

Foreign policy was no different. On issues involving diplomacy and defense, religious constituencies mobilized in greater numbers, with greater force, and to greater effect than they had in the past. Moreover, personal ties between secular governmental officials and religious communities proved to be unusually strong, giving Cold War diplomatic rhetoric an unusually strident moralistic tone. As Andrew Rotter has pointed out, three of the first four Cold War secretaries of state—Dean Acheson, John Foster Dulles, and Dean Rusk—were all sons of Protestant ministers.[13] Through such connections, religiosity, albeit often inadvertently, became an enduring feature of American Cold War foreign policy.

The very nature of the communist enemy, headquartered in Moscow but with the desire and potential to spread anywhere, even within the United States, was also important. Communism did not just threaten Americans' physical security—it threatened their very way of life. Anticommunists warned that communist repression of political and religious freedom presented a direct, existential threat to the United States. "[W]e stand for liberty, for the expansion of liberty," Daniel Patrick Moynihan, a leading neoconservative and US ambassador to the United Nations, argued in 1974 during the controversy over the Soviets' treatment of their Jewish population. "Anything less risks the contraction of liberty: our own included."[14] Communist tyranny was not an enemy the United States could defeat through force of arms alone. Against the avowed materialism and atheism of communist ideology, Americans reached for one of their most enduring and empowering values: religion and its free expression.

And yet, following the three phases of Soviet-American rivalry outlined above, the promotion of religious liberty was not a Cold War perennial. It bloomed and wilted as the Cold War itself did, reaching intense highs in the late

1940s and through the 1950s, a low in the era of détente, and a new high as détente came under attack at home in the 1970s and eventually collapsed with the Soviet invasion of Afghanistan in 1979. The pattern should not be surprising. When Americans felt threatened, either at home or abroad, they turned to religious faith for both solace and a solution.

Religious Liberty and World War II

As with many of the Cold War's defining contours, the theme of religious liberty was first shaped during World War II. Even before the United States had entered the war as a belligerent, President Franklin Roosevelt sought to define what it stood for in contrast to the ideology of Nazi Germany. Using his 1939 State of the Union address to respond to the 1938 Munich agreement, Roosevelt argued that America could not live in peace in a world dominated by tyranny. "Storms from abroad directly challenge three institutions indispensable to Americans," he warned in an echo of Woodrow Wilson, and indeed a much older tradition of conflating national security with the protection of ideological values as well as physical safety. "The first is religion. It is the source of the other two—democracy and international good faith." Religion was the wellspring of democracy and international society because, "by teaching man his relationship to God," it "gives the individual a sense of his own dignity and teaches him to respect himself by respecting his neighbors." Fascism and communism, not religion, were the anachronistic and atavistic forces in the world. "In a modern civilization," Roosevelt declared, "all three—religion, democracy and international good faith—complement and support each other. . . . The defense of religion, of democracy and of good faith among nations is all the same fight. To save one we must now make up our minds to save all."[15] Or, as he told Pope Pius XII later that year, "that which harms one segment of humanity harms all the rest."[16] Two years later, in girding the nation for the coming war, Roosevelt proposed that Americans would protect what he called the Four Freedoms; of these four basic essential conditions for a free society, Roosevelt included the Freedom of Worship.[17]

Unsurprisingly, given this strong presidential imprimatur, the importance of free religion to political liberty became a central theme in wartime religious discourse. "For liberty, like peace and war, is indivisible," the acclaimed journalist Anne O'Hare McCormick wrote shortly before American entry into the war. "It is impossible to grant freedom of worship without granting freedom of speech, freedom of the press, freedom of assembly. Religious liberty cannot exist without civil liberty, and vice versa."[18] In turn, the existence of a vibrant religious community was something of an insurance policy against tyranny, just as the existence of democracy was something of an insurance policy against religious persecution and atheism. It was, then, in the American national interest to ensure the spread of religion—especially religious freedom, through the separation of church from state—and political liberty as widely as possible. Otherwise, authoritarian alternatives, such as Nazism and Soviet communism, would destroy them both. "Wherever man is free, religion cannot remain in bondage," the Reverend John Sutherland Bonnell preached to his congregation in the Fifth Avenue Presbyterian Church at the height of the war. "The goal of the Four Freedoms will be realized only as we obey God's eternal laws and engage in ceaseless labors to this end with a vigilance that remains unabated throughout the years to come."[19] Indeed, in the autumn of 1941 Roosevelt discovered for himself the depth of Americans' support for religious liberty when he ran into staunch opposition, mostly from Catholics but also from conservative and even some liberal Protestants, to the extension of Lend-Lease aid to the Soviet Union; this controversy was itself a reprise of Catholics' angry protests in 1933 over Roosevelt's efforts to establish diplomatic relations with the Soviet Union.[20] Roosevelt then made matters much worse by claiming, rather spuriously, that while the Soviet Union might be atheist, its constitution at least adhered to a separation of church and state, thus protecting, at least in principle, the freedom of religious worship.[21]

With his keen political instincts and appreciation for the power of religion in politics, Roosevelt should have known better. As he himself had declared, the world was facing an especially dangerous threat from a new kind of totalitarian enemy that may have originated in Europe but posed a direct threat to freedom everywhere—including the United States. Though the source of the trouble lay far away, Americans assumed the threat to Europeans' liberty was a threat to the safety of their own. American Catholics and Protestants had little trouble linking themselves to their oppressed co-religionists in those parts of Europe under German or Soviet occupation, and American Jews, of course, felt religious persecution more acutely than anyone else could imagine. Thus there was something of a consensus, until then a rare occurrence in American religion, that the suppression of religion in Europe represented a grave threat that stretched across the oceans. Liberals and conservatives, modernists and fundamentalists, Reform and Orthodox: all agreed that the United States could not live in a world without the free expression of religious faith. In the words of the Inter-Faith Committee for Aid to the Democracies, one of the many ecumenical groups that emerged to support internationalism and defend "the fabric of Western civilization" during the war, "the leaders of totalitarian states have proved by their merciless persecution of religious communities that they cannot tolerate any faith except the paganism which glorifies their own race and their own persons."[22]

Drawing Dividing Lines in the First Cold War

As the Inter-Faith Committee's reference to the "paganism" of fascism suggests, Americans viewed modernist, totalitarian ideologies as competing belief systems, even new idolatrous religions that were horrific perversions of true biblical faith. This was indeed the Nazis' intention, though Hitler's ambition to create a new faith died in the ruins of Germany's wartime defeat and devastation.[23] In the early Cold War, communism came to supplant fascism as America's rival ideology. As Roosevelt's wartime difficulties with various religious communities illustrate, Americans already distrusted the Soviet Union and its communist ideology. What changed with the coming of the Cold War was that the Soviets were now feared as well as distrusted. Even more than Nazism, communism represented the nightmare inversion of the American ideal: command economy instead of free-market capitalism, people's dictatorship instead of liberal democracy, and atheism instead of religious faith. But communism extended its reach far wider than fascism ever did: by professing to have exclusive universal applicability, by claiming the future rather than the past, and by appealing to people's notions of social justice and equality, communism had a much broader resonance than fascism. As Odd Arne Westad has pointed out, the Soviet Union and the United States were promoting rival versions of modernity that competed for the world's allegiance.[24]

Most important for questions of religious freedom, communism did not profess a simple, reflexive materialistic atheism; despite claims to the contrary, it also breached the separate spheres of church and state by extending atheism at the expense of religious faith, and hence democracy. According to the Quaker activist Stewart W. Herman, church and state "are separated in the Iron Curtain countries." But while prohibitions on church involvement in politics were rigorously enforced, "the state—being totalitarian—retains an effective control over every expression of church life!"[25] Communism seemed to be innately expansionist and intolerant of any possible belief system that would compete for people's allegiance. Hence the clear and present danger of the communist threat. Communists stood, the evangelist Billy Graham proclaimed in 1949 at his first revival in Los Angeles, "against God, against Christ, against the Bible, and against all religion. Communism is not only an economic interpretation of life—Communism is a religion that is inspired, directed, and motivated by the Devil himself who has declared war against Almighty God."[26]

American Catholics concurred. Indeed, the anticommunist consensus actually stimulated a decline in anti-Semitism and anti-Catholicism among America's culturally hegemonic Protestants. After all, the main division of belief was now between atheism and religion rather than between rival faiths. While Protestant fundamentalists continued to fear Catholics almost as much as they did communists, other conservative Christians, such as the neo-evangelicals led by Billy Graham and Carl Henry, joined with other Christians and Jews to crusade against the communist menace. Thus while religion affected the character of US foreign policy during the Cold War, the Cold War was changing the face of American religion. The significance of this transformation was nothing short of revolutionary: anti-Catholicism had been an enduring staple of America's Protestant identity since the earliest colonial period; within a decade, it had vanished almost entirely.

And yet in the Cold War's early years, the exact terms of the debate over religious freedom and its place in the American worldview were not yet settled. Ironically, given their liberal views, mainline Protestants continued to harbor a fear of Catholicism's allegedly concentrated, authoritarian power. The Federal Council of Churches, the nation's largest and most important ecumenical group, a product of Social Gospel Progressivism, and a prominent advocate of the welfare state, declared in 1947 that the "critical and supreme political issue of today is that of the free society versus the police state." Such states sought to deny human dignity, and thus the will of God, by suppressing spiritual, intellectual, and political freedom through arbitrary state power. Against such forces, the FCC urged America to forge

> a world of free societies wherein all men, as the children of God, are recognized to have certain basic rights, including liberty to hold and change beliefs and practices according to reason and conscience, freedom to differ even from their own government and immunity from persecution or coercion on account of spiritual or intellectual beliefs.[27]

Yet the problem of autocracy, the FCC charged, was not confined to communist states. Anticommunist authoritarian nations, such as predominantly Catholic Spain and Argentina, were just as guilty of violating religious freedom, and hence just as dangerous to peace.[28] If liberty was indivisible, it was irrespective of which form of autocracy was its challenger.

Concerns about the compatibility of "American freedom and Catholic power," to quote the title of an alarmist bestseller about the supposed authoritarianism of American Catholics, were rooted firmly in traditional domestic political concerns that were then extended to suit a liberal Protestant fear of right-wing tyranny abroad.[29] Three of the nation's most liberal Protestant theologians—Harry Emerson Fosdick, a minister at New York's Riverside Church who had spearheaded the modernist attack on fundamentalism three decades before; Bromley Oxnam, a leading socialist and Methodist bishop; and Edwin T. Dahlberg, president of the Northern Baptist Convention and a leading pacifist—led the anti-Catholic charge. What galvanized them into action was not just a fear of fascist Catholics in Europe and Latin America who practiced what Dahlberg called "ecclesiastic totalitarianism," but fears that the First Amendment's wall of separation was crumbling at home.[30] Ignoring the warnings of the mainline Protestant establishment, in 1951 Truman decided to appoint, for the first time in American history, a permanent, official US ambassador to the Vatican. Protestants across the political and theological spectrums were furious. In a letter to Truman, Fosdick expressed his anger at "your violation of our basic American principle of the equality of all religious faiths in the eyes of our government." Fosdick warned the president that he spoke for millions of fellow Protestants, and that, "for conscience' sake, we cannot rest until this outrage is undone."[31]

Yet liberal Protestants were destined to lose their struggle to broaden the application of the religious liberty principle in US foreign policy. Americans may not have embraced dictators in Spain and Argentina, but neither did they fear them. Soviet communism, on the other hand, had a far-reaching espionage network operating within the United States and its allies, had the world's largest military seemingly poised to strike at Western Europe, and by 1949 had acquired its own atomic weapons. And as the Soviets' persecution of Christian clergy in Eastern Europe seemed to prove, religion itself faced a particularly dire threat from communism, what the *New York Herald Tribune* called "an identic pattern" that was "part of a larger effort to destroy resistance to Communist domination."[32] In 1948 Secretary of State Robert A. Lovett blasted the arrest of a Hungarian Roman Catholic Cardinal as a "sickening sham" that heralded communist ambitions to dominate Europe by force.[33]

Thus the promotion of religious freedom abroad was not a purely abstract notion. It became a specific weapon in America's Cold War arsenal and a goal to be pursued in opposition to communism, and was embraced as such by government officials. Just as Roosevelt had emphasized religion as an antidote to Nazism, Harry Truman, a devout if unchurched Baptist, made religious freedom an indispensable component of freedom itself, and thus also of America's new global grand strategy for the Cold War. "There is one thing that Americans value more than peace," he declared in March 1947, the same month his Truman Doctrine speech served as an unofficial declaration of Cold War. "It is freedom. Freedom of worship—freedom of speech—freedom of enterprise."[34] Playing on Americans' worst political fears and the paranoid political culture of the early Cold War, on another occasion Truman stressed that the free rights of the majority, around the world, were under threat from a fanatical, autocratic, atheist minority. "The greatest obstacle to peace is a modern tyranny led by a small group who have abandoned their faith in God," he declared in May 1950, shortly before the outbreak of the Korean War provided a confirmation of sorts. "These tyrants have forsaken ethical and moral beliefs. They believe that only force makes right. They are aggressively seeking to expand the area of their domination."[35]

In order to mount an attack on communism's global appeal, Truman wielded religion as a psychological and political weapon. Although the religious imagery of the Truman Doctrine and NSC-68 were not always explicit, their division of the world between good and evil mobilized a tradition of moral clarity and crusading zeal within American Protestantism that stretched back to the Puritans.[36] Most notably, Truman attempted to sponsor a conference of world religious leaders, to meet in Washington in 1948, that would "appeal to all *believers in God and human liberty* to join together to bring pressure of a common desire for peace upon the atheistic communistic government of Russia" by proclaiming their freedom to believe in their own faith, be it Christian, Muslim, or Jewish—even including, Truman boasted, "the top Buddhist and the Grand Lama of Tibet."[37] Others followed suit by adding religion to the otherwise hard-headed tools of diplomacy. In 1949, during the deliberations over the North Atlantic Treaty, Senator H. Alexander Smith, a member of the Foreign Relations Committee, feared the new alliance did not emphasize "the importance of our spiritual heritage" enough. "One of the big issues in the 'cold war,'" he wrote to his friend Charles P. Taft, was the contest "between the materialistic atheism of the Commies and America's fundamental faith in the guiding hand of God." Accordingly, Smith sponsored a resolution explicitly affirming NATO's Judeo-Christian foundations and respect for religious freedom.[38]

As the Cold War intensified in the late 1940s and into the 1950s, the promotion of religious liberty became increasingly important to the rhetorical and ideological underpinnings of US foreign policy. Building on Roosevelt and Truman's promotion of religious liberty as integral to democracy itself, John Foster Dulles, already a prominent statesman before becoming Dwight Eisenhower's secretary of state in 1953, elevated the defense of religion to the fore of American diplomacy. Dulles was not merely a politician or diplomat: he was also an influential layman in the Presbyterian Church, a leader of the ecumenical movement, and a successful international lawyer. Almost uniquely, he possessed the experience and expertise to combine law, religion, politics, and diplomacy and shape them into a highly effective ideological weapon.

For Dulles, the free expression of religion, protected by the official separation of church and state, was vital to the survival and spread of democracy. Religion was an expression not just of faith, but of morality, conscience, and community, without which no free society could hope to function. No democracy "can exist without law," Dulles believed, and "no law can exist without an ethos, . . . a sense of obligation in the conscience of the member of the community."[39] States that violated religious freedom, of their own people and of those they subjugated abroad, posed a security threat. "No political or social system should prevail," he told delegates at the inaugural convention of the World Council of Churches in

1948, unless it is in "accord with moral law" and supported "the opportunity of men to exercise their human rights and fundamental freedoms."[40]

As an ecumenical Protestant who had worked for the Federal Council of Churches during World War II, Dulles was predisposed to accepting people of faith—any faith—even though he also believed that Christianity offered the one true path to salvation. Dulles applied these beliefs as the head of the American delegation to the UN's founding assembly in 1945 in San Francisco: for him, only a broad, or ecumenical, system of collective security, grounded in universal human rights, could avert a third world war that would almost certainly destroy life on earth.[41] But as Cold War tensions escalated, and as it seemed that the Soviet Union, and later the People's Republic of China, were intent on sabotaging both the collective democratic will and the religious bases for moral conscience, Dulles began to believe that the United States and its like-minded allies simply could not work with communists; the threat they posed to the democratic way of life was too dangerous and implacable. Dulles outlined this more alarmist view when given the opportunity to address the congregation—his father's congregation—at the First Presbyterian Church of Watertown, New York:

> Orthodox communists believe that there is neither God nor moral law; that there is no such thing as universal and equal justice, and that human beings are without soul or sacred personality. They are free of the moral restraints and compulsions which prevail in a religious society and they think it quite right to use force and violence to make their way prevail. . . .
>
> Communists are, of course, entitled to have their own belief as to what is best for men, and they are entitled to try peacefully to bring their ideals into reality. That is the privilege of every human being. But since there is a God, since there is a moral law, since human personality is sacred, no human rulers can rightly use ruthless and violent methods and pitilessly crush all within their power who do not conform to their particular dictation.[42]

Thus motivated, Dulles abandoned his broad ecumenical vision, as embodied by the inclusive UN, for a much narrower one based on a common set of ideals, such as NATO; just as he had with the founding of the UN in 1945, Dulles worked for the Truman administration to help establish NATO in 1949.

As an especially zealous secretary of state—Arthur M. Schlesinger, Jr., dubbed him "the high priest of the Cold War"—Dulles practiced what he preached.[43] He tried to move beyond mere containment, a strategy which to some extent tolerated diplomacy, to isolation, most infamously by refusing to shake hands with

Chinese Premier Chou Enlai at an international conference in Geneva in 1954.[44] He also made religious liberty central to US foreign policy. In Korea and Vietnam, two nations artificially divided by the peculiar circumstances of the Cold War, he encouraged Christians in the communist north to flee to the anticommunist south. In both cases, Dulles intoned, "the driving force was a longing for religious freedom."[45] When Vietnam was partitioned at the seventeenth parallel in 1954, it was the US Seventh Fleet that orchestrated Operation Passage to Freedom, the flow of hundreds of thousands of Catholic refugees from north to south.[46] And in South Korea, South Vietnam, and Taiwan, Dulles worked hard to ensure that the authoritarian, unrepresentative Christians who ruled those largely non-Christian lands—respectively, the Methodist Syngman Rhee, the Roman Catholic Ngo Dinh Diem, and the Methodist Chiang Kai-shek—were secure. With the Cold War at its ideological height, religious liberty found itself at the heart of American foreign policy.

Declension and Revival

In the 1960s many of the ideological premises of America's Cold War diplomacy, including the promotion of religious liberty, receded dramatically. While many conservative Christians continued to criticize the Soviet Union and China for their ongoing violations of religious freedom, the Kennedy and Johnson administrations effectively dropped the issue altogether. The thawing of relations between Washington and Moscow was largely responsible for the softening of America's ideological stance. But the issue of religious freedom itself had become much more complicated for the simple reason that it was now America's allies that were committing much of the world's religious persecution. South Vietnam posed the gravest problem. In 1963 the Buddhists, who comprised nearly 90 percent of the population, revolted against the oppressive rule of the ruling Ngo family, who were Catholic. The trigger for the revolt was the Ngos' refusal to allow Buddhist monks in the city of Hue to fly traditional flags at their pagoda in honor of the Buddha's birthday. The uprising, which began in Hue in May 1963, quickly spread nationwide; the next month, the first Buddhist monk burned himself to death in protest. Americans were horrified; the Kennedy administration, knowing almost nothing of Vietnamese history and culture, was caught completely off-guard. "How could this have happened?" an aghast Kennedy asked an aide. "Who are these people? Why didn't we know about them before?"[47] Unfortunately for Kennedy, he was now seen as the patron and defender of a minority regime that oppressed the religious freedom of the majority of its citizens. Suddenly, wielding moralistic cudgels about the lack of religious liberty in the communist world did not seem like such a good idea.

Concern for the state of religious freedom abroad continued to fade as the war in Vietnam consumed Americans' attention and resources. Hawks simply wanted the war prosecuted with enough vigor to secure victory, which the Johnson administration's graduated escalation seemed unable to achieve. Doves, on the other hand, thought America should simply withdraw from Vietnam altogether. Many antiwar advocates, especially counterculture radicals and the New Left, did not blame communist North Vietnam, or even communist China, for the war, but they did blame the United States. Most shocking to many Americans was the large number of American religious leaders—Protestant ministers, Catholic priests, and Jewish rabbis—who protested the war not only on the traditional grounds of pacifism, but for the simple reason that they believed their country was wrong and even acting immorally.[48] An agonized Martin Luther King Jr., a Baptist preacher as much as a civil rights leader, publicly turned against the war in 1967, and thus against the president who had done more for the cause of black freedom than any other since Abraham Lincoln. In Vietnam, King was saying, Lyndon Johnson was no longer on the side of human freedom.[49] Rather than acting nobly as the defender of liberty around the world, America was now the oppressor in the eyes of many of its own people. Bogged down in debates at home over national identity and culpability, and diverted by the need to wage an increasingly frustrating war, Johnson and his advisers were not in a position to base their diplomacy on moral ideals such as the promotion of religious liberty. In 1966 a new Buddhist uprising against Ngo Dinh Diem's successor regime reinforced the point.[50]

By winning the presidency in 1968, Richard Nixon inherited these myriad problems, at home and abroad. Not only was the United States being fought to a stalemate by a largely preindustrial, partitioned third-world country in Southeast Asia, it was also reeling under a severe economic crisis, being challenged not only by adversaries but also by its closest allies—economically by Germany and Japan and diplomatically by France—and facing a Soviet Union that had recently attained parity in nuclear weapons.[51] Riots, protest, and racial strife at home powerfully reinforced America's global vulnerability.[52] With the help of his national security adviser, Henry Kissinger, Nixon devised a strategic response, détente, that included withdrawal from Vietnam, establishing relations with China, and bilateral trade and arms control with the Soviet Union. But doing so required Nixon and Kissinger to launch a revolutionary change in US foreign policy: no longer would the United States worry about the internal character or behavior of states; being realists, Nixon and Kissinger insisted that all states, be they liberal democracies or communist autocracies, pursued a common objective of security and responded in the same way to the dictates of power. Moscow's embrace of "godless communism" would not prevent Washington from treating it like any other state in the international system. Ideology, in other words, no longer mattered, and the promotion of religious freedom disappeared from American diplomacy.

Détente was a strategy based on nuance and negotiation; as Nixon and Kissinger framed it, the rationally calculated national interest determined foreign policy at the expense of unrealistic ideals. But as Kissinger himself later admitted, Americans were accustomed to a foreign policy based on the pursuit of ideals *and* interests and would not for long support a foreign policy that did not promote both.[53] Americans generally accepted the need for negotiations, but only so long as they led either to compromises by the enemy or the attainment of total world peace on America's basic terms.[54] When it seemed that détente was a tool for managing the Cold War rather than ending it, popular support plummeted. Not coincidentally, as amoral détente came under moralistic attack at home in the 1970s, the promotion of religious liberty roared back to life—with one key difference. While the promotion of religious values had remained important to Nixon's presidential rhetoric—it was he who first used the phrase "God bless America" to close a speech—the promotion of religious freedom abroad had not.[55] Religious freedom would inevitably require criticism of the Soviet Union and thus undermine superpower détente; and détente, after all, was the official foreign policy of the Nixon administration. Thus when Americans promoted religious freedom in the 1970s, they did so without the support of their president and secretary of state. In fact, Americans used religious freedom as a way to attack not only Soviet communism, but also their own president.

Unlike the salience of religious liberty in the early Cold War, when presidents and their administrations enshrined it as an abiding principle and objective in the name of anticommunism, in the 1970s religious liberty became a weapon that people outside the administration used to attack both enemies abroad and support for US foreign policy at home. Some of détente's attackers, such as the Israeli government, were even US allies.[56] There were several constants, though, most notably the target: Soviet communism. As with the persecution of Christians behind the Iron Curtain, the dispute once again turned on how communist regimes violated the religious freedom of their own people. But the persecuted faithful were now Jews as well as Christians, reflecting yet again how anticommunism helped cause a decline in American anti-Semitism. As one joint Christian-Jewish pro-Israel group proclaimed, "Where the liberation traditions of two great religious peoples converge, can freedom be far away?"[57]

At issue was the Soviet Union's decision not to allow Soviet Jews to emigrate to Israel, though in the United States this was tied strongly to a long history of vicious Russian anti-Semitism. In 1972 Nixon became the first American president since Roosevelt to visit the Soviet Union. At his Moscow summit with Leonid Brezhnev, Nixon pledged to extend Most Favored Nation (MFN) trading status to the Soviets, which would allow them to trade with the United States as freely as any other country. At a time when American power was at a low ebb, Nixon and Kissinger conceived of détente as a system of extending carrots and sticks in order to influence Soviet behavior. One of their most effective sticks was opening relations with communist China, whom the Soviet Union now regarded as its most dangerous enemy. Trade was their most important carrot because the Soviets were desperate for access to Western capital, credit, technology, and foodstuffs. The entire system of détente depended upon Nixon and Kissinger's ability to balance carrots with sticks, and the Soviets against the Chinese, in order to maximize American leverage in a time of vulnerability.[58]

Because it sought to de-escalate the Cold War, détente was initially popular among Americans. But when it became apparent that the de-escalation of the Cold War did not presage its end, and that its management actually required awkward compromises on matters of principle, such as the fundamental democratic freedoms of religion and movement, détente came under attack and rapidly lost popular support. Leading the charge were members of Congress—especially Senator Henry M. Jackson and Representative Charles Vanik—who refused on principle to support policies that tolerated infringements of American values. Partisan political advantage added to their motivation. In the 1970s, even with the emergence of a leftist critique of Israeli foreign policy, a majority of American Jews remained solidly Democratic, and so attacking détente, the policy of a Republican administration, on grounds of protecting both American values and Israeli security, held obvious political attraction.[59]

Jackson, a long-serving senator from Washington with presidential aspirations, was détente's most important and effective challenger. His campaign to modify détente by incorporating provisions to alter the Soviet Union's internal behavior—as opposed to Nixon and Kissinger's goal to influence the Soviets' external policies—deployed religious liberty as an essential precondition for democracy. The "struggle of Soviet Jews," Jackson declared at a rally in New York, "is in keeping with the noblest and most important of all American ideals, the ideal of freedom."[60] This kind of rhetoric was in keeping with the same ideological premises that had motivated Roosevelt, Truman, and Dulles in earlier decades. But Jackson went further, by incorporating universal human rights as the true foundation for international security and portraying the internal behavior of states as a matter of self-defense for all other states. According to Dorothy Fosdick, Jackson's longtime foreign policy aide, Jackson believed that "nations, especially powerful ones, that deny the basic freedoms deprive themselves of an effective public opinion to control their conduct—a situation that not only leaves their citizens unprotected from lawlessness and oppression, but is a menace to international peace."[61] Peace, Jackson maintained, was not simply the absence of war, nor even the management of international stability. "Without an increasing measure of individual liberty in the Communist world there can be no genuine détente," he told the Tucson Jewish Community Council in 1974, and

> there can be no real movement toward a more peaceful world. . . . For if new relations between East and West are to mature into long-term peaceful cooperation, there must be progress toward the freer movement of people and ideas between East and West, which is to say progress in the area of human rights and individual liberty.[62]

Or as Vanik argued during congressional hearings into détente, "I think the cause of freedom is helped everywhere" by pressuring the Soviets to allow their Jewish citizens to emigrate. "I think that it is a service for the liberty of all mankind that this effort is being made."[63] Enlightened self-interest of this kind simply resonated much more strongly than the Nixon administration's seemingly amoral détente.

Jackson did not just give speeches to friendly, like-minded audiences. He targeted détente where it was most vulnerable and where he was most effective: in Congress, using legislation that regulated trade with foreign countries. As he implored his colleagues, "while we're bargaining with the Russians over dollars and rubles, let's do some bargaining on behalf of helpless human beings. When we talk about free trade, let's talk about free people, too."[64] The Soviets needed MFN status; for this reason, it was one of the few areas in which Washington had nearly total leverage over Moscow. Jackson teamed up with Vanik, his counterpart in the House, to introduce what became known as the Jackson-Vanik amendment to the bill authorizing Nixon's trade negotiations with the Soviets. The Jackson-Vanik amendment stipulated that the United States would only confer MFN status when the Soviet Union lifted its restrictions on Russian Jews who wanted to emigrate to Israel; Jackson also hoped its provisions would cover persecuted Christians in the Soviet Union. Kissinger, now secretary of state, applied tremendous pressure upon Congress to reject the administration's critics, but the amendment passed easily. Vindicated, Jackson continued to press the Soviet Union on its repression of religious liberty. In 1976 he introduced another successful bill, cosponsored with Representative John Buchanan, Jr., that condemned the fact that "Christians and other religious believers in the Soviet Union are being persecuted simply because they desire to worship God according to the dictates of their conscience and the precepts of their faith rather than according to the dictates of the state." Introduced in May, the bill passed unanimously in the Senate and with only two dissenting votes in the House in October.[65]

Unrelenting political criticism of the Soviet Union's record on religious freedom was deep enough to transcend partisan lines. Democratic Representative Robert F. Drinan, a Jesuit priest from Massachusetts, actually favored the principle of détente because of its long-term potential to defuse Cold War tensions and ease the nuclear standoff. But he was not willing to support the practice of détente if it came at the expense of principles he thought more valuable: religious freedom in particular and universal human rights in general. Drinan's dual status as a cleric and critic of the Vietnam War added significant weight to his vision of a foreign policy centered on human rights. But as a Catholic priest, Drinan also projected a Judeo-Christian identity for America. In pressing for US support for Soviet Jews before the Jackson-Vanik amendment had been introduced, Drinan exhorted Nixon to express "the solidarity which should exist between all of those who worship the God of Abraham, of Isaac and of Jacob."[66] Although Drinan was a liberal, Catholic Democrat, his promotion of Judeo-Christian identity and universal adherence to human rights perfectly fit the temper of the evangelistic, confessional 1970s. Drinan believed that "only the Christians of the world, and particularly Christians in America, could so influence world opinion that Russia would simply be required both to allow Jews to emigrate if they so desire and to permit complete religious freedom in the Soviet Union."[67] Drinan's colleague in the House of Representatives, John Ashbrook, a deeply conservative Republican from Ohio, equally castigated the Soviet Union for its repression of religious freedom and the supporters of détente who excused Soviet repression in the name of geopolitical stability.[68]

Advocates of religious liberty in the 1970s couched their cause in the language of universal human rights, but when even a liberal, pro-choice Democrat like Drinan could emphasize the duty of "particularly Christians in America" to uphold freedom around the world, it was clear that patriotism and exceptionalism had survived America's humiliating defeat in Vietnam. The resurgence of exceptionalism and the Religious Right, in fact, had everything to do with putting the defeat of Vietnam, and the rest of the malaise associated with the 1970s, behind Americans for good.[69] And this was precisely the cause that helped sweep Ronald Reagan into the presidency in 1980. Despite his bellicose rhetoric and strident image, Reagan had always been more politician than ideologue. The secret of his tremendous success was in his uncanny ability to bridge the gap, sometimes vast, between rhetoric and reality. On many issues near and dear to the Religious Right's heart, such as abortion, Reagan actually delivered precious little despite his close relationship with many Christian conservative leaders. But on foreign policy, where the president and the Religious Right shared a confluence of interests, Reagan was able to deliver almost everything for which anticommunist advocates of religious liberty clamored. As he declared in his speech accepting the Republican Party's presidential nomination in the summer of 1980:

> Can we doubt that only a Divine Providence placed this land, this island of freedom, here as a refuge for all those people in the world who yearn to breathe freely: Jews and Christians enduring persecution behind the Iron Curtain, the boat people of Southeast Asia, of Cuba and Haiti, the victims of drought and famine in Africa, the freedom fighters in Afghanistan and own countrymen held in savage captivity?[70]

The poisonous scourges of human freedom—drought, famine, but above all the communists of the world, from Eastern Europe to Cuba to Afghanistan to Southeast Asia, where they held Americans in "savage captivity"—faced their antidote, Reagan promised, in the United States.

Reagan rode two waves in heightening the ideological tensions of the Cold War. The first, domestic, was in reaction to détente and Jimmy Carter's notion that America had entered an era of limitations. The second was international in origin and nature, as the world, including America, witnessed an explosive growth of conservative religiosity. Reagan's natural ally in riding this second wave was Pope John Paul II, a native of Poland who had his own reasons for mounting a crusade against communist persecution of religion. In US foreign policy, the two waves crested in a speech Reagan gave to the National Association of Evangelicals in 1983. The basis of peace and democracy, Reagan declared, was "a commitment to freedom and personal liberty that, itself, is grounded in the much deeper realization that freedom prospers only where the blessings of God are avidly sought and humbly accepted." Reagan knew this, he claimed, simply by being an American, because the "American experiment in democracy rests on this insight." Because communists believed that "[m]orality is entirely subordinate to the interests of class war" and because they "preach the supremacy of the state [and] declare its omnipotence over individual man," Reagan proclaimed the Soviet Union to be the source and "focus of evil in the modern world."[71] The Soviets' abridgement of religious freedom, then, was not just abhorrent to American values; it was a threat to American security and world peace.

Though the times had changed dramatically, and the Cold War itself had evolved through three distinct phases, there was little to distinguish Reagan's meaning from those of Franklin Roosevelt and Harry Truman decades before. Indeed, while the term "Cold War" defines the global struggle between the United States and the Soviet Union from the late 1940s to the late 1980s, Roosevelt had already established the ideological, political, and strategic framework of America's Cold War in preparation for World War II; and in turn, FDR had simply built upon a much older tradition of American republicanism that saw ideals and interests as indivisible.[72] Americans believed religious freedom, at home and abroad, was essential in its own right; but even more, they believed it was integral to human freedom overall. Without religion, morality was empty, fraudulent, even dangerous because it lacked a true moral compass that only faith could provide; without morality, democracy was meaningless; and without religious freedom, political freedom was impossible. This line of argument had been central to American political thought and religious discourse for two centuries. Little wonder, when galvanized by the intense ideological fires of the Soviet-American rivalry and the looming shadow of the communist threat, that it became such a central component to US foreign policy in the Cold War.

Notes

1. For variations on this thematically chronological scheme, see Fred Halliday, *The Making of the Second Cold War*, 2nd ed. (London, 1986); Vladislav Zubok and Constantine Pleshakov, *Inside the Kremlin's Cold War: From Stalin to Khrushchev* (Cambridge, MA, 1996), 236–237; John Lewis Gaddis, *We Now Know: Rethinking Cold War History* (Oxford, 1997), pp. 291–292; Marc Trachtenberg, *A Constructed Peace: The Making of the European Settlement, 1945–1963* (Princeton, 1999), pp. 352, 379–382, 398–402; James G. Hershberg, "The Crisis Years, 1958–1963" in Odd Arne Westad (ed.), *Reviewing the Cold War: Approaches, Interpretations, Theory* (London, 2000), pp. 319–320; Jennifer W. See, "An Uneasy Truce: John F. Kennedy and Soviet-American Détente, 1963," *Cold War History*, 2 (2002), pp. 161–194; and Andrew Preston, *The War Council: McGeorge Bundy, the NSC Staff, and Vietnam* (Cambridge, MA, 2006), pp. 54–55.
2. The phrase comes from Thomas Bender, *A Nation Among Nations: America's Place in World History* (New York, 2006), which seeks to challenge historiographical notions of American exceptionalism (that is, that America was somehow different and apart from the rest of the world). Interestingly, and not coincidentally, Bender's narrative, which begins in the colonial period, peters out with the onset of World War II—in other words, right at the moment when the United States was becoming something much, much more than merely "a nation among nations."
3. On the need to keep the Cold War, to some extent, centered on the United States and American power, see Campbell Craig and Fredrik Logevall, *America's Cold War: The Politics of Insecurity* (Cambridge, MA, 2009).
4. Harry Truman quoted in Elizabeth Edwards Spalding, *The First Cold Warrior: Harry Truman, Containment, and the Remaking of Liberal Internationalism* (Lexington, 2006), p. 209; George H. W. Bush quoted in Melvyn P. Leffler, *For the Soul of Mankind: The United States, the Soviet Union, and the Cold War* (New York, 2007), p. 3. For an excellent analysis of the unusually ideological and cultural nature of the Cold War, see Walter L. Hixson, *Parting the Curtain: Propaganda, Culture, and the Cold War, 1945–1961* (New York, 1997).
5. For a fuller exploration of this theme, see Anders Stephanson, "Liberty or Death: The Cold War as US Ideology" in Westad (ed.), *Reviewing the Cold War*, pp. 81–100.
6. See, respectively, Gaddis, *We Now Know*, pp. 288–289; Aaron Friedberg, *In the Shadow of the Garrison State: America's Anti-Statism and Its Cold War Grand Strategy* (Princeton, 2000); and Lloyd C. Gardner, *Pay Any Price: Lyndon Johnson and the Wars for Vietnam* (Chicago, 1994).
7. Quoted in Rick Perlstein, *Nixonland: The Rise of a President and the Fracturing of America* (New York, 2008), p. 153.
8. Frank Lambert, *The Founding Fathers and the Place of Religion in America* (Princeton, 2003), pp. 231–232, 241–246.

9. For an outline of this argument, see Peter L. Berger, "Afterword" in *Articles of Faith, Articles of Peace: The Religious Liberty Clauses and the American Public Philosophy*, ed. James Davison Hunter and Os Guinness (Washington, DC, 1990), p. 118; or Franklin I. Gamwell, *The Meaning of Religious Freedom: Modern Politics and the Democratic Resolution* (Albany, 1995). On Madison, see his "Memorial and Remonstrance against Religious Assessments," June 20, 1785, *The Papers of James Madison*, vol. 8 (Chicago, 1973), pp. 298–304.
10. See, for example, Carl J. Friedrich and Zbigniew K. Brzezinski, *Totalitarian Dictatorship and Autocracy*, 2nd ed. (New York, 1966), pp. 299–315.
11. Robert Wuthnow, *The Restructuring of American Religion: Society and Faith since World War II* (Princeton, 1988). On the 1950s, see J. Ronald Oakley, *God's Country: America in the Fifties* (New York, 1986), pp. 319–327; and Mark Silk, *Spiritual Politics: Religion and America since World War II* (New York, 1988). On the 1970s, see Bruce J. Schulman, *The Seventies: The Great Shift in American Culture, Society, and Politics* (New York, 2001), pp. 92–96.
12. Wuthnow, *Restructuring of American Religion*. See also Garry Wills, *Head and Heart: American Christianities* (New York, 2007).
13. Rotter, *Comrades at Odds: The United States and India, 1947–1964* (Ithaca, 2000), p. 221. Acheson's father was an Episcopalian Bishop in Connecticut, Dulles's a Presbyterian minister in upstate New York, and Rusk's an ordained Presbyterian minister in Georgia, although he never actually had his own church.
14. Moynihan, "Was Woodrow Wilson Right?" *Commentary*, May 1974, pp. 30–31.
15. Roosevelt, "Annual Message to the Congress," January 4, 1939, *Public Papers and Addresses of Franklin D. Roosevelt*, vol. 8, *War and Neutrality, 1939* (New York, 1941), pp. 1–2.
16. Quoted in Robert Dallek, *Franklin Roosevelt and American Foreign Policy*, 2nd ed. (New York, 1995), p. 215.
17. On the Four Freedoms, which along with the August 1941 Atlantic Charter provided Americans with a general ideological blueprint for the war, see Elizabeth Borgwardt, *A New Deal for the World: America's Vision for Human Rights* (Cambridge, MA, 2005).
18. McCormick, "Religious Freedom in the Soviet Union," *The New York Times*, October 6, 1941, p. 16 (hereafter *NYT*).
19. Bonnell, "Religious Liberty Seen as War Goal," *NYT*, December 13, 1943, p. 16.
20. Dallek, *Franklin Roosevelt and American Foreign Policy*, pp. 79–80.
21. On the controversy over whether the Soviet Union respected religious freedom, and thus whether the United States should extend Lend-Lease aid in the summer of 1941, see Steven Merritt Miner, *Stalin's Holy War: Religion, Nationalism, and Alliance Politics, 1941–1945* (Chapel Hill, 2003), pp. 224–228; and David S. Foglesong, *The American Mission and the "Evil Empire": The Crusade for a "Free Russia" since 1881* (Cambridge, 2007), pp. 87–88.
22. Inter-Faith Committee for Aid to the Democracies press release, July 15, 1941, Henry Sloane Coffin Papers, Box 3, Folder 33, Special Collections, Burke Theological Library, Union Theological Seminary, Columbia University, New York, NY (hereafter UTS).
23. On Nazism as a quasi-religious system of faith, see Emilio Gentile, *Politics as Religion*, trans. George Staunton (Princeton, 2006); and Michael Burleigh, *Sacred Causes: Religion and Politics from the European Dictators to Al Qaeda* (London, 2006).
24. Westad, *The Global Cold War: Third World Interventions and the Making of Our Times* (Cambridge, 2005), pp. 8–72.
25. Information Service Bulletin of the National Council of Churches, "The Church Behind the Iron Curtain," April 11, 1953, Robert Cushman Papers, Box 11, University Archives, William R. Perkins Library, Duke University, Durham, NC.
26. Quoted in Martin E. Marty, *Modern American Religion*, Vol. 3, *Under God, Indivisible, 1941–1960* (Chicago, 1996), p. 152.
27. Federal Council of the Churches of Christ in America (FCC) booklet, "Cross-Roads of American Foreign Policy," July 1, 1947, John Foster Dulles Papers, Box 284, Seeley G. Mudd Manuscript Library, Princeton University, Princeton, NJ.

28. "Church Body Shies at Parley on Reds," *NYT*, March 12, 1949, p. 4; FCC press release, March 17, 1949, FCC Archives, Box 18, Folder 17, Presbyterian Historical Society, Philadelphia (hereafter FCC-PHS).
29. Paul Blanshard, *American Freedom and Catholic Power* (Boston, 1949).
30. "Meeting of Protestant Clergymen with Myron C. Taylor at Union Club, New York," October 20, 1947, Myron C. Taylor Papers, Box 3, Rare and Manuscript Collections, Carl A. Kroch Library, Cornell University, Ithaca, NY.
31. Harry Emerson Fosdick to Truman, October 22, 1951, Harry Emerson Fosdick Papers, Series IIA, Box 10, Folder 11, UTS.
32. "Red State vs. the Church: Communists' Attacks on Catholics Behind Iron Curtain Fit a Pattern," *New York Herald Tribune*, July 2, 1949, p. 1.
33. "Lovett Deplores Cardinal's Arrest in Budapest as a Sickening Sham," *NYT*, December 30, 1948, p. 1.
34. Truman, "Address on Foreign Economic Policy, Baylor University," March 6, 1947, *Public Papers of the Presidents of the United States: Harry S. Truman, 1947* (Washington, DC, 1963), p. 169.
35. Quoted in Spalding, *First Cold Warrior*, p. 212.
36. Emily S. Rosenberg, "U.S. Cultural History," in *American Cold War Strategy: Interpreting NSC 68*, ed. Ernest R. May (Boston, 1993), pp. 160–64; Stephanson, "Liberty or Death," pp. 81–100.
37. Memo for the record, October 26, 1948, Taylor Papers, Box 3, Cornell (emphasis in original); Harry Truman to Bess Truman, October 2, 1947, in *Dear Bess: The Letters from Harry to Bess Truman, 1910–1959*, ed. Robert H. Ferrell (New York, 1983), pp. 551–552.
38. H. Alexander Smith to Charles P. Taft, June 1, 1949, and enclosed copy of "Senate Resolution on Interpretation of North Atlantic Treaty," May 27, 1949, Box 16, Folder 5, FCC-PHS. On the remarkable course of Smith's faith-based political life, see William Inboden, *Religion and American Foreign Policy, 1945–1960: The Soul of Containment* (Cambridge, 2008), pp. 190–225.
39. Dulles, "Our Christian Witness in a World at War," 1939, Dulles Papers, Box 281, Princeton. For the best examinations of Dulles's faith, see Ronald W. Pruessen, *John Foster Dulles: The Road to Power* (New York, 1982); Mark G. Toulouse, *The Transformation of John Foster Dulles: From Prophet of Realism to Priest of Nationalism* (Macon, GA., 1985); and Inboden, *Religion and American Foreign Policy*, pp. 226–256.
40. Dulles address to the World Council of Churches, Amsterdam, August 24, 1948, Dulles Papers, Box 295, Princeton.
41. See John S. Nurser, *For All Peoples and All Nations: The Ecumenical Church and Human Rights* (Washington, DC., 2005), pp. 49–68.
42. Dulles address to the First Presbyterian Church of Watertown, August 28, 1949, Dulles Papers, Box 297, Princeton.
43. Schlesinger, Jr., *The Cycles of American History* (Boston, 1986), p. 394.
44. Richard H. Immerman, *John Foster Dulles: Piety, Pragmatism, and Power in U.S. Foreign Policy* (Wilmington, 1999), p. 93.
45. Quoted in Seth Jacobs, *America's Miracle Man in Vietnam: Ngo Dinh Diem, Religion, Race, and U.S. Intervention in Southeast Asia* (Durham, 2004), p. 10.
46. Seth Jacobs, "'Our System Demands the Supreme Being': The U.S. Religious Revival and the 'Diem Experiment,' 1954–55," *Diplomatic History*, 25 (2001), pp. 614–618.
47. Quoted in Preston, *War Council*, p. 120.
48. The best overview of the antiwar movement is Tom Wells, *The War Within: America's Battle Over Vietnam* (Berkeley, 1994). On religious opposition to the war, see Mitchell K. Hall, *Because of Their Faith: CALCAV and Religious Opposition to the Vietnam War* (New York, 1990); and Patricia McNeal, *Harder than War: Catholic Peacemaking in Twentieth-Century America* (New Brunswick, 1992), pp. 131–172.
49. See Simon Hall, *Peace and Freedom: The Civil Rights and Antiwar Movements of the 1960s* (Philadelphia, 2005); and Harvard Sitkoff, *King: Pilgrimage to the Mountaintop* (New York, 2008).

50. On Buddhist political activism in South Vietnam during the war, see Robert J. Topmiller, *The Lotus Unleashed: The Buddhist Peace Movement in South Vietnam* (Lexington, 2002). On the 1963 Buddhist crisis, see David Kaiser, *American Tragedy: Kennedy, Johnson, and the Origins of the Vietnam War* (Cambridge, MA, 2000), pp. 213–247; and Howard Jones, *Death of a Generation: How the Assassinations of Diem and JFK Prolonged the Vietnam War* (New York, 2003), pp. 247–267. For the 1966 Buddhist crisis, see Frances FitzGerald, *Fire in the Lake: The Vietnamese and the Americans in Vietnam* (Boston, 1972), pp. 345–364.
51. On the crisis of hegemony facing the United States in the late 1960s and early 1970s, see the essays in Fredrik Logevall and Andrew Preston (eds.), *Nixon in the World: American Foreign Relations, 1969–1977* (New York, 2008).
52. On the domestic origins of détente, see Jeremi Suri, *Power and Protest: Global Revolution and the Rise of Détente* (Cambridge, MA, 2003).
53. Henry Kissinger, *Diplomacy* (New York, 1994), pp. 743, 761.
54. Fredrik Logevall, "A Critique of Containment," *Diplomatic History*, 28 (2004), pp. 473–499.
55. David Domke and Kevin Coe, *The God Strategy: How Religion Became a Political Weapon in America* (New York, 2008), p. 61.
56. Noam Kochavi, "Idealpolitik in Disguise: Israel, Jewish Emigration from the Soviet Union, and the Nixon Administration, 1969–1974," *International History Review*, 29 (2007), pp. 550–572.
57. National Interreligious Task Force on Soviet Jewry, "Easter People Renew the Freedom Gift of God with Passover People," March 1974, Cushman Papers, Box 11, Duke.
58. On the premises of the Nixon-Kissinger grand strategy, see Raymond L. Garthoff, *Détente and Confrontation: American-Soviet Relations from Nixon to Reagan*, rev. ed. (Washington, 1994); Jussi M. Hanhimäki, *The Flawed Architect: Henry Kissinger and American Foreign Policy* (New York, 2004); and John Lewis Gaddis, *Strategies of Containment: A Critical Appraisal of American National Security Policy during the Cold War*, rev. ed. (New York, 2005), pp. 272–341.
59. On the enduring Democratic loyalties of American Jews during the era, see Joshua Michael Zeitz, "'If I am not for myself . . .': The American Jewish Establishment in the Aftermath of the Six Day War," *American Jewish History*, 88 (2000), pp. 253–286.
60. Henry M. Jackson statement to the Soviet Jewry Rally, New York, May 6, 1973, Henry M. Jackson Papers, Series 6, Box 10, Folder 23, Special Collections, Allen Library South, University of Washington, Seattle (hereafter UW).
61. Fosdick, "Introduction" in *Staying the Course: Henry M. Jackson and National Security* (Seattle: University of Washington Press, 1987), p. 9.
62. Jackson statement to the Jewish Community Council Dinner, Tucson, February 9, 1974, Series 6, Box 10, Folder 104, Jackson Papers, UW.
63. US Congress, House Committee on Foreign Affairs, Subcommittee on Europe, *Soviet Jewry. Hearings, Ninety-second Congress, first session. November 9 and 10, 1971* (Washington, DC., 1972), p. 92.
64. Jackson press release—statement made in Denver, March 31, 1973, Series 6, Box 10, Folder 13, Jackson Papers, UW.
65. *Congressional Record—Senate*, October 1, 1976.
66. "Nixon Asked to Plead for Soviet Jews," *NYT*, March 21, 1972, p. 20.
67. Drinan Report, "Conversations in Rumania and Israel," n.d., Robert F. Drinan Papers, Israel Series, Box 1, Burns Library, Boston College, Chestnut Hill, MA.
68. "World Council of Churches—A Case of Pinkeye," *Congressional Record—House*, December 18, 1975; "Will WCC Come Back to Reality?" *Washington Star*, January 3, 1976.
69. See especially William Martin, *With God On Our Side: The Rise of the Religious Right in America* (New York, 1996); Schulman, *Seventies*, pp. 193–252; David Farber, "The Torch Had Fallen" in Beth Bailey and David Farber (eds.), *America in the Seventies* (Lawrence, KS: University Press of Kansas, 2004), pp. 9–28; and Paul Boyer, "The Evangelical Resurgence in 1970s American Protestantism" in Bruce J. Schulman and Julian E. Zelizer (eds.), *Rightward Bound: Making America Conservative in the 1970s* (Cambridge, MA, 2008), pp. 34–43.

70. Ronald Reagan, acceptance speech at the Republican National Convention, "Time to Recapture Our Destiny," Detroit, July 17, 1980, http://www.reaganlibrary.com/reagan/speeches/speech.asp?spid=18 (accessed August 16, 2008).
71. Ronald Reagan, "Remarks at the Annual Convention of the National Association of Evangelicals in Orlando, Florida," March 8, 1983, *Public Papers of the Presidents of the United States: Ronald Reagan, 1983*, Book I (Washington, DC, 1984), pp. 359–360, 362, 363.
72. For this longer history, see Stephanson, "Liberty or Death."

8

God, the Bomb, and the Cold War

The Religious and Ethical Debate Over Nuclear Weapons, 1945–1990

PAUL S. BOYER

The atomic bombs that obliterated Hiroshima and Nagasaki in August 1945 marked not only a quantum leap in the technology of warfare, but also a radically new stage in an ongoing discourse over what ethical constraints warring nations should observe. This chapter examines the ethical and religious debates over nuclear weapons that unfolded from 1945 through more than four decades when the world's stock of nuclear weapons, vastly more lethal than the bombs of 1945, increased exponentially, and bomb delivery systems grew ever more sophisticated.

In some respects, this discourse transcends the Cold War and its technological corollary, the superpower nuclear arms race. Moral reflections on killing in wartime are as old as civilization, and, as we shall see, ethical uneasiness over Allied bombing practices in World War II arose well before Hiroshima. Further, in its distinctly "nuclear" form (now sometimes subsumed under the term "weapons of mass destruction"), the debate survived the collapse of the Soviet Union and indeed it continues still.[1]

Nevertheless, nuclear menace and the ethical issues it posed are inextricably linked to the Cold War (however defined or dated). Indeed, these realities bear directly on this book's central purpose: to seek fresh critical perspectives on that conflict. The framing essays by Anders Stephanson, Odd Arne Westad, Philip Mirowski, and Steven Belletto are all illuminated, and sometimes challenged, when the nuclear arms race and its accompanying ethical discourse enter the equation.

Down to 1962, Stephanson argues, the "coldwar" ideological construct (to use his coinage) gave Washington policymakers a compelling rationale for engineering America's emergence as a dominating global power. In this construct, the Soviet Union was demonized as the absolute, implacable enemy. Diplomacy was useless; only military confrontation and worldwide "containment" would suffice. Down to 1949, one might add, the crucial technological underpinning of this apocalyptic worldview was America's sole possession of the atomic bomb. The absolute weapon called forth the absolute enemy. Once the Soviets acquired the bomb, and on through the 1950s, the coldwar" imagery of absolute, ever deepening menace, centered in the Kremlin, continued to shape US nuclear-weapons policy, justifying the hydrogen-bomb project, mounting stockpiles of nuclear weapons, and Pentagon nuclear-warfighting scenarios. All this, in turn, spawned the ethical debates explored in this chapter.

After the Cuban Missile Crisis, Stephanson contends, the dawning realization that a nuclear war could actually destroy civilization played a key role (along with the Sino-Soviet split and the Vietnam War) in shattering the basic assumptions underlying Washington's apocalyptic rationale for endless confrontation. "[N]uclear weapons," he writes, "turn out to be very effective ideology killers." The present chapter somewhat complicates this component of Stephanson's argument. Firstly, from August 1945 onward, ethicists, religious figures, and cultural creators repeatedly emphasized the horrendous human toll and even global destruction that nuclear war could produce. This was hardly a realization that suddenly burst into general awareness in October 1962. (Though the missile crisis certainly did, as Stephanson writes, make the risks "chillingly concrete and explicit.") Secondly, from a broader cultural view, the caricature of the Soviet Union as a Grendel-like monster that underlay US policymakers' Cold War rationale for globalizing US power (in Stephanson's reading) did not vanish after 1962, despite talk of détente. Having deeply penetrated the national consciousness, it could not be turned off like a spigot. As this chapter argues, for millions of Americans the bogeyman view of Russia survived in full force beyond 1962. Hal Lindsey's bestselling 1970 Bible-prophecy popularization *The Late Great Planet Earth* found both nuclear war and Russia's destruction foretold in Scripture. If the apocalyptic worldview was, as Stephanson suggests, simply "lurking ideologically in the background" awaiting President Reagan's vivifying wand, it was a very powerful lurking reality. In fact, it loomed large in American thought through the 1960s and 1970s, constraining policymakers' options, fueling ethical debates, and influencing US strategic thinking despite the partial normalization of superpower relations and intermittent arms-control negotiations.

Key themes in Odd Arne Westad's chapter, too, gain salience when viewed from the perspective of the nuclear arms race and its accompanying ethical discourse. In urging a "pluralist" approach to Cold War studies, Westad quotes William Appleman Williams's inclusion of "anticipations of Utopia [and] messianic idea lism" among the factors shaping Cold War thinking. Both those Americans who repudiated US nuclear policies on moral grounds and dreamed of world peace, and those who saw nuclear war and Russia's destruction as the prophesied prelude to the Millennium, fall within this rubric, underscoring Westad's call for attention to the broader cultural and ideological currents that molded popular opinion and influenced public policy during the Cold War.

Westad's proposed "decentering" of Cold War studies perhaps does run the risk, as Stephanson cautions, of marginalizing the major players and their actions. Nevertheless, I do welcome Westad's more capacious understanding of the field, encompassing as it does the ethicists, religious figures, and cultural creators who populate this chapter. The multinational component of Westad's decentering project holds promise as well. For students of the Cold War's intellectual and cultural ramifications, no less than for those who focus on strategy, politics, and economics, a more comparative, transnational perspective is likely to yield valuable insights.

Philip Mirowski's discussion of the Cold War's effects on US intellectual life and academic disciplines, particularly the social sciences, is similarly deepened as one incorporates the nuclear reality. Even before the Cold War began (as I noted in *By the Bomb's Early Light* [1985]), the atomic bombing of Japan produced urgent calls for social science research on strategies for avoiding the nightmare of atomic annihilation that the physicists had bequeathed to humanity.

Mirowski's discussion of the multidisciplinary institutes founded to address Cold War-related issues also links directly to this chapter, since nuclear strategy centrally preoccupied several such centers. As strategists at the RAND Corporation and other think tanks spun out ever more rococo deterrence doctrines, Americans troubled by the ethical implications of nuclear weapons felt increasingly intimidated by the arcane theories and specialized vocabulary emanating from these hermetic enclaves. With their scientific pretensions, the think-tank strategists rarely addressed ethical considerations. In Lawrence Freedman's comprehensive history *The Evolution of Nuclear Strategy* (1981 and later editions), the words "ethics," "religion," and "morality" are absent from the index.

Finally, this chapter also bears directly on Steven Belletto's view of the Cold War as a "rhetorical field" and his discussion of the proto-postmodernist novelists and critics of the 1950s and 1960s who challenged the "reality" conjured up by the Cold War ideologues. The ethicists and cultural creators examined below shared in this subversive opposition to the dominant Cold War narrative, challenging the moralistic presumptions of official versions of America's global mission. No less than Salinger, Kerouac, and Bishop, the ethicists, religious figures, writers, and moviemakers who questioned the dominant nuclear discourse helped create those "cracks in the consensus culture" noted by Belletto. They, too, insisted that "what was being called reality by those in power was merely one way to view reality." Indeed, from their perspective, the power-wielders' version of reality was not only epistemologically dubious, but morally troubling.

As our understanding of the Cold War and the Nuclear Age expands, we are becoming aware that journalists, theologians, physicians, filmmakers, composers, novelists, poets, and TV producers, no less than politicians, diplomats, Pentagon planners, and think-tank strategists, have played a role in shaping the discourse.

Confronting Hiroshima and Nagasaki: The Debate Begins

The initial ethical debate over the atomic bomb focused on the immediate reality of two cities' destruction.[2] Most Americans, along with most editorial writers and other opinion molders, initially accepted President Truman's argument: the atomic bombs had ended the war and saved countless lives that would have been lost in a US invasion of Japan. Truman also cited the principle of retribution: the atomic bomb was just recompense for Japan's Pearl Harbor attack and wartime atrocities.

Despite wartime passions and the euphoria of victory, however, the atomic bombing of Japan stirred ethical unease. Truman's argument that Japan's misdeeds justified any American response, however disproportionate, challenged a long tradition of Christian ethical pronouncements on war, codified in the so-called just-war doctrine. This troubled critics at the time, and would provoke much soul-searching as the debate unfolded.

For pacifists, the atomic bomb simply underscored the moral repugnance of war itself. Harry Emerson Fosdick, pastor of New York's Riverside Church, in a protest letter he and other pacifists addressed to Truman, and in a nationally broadcast radio sermon reprinted in his *On Being Fit to Live With* (1946), highlighted the ethical problem in Truman's position: "When our self justifications are all in, every one of us is nonetheless horrified at the implications of what we did. Saying that Japan was guilty and deserved it, gets us nowhere. The mothers and babies of Hiroshima and Nagasaki did not deserve it." The "mass murder of whole metropolitan populations," Fosdick continued, violated "every moral standard the best conscience of the race ever has set up." The pacifistic Protestant magazine *Christian Century* echoed Fosdick in an August 29, 1945, editorial, "America's Atomic Atrocity." Truman's "brutal disregard of any principle of humanity," it charged, was morally "indefensible."[3]

Not only pacifists recoiled against Truman's action. The critics included future secretary of state John Foster Dulles. A Wall Street lawyer in 1945, Dulles was also a prominent Presbyterian layman and chair of the Commission on a Just and Durable Peace of the Federal Council of Churches (FCC), a liberal Protestant ecumenical body. On August 9, before news of the Nagasaki bombing,

Dulles and Methodist Bishop G. Bromley Oxnam, the FCC's president, issued a joint statement opposing further atomic bombings. "If we, a professedly Christian nation, feel morally free to use atomic energy in that way," they declared, "men elsewhere will accept that verdict . . . and the stage will be set for the sudden and final destruction of mankind." Reverend John Haynes Holmes of New York's nonsectarian Community Church went further, describing the atomic bombings as "the supreme atrocity of the ages; . . . a crime which we would instantly have recognized as such had Germany and not our own country been guilty of the act." Leading periodicals of major liberal Protestant denominations were equally outspoken.[4]

The first extended Protestant moral critique of the atomic bombing of Japan was a 1946 report by a twenty-two-member panel of the Federal Council of Churches chaired by Robert L. Calhoun, professor of historical theology at Yale. The panel, all from US Protestantism's liberal wing, included Reinhold Niebuhr, Henry P. Van Dusen, and John C. Bennett of New York's Union Theological Seminary and Roland H. Bainton and H. Richard Niebuhr of Yale, along with other theologians, philosophers, and church historians. "We would begin with an act of contrition," the panel said; "[T]he surprise bombings of Hiroshima and Nagasaki are morally indefensible. . . . We have sinned grievously against the laws of God and the people of Japan." As partial expiation, they urged aid to "the survivors of those two murdered cities."[5]

Roman Catholic commentators invoked just-war doctrine, with its roots in Catholic moral discourse. First formulated by St. Augustine and elaborated by successive theologians and popes, this doctrine by the twentieth century had been codified in a series of principles. To pass ethical muster, a war must be in a just cause and declared by a competent authority only after all alternatives have been explored, and the justice of the cause must outweigh the war's physical and moral cost. The doctrine also included standards for the *conduct* of war, and these proved particularly germane to the post-1945 debate. The combatants must pursue reconciliation and not commit needlessly destructive acts or impose extreme demands (e.g., "unconditional surrender") for a restoration of peace. The means employed must be proportionate to the ends sought and innocent civilians must never be targeted.[6] To be sure, these principles raised many interpretive questions, and they had been violated repeatedly, most recently in the attacks on civilians by all the belligerents in World War II, even before Hiroshima and Nagasaki. Nevertheless, just-war doctrine remained a touchstone in the post-1945 ethical debate over nuclear weapons.

Citing just-war principles, Catholic commentary on the atomic bombing of Japan was uniformly critical. Hiroshima and Nagasaki, said *Commonweal*, a weekly edited by lay Catholics, "are names for American guilt and shame." The Jesuit journal *America* concurred in a belated but vigorous 1947 essay by Edgar

R. Smothers, S.J. The argument that the atomic bomb shortened the war, Smothers wrote, "collapses against a primary principle of sound morality: no end—however good, however necessary—can justify the use of an evil means." By substituting "national pragmatism" for moral principle, he declared, "the United States committed an enormous wrong at Hiroshima, and duplicated it at Nagasaki."[7]

A few secular voices echoed this judgment, even in unlikely venues. In a 1948 essay in the professional journal *Air Affairs,* the cultural critic Lewis Mumford denounced the "genocide" initiated by the wartime firebombings of enemy cities and continued at Hiroshima and Nagasaki. The atomic bomb, wrote Mumford, simply "wrapped up this method of extermination in a neater, and possibly cheaper package."[8] This ethical revulsion found expression, too, in the *New Yorker* magazine, whose August 31, 1946, issue featured a single essay, "Hiroshima," by journalist John Hersey. The son of Protestant missionaries to China, Hersey made his moral perspective clear by abandoning distancing abstractions to focus on six individuals' experience of the bomb. (One was a Methodist minister, Kiyoshi Tanimoto, and another a German Jesuit missionary, heightening the impact for Western readers.) Soon published in book form, *Hiroshima* exerted a profound impact that rested in part on Hersey's unstated but unmistakable ethical position: the atomic bombing of Hiroshima was a moral catastrophe that must weigh on the national conscience. *Christian Century*'s reviewer found it "excruciating" to identify himself, "as every American must, with the hand that tripped the bomb release that sent compound tragedy hurtling into the unsuspecting city." Based on the letters he received, Hersey later wrote, *Hiroshima* "[gave] many readers their first sense of real guilt about the bomb."[9]

Despite the *Christian Century* reviewer's claim, not "every American" shared his sense of guilt. Indeed, the criticism by religious leaders and others did *not* reflect the typical response. Approval ratings for the atomic bombing of Japan stood at 85 percent in August 1945. In a poll later that year, 77 percent approved, of whom 23 percent said the United States "should have quickly used many more of the bombs before Japan had a chance to surrender."[10] For most Americans at the time, in short, the assertion that "the atomic bomb ended the war and saved American lives," coupled with Truman's retribution argument, appears to have provided sufficient moral justification for its use.

Crucial to America's postwar moral engagement with nuclear weapons is the fact that the atomic bomb first entered the national consciousness at the climax of a conflict that for most Americans had absolute moral clarity. If ever a war was justified, they believed, it was the one against Nazi Germany and its allies. Further, US leaders had defined this as a "total war," waged not only against the enemies' armies and military infrastructure, but against their entire societies. By this logic, cities became legitimate targets. The firestorm destruction of Dresden in February 1945 and Tokyo in March occurred months before Hiroshima. This, too, shaped postwar thinking about the ethical implications of nuclear weapons.

As Catholic and liberal Protestant leaders wrestled with the ethical challenge of the atomic bomb, some evangelical Protestant writers found a different meaning in the new weapon. The atomic bomb and even mass annihilation in a future nuclear holocaust, they proclaimed, were foretold in biblical prophecies. Many quoted II Peter 3:10: "[T]he heavens shall pass away with a great noise, and the elements shall melt with fervent heat, the earth also and the works that are therein shall be burned up." A 1945 country-music song, Fred Kirby's "Atomic Power," evoking images of "brimstone fire" raining down in a "day of judgment," linked the Bomb directly to end-time beliefs. Even President Truman, reflecting on the July 1945 Alamogordo test, mused: "It may be the fire destruction prophesied in the Euphrates Valley Era, after Noah and his fabulous Ark."[11]

Philadelphia's Donald Grey Barnhouse, a popular radio preacher, explored the bomb's prophetic significance in his *Eternity* magazine in December 1945. While some hoped international agreements would prevent atomic war, Barnhouse wrote, "It is already too late. The threads of inevitability have been caught in the mesh of the hidden gears of history and the divine plan moves toward the inexorable fulfillment." In "This Atomic Age and the Word of God," a tract of November 1945, Wilbur M. Smith of Chicago's Moody Bible Institute marshaled biblical passages that he claimed foretold the atomic bomb and future atomic destruction. Excerpted in *Reader's Digest* and expanded into book form in 1948, Smith's work provided a template for countless future prophecy popularizers.[12]

While some religious writers found atomic annihilation foretold in scripture, others turned to the larger moral implications of the nuclear future. The Cold War both complicated and added urgency to their reflections.

The Ethics of Atomic Weapons in the Early Cold War Era

Although Catholic and liberal Protestant leaders widely deplored America's atomic bombing of Japan, consensus faded when they turned to the postwar era. The 1946 Calhoun Commission report, after unanimously condemning the Hiroshima and Nagasaki bombing, split three ways over the larger issue of the moral status of atomic weapons. The first group, comprising religious pacifists, held that "the atomic bomb has revealed the impossibility of a just war, and has shown the necessity for repudiation of all support of war by the Church." A second group, while rejecting pacifism, categorically condemned the use of atomic weapons against civilians. The third group refused to condemn outright any future use of atomic bombs, noting that in some circumstances "the only effective restraint upon would-be aggressors might be fear of reprisals. . . . [T]his possible restraint should not be removed in advance."[13] Here, in embryo, emerged the debate over nuclear deterrence that would eventually dominate the discourse.

The most comprehensive early attempt to formulate a Catholic position on nuclear weapons was "The Ethics of Atomic War" (1947) by the Catholic Association for International Peace, a body chaired by a Jesuit theologian and including such well-known churchmen as John Courtney Murray, S. J., editor of the Jesuit *Theological Journal,* and Fulton J. Sheen, host of a popular radio program, *The Catholic Hour*. Under just-war doctrine, this report concluded, deliberately targeting civilians—whatever the weapon involved—was "simple murder." But like the Protestant Calhoun Commission, these Catholic moralists resisted a categorical denunciation of nuclear weapons and even qualified their condemnation of attacking civilians. If an enemy had already launched an atomic attack or was poised to invade, they suggested, atomic bombing enemy cities would be "morally defensible" provided the purpose was truly defensive and the bombs did not actually *target* civilians, but the enemy's "military productive capacity." Millions might die, the report conceded, but as an unintended side-effect, not a primary objective, and thus the deaths would be "outweighed by the good obtained, the salvation of the innocent country." Reason, not emotion, the authors insisted, must guide such calculations.[14]

As the 1940s ended, the ethical discussion about nuclear weapons faded. In October 1949, *Christian Century* observed: "The churches have been nibbling at the problem of the morality of atomic warfare . . . ever since Hiroshima, and so far they have gotten exactly nowhere. Perplexed by doubts and divided in mind, . . . they have reached a tacit understanding . . . to blanket in silence this most crucial of all the political issues affecting the fate of mankind."[15]

The reasons seem clear. 1950 found the Cold War in full swing. Communists ruled in China; the Russians had tested an atomic bomb; the Korean War was underway (and going badly); government and media voices warned of possible nuclear war with the Soviets and urgently called for US atomic supremacy. Responding to these alarms, Americans overwhelmingly supported President Truman's January 1950 decision to build the hydrogen bomb, a thousand times more powerful than the Hiroshima bomb. In an August 1950 poll, 28 percent of Americans favored using atomic bombs in Korea. In December 1950, *U.S. News* noted a "wave of demand" for atomic bombing the Chinese troops who had entered the war in massive numbers a few weeks earlier. By November 1951, as the war dragged on, 51 percent supported atomic bombing "military targets." A country song of the day, "When That Hell Bomb Falls," mingled images of nuclear destruction with the wish that God would "lend a helping hand" in Korea.[16]

While the earliest postwar ethical discussion of future atomic war spoke only generically of "enemies" and "would-be aggressors," Russia soon replaced such abstractions, as Cold War alarms and the ethical debate over nuclear weapons gradually converged. Some even advocated a preemptive nuclear strike on Russia, to thwart the spread of atheistic communism. In "Advice to Joe" (1951), country singer Roy Acuff predicted that Stalin would regret his aggressions when Moscow lay in ashes. In *The Atomic Bomb and the End of the World* (1954), the evangelist Hyman Appelman, a Jewish Christian, noted the strength of this view, while rejecting it: "They tell us that . . . America ought to bomb Russia right now, and stop the Communistic forces in a preventive war. No! A thousand times, No! God grant that America may never be the aggressor. . . . I had rather see ten Pearl Harbors than have America bomb any enemy country first."[17]

In this charged political environment, the few religious leaders who addressed the issue (apart from Quakers and other pacifists) mainly defended stockpiling and possibly using nuclear weapons. *The Christian Conscience and Weapons of Mass Destruction*, the 1950 report of yet another Federal Council of Churches commission, illustrates the shift. The body now included a member of the US Atomic Energy Commission and other laymen identified with Washington's nuclear weapons program. While carryover members from the earlier Calhoun Commission included Reinhold Niebuhr, now a militant Cold Warrior, several prominent pacifists were dropped.

The Christian Conscience and Weapons of Mass Destruction contained eloquent passages deploring war but, unlike the Calhoun Commission, expressed no guilt for the atomic bombing of Japan. While nuclear weapons raised ethical issues of "terrible dimensions," the commission found, these were not of "an absolutely different moral category" from general questions regarding the use of violence. Ethically, the motive, not the weapon, is the key consideration, and one cannot "draw this moral line in advance, apart from all the actual circumstances." In effect, the report endorsed the Truman Administration's defense of atomic and thermonuclear bombs as legitimate weapons of war:

> For the United States to abandon its atomic weapons, or to give the impression that they would not be used, would leave the non-Communist world with totally inadequate defense. For Christians to advocate such a policy would be for them to share responsibility for the worldwide tyranny that might result. . . . American military strength, which must include atomic weapons as long as any other nation may possess them, is an essential factor in the possibility of preventing both world war and tyranny. If atomic weapons or other weapons of parallel destructiveness are used against us or our friends in Europe or Asia, we believe that it

> could be justifiable for our government to use them in retaliation with all possible restraint.

This insistence on the moral right of nuclear retaliation, observed Robert Calhoun in dissent, while defensible on "political and cultural grounds," could "scarcely be regarded as distinctly Christian." The only other dissenter, Georgia Harkness, a theologian at a Methodist seminary in Chicago, dismissed talk of "[nuclear] retaliation with all possible restraint" as oxymoronic.[18]

By the early 1950s, the few Roman Catholic pronouncements on nuclear weapons also generally supported their use in certain circumstances. Edmund A. Walsh, S.J. of Georgetown University even justified a preemptive nuclear strike if a nation had "sound reason to believe" an enemy attack was imminent: "Neither reason nor theology nor morals requires men or nations to commit suicide by requiring that we must await the first blow," he wrote. Just-war doctrine offered no basis for a categorical condemnation of nuclear weapons, agreed Francis J. Connell, dean of theology at Catholic University.[19]

After declining during the Cold War's intense early stage, ethical commentary on nuclear weapons revived in the later 1950s and early 1960s, in both frequency and critical bite. This upsurge paralleled a broader resurgence of political activism and cultural attention to nuclear issues. Beginning with the 1954 US H-bomb tests that spread radioactivity across the South Pacific, public attention to the nuclear threat intensified, focused now not only on nuclear war, but on deadly radioactive fallout. As a test-ban movement gained momentum, novelists, science-fiction writers, magazine editors, moviemakers, and TV producers addressed these issues.[20]

In this climate, the ethical debate resumed, including books with such titles as *War and the Christian Conscience, War and Christianity Today, God and the H-Bomb, Morality and Modern Warfare,* and *Morals and Missiles*. Scores of articles on this theme appeared in theological and philosophical journals and in the secular press.[21] This renewed ethical scrutiny included Pope John XXIII's encyclical *Pacem in Terris* (1963) with its eloquent description of nuclear fear and the hazards of nuclear testing; its urgent call for disarmament; and its unequivocal pronouncement: "Nuclear weapons must be banned." Vatican II, the early 1960s' council of Catholic bishops, reinforced the point, describing the nuclear arms race as "one of the greatest curses" confronting humanity, "an act of aggression against the poor and a folly which does not provide the security it promises."[22]

In the early 1960s the Trappist monk Thomas Merton, author of *The Seven-Storey Mountain* (1948), a spiritual autobiography, called nuclear weapons "the most crucial moral and religious problem in twenty centuries of [Christian] history." Theologians who justified the nuclear arms race, thundered Merton, were contributing to

> the slow corruption of the Christian ethical sense by . . . juggling with moral clichés devoid of serious content, and the weakening of genuine human compassion. The scandalous consequences of this has been not only confusion, inertia, indecision, and even culpable silence on the part of many Christian spokesmen, but worse still, some Christian leaders have actively joined in the cold war and . . . bless nuclear war as a holy and apocalyptic crusade. . . . It is absurd and immoral to pretend that Christendom can be defended by the H-bomb. . . . The immediate responsibility of Christians is to contribute whatever they can to an atmosphere of sanity and trust in which negotiation and disarmament may eventually become feasible.[23]

This surge of religious commentary faded by the mid-1960s, again paralleling a larger decline in nuclear awareness after the 1963 Limited Nuclear Test Ban Treaty halted the atmospheric tests that had stirred such fear. This treaty also offered hope of further negotiations and an easing of US-Soviet tensions. With these developments, and the emergence of other urgent issues, especially the Vietnam War, ethicists' attention to nuclear weapons somewhat diminished.[24]

The Dilemma of Deterrence

The muted post-1963 moral discourse about nuclear weapons also reflected the fact that *deterrence* was now America's stated nuclear strategy.[25] If the US nuclear buildup had challenged ethicists and theologians in the fraught climate of the early Cold War, the morality of threatening nuclear retaliation as a means of deterring attack and thereby *preventing* nuclear war proved still more troubling.

Bernard Brodie, a Yale political scientist, formulated an embryonic version of deterrence theory in *The Absolute Weapon: Atomic Power and World Order* (1946), and the early religious debate over deterrence dates from this period. The pacifist A. J. Muste criticized the Calhoun Commission members who defended stockpiling atomic bombs for deterrent purposes. Talk of preventing atomic war by threatening atomic reprisal, wrote Muste, had "an ugly and sinister sound, especially when it comes from Christian lips." Religious leaders justifying this position, he asserted, were "handing a blank check to the militarists"; their ultimate guilt could be "far greater than that which rests upon the Nazis."[26]

Albert Wohlstetter of the RAND Corporation, an influential California think tank with close ties to the Pentagon, elaborated deterrence theory in a 1954 study later published as "The Delicate Balance of Terror." But it was in the 1960s, during Robert McNamara's tenure as secretary of defense, that deterrence became the cornerstone of US nuclear strategy. "The major mission of the

Strategic Retaliatory Forces," McNamara told the House Armed Services Committee in 1963, "is to deter war by their capability to destroy the enemy's war-making potential, including not only his nuclear strike forces and military installations, but also his urban society, if necessary." In the language of nuclear strategy, this meant that the US response would include both a *counterforce* attack on the Soviet military and, "if necessary," a *countervalue* attack against major cities.[27]

According to this doctrine, the sole function of America's nuclear arsenal was to deter a nuclear attack, or, as McNamara testified in 1968, to maintain a nuclear capability that could absorb a Soviet assault and still inflict "Assured Destruction" on the attacker. Fear of such retaliation, argued deterrence theorists, would inhibit Russia from ever launching a nuclear strike, since its own society would be destroyed in consequence.[28] In the mirror-image world of nuclear strategy, deterrence theory made sense for both sides—as the Soviets acknowledged in 1972 by signing the Anti-Ballistic Missile (ABM) Treaty, by which each side limited itself to two missile-defense installations (later reduced to one), in effect opening itself to annihilation should it ever be so insane as to initiate a nuclear attack.

Deterrence doctrine vastly complicated the ethical issues surrounding nuclear weapons. No longer was it sufficient or even relevant simply to denounce nuclear war, since deterrence theorists themselves proclaimed preventing such a war as their only purpose. But what if deterrence failed? Would Washington indeed unleash the promised retaliation, possibly killing millions? McNamara insisted on America's "unwavering will" to do just that. Presidential adviser Walt Rostow in 1964 declared: "Credible deterrence in the nuclear age lies in being prepared to face the consequences if deterrence fails . . . up to and including all-out nuclear war."[29]

Threatening and preparing for mass slaughter, even as a preventive strategy, posed agonizing ethical problems, but a few theologians did endorse deterrence doctrine. Reinhold Niebuhr, now a tough-minded Cold War "realist," declared in 1959: "To serve peace we must threaten war, without blinking the fact that the threat may be a factor in precipitating war."[30] However, many theologians and ethicists, not only from the historic peace churches (Quaker, Mennonite, Brethren) but also Roman Catholics and mainstream Protestants, rejected a strategy predicated on threats to annihilate an entire society. In 1965, citing just-war doctrine, Vatican II declared: "Any act of war aimed indiscriminately at the destruction of entire cities . . . along with their population is a crime against God and man himself. It merits unequivocal and unhesitating condemnation." What, then, could one say of a strategy founded on proclaiming one's readiness to commit such an act if deterrence failed? A writer in *Commonweal* in 1971 found the whole concept "obscene." What if human error or a technical malfunction triggered an attack or created the mistaken impression that one was underway? Could a single madman bring on the ultimate cataclysm, as Stanley Kubrick (a student of deterrence theory) suggested in his 1964 film *Dr. Strangelove*? Some found retaliatory threats against Russian civilians especially repugnant, since they had so little voice in Moscow's actions.[31]

In *Nuclear Policy for War and Peace* (1960), Thomas E. Murray Jr., a former member of the US Atomic Energy Commission and prominent Catholic layman, passionately rejected deterrence theory. America's massive nuclear arsenal, built in the name of deterrence, he wrote, "has grown increasingly offensive to the moral conscience." The effort to end "the dominion of terror" these weapons had created, Murray wrote, "is not alien to the purposes of God."[32]

But ethical challenges to countervalue deterrence could be problematic. In a 1959 essay reaffirming Catholic just-war doctrine amid rising antinuclear protests, John Courtney Murray condemned the "atrocities of Hiroshima and Nagasaki" and echoed Pope Pius XII in rejecting any nuclear strategy that deliberately targeted civilians. But Father Murray also criticized the absolutist position "that all use of atomic weapons in war is, somehow, in principle, evil." Challenging "the vulgar pacifism . . . so common today," he insisted: "There are greater evils than the physical death and destruction wrought in war." With the 1956 Soviet invasion of Hungary fresh in memory, Murray insisted that nuclear retaliation to aggression "remains possible and may prove to be necessary," and "since nuclear war may be a necessity, it must be made a possibility." In this spirit, he called for a sustained effort—technological, strategic, and ethical—to bring nuclear weapons under the moral umbrella of just-war doctrine. "To say that the possibility of limited [nuclear] war cannot be created by intelligence and energy, under the direction of a moral imperative, is to succumb to some sort of determinism in human history." While conceding that America's nuclear-weapons program and targeting strategies were "to a considerable extent hidden from the public knowledge," Murray nevertheless saw hope that some forms of nuclear war could be made ethically defensible. Meanwhile, he urged pursuit of the Church's historic role: "[T]o condemn war as evil, to limit the evils it entails, and to humanize its conduct as far as possible."[33]

Paul Ramsey, a Methodist layman and religion professor at Princeton, similarly advocated a "limited nuclear war" alternative to countervalue deterrence. In his books *War and the Christian Conscience* (1961) and *The Just War* (1968), Ramsey rejected as immoral a doctrine based on multi-megaton bombs and the threat of mass civilian slaughter, arguing instead for a deterrence strategy involving "rational nuclear armaments"—which he defined as bombs in the range of the one that obliterated Hiroshima, or smaller—targeting not cities but military installations. "[T]he collateral civilian damage" could be massive, he conceded, but since civilians had not been deliberately targeted, such an attack (if deterrence failed) would meet just-war criteria.[34]

Ramsey's qualified defense of a limited nuclear warfighting capability pleased Pentagon strategists unhappy with countervalue deterrence theory, predicated as it was on a massive spasm of retaliatory destruction if deterrence failed. As early as 1957, Henry Kissinger in *Nuclear Weapons and Foreign Policy* had criticized John Foster Dulles's "massive retaliation" threat as unconvincing and called for an actual nuclear warfighting capability encompassing a range of weapons. Many Pentagon planners and think-tank strategists never accepted the operational implications of deterrence theory, and proposals for counterforce nuclear weapons and delivery systems continued to proliferate. Even after McNamara endorsed deterrence doctrine, the Pentagon's nuclear targeting system, SIOP (Single Integrated Operational Plan), targeted Soviet military sites and missile bases, reflecting not only countervalue deterrence principles but also the desire to prevail in an actual nuclear war. In the early 1970s, when Defense Secretary James Schlesinger advocated an expanded counterforce strategy labeled "Flexible Response," he and other officials, including Fred C. Iklé, head of the Arms Control and Disarmament Agency, cited the ethical arguments against countercity deterrence advanced by religious writers like John Courtney Murray and Paul Ramsey. Enlarging US strategic doctrine beyond mere deterrence, Schlesinger called for a range of strategic weapons and targeting options to convince Moscow of America's determination to win a nuclear war, should one occur.[35] This underscored the problem with the counterforce approach: it could plausibly be seen as a strategy not for preventing, but for actually *fighting*, a nuclear war. Yet its proponents presented it as a response to the ethicists' critique of deterrence doctrine!

A notable intervention in this debate was *Just and Unjust Wars: A Moral Argument with Historical Illustrations* (1977) by the Harvard political theorist Michael Walzer. A onetime Vietnam War protester, Walzer offered reflections on ethics and war, with examples from ancient Greece through Vietnam. In the section on nuclear issues, after a brief but incisive critique of Truman's rationale for the atomic bombing of Hiroshima and Nagasaki, Walzer turned to deterrence theory. Like most ethical theorists, he found it morally unacceptable—indeed "murderous" and criminal. To deter an attack by threatening to exterminate masses of innocent people, he suggested, is like deterring murder by threatening to kill a murderer's family and friends. No one may actually *want* to kill the civilians who would die in a retaliatory attack if deterrence failed, yet "[t]hat is the stated policy of our government; and thousands of men, trained in the techniques of mass destruction and drilled in instant obedience, stand ready to carry it out. And from the perspective of morality, the readiness is all."[36]

Yet Walzer saw no short-term alternative. The prospect of mutual destruction in a nuclear war, he wrote,

> has faced mankind since 1945. . . . Deterrence is a way of coping with that condition, and though it is a bad way, there may well be no other that is practical in a world of sovereign and suspicious states. We threaten evil in order not to do it, and the doing of it would be so terrible that the threat seems in comparison to be morally defensible. . . . [N]uclear weapons are politically and militarily unusable only because and insofar as we can plausibly threaten to use them in some ultimate way. And it is immoral to make threats of that kind.[37]

Or, as Woody Allen mused: "Now more than anytime in history, mankind faces a crossroad. One path leads to despair and utter hopelessness. The other, to total extinction. Let us pray we have the wisdom to choose correctly."

Walzer rejected the argument of those who tried to escape the paradox of deterrence by embracing a counterforce strategy limiting the retaliation to military targets. By suggesting that nuclear war might be "winnable," he contended, such a strategy actually increased its likelihood. And even an attack on "military targets" could produce civilian casualties grotesquely disproportionate to any legitimate purpose. (President Truman, after all, announcing the Hiroshima bombing, had called the city a "military base," and by the 1960s the Pentagon had identified more than 40,000 "military targets" across the Soviet Union and sixty in Moscow alone.[38]) Further, in an actual superpower nuclear exchange, even an initial measured response would almost certainly escalate to all-out confrontation.

Walzer sharply criticized Paul Ramsey's argument for a counterforce strategy (permissible on just-war grounds) that would nevertheless cause such heavy "collateral" civilian casualties as to retain the deterrent value of the present immoral strategy. Commented Walzer:

> [L]ike other deterrent theorists, [Ramsey wants] to prevent nuclear attack by threatening to kill very large numbers of innocent civilians, but unlike other deterrent theorists, he expects to kill these people without aiming at them. That may be a matter of some moral significance, but it does not seem significant enough to serve as the cornerstone of a justified deterrent. . . . Surely anyone designing such a strategy must accept moral responsibility for the effects on which he is so radically dependent.[39]

Moral casuistry offered no escape from the ethical problems with deterrence. "[T]he reason for our hesitancy and self-doubt," concluded Walzer, "is the monstrous immorality that our policy contemplates, an immorality we can never hope to square with our understanding of justice in war. Nuclear weapons explode the theory of just war." Yet despite Cold War suspicions, Walzer tentatively suggested, alternatives to Wohlstetter's "delicate balance of terror" might be devised. Because "[n]uclear war is and will remain morally unacceptable . . ., we must seek out ways to prevent it," he wrote, "and because deterrence is a bad way, we must seek out others. . . . [T]he readiness to murder is balanced, or should be, by the readiness not to murder, not to threaten murder, as soon as alternative ways to peace can be found." What might these be? Walzer avoided this crucial question. "It is not my purpose here to suggest what the alternatives might look like," he concluded.[40]

The increasingly arcane nature of nuclear strategy further inhibited ethical discourse. In the early postwar years, as historian Gregg Herken and others have shown, "nuclear strategy" was fairly simple (if unnerving): build more bombs, identify more targets.[41] As deterrence theory in its various permutations evolved, however, strategic analysis became a quasi-scientific pursuit with its own forbidding vocabulary and theoretical constructs, dominated by Pentagon specialists and civilian theorists based at universities or think tanks such as the RAND Corporation. Conveying "the impression of holding membership in a closed club" (as a *New Yorker* writer observed in 1971), these strategists moved in their own intellectual orbit. One critic, calling them "the new priesthood," noted that even in academia, with its tradition of open inquiry, "they enjoy a privileged area of argument and can always retreat to a sanctuary of secret dataland."[42] As nuclear strategy grew more rarified, religious leaders and ethicists proved reluctant to offer judgments that might appear hopelessly naïve or ill-informed.

For Americans existing in the shadow of the bomb, deterrence doctrine offered hope that the nuclear arms race would soon reach a point of stasis. Once each side possessed a secure retaliatory capability, the race would end in a tie. Nuclear warheads in their thousands would remain, but they would simply rest in their silos, bombers, and submarine bays, endlessly deterring. Thanks to deterrence theory (and an easing of Cold War tensions), editorialized *Business Week* in 1968, "living with the atomic bomb has turned out to be less frightening than it once seemed."[43] The continued build-up of each side's nuclear arsenals—summed up in the phrase "overkill"—belied such confidence, but the hope remained.

Nuclear Fears, Russia's Fate, and Bible Prophecy

While ethicists and theologians struggled with deterrence theory, prophecy believers continued to find nuclear war foretold in the Bible. "The dread reality of guided missiles and nuclear weapons," wrote one in 1956, had stimulated interest in prophecy. At a 1956 prophecy conference, a speaker quoted a passage from Zechariah describing the fate of combatants in a future war: "Their flesh shall consume away while they stand upon their feet, and their eyes shall consume away in their holes, and their tongue shall consume away in their mouths." Ever-proliferating nuclear weapons, he went on, "have made real this passage of Scripture." *The God of the Atom,* a film in Moody Bible Institute's "Sermons from Science" series, offered a dollop of physics, described the effects of nuclear war, and concluded by asserting that Bible prophecy foretold the entire process.[44]

Cold War prophecy popularizers also insisted that a passage in Ezekiel prophesying the obliteration of the armies of "Gog," a northern kingdom that attacks Israel, must refer to Russia. Via radio, television, paperback books, and local pulpits, prophecy interpreters proclaimed Russia's foreordained annihilation, perhaps in a nuclear World War III.[45]

Nuclear war and Russia's obliteration loom large in Hal Lindsey's *The Late Great Planet Earth* (1970), a popularization of Bible prophecy that became *the* nonfiction bestseller of the 1970s. Assuming that all scriptural allusions to fiery destruction and mass suffering foreshadowed nuclear war, Lindsey relentlessly turned the Bible into a manual of atomic-age combat: Zechariah's image of human flesh "consuming away" portrays "exactly what happens to those who are in a thermonuclear blast"; the falling stars and stinging locusts of Revelation are warheads fired from space platforms and helicopters spraying nerve gas; the scorching heat and bodily sores mentioned in Revelation describe the blast and radiation effects observed at Hiroshima and Nagasaki. Combining Ezekiel's account of Gog's destruction and biblical prophecies of "fire and brimstone," Lindsey also confidently predicted Russia's "utter and complete decimation" in the near future, probably in "a nuclear exchange of ballistic missiles."[46]

Commenting on *The Late Great Planet Earth,* Michael Barkun has observed: "As the exclamation points march forward, it becomes clear that Lindsey finds these prospects enormously attractive. His prose pants with scarcely a word of sympathy for the hundreds of millions killed or maimed. For him, the [fulfillment of prophecy] . . . is grand, cosmic theatre, the ultimate Hollywood spectacle."[47]

To be sure, some evangelicals rejected Lindsey's lurid end-time scenario. One ridiculed it as "a farrago of nonsense."[48] Nevertheless, Lindsey and other televangelists and paperback writers who promulgated this interpretation unquestionably influenced American views of the nuclear arms race and the Cold War, with direct ethical implications: if nuclear war and Russia's annihilation are God's will, then conventional moral assessment becomes irrelevant, and efforts to promote disarmament or ease Cold War tensions are not only pointless, but direct challenges to the divine plan.

The Early 1980s: The Ethical Debate Revives

The early 1980s brought a fresh surge of ethical commentary on nuclear weapons. As before, this cycle reflected broader political and cultural trends. Although President Jimmy Carter (1977–81) was urging the elimination of nuclear weapons, that hope quickly faded. By the late 1970s the Americans and the Soviets had deployed some 50,000 nuclear weapons with their accompanying delivery systems, including MIRVs (multiple independently targetable reentry vehicles)—ballistic missiles fitted with up to ten warheads. In 1979, responding to Soviet missile deployments thought to threaten America's second-strike capability, Carter approved a basing system for the new MX ("Peacekeeper") missiles that involved shuttling 200 of them among 4,600 launch sites in the West. (Each MX's ten warheads had a 300-kiloton yield—twenty times that of the Hiroshima bomb.)[49]

In 1979, too, Carter signed a presidential directive (PD-59) authorizing a counterforce targeting strategy (echoing James Schlesinger's "Flexible Response" doctrine) aimed at Russia's political/military nerve centers, nuclear and conventional forces, and industrial complexes. While Defense Secretary Harold Brown defined the purpose as strictly deterrence, some charged that PD-59 also sought a US nuclear war-fighting capacity. Also in 1979, reacting to Moscow's invasion of Afghanistan and to pressure from a hawkish lobby called the Committee on the Present Danger, Carter withdrew a US-Soviet arms-control treaty, SALT II, from the Senate.[50] Amid these developments, nuclear anxieties intensified.

Fear escalated as Ronald Reagan assumed the presidency. The early Reagan years saw major military-spending increases, including nuclear-weapons appropriations. As Secretary of State Al Haig mused about a nuclear response if the Soviets invaded Western Europe, the administration promoted civil-defense planning. Addressing an evangelical gathering, Reagan labeled the Soviet Union "the focus of evil in the modern world."[51]

Amid deepening anxiety, antinuclear activists called for a mutual, verifiable freeze on nuclear-weapons development and deployment while disarmament talks proceeded. In 1982, as the campaign attracted broad support and generated mass rallies, several states passed nuclear-freeze referenda and more than 130 Congress members endorsed the cause.[52] Rising antinuclear sentiment found expression in popular culture, including movies, novels, and TV programs. In the 1983 film *WarGames,* a teenage computer geek (Matthew Broderick) nearly triggers a thermonuclear war when he accidentally hacks into the Air Force's SIOP computer. In William Prochnau's novel *Trinity's Child* (1983), Moscow answers an unidentified nuclear missile strike on a Russian city with a limited nuclear attack on America, confronting US officials with the agonizing choice of standing down or launching an all-out nuclear counterattack—the classic dilemma of deterrence doctrine. In *The Day After* (1984), a widely viewed ABC television special, the Soviets launch a nuclear attack on the United States after a confrontation in Europe spirals out of control.[53]

In this climate, ethical opposition to nuclear weapons again found its voice. In 1982, Rabbi Alexander Schindler, head of the Union of American Hebrew Congregations, predicted: "Nuclear disarmament is going to become the central moral issue of the '80s, just as Viet Nam [*sic*] was in the '60s." After years of relative silence, church bodies once more denounced the nuclear arms race. Even among evangelicals, generally supportive of Reagan, dissident voices were heard. Ronald Sider, founder of Evangelicals for Social Action, made the biblical case against nuclear weapons in a 1982 book. Revivalist Billy Graham, who in the 1950s had exploited nuclear terror to win converts, now urged Christians to work for peace.[54]

Books and articles, conferences, symposia, and study commissions explored the morality of the nuclear arms race. Secular periodicals joined the debate. Both the liberal *New Republic* and the conservative *National Review* devoted special issues to the topic.[55] A new attentiveness to nuclear matters arose in local churches, on college campuses, and in grassroots community groups.

In *The Fate of the Earth* (1982), a secular version of the prophecy writers' apocalyptic scenario, journalist Jonathan Schell envisioned a post–nuclear war world devoid of human life—"A Republic of Insects and Grass." Nuclear weapons "grew out of history, yet they threaten to end history," he wrote; "[M]ade by men, . . . they threaten to annihilate man." After documenting the destructive potential of the superpowers' nuclear arsenals, Schell called for a tripartite moral reformation: recovery of "the ancient principle of the sacredness of human life"; embrace of "the ecological principle [of] respect for the earth"; and "respect for God or nature, or whatever one chooses to call the universal dust that made, or became, us." Even the *possibility* of a world-destroying holocaust, Schell argued, demanded a radical response: world government. Americans must renounce not only deterrence doctrine and nuclear weapons, but national sovereignty itself. Reviewers praised Schell's harrowing vision of nuclear war's consequences, but skeptics dismissed his proposed solution as "wildly Utopian" or at least as evidence of "political naïveté."[56]

In *The Abolition* (1984), Schell conceded the unlikelihood of achieving world government anytime soon, and even endorsed a form of deterrence: in a nuclear-free world, the *knowledge* that other nations could build nuclear weapons would act as a "weaponless deterrence." But he adamantly insisted on the ethical unacceptability of the current situation: "[I]mmorality is inherent in the very possession of tens of thousands of nuclear weapons, whatever the doctrine. There is no conceivable way that these can be used without mass slaughter on an incalculable scale, and no theoretical sophistry can eliminate this basic fact."[57]

However implausible its political prescriptions, Schell's jeremiad remains significant as a *cri de coeur* against the existential and moral consequences of a strategic doctrine requiring multiplied thousands of nuclear weapons capable of destroying human life many times over. "Through the balance of terror," he wrote, "we all . . . hold a dagger to the hearts of those nearest and dearest to us as well as . . . those far away." In rejecting nuclear weapons, he went on, "we resolve to escape this pervasive corruption of our lives. We resolve to clear the air of the smell of burning flesh."[58] The prophecy believers foresaw a new age through divine intervention; Schell, in a scarcely less apocalyptic mode, anticipated it through a mass conversion, as people everywhere embraced the vision of a nuclear-free world. His very title, *The Abolition,* evoked the religiously inspired reform movement that had earlier battled another great evil, slavery.

Some went beyond rallies and pronouncements to civil disobedience. In 1980 the Berrigan brothers, Daniel and Philip, Catholic priests and veteran antiwar activists, formed the Plowshares Movement, evoking the biblical passage "They shall beat their swords into plowshares" (Isaiah 2:4). Entering a Pennsylvania General Electric plant that manufactured nuclear-missile components, they and six others symbolically hammered on some nose cones, and were arrested and imprisoned. (A 1982 film starring Martin Sheen told the story.) Leroy Matthiesen, the Catholic bishop of Amarillo, Texas, home of a hydrogen-bomb assembly facility, addressed a plea to its employees: "We urge individuals involved in the production and stockpiling of nuclear bombs to consider what they are doing, to resign from such activities, and to seek employment in peaceful pursuits." Seattle's Catholic bishop, Raymond Hunthausen, announced that he was withholding half of his federal income taxes to protest the US nuclear-weapons stockpile.[59]

In 1983 came *The Challenge of Peace,* a 103-page pastoral letter by the American Catholic bishops, issued after exhaustive study and consultations with Pope John Paul II, Secretary of Defense Caspar Weinberger, National Security Adviser William Clark, and others. The principal author, Reverend J. Bryan Hehir, a Harvard Divinity School PhD., headed the Social Development and World Peace department at the US Catholic bishops' Washington headquarters. Accessibly written and issued as an inexpensive paperback, *The Challenge of Peace* was widely studied in Catholic parishes and attracted broad media attention.[60]

Building on scriptural passages, just-war doctrine, and papal pronouncements, the bishops unequivocally condemned the nuclear arms race and called for redoubled effort to reduce the physical and moral risks of nuclear war. "Under no circumstances," they declared, echoing Vatican II, "may nuclear weapons or other instruments of mass slaughter be used for the purpose of destroying population centers or other predominately civilian targets." Any first use of nuclear weapons, even to repel a Russian invasion of Western Europe, they judged "morally unjustifiable." As for a nuclear deterrent confined to military targets (as earlier advocated by John Courtney Murray and Paul Ramsey), they professed themselves "highly skeptical." Even a war "defined as limited by strategists," they noted, could produce untold civilian casualties.[61]

As for deterrence doctrine as a whole, the bishops speculated that it had become "the driving force in the superpower arms race." Rehearsing the ethical case against threatening a sinful act, even for a moral reason, they echoed Walzer in giving nuclear deterrence only "a strictly conditional moral acceptance," tolerable only if coupled with serious disarmament efforts. After suggesting specific steps toward this goal, including a negotiated freeze on developing or deploying more nuclear weapons, they concluded by urging a dramatic initiative: a UN-sponsored "international task force for peace; . . . with membership open to every nation, . . . with one sole agenda: the creation of a world that will one day be safe from war." "Let us have the courage to believe in the bright future and in a God who wills it for us," the bishops concluded, "not a perfect world, but a better one. The perfect world, we Christians believe, is beyond the horizon, in an endless eternity where God will be all in all. But a better world is here for human hands and hearts and minds to make."[62]

This early 1980s ethical discourse proved short-lived. In March 1983, responding to the freeze campaign, the forthcoming Catholic bishops' statement and other pronouncements by religious bodies, and the wave of cultural productions expressing widespread nuclear fears, President Reagan in a televised address declared that he shared the concerns of the antinuclear movement. But instead of endorsing the nuclear freeze, Reagan proposed a Strategic Defense Initiative (SDI) to develop a missile-defense system to render America invulnerable to attack. Critics quickly noted that missile defense contradicted deterrence doctrine and that such a system would free the United States to launch a nuclear first strike without fear of retaliation. But whatever its strategic implications or technological hurdles, Reagan's speech served its immediate political purpose. As Americans debated SDI, the freeze campaign faded, and with it this renewed wave of ethical commentary on nuclear weapons.[63]

Nuclear Ethics (1986), by Harvard political scientist Joseph S. Nye Jr., offered an austere coda to this latest cycle of moral discourse. Nye criticized nuclear strategists who ignored moral considerations, accusing them of betraying the very values they professed to defend. His main target, however, were those like Jonathan Schell who invoked "absolute moral judgments" to denounce nuclear weapons and deterrence doctrine without engaging the "empirical facts" of the actual strategic situation and who conflated possibilities with absolute certainties. The (allegedly) remote prospect of all-out nuclear war hardly justified

Schell's radical prescriptions, Nye insisted. Nor need a limited nuclear war inevitably escalate.[64] The moralists who pronounced deterrence theory unethical, Nye concluded, had "fail[ed] in the overall thrust of their argument" and needed "to dirty their hands with some knowledge about nuclear strategy." To this end, he offered a detailed discussion of probability theory and current strategic debates. While crediting the freeze campaigners with moderating the Reagan administration's stance on nuclear issues, he criticized their "hysteria," "shrill invective," "snide attributions of bad motives," and general lack of intellectual rigor.[65]

Nye's skepticism reflected the perspective of an academic specialist and government insider immersed in the arcana of targeting strategy and US-Soviet strategic relations. To be taken seriously, he added, moralists' discussion "must rest on careful causal assessments of the relative risks of different deterrence policies and the alternatives to them, including an awareness of the broad bands of uncertainty that will necessarily be involved." "The first step in moral reasoning about nuclear weapons," he wearily cautioned, "should be not to expect too much."[66]

While acknowledging the awesome risks and moral ambiguities of deterrence doctrine, Nye defended it as essential to American security: "We can give survival of the species a very high priority," he asserted, "without giving it the paralyzing status of an absolute value. Some degree of risk is unavoidable if individuals or societies are to avoid paralysis and enhance the quality of life beyond mere survival." Planning for limited nuclear war is essential, too, he wrote, "if a political leader is to have any choices between capitulation and an all-out spasm of total devastation."[67]

Nye offered thoughtful insights and sought to bring both intellectual rigor and moral awareness to strategic issues. He acknowledged that spending on nuclear weapons diverted resources from urgent social needs—another factor in the moral calculus of the debate. Further, he conceded, if deterrence failed, the principles of proportionality and sparing civilians would go out the window: "[D]eterrence depends on some prospect of use, and use involves some risk that just war limits will not be observed." In considering nuclear ethics, he argued, a relativist approach is more useful than absolutist positions.[68]

In the long run, Nye argued, the most promising strategy lay in carefully calibrated measures, overseen by knowledgeable experts of moral sensibility (people like Joseph S. Nye Jr., one might say), to maintain a "managed balance of power and nuclear risk reduction" while pursuing patient efforts to diminish risk and ease Cold War tensions. In this task, neither "amoral strategists," "moral absolutists," nor "apocalyptic activists" were particularly helpful.[69]

Even as Nye's book appeared, US-Soviet relations were evolving rapidly, with profound implications for the forty-year discourse addressed in this chapter. In

1985–88, the Cold Warrior Reagan improbably met three times with Soviet premier Mikhail Gorbachev, head of the erstwhile "evil empire," reviving the arms control process. By 1990, the Soviet Union had collapsed and the Cold War had ended. Nuclear concerns continued, but focused now less on the nightmare of global thermonuclear war than on nuclear proliferation, the security of fissile material, conflicts between regional nuclear powers, and terrorism by radical groups little influenced by the constraints of deterrence doctrine.[70]

As one steps back from this extended "nuclear ethics" discourse, its cyclical nature, its multipolarity, and the many outlets through which it found expression are striking. Surging when nuclear fears and activism intensified, it became more muted at other times. Further, no single religious or ethical stance gained dominance. Most religious leaders and ethicists condemned the atomic bombing of Hiroshima and Nagasaki, but no consensus emerged on other issues. Some condemned all future use or even threatened use of nuclear weapons; others defended the threat of nuclear retaliation as an essential deterrent. Still others judged preparation for nuclear attacks on military targets (though massive civilian casualties might result) morally preferable to the explicit annihilation threat undergirding classic countervalue deterrence theory. Prophecy popularizers, meanwhile, encouraged moral passivity by portraying a nuclear apocalypse as foreordained by God.

While I have foregrounded the pronouncements of clerics, theologians, and academics, a full survey of the moral response to nuclear weapons would include magazine writers and newspaper editorialists; physicians like Robert Jay Lifton and Helen Caldicott; novelists like Tim O'Brien (*The Nuclear Age*); poets (Randall Jarrell, Robert Lowell, and Allen Ginsberg among others); filmmakers like Stanley Kramer (*On the Beach*) and Stanley Kubrick (*Dr. Strangelove*); and artists like Jacob Lawrence.[71] This company would also encompass science-fiction writers like Ray Bradbury (*The Martian Chronicles*) and Walter Miller Jr. (*A Canticle for Leibowitz*); the muralists Iri and Toshi Maruki, creators of the powerful "Hiroshima Panels"; the Japanese TV producers of *Unforgettable Fire*, based on the memory paintings of A-bomb survivors; and musical satirists like Tom Lehrer ("We'll All Go Together When We Go") and Randy Newman ("Political Science"). Such a survey would take in musical composers—Krzysztof Penderecki (*Threnody to the Victims of Hiroshima*), James Yannatos (*Trinity Mass*), Philip Glass (*Plutonium Ode*), John Adams (*Doctor Atomic*), and others. It would even include the planners of an early-1980s' "Perspectives on Nuclear War" course at the University of Wisconsin-Madison, where the final meeting consisted of a slide show of art treasures and the playing of a movement from a Schubert string quartet. The point was obvious: this, too, could be lost in a nuclear war.

Yet, as I have cautioned, one cannot assume that these ethical responses mirrored larger social attitudes. The views of ethicists, religious leaders, and cultural creators are significant components of a society's moral history, but an unreliable guide to the views of the whole population. The overwhelming popular approval of the atomic bombing of Japan as religious leaders condemned it, and the clamor for dropping atomic bombs in the Korean War, underscore the gap between the ethical discourse of a few and broader public attitudes.

Assessing the impact of this moral discourse on policymakers and strategists is equally problematic. Some did articulate ethical concerns. In 1959, amid widespread agitation for a nuclear test ban, George Kennan, a Presbyterian layman and influential early-postwar policymaker, published an essay expressing grave qualms both about America's World War II bombing campaigns and current nuclear strategy:

> In . . . the bombing of Dresden and Hamburg, to say nothing of Nagasaki and Hiroshima, Americans went beyond what it seems to me the dictates of Christian conscience should have allowed (which is not to say that I think their problem was an easy one).
>
> I regret as an American and as a Christian, that these things were done. I think it should be our aim to do nothing of the sort in any future military encounter. If we must defend our homes, let us defend them as well as we can in the direct sense, but let us have no part in making millions of women and children and noncombatants hostages for the behavior of their own governments.
>
> It will be said to me: This means defeat. To this I can only reply: I am skeptical of the meaning of "victory" and "defeat" in their relation to modern war between great countries. To my mind the defeat is war itself. In any case it seems to me that there are times when we have no choice but to follow the dictates of our conscience, to throw ourselves on God's mercy, and not to ask too many questions.[72]

Kennan's reflections, of course, came after he had left government service. Instances of sitting leaders bringing ethical considerations explicitly into the policymaking process are rare. Of course, officials always *claim* to be guided by high moral principles and seek to persuade ethicists of that fact.[73] And they welcome moral arbiters who endorse their views, as James Schlesinger welcomed Paul Ramsey's support for a counterforce targeting strategy. But rhetorical affirmations and cherry-picking arguments to support predetermined positions differs from a serious engagement with the moral implications of one's policy choices. When Robert McNamara was asked in 1985 if he could recall any religious or ethical writing (or work of the imagination) that had influenced him as secretary of defense, he candidly answered no; his reading had consisted of reports and statistical analyses. In *Nuclear Ethics*, Joseph Nye acknowledged the chasm separating moralists and strategists. "The moralists formulate fine principles that seem to the strategists about as relevant to a foreign policy as a belief in the tooth fairy is to the practice of dentistry." Yet ethical considerations inevitably intrude, for reasons of domestic politics if nothing else. As the hawkish strategist Colin S. Gray acknowledged in 1985: "[T]he ability of a democracy to sustain an adequate military posture year after year . . . is not unrelated to the popularly perceived compatibility of moral values with defense policy."[74]

When the caveats are acknowledged, the ethical discourse explored in this chapter remains a significant and neglected part of America's Cold War history. The atomic bomb and the nuclear arms race led theologians, ethicists, philosophers, political scientists, and prophecy popularizers—along with a host of cultural creators—to reflect on the Bomb's larger implications for humanity's slim reserves of moral capital and for the centuries-long effort to confine war within ethical bounds. The participants in this discourse addressed troubling issues that those in power mostly preferred to avoid. When Democratic presidential candidate Adlai Stevenson in 1956 urged a halt in US atmospheric nuclear testing, President Eisenhower harrumphed: "[W]eapons policy is manifestly not a subject for detailed public discussion."[75] The religious leaders and ethicists considered in this chapter decidedly disagreed. Nothing could be *more* appropriate for public discussion, they believed, than strategic policies that could determine the fate of countless human beings and even threaten human survival itself. Their discourse varied in perspective and profundity, but cumulatively it helped shape America's intellectual, cultural, and political history in the second half of the twentieth century. This, too, is part of the Cold War's complex legacy.

Notes

1. See, for example, Sohail H. Hashmi and Steven P. Lee (eds.), *Ethics and Weapons of Mass Destruction* (Cambridge, 2004); George Cotkin, *Morality's Muddy Waters: Moral Quandaries in Modern America* (Philadelphia, 2010), esp. Chap. 2, "A Sky That Never Cared Less" (pp. 35–76); Jonathan Granoff, "Nuclear Weapons, Ethics, Morals, and Law," *Brigham University Law Review*, Vol. 2000, No. 4 (2000), 1413–1442; Francis A. Boyle, *The Criminality of Nuclear Deterrence* (Christchurch, NZ, 2002).
2. Paul Boyer, *By the Bomb's Early Light: American Thought and Culture at the Dawn of the Atomic Age* (New York, 1985; reprinted 1994), esp. pp. 179–240, 334–351.
3. Harry Emerson Fosdick, *On Being Fit to Live With: Sermons on Postwar Christianity* (New York, 1946), pp. 20, 76, 77; "America's Atomic Atrocity," *Christian Century*, August 29, 1945, pp. 974–975.
4. "Churchmen Speak on Atomic Bomb," *Federal Council Bulletin*, September 1945, p. 6; Holmes, "Editorial Comment," *Unity*, September 1945, pp. 99–100; Boyer, *By the Bomb's Early Light*, p. 201.

5. Federal Council of the Churches of Christ in America, Commission on the Relation of the Church to the War in the Light of the Christian Faith, *Atomic Warfare and the Christian Faith* (New York, 1946), pp. 11, 12, 19.
6. Frederick H. Russell, *The Just War in the Middle Ages* (Cambridge, 1975); James T. Johnson, *Just War Tradition and the Restraint of War: A Moral and Historical Inquiry* (Princeton, 1981); National Conference of Catholic Bishops, *The Challenge of Peace: God's Promise and Our Response* (Washington, DC, 1983), pp. 26–34.
7. "Horror and Shame," *Commonweal*, August 24, 1945, pp. 443–444; Edgar R. Smothers, S.J., "An Opinion on Hiroshima," *America*, July 5, 1947, pp. 379–380. Smothers' 1947 criticism of Truman's A-bomb decision is particularly noteworthy, since by then the Cold War was underway and *America*, intensely anticommunist, generally supported the Truman administration's tough anti-Soviet policies.
8. Mumford, "Atom Bomb: 'Miracle' or Catastrophe?" *Air Affairs*, July 1948, pp. 327, 328.
9. Russell S. Hutchinson, "Hiroshima," *Christian Century*, September 25, 1946, pp. 1151; John Hersey to Paul Boyer, January 24, 1985, in author's possession.
10. Sydnor H. Walker (ed.), *The First One Hundred Days of the Atomic Age* (New York: Woodrow Wilson Foundation, 1945), p. 35; "The *Fortune* Survey," *Fortune*, December 1945, p. 305.
11. Charles Wolfe, "Nuclear Country: The Atomic Bomb in Country Music," *Journal of Country Music*, 7 (January 1978), pp. 7, 9, 10–11, 12–13; Truman diary jottings, July 16 and 25, 1945, in Robert H. Ferrell (ed.), *Off the Record: The Private Papers of Harry S. Truman* (New York, 1982), pp. 52–53, 55, 56. Truman evidently conflated the New Testament prophecy of the earth's fiery destruction (II Peter 3:10) and the Genesis account of Noah's flood. For more on prophecy writers' interpretation of the atomic bomb, see Paul Boyer, *When Time Shall Be No More: Prophecy Belief in Modern American Culture* (Cambridge, 1992), pp. 115–151.
12. Donald Grey Barnhouse, "Tomorrow: Current Events in the Light of the Bible," *Eternity*, December 1945, pp. 505, 534; Wilbur M. Smith, *This Atomic Age and the Word of God* (Boston, 1948).
13. *Atomic Warfare and the Christian Faith*, pp. 12, 13.
14. Wilfred Parsons, S. J. and the Ethics Committee, "The Ethics of Atomic War," Catholic Association for International Peace, *Peace in the Atomic Age* (Washington, DC, 1947), pp. 9, 10, 11, 12, 13.
15. "The Moral Revolt of the Admirals," *Christian Century*, October 26, 1949, pp. 1256–1257.
16. George H. Gallup (ed.), *The Gallup Poll: Public Opinion, 1935–1971* (3 vols., New York, 1972), II, pp. 894–895, 938, 1027; "A-Bomb Will Not Beat China: Crowded Military Targets Scarce in Far East," *U.S. News and World Report*, December 8, 1950, p. 23; Wolfe, "Nuclear Country," p. 19.
17. Ibid., 19; Hyman J. Appelman, *The Atomic Bomb and the End of the World* (Grand Rapids, 1954), pp. 17–18.
18. "The Christian Conscience and Weapons of Mass Destruction: Report of a Commission Appointed by the Federal Council of Churches of Christ in America," extract in *Christian Century*, December 13, 1950 (including list of members), pp. 1489–1491.
19. Gordon C. Zahn, "The A-Bomb: Moral or Not?" *Commonweal*, September 29, 1950, p. 607 (quoting Connell); "How About the Bomb?" *Time*, December 18, 1950, p. 50 (quoting Walsh).
20. Boyer, *By the Bomb's Early Light*, pp. 352–355.
21. A popular myth holds that the debate in these years focused on the morality of shooting a neighbor trying to enter one's fallout shelter in a nuclear attack. While one Jesuit theologian did defend the ethics of such action (Laurence McHugh, S.J., "Ethics at the Shelter Doorway," *America*, 105 [September 30, 1961], pp. 824–827), the nuclear-ethics discourse of this period was far more wide-ranging.
22. *Pacem in Terris: Peace on Earth: Encyclical Letter of Pope John XXIII* (New York: America Press, 1963), Sec. 109–113; [Vatican Council II], *De ecclesia in mundo huius temporis: The*

Pastoral Constitution on the Church in the Modern World. Promulgated by Pope Paul VI (Glen Rock, NJ, 1967), Sec. 81.

23. Thomas Merton, "Christian Ethics and Nuclear War" in Merton, *The Nonviolent Alternative*, edited with an introduction by Gordon Zahn (New York, 1980), pp. 83, 86, 87 (revised edn. of *Thomas Merton on Peace*, originally published in 1971).
24. Paul Boyer, "From Activism to Apathy: The American People and Nuclear Weapons, 1963–1980," *Journal of American History*, 70/4 (1984), pp. 821–844.
25. Ibid., pp. 832–835.
26. Brodie, "War in the Atomic Age," in Brodie (ed.), *The Absolute Weapon: Atomic Power and World Order* (New York, 1946), pp. 21–69; A. J. Muste, *Not by Might: Christianity the Way to Human Decency* (New York, 1947), pp. 163, 164, 166, 167.
27. *Statement of Secretary of Defense Robert S. McNamara before the House Armed Services Committee . . . January 30, 1963*, in *The American Atom: A Documentary History of Nuclear Politics from the Discovery of Fission to the Present*, ed. Philip Cantelon, Richard Hewlett, and Robert Williams, 2nd ed. (Philadelphia, 1992), p. 223. See also David Rosenberg, "The Origins of Overkill: Nuclear Weapons and American Strategy, 1945–1960," *International Security*, 7/4 (1983), pp. 3–71.
28. *Statement of Secretary of Defense Robert S. McNamara before the Senate Armed Services Committee . . . Prepared January 22, 1968* (Washington, D.C., 1968), pp. 47, 54.
29. *Statement of Secretary of Defense Robert S. McNamara Before the Senate Armed Services Committee*, 47; W. W. Rostow, "The Test: Are We the Tougher?" *New York Times Magazine*, June 7, 1964, pp. 112, 113.
30. Niebuhr, "From Progress to Perplexity" in *The Search for America*, ed. Huston Smith (Englewood Cliffs, NJ, 1959), p. 144, quoted in Paul Ramsey, *War and the Christian Conscience: How Shall Modern War Be Conducted Justly?* (Durham, 1961), p. 5.
31. "Pastoral Constitution on the Church and the Modern World" in *The Documents of Vatican II*, ed. Walter M. Abbott (New York, 1966), p. 294; Edward S. Boylan, "Is the ABM Moral?" *Commonweal*, June 11, 1971, p. 304. See also Morton A. Kaplan (ed.), *Strategic Thinking and Its Moral Implications* (Chicago, 1973); Thomas Nagel, "War and Massacre," *Philosophy and Public Affairs*, 1 (1972), pp. 123–144; and J. Bryan Hehir, "The Just-War Ethic and Catholic Theology: Dynamics of Change and Continuity" in Thomas A. Shannon (ed.), *War or Peace: The Search for New Answers* (Maryknoll, NY, 1980), pp. 15–39. Philip Green, *Deadly Logic: The Theory of Nuclear Deterrence* (Columbus, 1966), including Green's bibliographic essay, is useful on pre-1966 critiques of deterrence theory.
32. Murray, *Nuclear Policy for War and Peace* (Cleveland, 1960), p. 241.
33. John Courtney Murray, S.J., "Remarks on the Moral Problem of War," *Theological Studies*, 20 (March 1959), 40–61, quoted passages 45, 50, 54, 57, 58. My thanks to Daniel Gerster who brought this essay to my attention. This essay extended the similar argument advanced in the 1947 report of the Catholic Association for International Peace, discussed above, to which Murray belonged.
34. Ramsey, *War and the Christian Conscience*, esp. pp. 273–304 ("rational nuclear armaments" quote, p. 292); Ramsey, *The Just War: Force and Political Responsibility* (New York, 1968; new edn 2002), p. 252 ("collateral civilian damage" quote).
35. Henry A. Kissinger, *Nuclear Weapons and Foreign Policy* (New York, 1957; abridged Doubleday paperback edn, 1958), esp. pp. 103–168; *Report of the Secretary of Defense, James R. Schlesinger on the FY1975 Defense Budget* (Washington, DC, 1974); Fred C. Iklé, "Can Nuclear Deterrence Last Out the Century?," *Foreign Affairs*, 51, 2 (January 1973); Freedman, *The Evolution of Nuclear Strategy*, 2nd edn., pp. 377–382; Douglas P. Lackey, "The American Debate on Nuclear Weapons Policy, A Review of the Literature, 1945–1985," *Analyse & Kritik*, 9, 1–2 (1987), pp. 7–46, online at www.analyse-und-kritik.net/1987-1-2/AK_Lackey_1987.pdf (accessed November 18, 2009), pp. 21–23, 31–34. See also Charles L. Glaser, "Why Do Strategists Disagree about the Requirements of Strategic Nuclear Deterrence?" in Lynn Eden and Steven Miller (eds.), *Nuclear Arguments: Understanding the Strategic Nuclear Arms and Arms Control*

Debates (Ithaca, 1989); McGeorge Bundy, "Strategic Deterrence Thirty Years Later: What Has Changed?" in Christoph Bertram (ed.), *The Future of Strategic Deterrence* (London, 1981), p. 8; Michael Mandelbaum, *The Nuclear Question: The United States and Nuclear Weapons, 1946–1976* (Cambridge, 1979), pp. 202–203.

36. Walzer, *Just and Unjust Wars: A Moral Argument with Historical Illustrations*, 3rd ed. (New York, 1990), p. 272.
37. Ibid., pp. 274, 278.
38. *The Challenge of Peace*, p. 57.
39. Walzer, *Just and Unjust Wars*, pp. 279, 280.
40. Ibid., pp. 282, 283.
41. Herken, *The Winning Weapon: The Atomic Bomb in the Cold War, 1945–1950* (New York, 1980) and *Counsels of War* (New York, 1985); Paul Boyer, "'The Fences are Gone,' American Policymaking in the Dawn of the Nuclear Age," *Reviews in American History*, 10 (1982), pp. 448–453.
42. Daniel Lang, "A Reporter at Large: The Supreme Option," *New Yorker*, January 9, 1971, p. 52; Ralph E. Lapp, *The New Priesthood: The Scientific Elite and the Uses of Power* (New York, 1965), p. 36. See also Roy Licklider, *The Private Nuclear Strategists* (Columbus, 1971), pp. 33–36, 160, and Arthur Herzog, *The War-Peace Establishment* (New York, 1965), pp. 3–99.
43. "Can Talk Stop the Arms Race?" *Business Week*, July 13, 1968, p. 31.
44. Gerald B. Stanton, *Kept from the Hour: A Systematic Study of the Rapture in Bible Prophecy* (Grand Rapids, 1956), p. 12; W. R. Wallace, "Shadows of Armageddon" in William Culbertson and Herman B. Centz (eds.), *Understanding the Times: Prophetic Messages Delivered at the Second International Congress on Prophecy, New York City* (Grand Rapids, 1957), pp. 187–188, 189; Moody Bible Institute, *Moody Science Classics: God of the Atom* (Chicago, 1998), videotape edition of 1957 film. On the prophetic interpretation underlying these beliefs, and their foreign-policy implications, see the following, by Paul Boyer: *When Time Shall Be No More*, pp. 1–18, 80–100; "The Apocalyptic in the Twentieth Century" in Christopher Kleinhenz and Fannie J. LeMoine, eds., *Fearful Hope: Approaching the Millennium* (Madison, 1999), pp. 149–169; and "Biblical Prophecy and Foreign Policy" in Claire Badaracco (ed.), *Quoting God: How Media Shape Ideas About Religion and Culture* (Waco, 2005), pp. 107–122.
45. For a more extended discussion of the many popular prophecy works foretelling Russia's destruction, see Boyer, *When Time Shall Be No More*, pp. 152–180.
46. Lindsey, *The Late Great Planet Earth* (New York, 1973), pp. 60, 149, 150, 163, 164.
47. Michael Barkun, "Nuclear War and Millenarian Symbols: Premillennialists Confront the Bomb," paper given before the Society for the Scientific Study of Religion, October 1985, p. 24 (quoted by permission).
48. James Barr, *Fundamentalism* (Philadelphia, 1977), pp. 206, 207. See also D. S. Russell, *Apocalyptic Ancient and Modern* (Philadelphia, 1978), p. 64.
49. "The Politics of Armageddon: the Scowcroft Commission and the MX Missile" in Kenneth Kitts, *Presidential Commissions and National Security* (Boulder, 2006). Because of public protests, only fifty MX missiles were deployed, in fixed silos rather than in the mobile-basing configuration. The last one was retired in 2005. Wade Boese, "United States Retires MX Missile," *Arms Control Today*, October 2005, online at www.armscontrol.org/act/2005_10/OCT-MX. Accessed August 7, 2008.
50. J. Peter Scoblic, *U.S. vs. Them: How a Half-Century of Conservatism Has Undermined America's Security* (New York, 2008), pp. 98–101, 109–111; William E. Odom, "The Origins and Design of Presidential Decision-59: A Memoir" in Henry Sokolski (ed.), *Getting MAD: Nuclear Mutual Assured Destruction, Its Origins and Practice* (Carlisle, 2004). See also Fred Kaplan, *The Wizards of Armageddon* (Stanford, 1991) and Lawrence Freedman, *The Evolution of Nuclear Strategy*, 3rd ed. (Basingstoke, 2003).
51. Robert Scheer, *With Enough Shovels: Reagan, Bush, and Nuclear War* (New York, 1982); Paul Boyer (ed.), *Reagan as President: Contemporary Views of the Man, His Politics, and His*

Policies (Chicago, 1990), pp. 165–169 (National Association of Evangelicals address), quote on p. 168.

52. Lawrence Wittner, *The Struggle Against the Bomb*, Vol. 3 (Stanford, 2003), pp. 175–177; Thomas Rochon and David Meyer (eds.), *Coalitions & Political Movements: The Lessons of the Nuclear Freeze* (Boulder, 1997).
53. For a more extended discussion of nuclear themes in 1980s' popular culture see Paul Boyer, *Fallout: A Historian Reflects on America's Half-Century Encounter with Nuclear Weapons* (Columbus, 1998), pp. 199–225.
54. "Thinking About the Unthinkable," *Time*, March 29, 1982, online at http://www.time.com/time/magazine/article/0,9171,953406-1,00.html (accessed May 23, 2008), Schindler quote; Ronald Sider and Richard Taylor, *Nuclear Holocaust & Christian Hope* (New York, 1982); Billy Graham, *Approaching Hoofbeats: The Four Horsemen of the Apocalypse* (Waco, 1983).
55. Leon Wieseltier, "Nuclear War, Nuclear Peace: A New Argument on the Predicament of Our Age," *New Republic*, January 10 & 17, 1983; Michael Novak, "Moral Clarity in the Nuclear Age," *National Review*, April 1, 1983.
56. Jonathan Schell, *The Fate of the Earth* (New York, 1982), pp. 3, 174, 177, 178, 181–231; Strobe Talbott, "Arguments Against MADness," *Time*, June 11, 1984 ("wildly Utopian"); Andrew J. Pierre, *Foreign Affairs*, Fall 1984 ("political naïveté").
57. Schell, *The Abolition* (New York, 1984), p. 56; Joseph Nye, *Nuclear Ethics* (New York, 1986), p. 94 (quoting Schell, "weaponless deterrence"). Like Hersey's *Hiroshima*, Schell's books originally appeared as *New Yorker* essays.
58. Schell, *The Abolition*, quoted in Talbott, "Arguments Against MADness."
59. Murray Polner and Jim Grady, *Disarmed and Dangerous: The Radical Lives and Times of Daniel and Philip Berrigan* (New York, 1997); A. G. Mojtabai, *Blesséd Assurance: At Home with the Bomb in Amarillo, Texas* (Boston, 1986), pp. 52–55, quoted passage, p. 55; "Seattle's Bishop Resumes Control," *The New York Times*, May 28, 1987.
60. *The Challenge of Peace*; webpage of Harvard International Relations Council, http://athome.harvard.edu/programs/irw/bio.html, accessed May 23, 2008 (Hehir biographical information).
61. *The Challenge of Peace*, pp. 46, 48, 50. Like Walzer, the bishops dismissed Paul Ramsey's distinction between mass civilian casualties resulting from deliberately targeting them, and comparable casualties caused by an attack ostensibly aimed at military targets. Only "moral casuistry," they said, could "justify using a weapon which 'indirectly' or 'unintentionally' killed a million innocent people because they happened to live near a 'militarily significant target'" (p. 61).
62. *The Challenge of Peace*, 53, 58, 59, 102–103.
63. Boyer (ed.), *Reagan as President*, pp. 206–219; Boyer, "Selling Star Wars: Ronald Reagan's Strategic Defense Initiative" in Kenneth Osgood and Andrew Frank (eds.), *Selling War in a Media Age: The Presidency and Public Opinion in the American Century* (Gainesville, 2010), 196–223.
64. Nye, *Nuclear Ethics*, pp. 15, 50–51, 63, 91 (quoted phrases), pp. 93–97.
65. Ibid., quoted phrases on pp. xii, 11, 79, 92. See also pp. 62–70, 78, and 108–120.
66. Ibid., pp. 80, 92.
67. Ibid., pp. 45–46, 105; reviews by Walter Goodman, *New York Times*, April 7, 1986, p. 17; James Stegenga, *American Political Science Review*, 81/4 (1987).
68. Nye, *Nuclear Ethics*, p. 52 (quoted passage), p. 79.
69. Nye, *Nuclear Ethics*, pp. 13, 129–130.
70. The 1989 documentary collection *Nuclear Arguments*, cited above (n. 34), focused entirely on strategic issues, ignoring ethical considerations.
71. In the early 1980s, during the nuclear weapons freeze campaign, the Limited Editions Book Club invited Jacob Lawrence, known for his Depression-era paintings of African Americans, to illustrate a book of his choice. He selected John Hersey's *Hiroshima*, which he was rereading at the time. Robert Cozzolino, Curator of Modern Art, Pennsylvania Academy of Fine Arts, e-mail to author, May 19, 2008.

72. Kennan, "Foreign Policy and Christian Conscience," *Atlantic Monthly*, May 1959, online at www.theatlantic.com/doc/195905/christianity-foreign-policy. Accessed May 7, 2008.
73. See, for example, the efforts of National Security Advisor William Clark and Secretary of Defense Caspar Weinberger to persuade the Catholic bishops that US nuclear warplanning did "not target the Soviet civilian population as such"—*The Challenge of Peace*, pp. 56, fn. 81.
74. Author interview with Robert McNamara, October 3, 1985, transcript in author's possession; Nye, *Nuclear Ethics*, p. 11; Colin Gray, "Strategic Defense, Deterrence, and the Prospects for Peace," *Ethics*, 95 (1985), p. 661.
75. Eisenhower quoted in Ramsey, *War and the Christian Conscience*, p. 290.

9

Blues Under Siege

Ralph Ellison, Albert Murray, and the Idea of America

DANIEL MATLIN

The field of Cold War history has become less exclusively occupied with high-political machinations in Moscow and Washington and increasingly hospitable to multiple, decentered narratives stretching across a more global terrain. Amid this proliferation of alternative perspectives, one countervailing force for convergence has been an emphasis on the importance of American ideology and self-perception to the conflict's origins and character. Odd Arne Westad and Anders Stephanson may differ as to the Cold War's chronological and geographic scope, but both identify the study of ideology as, in Westad's words, "perhaps the most useful" contribution that can be made, at this point, within a field that "has often ignored ideas as the basis for human action."[1] Ideology, it was long assumed, accounted only for Soviet aggression, and most historians accepted Daniel Bell's assurance that American ideology in the postwar period was conspicuous only by its absence.[2] Though Westad has pioneered Cold War historiography's newly global reach, nevertheless he "to some extent go[es] along with Anders Stephanson's contention that the Cold War may profitably be seen as a U.S. ideological project," and adds that "it was to a great extent American ideas and their influence that made the Soviet-American conflict into a *Cold War*."[3]

A related development is the challenge to "Cold War determinism" posed in this volume by Peter Mandler and elsewhere by David Engerman and Joel Isaac. As these historians demonstrate, reification of "the cold war" as an autonomous agent responsible for postwar America's every trait has distorted our picture of the era's politics and diplomacy and of its intellectual, cultural, and social life.[4] This is not to deny that the events and contexts that defined the Cold War exerted a powerful, often pernicious influence on many historical actors and institutions, but rather to counterbalance our sense of the Cold War's capability to produce America with greater understanding of America's capability to produce the Cold War. Such a purpose underlies a move toward a relative *longue durée*, manifest in Stephanson's efforts to locate the Cold War's origins in the adaptation of longstanding American traditions of ideology and self-perception to the changed circumstances of the postwar world.[5] Moreover, as the character of the Cold War is increasingly understood as an outcome of American ideology, so the frontiers of Cold War historiography shift further into the territories of intellectual and cultural history. The natural sciences, human sciences, arts, and religious life of the period are no longer regarded merely as symptomatic of the Cold War's ability to penetrate the mind, but are also seen to offer historians points of entry into the ideas that gave the Cold War its shape. As Steven Belletto points out in this volume, scholarship on the Cold War emanating from literary and cultural studies has revealed "a dynamic—rather than simply causal—relationship between political norms and aesthetic production."[6]

Central to these undertakings is the question of "what it was about the United States and its self-conception that made the Cold War a natural way of being toward the world."[7] In this context, I wish to draw attention to a subset of Americans whose conceptions of the United States hold particular value to the study of American ideology of the Cold War era. The subset—African-American intellectuals of the decades following World War II—commends itself to students of American self-perception not least because of the widespread expectation that arose during those years that black people stood, for the first time, within sight of a meaningful American citizenship. What America and its citizenship meant were matters on which black intellectuals concentrated their energies with heightened urgency.

Among the most impassioned voices in this discourse were Ralph Ellison and Albert Murray, two writers whose close friendship nurtured shared ideas about America and its promise of "freedom." In what follows, I argue that Ellison and Murray regarded the United States as the steward of a particular notion of freedom. To them, freedom inhered not only in the rights afforded by democratic citizenship, but also in the very belief that individual agency might defy the constraints of circumstance—a conviction or disposition that they termed "heroism." Their idea of America was no mere calculated rationalization of the United States' postwar globalist ambitions. It fortified Ellison's and Murray's enthusiasm for the civil rights movement no less than it compelled their endorsement of America's assertive geopolitical stance. Moreover, it constituted Ellison's and Murray's variation on a theme deeply rooted in American thought.

In locating the Cold War within the historical sweep of American ideology and self-perception, Stephanson calls attention to a "tradition that perhaps can best be described as 'freedom under siege.'" The meanings imparted to "freedom" have been ceaselessly revised, but "freedom is always under threat" from a "negative agent," itself reconstituted as the despotism of George III, the slavocracy, German militarism, and eventually the specter of communism. Intimately entwined with American articulations of classical republicanism, this tradition has been as much concerned with dangers to freedom emanating from within the polity as with the hostile designs of foreign powers—not least on the grounds that any weakening of "community virtue" would increase the republic's vulnerability to external threats.[8] Ellison's and Murray's writings belong to this tradition, and their notion of an embattled freedom resonated with the United States' ideological confrontation with communism. Yet communism itself comprises only one manifestation of the negative agent that stalks their writings. Besieging the heroic disposition integral to their distinctive notion of freedom, they believed, was the more fundamental and pervasive threat of determinism, conceived as the very denial of creative human agency.

If Ellison's and Murray's conception of America shaped (as well as was shaped by) their attitudes toward the civil rights struggle and the Cold War, by the mid-1960s a younger cohort of radical black intellectuals offered a very different assessment of these domestic and geopolitical upheavals, grounded in a sharply divergent idea of America. The "second phase" of the Cold War, in Westad's periodization, prolonged the conflict beyond the stabilization of European borders in the early 1960s by shifting the locus of superpower rivalry to the theaters of decolonization in Asia, Latin America, and Africa.[9] To militant African-American intellectuals such as Amiri Baraka, who renounced all faith in America's commitment to "freedom" along with his "slave name," LeRoi Jones, the United States' efforts to control the dynamics of decolonization appeared wholly consistent with what they deemed to be a congenital, ineradicable American propensity for oppression.[10] Indeed, the civil rights movement and the Cold War combined to reignite debate over the very possibility of black identification with America.

One forum in which this debate among African-American intellectuals assumed an especially clamorous tone was their writings about black music, which are replete with commentary, explicit and inferential, on the nature of America and on the Americanness (or otherwise) of its black inhabitants. For Ellison and Murray, the blues and its offspring, jazz, were the clearest expressions of the heroic American conception of freedom. As such, these musical forms embodied the indissoluble conjunction between "Negro" and "American" cultures, and indeed political destinies. In what follows, I draw primarily on Ellison's and Murray's writings about the blues and jazz in order to explicate their idea of America, with Baraka's black nationalist commentaries on music offering a counterpoint at intervals along the way. The first section of this chapter establishes Ellison's and Murray's claims about the relationship between black people and America as part of an ongoing conversation among black intellectuals, and recounts the developments in postwar African-American music that prompted many of their reflections on the United States. In the second section, I argue that Ellison's and Murray's distaste for these musical innovations signaled their concern that deterministic modes of thinking—which they also discerned in contemporary African-American literature and in the social sciences—were corroding the heroic disposition and imperiling American freedom. Finally, while considering the challenge to their views posed by black nationalism in the 1960s, I demonstrate how Ellison's and Murray's idea of America countenanced both civil rights reforms and America's assertive Cold War stance as vital to the cause of freedom.

Taking my cue from the move against "Cold War determinism," I wish to suggest that the visions of America projected by black intellectuals in the postwar decades need to be understood not merely as *responses* to the events and climate of the Cold War—though to some extent they undoubtedly were—but also as *constituting* in themselves an important part of the fabric of American thought and culture from which the Cold War—and the domestic opposition to it—was cut. In this manner, I hope to demonstrate how the study of black intellectuals can make its contribution to the inquiry conceived by Stephanson, Westad, and others; and, more broadly, how extending this inquiry's remit further into the domains of intellectual and cultural history might bring to the surface more of the materials from which an American "ideological project" derived its form.

We Who Are Dark

African-American intellectuals in the decades following World War II harbored profoundly, often bitterly divergent political convictions. Yet whatever those convictions were, their diagnoses and prognoses regarding both civil rights and the Cold War were grounded in their fundamental conceptions of the character of America and the possibilities of a "Negro-American" or "black-American" identity. Disagreements concerning civil rights and black power most visibly concerned the place of black people within America, while the controversies of the Cold War overtly addressed America's place in the wider world. Both discussions, however, hinged on the nature of the United States as imagined by a section of its population that had long claimed a privileged insight as the ironic consequence of its unprivileged status. W. E. B. Du Bois had written at the turn of the twentieth century of black people's "second-sight in this American world." In 1926 he reasserted his belief that "we who are dark can see America in a way that white Americans can not."[11]

These words reverberated in 1969, when Ralph Ellison—a writer not much given to racial mystique—stated that there were "many aspects of American life which can only be described, analyzed, and defined by black intellectuals, for no other group possesses an adequate perspective or so urgent a need." Along with this peculiar privilege, Ellison reflected three years later, came a heightened responsibility:

> If we can't look out upon this nation and foresee where problems are going to surface, no one can. . . . Remember that Americans have run from understanding the cost of this great country. We have paid much of that cost. Having paid it, we have the obligation to accuse, to prescribe, and to rectify.

Not all black writers felt this obligation—to act as America's conscience and to forecast impending threats to its survival—as the corollary of their unsolicited "second-sight."[12] By the mid-1960s, the fundamental premise of the established civil rights organizations—that America could be brought to its moral senses and that the federal polity (if not the Southern states) was after all concerned with such matters as rights and freedoms—induced patent skepticism, even ridicule, among some black thinkers and activists. Doubtful of the American commitment to democracy at home, the twenty-nine-year-old writer LeRoi Jones (later Amiri Baraka) in 1963 found the United States' posture as a global champion of freedom to be stretching credulity:

> It is no secret that the West, and most particularly the American system, is in the position now of having to defend its values and ideas against totally hostile systems. The American Negro is being asked to defend the American system as energetically as the American white man. There is no doubt that the middle-class Negro is helping and will continue to help in that defense. But there is perhaps a question mark in the minds of the many poor blacks (which is one explanation for the attraction of such groups as the Black Muslims) and also now in the minds of many young Negro intellectuals. *What is it that they are being asked to save?* It is a good question, and America had better come up with an answer.[13]

Jones's attitude toward the United States' global stance was thus tightly bound up with his response to the treatment of black people in America. Both, he believed, were testimony to what he called "the essential nature of this country."[14]

The interrelation between civil rights and the Cold War—once the subjects of discrete historical literatures—is now the theme of a host of impressive studies. In the arena of international history, Mary Dudziak, Thomas Borstelmann, and others have detailed how the imperative to project the United States' image as a global guarantor of democracy both spurred the pace of domestic civil rights reform and contained that reform within boundaries consonant with Cold War-era liberalism.[15] From within African-American history, scholars including Kevin Gaines, Peniel Joseph, Timothy Tyson, and Robin Kelley and Betsy Esch emphasize the internationalist character of black protest in the United States during these years. Their work captures the linkages, real and imagined, between such protest and African, Asian, and Latin American movements for "self-determination" at a moment when the emergence of new, "non-aligned" states disrupted American visions of global order.[16] These multiple lines of investigation indicate some fruitful ways in which future scholarship might bridge the gap between the Cold War as American ideology and policy and the global dimensions and disparate locales of the Cold War's "second phase." They also suggest the value of exploring interconnections between black people's expectations of American citizenship and their attitudes toward America's figurative citizenship in the world. In this regard, the writings of black intellectuals reveal how longstanding problematics in African-American thought concerning America's "essential nature" informed black responses to postwar developments at home and abroad. At stake in both civil rights and the Cold War was the recurrent question of the possibility of black identification with America.

In the most habitually quoted passage of the most renowned text in African-American letters, *The Souls of Black Folk* (1903), Du Bois had addressed himself precisely to this question:

> One ever feels his two-ness,—an American, a Negro; two souls, two thoughts, two unreconciled strivings; two warring ideals in one dark body, whose dogged strength alone keeps it from being torn asunder.... He simply wishes to make it possible for a man to be both a Negro and an American, without being cursed and spit upon by his fellows, without having the doors of Opportunity closed roughly in his face.

The concept of "two-ness" or "double-consciousness" that became Du Bois's signature trope, and that has percolated through a century's theorization about race and identity, was grounded in deep uncertainty as to America's capacity to incorporate "black folk" within the bounds of what was American.[17] By the 1960s, which marked a crest of dissension over the trajectory of black political and cultural activity, African-American intellectuals appeared increasingly divided between those who regarded "double-consciousness" as premised on a false dichotomy and those who diagnosed it as a pervasive schizophrenia for which the antidote entailed cultivation of the authentic racial self.

In the former camp, Ellison and his close friend Albert Murray maintained that to try to separate the "black" from the "American" was, as Ellison put it, "to attempt delicate brain surgery with a switchblade."[18] Despite the strictures of segregation, Murray elaborated, American culture was "irrevocably composite" and "incontestably mulatto." Culturally, at least, integration had already happened. Not only were "US Negroes" categorically an American people; they were, as Murray titled his first book, "*The Omni-Americans*"—a people whose ethic of dogged determination and spirit of improvisation comprised the quintessence of the American national character.[19] Meanwhile, in the starkest possible rejoinder to any idealization of a "mulatto" single-consciousness, Amiri Baraka recast Du Bois's "two warring ideals" such that the "American" antagonist was reduced to a repressive "white" agent whose effect was to suffocate black authenticity:

> Du Bois said we always have the double consciousness. We trying to be Black and meanwhile you got a white ghost hovering over your head that says if you don't do this you get killed, if you don't do this you won['] t get no money, if you don't do this nobody will think you're beautiful. . . . That's the ghost, you tryin' to be Black and the ghost is telling you to be a ghost.[20]

Ironically, the imagery of Baraka's self-consciously anti-American pronouncements often exemplified postwar America's therapeutic turn.[21] Baraka, and many others within the black power and black arts movements in which he had become a leading figure, reconceived "double-consciousness" as a racial neurosis, a bipolarity potentially no less destructive than the conflict between superpowers. The therapeutic response to America's psychic tyranny was, indeed, conjoined with the rising challenge to America's geopolitical authority from the nonaligned nations. No black person of healthy mind, Baraka believed, would "defend the American system" against such a challenge.[22]

Writing about music, it has been said, is like dancing about architecture.[23] Yet the former has proven the more popular vocation. Each of the authors mentioned thus far was concerned with the interpretation of black music, not least when they argued over the relationship of black culture to the American whole. Du Bois had embedded "double-consciousness" within the very structure of *The Souls of Black Folk* by prefacing chapters of the book with lyrics of black "sorrow songs" as well as selections of white American and European music and verse. It was in *Blues People: Negro Music in White America* (1963) that Jones asked what kind of America black people were being "asked to save," and in a review of the same book that Ellison likened the separation of "black" and "American" to the work of an erratic neurosurgeon. For Murray, as for Ellison, the blues idiom that infused jazz was "a major American innovation of universal significance and potential."[24] Moreover, it was in their pronouncements about the character of the blues and the postwar reinvention of jazz that Ellison and Murray offered some of their most revealing remarks about the nature of America and the meaning of freedom.

Jazz blew into the postwar world in a fractious, paradoxical state. Since the mid-1930s, big swing bands such as those led by Duke Ellington, Benny Goodman, Tommy Dorsey, and Glenn Miller had popularized the music as never before, with a near monopoly over America's dance-floors and an optimistic, propulsive syncopation that buoyed audiences' spirits through the Depression and World War II. A music that had first sounded at the Saturday night fish fries, Sunday lawn parties, steamboat jamborees, and, reputedly, the bordellos of early twentieth-century black and Creole New Orleans had achieved a level of recognition—and undergone a transformation—unimaginable to its early practitioners.[25] Beamed out to soldiers on armed services' radio and enlisted into military dance bands, swing's patriotic credentials were finally assured when the airplane carrying Captain Glenn Miller disappeared over the English Channel late in 1944. Yet as dominant as the big bands had been, their demise in the immediate postwar years was just as swift, and almost as deadly, as Miller's. Disputes between record companies and musicians' unions yielded a wartime recording blackout, which in turn prompted radio broadcasters to diversify their musical fare and helped launch the postwar success of the country and western and rhythm and blues styles. The closure of many ballrooms combined with the rising cost of travel and declining entertainment spending to undermine the viability of large bands and orchestras.[26]

Many jazz musicians and critics now believed, moreover, that too high a price had been paid in musical integrity for jazz's popularization in the swing era. And by no means had the benefits of jazz's growth accrued equally to black musicians, composers, and bandleaders as to their white counterparts, whose superior fame and fortune within a genre that owed its existence to black innovation seemed, to some, as perverse as a segregated US Army fighting a "war for democracy." Out of these altered sensibilities and circumstances emerged two musical responses. A "Dixieland" revival took off, fueled by nostalgia for the raucous, unsmoothed sonorities of pre-swing-era jazz combos. Eager prospectors journeyed south to locate the aging veterans of early New Orleans bands and soon claimed to have struck gold in the person of Bunk Johnson, a toothless onetime trumpeter whom they coaxed from the Louisiana rice fields and furnished with a set of dentures and a new horn.[27] Meanwhile, in wartime after-hours sessions and backroom jams in Harlem and other hotspots, a more innovative response to jazz's stylistic impasse was taking shape. From Charlie Parker's alto saxophone, Dizzy Gillespie's trumpet, and the experimentation of numerous other instrumentalists came the breakneck tempos, jagged rhythms, and complex harmonic extensions that defined "bebop" as a music of aesthetic and social restlessness. It was a music firmly settled in, if still unsettled by, the life of the northern cities to which many of its originators had only recently arrived.[28]

In an essay first published in *Esquire* in 1959, Ralph Ellison reflected on bebop's incubation during the early 1940s in jam sessions at Minton's Playhouse in Harlem. This musical stirring was, Ellison wrote,

> a texture of fragments, repetitive, nervous, not fully formed; its melodic lines underground, secret and taunting; its riffs jeering—"Salt peanuts! Salt peanuts!"—its timbres flat or shrill, with a minimum of thrilling vibrato. Its rhythms were out of stride and seemingly arbitrary, its drummers frozen-faced introverts dedicated to chaos.[29]

Raised in Oklahoma City, Ellison had made his way to New York in 1936 and it was there, in the late 1940s, that he befriended Albert Murray. The two aspiring writers had overlapped as undergraduates at Alabama's Tuskegee Institute in the mid-1930s, but Murray, two years younger, had revered Ellison from a distance. A native of Mobile County, Alabama, Murray was now enrolled in a master's program in literature at New York University, while Ellison was occupied with drafting the work that, on its publication in 1952 as *Invisible Man*, almost instantly entered the canon of Great American Novels.[30] The two men had much in common besides their education and northward migrations, including a ravenous appetite for the modernist fiction of William Faulkner, Ernest Hemingway, André Malraux, and Thomas Mann, and a deep affinity for jazz. Both would give black musical expression prominence in their fiction and their critical explorations of the American experience. Murray's career in letters was slower than Ellison's to take off, and less stellar when it did. Nevertheless, he earned a reputation during the 1960s and 1970s as a sophisticated theorist of African-American aesthetics and was eventually anointed by Henry Louis Gates Jr. as the "foremost cultural explicant of black modernism."[31]

At first sight, the pairing of Ellison and Murray uncannily mirrors bebop's leading partnership of Parker and Gillespie, also forged in the 1940s. Ellison, born in 1913 in Oklahoma, and Parker, born in 1920 and raised in Kansas City, Missouri, both hailed from states whose histories combined segregation and westward expansion, while Murray, born in Alabama in 1916, and Gillespie, born in Cheraw, South Carolina, in 1917, were sons of the Deep South.[32] However, while the four men were born within the space of just seven years and undertook a common northward journey to New York, even the marginal seniority of Ellison and Murray assumed the character of a generational fault line in jazz history. The literary pairing were never reconciled to the changes wrought by bebop on the music they had grown up hearing, playing (at least in Ellison's case—he had majored in music at Tuskegee and had shown promise as a trumpeter), and dancing to.[33] Devotees of Duke Ellington and Count Basie, the most inventive and serious-minded African-American composers and bandleaders amid the flood of swing music, Ellison and Murray had formed their lifelong musical attachments in the 1930s and were disconcerted by jazz's postwar direction.[34]

Hostility toward bebop was scarcely unusual in a postwar jazz scene torn between so-called "progressives" and "moldy-figs."[35] *Time* magazine emphasized the new music's illicit, subcultural aura, in contrast to swing's hard-won mainstream credentials, when it dismissed bebop in 1946 as "hot jazz overheated, with overdone lyrics full of bawdiness, references to narcotics, and doubletalk."[36] A primarily instrumental music, bebop had few "lyrics" as such, but its very name testifies to the esoteric argot that was part of its milieu. As the jazz historian Ingrid Monson has noted, the beboppers' "unorthodox clothing, their refusal to speak in mainstream English to mixed crowds, and their refusal to play at mainstream dance tempos all announced to wartime audiences that the terms of participation in the jazz scene were shifting."[37] The historian Lewis Erenberg also stresses that bebop "was more than a technical innovation in form." World War II "magnified awareness among young blacks of their secondary racial and economic status in a new culture symbolized by Glenn Miller's [all-white] band," and indeed bebop's very complexity seemed to contest swing's facile assertion of a cohesive, pluralistic America.[38] For LeRoi Jones, writing in the early 1960s, "the moderns, the *beboppers*" had restored jazz to its rightful place "outside the mainstream of American culture." Among the black middle class, Jones believed, the "willfully harsh, *anti-assimilationist* sound of bebop fell on deaf or horrified ears, just as it did in white America."[39]

Paradoxically, bebop played a pivotal role in jazz's appropriation as an iconic American cultural form and a "Sonic Weapon" in Cold War diplomacy.[40] As their designation as "moderns" intimated, the beboppers' rebellion against the hackneyed conventions of swing, their harmonic experimentation, and the increasing autonomy of their rhythmically complex music from dance all served to promote jazz's reception as "art music."[41] While subsequent developments in postwar jazz such as the "West Coast" or "cool" tendency of the 1950s diverged in certain respects from bebop's fervent style, most were nonetheless indebted to bebop's harmonic innovation and its predominantly small-band dynamic, which amplified the virtuosity of the instrumental soloist against the backdrop of a pared-down rhythm section. Predictably enough, it was a white jazz musician, the Californian, classically trained pianist and composer Dave Brubeck, who would adorn the cover of *Time* in November 1954. An accompanying article assured readers that "Jazz as played by Brubeck and other [white] modernists (Gerry Mulligan, Chet Baker, Stan Getz, Shorty Rogers) is neither chaotic nor abandoned. It evokes neither swinging hips nor hip flasks. It goes to the head and the heart more than to the feet."[42]

Nevertheless, the enlistment of jazz into Cold War cultural diplomacy had to make room for black artists if it was to achieve one of its principal aims. In the words of Willis Conover, whose "Music USA" programs were broadcast across the Middle East, Asia, and Africa on *Voice of America* from 1955, jazz was uniquely capable of correcting "the fiction that America is racist."[43] So it was that Dizzy Gillespie—perhaps the bebopper least associated with "narcotics" and most widely recognized as a dependable professional—was dispatched, with his band, to the Middle East and South Asia in 1956 as a cultural ambassador under the auspices of the US State Department, in the first of many such official jazz tours astutely chronicled by Penny Von Eschen.[44] On the heels of the conference of nonaligned nations in Bandung, Indonesia, in 1955, the jazz tours and broadcasts assumed a prominent role in the United States' ensuing global charm offensive.

The participation of African-American musicians, including Ellington and Armstrong, did not signify their concurrence that American racism was a "fiction." Rather, the musicians welcomed as progress the recognition of jazz as a serious art form and saw in the expeditions a unique means of sustaining large touring bands that now struggled for survival at home.[45] Though their politics were by no means of a kind, the musicians were rarely unquestioning of the mantras of Cold War-era liberalism. Gillespie would wage an initially humorous but ultimately pointed campaign for the US Presidency in 1964, advocating withdrawal from Vietnam and recognition of the People's Republic of China.[46] Armstrong, though he would perform under the State Department's banner in the Congo in 1960 just months before the assassination of Patrice Lumumba, canceled his scheduled tour of the USSR in 1957 as a protest against President Eisenhower's reluctance to intervene in the Little Rock integration crisis.[47]

Underlying jazz's newly minted diplomatic status was a reading of its creative dynamics as a metaphor for the workings of American democracy, and as their archetypal product. US Representative Frank Thompson Jr., one of the "goodwill" tours' leading congressional advocates, set out the theory in 1956. "The way jazz works," Thompson explained, "is exactly the way a democracy works. *In democracy, we have complete freedom within a previously and mutually agreed framework of tempo, key, and harmonic progression.*"[48] Celebrations of jazz as a democratic conversation among equals tended to disregard the fact that bands almost invariably have their leaders or "frontmen," and their "sidemen" (and the gendered language attests to a further axis of inequality within a jazz world in which women appeared as vocalists, if at all). The authority wielded by some bandleaders made them less akin to elected executives held in check by orchestral legislatures than to tyrants who, to take the bassist Charles Mingus as an admittedly extreme example, unleashed physical violence at the hint of an unwelcome chord out of the assembly.[49] Still, jazz was widely deemed a fitting musical mascot to parade in defiance of Soviet rigidity and repression. As the historian Scott Saul points out, an article in *The New York Times* in 1955 explaining the purpose of the forthcoming tours "hammered five times on the term 'individual' and its cognates—for instance in the tortuous expression that 'individual Americans' (meaning jazz musicians with individual styles) would continue to lure Europeans to their performances."[50]

Something Awful Must Be Happening

That jazz comprised a democratic forum for personal expression was a belief that Ellison and Murray shared. Yet postwar developments in the music generally left them cold, and bebop was for them more an object of embarrassment than a worthy cultural representative on the world stage. Publicly optimistic about American democracy's potential to iron out its defects and fulfill its promise, Ellison confidentially read the changing timbre of jazz as an alarming barometer of national virility. While his essays implied a lukewarm toleration of Charlie "Bird" Parker and the bebop phenomenon, privately he decried jazz's recent transformation.[51] In a letter of 1959 to Murray, omitted from their published correspondence, Ellison, then teaching courses on American literature at Bard College, uncorked his frustration.[52] The records that his enthusiastic students played him were

> teen-age embarrassment and birdshit. When so many musicians can stand up in public and make their horns sound so miserable and self-pitying, castrated and flat, something awful must be happening to the country; something no one has named or even begun to grasp. The stuff sounds gutless and homo. . . . Thank God for old Duke.[53]

Perhaps more prominent in the minds of Americans in 1959 were the Soviets' launch of Sputnik two years previously, the meager growth of the economy since the recession of 1958, the gathering revolution in Cuba, and the alleged "missile gap."[54] Yet the same undertone of anxiety that weighed down an overtly optimistic society, and that impelled John F. Kennedy's barbs at the Eisenhower administration's complacency, found its analogue in Ellison's distaste for the eviscerated masculinity he detected in the jazzmen of the day. Three years later, Ellison would voice this distaste more publicly, if also more guardedly, in an essay that tempered its praise for Parker's "brilliance and imagination" with charges of "self-deprecation and self-pity."[55]

Such terms as "gutless" and "self-pitying" drew their meaning from a constellation of beliefs that Ellison and Murray held in common. By the 1950s, both were partisans of "heroism," a concept that they counterposed against determinism as a means of comprehending the nature of their society and as an ethic by which to live. The starkly gendered language in which these authors championed heroism and traduced determinism was redolent of America's persistently masculine lexicon of republican citizenship as well as the sexually charged imagery of the blues.[56] Indeed, it was largely as a result of the historic denial to African Americans of a status of citizenship idealized by the wider society as an attribute of "manhood" that black political discourse so often exhibited a preoccupation with the assertion of masculinity.[57]

Ellison's advocacy of heroism against determinism both indexed and expedited the recanting of his prewar Marxism, a transition brashly announced by *Invisible Man*'s caustic depiction of "the Brotherhood."[58] By contrast, Murray, who spent the 1950s in the US Air Force managing technical operations in North Africa and teaching geopolitics courses in the ROTC program back at Tuskegee, had no obvious youthful radicalism to recant. After retiring from the military in 1962 at the rank of major, Murray returned to New York and joined with Ellison in detailing the relationship of black culture to the American whole.[59]

The essays collected in Ellison's *Shadow and Act* (1964), those sewn together in Murray's first published volume, *The Omni-Americans* (1970), and Murray's subsequent studies *The Hero and the Blues* (1973) and *Stomping the Blues* (1976) all located within black American musical expression the essence of a heroic sensibility.[60] For these writers, the folk-derived blues idiom encapsulated the ethic of heroism that animated the adventurous quality of American experience. As Ellison put it, Americans "might well be a people whose fundamental attitude toward life is best expressed in the blues."[61] Drawing on Constance Rourke's *American Humor: A Study of the National Character* (1931), a work that both men revered for its appreciation of black Americans' "irreverent wisdom" and "adroit adaptations" as suitable "emblems for a pioneer people," Murray defined the blues tradition as one of "confrontation and improvisation—that is, to use Rourke's word, of "resilience."" This black-originated tradition was "indigenous to the United States, along with the Yankee tradition and that of the backwoodsman."[62]

The heroic persona was, Murray acknowledged, in part a legacy of the ancients and a staple of literary inventions as various as Thomas Mann's *Joseph and His Brothers* and contemporary detective fiction. Yet in the modern world, heroism seemed to Ellison and Murray to have been most powerfully motive in the "futuristic drama of American democracy" and continental expansion.[63] Ellison's parents had been "pioneers in a young state," and he regarded the American novel itself as "a conquest of the frontier; as it describes our experience, it creates it."[64] Blues heroism, then, was as stridently American and as ambiguously universal as Ellison's extraordinary phrase of 1968, "the national human predicament."[65]

In what he confessed was a "shamelessly nostalgic outburst," Ellison had paid tribute in 1958 to the blues singer Jimmy Rushing, whose performances Ellison recalled from his youth. Where Parker's tone was self-pitying, Rushing's voice broke through the hardships of black life in Oklahoma City and entered into an emboldening dialectic with his audience:

> We were pushed off to what seemed to be the least desirable side of the city . . . yet there was an optimism within the Negro community and a sense of possibility which, despite our awareness of limitation (dramatized so brutally in the Tulsa riot of 1921), transcended all of this, and it was this rock-bottom sense of reality, coupled with our sense of the possibility of rising above it, which sounded in Rushing's voice.

Noting that the "feeling of communion" between singer, musicians, and dancers was deepest when Rushing's voice "began to soar with the spirit of the blues," Ellison suggested that the "thinness of much of so-called 'modern jazz' is especially reflective of this loss of wholeness."[66] In 1969 Ellison would valorize Ellington and Armstrong as "stewards of our vaunted American optimism" who had lifted "our morale" during the Depression with their "triumphant" sound. "For us, Duke was a culture hero."[67]

To Ellison and Murray, the "optimism" and "sense of possibility" conjured through music by Rushing, Ellington, and Armstrong comprised heroism's vital qualities. For the artist, the slave, the citizen, and society, freedom itself subsisted in the very aspiration to achieve a conquest. One became heroic, in Murray's words, "by confronting and slaying dragons."[68] Those beasts might appear on the harsh terrains of the Western frontier or on a depressed city block, in one's own self-doubt or in the enmity of others. As Ellison wrote of heroism's most audible expression, "the blues is an art of ambiguity, an assertion of the irrepressibly human over all circumstance, whether created by others or by one's own human failings."[69]

Yet besieging this heroic ethic, in Ellison's and Murray's view, was an insidious force in American life that bore no minor relation to the United States' embattled global position. The negative agent, determinism, sounded in the purportedly disconsolate tone of Parker's horn, with its resignation to human frailty before systemic power. It was this tone that had prompted Ellison's remark to Murray that "something awful must be happening to the country." In the same letter of 1959, Ellison had lamented of the current crop of black musicians that even their record sleeves smacked of the kind of "photo-castration" that the white author, photographer, and patron Carl Van Vechten had perpetrated on his black subjects during the Harlem Renaissance. Reducing bebop to a cult of victimhood and alienation, Ellison concluded with contempt that "these guys are doing to themselves, out of self hate and a child-like self-assertion, exactly what all the years of slavery and second-class citizenship couldn't do—they've killed their own rich Negro sense of life and become zombies."[70]

Bebop's affront to the jazz tradition was, however, but one symptom of the pervasive loss of that heroic optimism without which there could be no freedom. In a testy exchange with the socialist critic Irving Howe in 1963 and 1964, Ellison denounced a black literary style that he considered no less self-pitying than Parker's musical style. Ellison rounded on his early mentor, the novelist Richard Wright, and on sympathetic "sociology-oriented" critics such as Howe who believed, according to Ellison, "that unrelieved suffering is the only 'real' Negro experience":

> For there is also an American Negro tradition which teaches one to deflect racial provocation and to master and contain pain. It is a tradition which abhors as obscene any trading on one's anguish for gain or sympathy; which springs not from a desire to deny the harshness of existence but from a will to deal with it as men at their best have always done. It takes fortitude to be a man, and no less to be an artist.[71]

As his barbed reference to "sociology-oriented critics" attests, Ellison believed that the unheroic subjectivity of victimhood was sanctioned and sustained by the increasing prestige of the social sciences within American culture. As early as 1944, Ellison had assailed social scientists' preoccupation with black "social pathology" and their blindness to black creativity. Objecting to Gunnar Myrdal's claim in *An American Dilemma* that most aspects of black life were "secondary reactions to more primary pressures from the side of the dominant majority," Ellison asked: "Are American Negroes simply the creation of white men, or have they helped to create themselves out of what they found around them? Men have made a way of life in caves and upon cliffs; why cannot Negroes have made a life upon the horns of the white man's dilemma?"[72]

By the 1960s, both Ellison and Murray espoused what Richard King aptly calls "an ongoing (and sometimes tiresome) hostility to social scientific accounts of black life and its institutional inadequacies."[73] In an interview published in 1965, Ellison censured the African-American social psychologist Kenneth B. Clark for neglecting "the heroic side" of black people's lives and their struggle for citizenship.[74] Murray would later recall that his first book, *The Omni-Americans*, had grown out of his concern with "the nature of heroic action" and his rejection of the bleak generalizations and "materialist, biased oversimplifications of social science in the United States."[75] The book tore into what Murray called the "social science fiction" of Clark and others, and into "social science fiction fiction," namely the novels of Richard Wright, James Baldwin, Claude Brown, and other authors whom Murray deemed hostages to the "pseudo-psychiatric nonsense about black self-hatred and self-rejection."[76] Charging that "most American social science theorists and technicians" were "nothing if not Marx-Freud oriented," Murray gave his critique of determinism a decidedly nativist edge.[77] If the "vaunted optimism" of American life was epitomized in the heroic ethic of the blues, the materialist "oversimplifications" of social science and the ethic of victimhood in the literature that it inspired seemed, to Murray, to sag with the weight of European pessimism. Thus Baldwin, with his mournful depictions of Harlem as a "black ghetto," had eschewed "US Negro tradition" and now wrote like a "New York Jewish intellectual of immigrant parents." According to Murray, moreover, the "impertinence" of "European refugees" was "more infuriating to multigeneration US Negroes" than "even the most degenerate rituals of the South."[78]

Years later, Murray traced his antipathy toward the social sciences back to the 1930s, when he had been "coming of age" as an aspiring writer "just at the time when social engineering, in the form of communism, socialism, and so forth, was invading America, coming into American consciousness." Wright's fiction, he claimed, was emblematic of "this compromising of individuality, and individual liberty."[79] For Murray, Wright's Marxism and Baldwin's disregard for "US Negro tradition" were intelligible only as consequences of America's "invasion" by the intrinsically un-American methodologies of the social sciences and social engineering (imported, presumably, by the European refugees of the 1930s).

The Greatest Stuff in the World

At a time when both modern jazz and the social sciences were subjected to attempts at appropriation by the Cold War state, Ellison and Murray derided them as manifestations of a baleful determinism.[80] Yet far from signifying Ellison's and Murray's dissent from the tenets of American self-conception that "made the Cold War a natural way of being toward the world," this derision exemplified a tendency toward moral and social self-critique that was itself characteristic of the tradition of "freedom under siege." Ellison's apprehension in 1959 that "something awful must be happening to the country" only deepened his devotion to what he considered to be authentically American ideals. Believing that determinism posed an existential threat to the heroic faith in human agency, Ellison and Murray looked favorably on the United States' avowed commitment during the 1960s to the expansion of freedom both at home and abroad.

As the literary historian Ross Posnock has argued, contrary to "received wisdom," Ellison's postwar disavowal of Marxism and black nationalism did not signify "political disenchantment and aesthetic refuge." Though Daniel Bell described Ellison, along with James Baldwin, as a "cousin" in the *Partisan Review* family, and many commentators have since ascribed to Ellison a Lionel Trilling-like retreat from the political, Posnock seeks to acquit Ellison on all such charges.[81] He foregrounds the "commitment to action" in Ellison's writings and acutely discerns a kinship between this commitment as expressed by the protagonist of *Invisible Man* ("I believe in nothing if not in action") and Hannah Arendt's exposition of classical republican virtues as the essence of "political action."[82] Indeed, Ellison repeatedly invoked the social responsibilities of the novelist in terms of the obligations of citizenship. In undertaking to write a novel, he stated in 1955, he had accepted "the responsibilities inherited by those who practice the craft in the United States," among which was "the shaping of the culture as I should like it to be."[83] Or, as he put it in 1983, the novelist's role was "to sensitize the nation's ever-floundering conscience," so that "even when concerned mainly with the perfection of his art, the novelist finds himself compelled to consider the moral and political consequences of his fiction."[84]

Ellison's concern for the moral health of the Republic and his admiration for the "heroic" conduct of the civil rights movement certainly qualify his reputation for political quietism.[85] However, if Posnock demonstrates that Ellison was never the apolitical "cold-war high modernist" depicted by many, he is less successful in using Ellison's republicanism to distance the author from "cold-war liberalism."[86] Indeed, Stephanson identifies the "classical republican tradition" as one source of the American belief in "freedom under siege" from which the Cold War derived its character. This republicanism held that "freedom, indissolubly linked to community virtue, is always under threat from the inherent tendency to corruption and degeneration." For George Kennan, Stephanson infers, "domestic ignorance, the corruptions of mass consumption and evils of laxity offered the materials for a veritable Jeremiad on domestic decline, a threat ultimately far more important to him than the actual Soviet one."[87] For Ellison, the American novelist's responsibility was precisely to deliver a jeremiad—to keep alive in the minds of citizens their "obligation of carrying out and fulfilling that vision of democratic freedom" bestowed by the Republic's "sacred documents." And just as there existed from the outset a "flaw" in America's "hopeful project," so, in American fiction from Mark Twain to William Faulkner and beyond, "the Negro and his status have always stood for that moral concern" that compels the novelist.[88]

However pertinent Ellison's and Arendt's overlapping notions of citizenship might have been to the 1960s' vogue for participatory democracy, it is little wonder that, as Posnock observes with a perceptible sense of injustice, they "enjoyed nearly antithetical reputations" among the New Left.[89] Ellison's talk of the "magic" of the Declaration of Independence, the Constitution, and the Bill of Rights was deeply unfashionable among radical and youth movements during an era in which, particularly in light of the war in Vietnam, black nationalists and many on the Left characterized the United States as intrinsically malignant.[90] Whereas Martin Luther King Jr. had offered his audience at the Lincoln Memorial in 1963 "a dream deeply rooted in the American dream," his belief that there remained "funds in the great vaults of opportunity of this nation" was widely renounced within the black power movement that swelled toward the decade's end.[91]

Many black power advocates in fact rejected self-definition as "Americans," some styling themselves as "Africans" while others identified with a global "colored" or "third world" community under the symbolic revolutionary leadership of Mao Zedong.[92] The roll call of black writers and artists such as Du Bois, Maya Angelou, and Julian Mayfield who emigrated to Kwame Nkrumah's Ghana testifies to the waning belief in some black intellectual quarters in the 1960s that one could, as Du Bois himself had hoped at the turn of the century, "be both a Negro and an American."[93] Neither was profound disillusionment with America's democratic promise confined to the ranks of dogmatic black nationalists. The artist Romare Bearden, whose stylizations of African-American life in collage were much admired by Ellison and Murray, believed that "Western society, and particularly that of America, is gravely ill and a major symptom is the American treatment of the Negro."[94] Disgusted with the war in Vietnam and its deleterious effect on the movement for social justice at home, a fraught Martin Luther King telephoned Atlanta's Ebenezer Baptist Church from his Memphis hotel room hours before his assassination on April 4, 1968, to convey the title of the sermon he intended to deliver the following Sunday: "Why America May Go to Hell."[95]

Among jazz musicians, black nationalism galvanized a swathe of the 1960s avant-garde to contest the music's appropriation as an emblem of the American "way of life." The saxophonist Archie Shepp expressed solidarity not only with the struggle against racism at home, but also with the United States' Cold War adversaries abroad. "Our vindication will be black," he expounded, "as the color of suffering is black, as Fidel is black, as Ho Chi Minh is black."[96] Baraka detected in John Coltrane's reworking of such standards as "My Favorite Things" an attempt to "do away with weak Western forms" by "murder[ing] the popular song," and heard in the experimentation of Shepp, Sun Ra, and others an effort to redirect jazz toward "Eastern" melodic motifs as well as the music's original "African influences."[97] His study *Blues People* (1963), which set out to narrate the history of African Americans by chronicling the transformation of their music from the slave songs to the jazz avant-garde, had characterized the blues as a music that could only have emerged in response to the conditions of American life as experienced by the slaves and their descendants. Yet even at this early stage of his journey from New York's interracial bohemia to a strident black separatism, Jones, as he then was, unmistakably cast the blues as a music and an ethic of *resistance* to America—a repository of black authenticity that periodically reasserted itself against the predations of the American "mainstream," as in the case of bebop or the "free jazz" of the contemporary avant-garde.[98]

All of this was anathema to Ellison. "The tremendous burden of sociology that Jones would place upon this body of music," he quipped in the *New York Review of Books*, "is enough to give even the blues the blues." Objecting to Jones's affirmation of bebop as an "antimainstream" music that had salvaged jazz from the dilution of its blackness in the swing era, Ellison countered with his syncretic theory of American culture. Slavery and segregation notwithstanding, freedom to make what they would of the cultural materials surrounding them was what black Americans had enjoyed "in place of [political] freedom."[99] Moreover, there had never been a "mainstream of American music," capable of diluting black forms, to which black creativity had not already contributed. In *Blues People*, Ellison felt, Jones had hit upon the exact problem—the ubiquitous "confusion" over black people's "American identity"—only to deepen it.[100]

Underpinning these divergent perspectives on black music were antithetical conceptions of America and the possibilities inherent in its citizenship. What was the nature of the country, Jones asked at the end of *Blues People*, that its black inhabitants were "being asked to save" from the threat of "totally hostile systems"?[101] The answer intimated by the preceding pages of his book was that it was the same America *against* which black people had struggled with their lives and their music for more than three hundred years. By 1964, Jones claimed that segregation maintained "an absolute gulf that separates white from black," which in turn "spawns, continues, *separate* cultures." In an essay entitled "The Last Days of the American Empire (Including Some Instructions for Black People)," Jones counseled that "there is *no chance* that the American white man will change." The America that civil rights leaders sought to enter "as if it were paradise" was in fact only a "deep stinking hole," and the "sparkling democratic utopias of the future" peddled by white liberals were, and always had been, dreams "in the dust of never-never land."[102] Mississippi, Harlem, and the Congo were all corners of the same ruthless "worldAmerica [*sic.*]," the only variation being "the method the white man employs to suppress and murder." And yet, even as he prophesized Lyndon Johnson as "a war criminal of the not so distant future," Jones regarded the American "power structure" as increasingly "desperate" in the face of "liberation fronts" emerging across the globe.[103]

Ellison, meanwhile, came to regard Johnson's presidency as confirmation that "the white man" would indeed change. In an essay first published in 1968, he speculated that his fondness for the Texan was mediated by the "old slave-born myth" of "the flawed white Southerner" who is "redeemed," and who "will do the right thing however great the cost, whether he likes Negroes or not, and will move with tragic vulnerability toward the broader ideals of American democracy." Likening the distrust many of his fellow intellectuals harbored toward this "Texan intoning the values of humanism" to the proverbial suspicion of a "Greek bearing gifts," Ellison explained that it was his "own interests and background" that compelled him to "bear witness" to the contrary.[104] He, too, was "concerned about the war in Vietnam and would like to see it ended." And yet,

> I am also familiar with other costly wars of much longer duration right here at home—the war against poverty and the war for racial equality—and therefore I cannot so easily ignore the changes that the President has made in the condition of my people and still consider myself a responsible intellectual. My sense of priorities is necessarily different.[105]

While many liberals and civil rights activists, most notably King, excoriated Johnson precisely for the damage inflicted on the war on poverty by the war in Vietnam, Ellison appeared content with the president's assurance that there could be both guns and butter. Moreover, his stated wish to see the war in Vietnam "ended" overlay a decidedly hawkish subtext. At the invitation of Paul Douglas, the former US senator from Illinois, Ellison had in 1967 joined the misleadingly named Citizens Committee for Peace with Freedom in Vietnam, an "elite pro-war group" that numbered Presidents Truman and Eisenhower among its members.[106] Writing to thank Johnson for a brief audience and a signed photograph that same year, Ellison invoked the language of heroism, suggesting that "a broad capacity for making the unbelievable a reality is a mark of your personal style, and the nation is fortunate that this is so."[107]

The "unbelievable" that the president had signed into reality with the civil rights and voting rights legislation was the very "magic" conceived in America's founding documents. What one listened for in the utterances of a president, Ellison remarked in his 1968 essay, was "his awareness of the hopes and values of a diverse people struggling to achieve the American promise in their own time," and Johnson's speech "To Fulfill These Rights," delivered at Howard University in 1964, had "spelled out the full meaning of integration for Negroes" with singular purpose.[108] The nature of Ellison's admiration for Johnson divulges the essence of his own "Cold War liberalism." Just as the president's commitment to civil rights abjured any contraction of the American democratic promise, so his stubborn pursuit of military victory in Vietnam seemed to Ellison to encapsulate the "vaunted optimism" that propelled America's stewardship of human freedom.

In 1955 Ellison had already recognized that American democracy's newly global purview thrust its own core moral concern, that of "the Negro and his status," further in the direction of universality:

> Our so-called race problem has now lined up with the world problems of colonialism and the struggle of the West to gain the allegiance of the remaining non-white people who have thus far remained outside the Communist sphere; thus its possibilities for art have increased rather than lessened. Looking at the novelist as manipulator and depictor of moral problems, I ask myself how much of the achievement of democratic ideals in the United States has been affected by the steady pressure of Negroes and those who were sensitive to the implications of our condition, and I know that without that pressure the position of our country before the world would be much more serious even than it is now.[109]

Summoned in 1966 to testify before a US Senate subcommittee on the urban crisis, the congruence between Ellison's positions on civil rights and Vietnam became explicit. Jacob Javits, the liberal Republican senator from New York, put it to Ellison that the predicament of urban blacks was not simply a "Negro crisis," but a "national crisis" much like the United States' situation in Vietnam. Javits saw "no reason, with all respect, why one can't be strongly back of our policy there and strongly back of our policy here." "I certainly agree, Senator," came Ellison's reply, to which he added that such crises as war and economic depression, though tragic, often bore the consolation for "the Negro" that "democracy spreads."[110] As civil rights marchers pitted their bodies against segregation, and black city dwellers struggled against the cruelties of their urban environment, and blues singers intoned survival and transcendence, and novelists protected the very belief in heroic action from the limiting concepts of determinism and victimhood, so Ellison, with optimism, demanded "freedom" in Vietnam. From the perspective of Cold War liberalism, the very peculiarity of the United States was, after all, its singular historical role in substantiating an aspiration toward freedom that was potentially universal. The alignment of America's "so-called race problem" with the "world problems" of colonialism and totalitarianism rendered visible that embattled striving after freedom that Ellison surely had in mind when he wrote of "the universality of Harlem life and the 'harlemness' of the national human predicament."[111]

The potential for coexistence between the Republican language of political action and the tenets of Cold War liberalism is perhaps even more striking in Murray's elaboration of heroic virtue:

> Heroism, which is, among other things, another word for self-reliance, is not only the indispensable prerequisite for productive citizenship in an open society; it is also that without which no individual or community can remain free. Moreover, as no one interested in either the objectives

> of democratic institutions or the image of democratic man can ever afford to forget, the concept of free enterprise has as much to do with adventurous speculations and improvisations in general as with the swashbuckling economics of, say, the Robber Barons.[112]

Thus did blues capitalists launch daring melodic flights over the market's riffs and changes. A constant refrain of Murray's writing, meanwhile, was that black nationalists who renounced America as "the White Man's country" capitulated to "the propagandists of white supremacy." Enraged "black militants" spoke of liberation "as if one could exercise the right of redress without first claiming one's constitutional identity as citizen!"[113] Their claim to an "African" identity appeared to Murray a comic, if disastrous, folly. "Who's greater than the United States! And we are an inextricable part of that," he told an interviewer in 1994. "And you're going to give up all of that, the greatest stuff in the world, to go back and claim you don't have a pisspot on the left-handed side of the Nile? Of the Zulu River? That just seems ridiculous to me."[114]

Even as slaves, Murray had stated in *The Omni-Americans*, blacks in the United States had been "*living in the presence of more human freedom and individual opportunity than they or anyone else had ever seen before*. That the *conception* of being a free man in America was infinitely richer than any notion of individuality in the Africa of that period goes without saying."[115] Always more of a polemicist (and a chauvinist) than Ellison, Murray nonetheless shared with his friend the belief that black people were at their most characteristically American—were, indeed, the very epitome of the American—when asserting their rights as citizens. "The most dramatic fight for American ideals," Ellison had written in 1958, "is being sparked by black Americans." Far from pitching their art and their lives against America, as Baraka claimed, theirs was "the most authoritative rendering of America in music."[116]

Since his death in 1994, as the politics of the Cold War were giving way to those of the "culture wars," Ellison has been fought over, and against, without mercy. The latest major scholarly treatment of his life has been greeted by one reviewer as nothing less than "a lynching" by the coarse rope of "political correctness."[117] Yet an array of liberal and neoconservative commentators have claimed Ellison's mantle with equal fervor as they offer up competing interpretations of his American nationalism, his cosmopolitanism, his affirmation of black culture, and his straining against the strictures of race. Scholarship now presents us with many Ralph Ellisons to explore, pick apart, rebuke, and revere—the democrat, the snob, the artist, the political theorist, the radical, the conservative, and many more. One devotee who seems to trouble each of these categories in a not dissimilar fashion is the columnist and pundit Stanley Crouch. A repentant former admirer of Baraka, in the 1970s Crouch acquired a new "mentor" in the person of Murray, and credits Ellison's writings, too, with clearing his path away from black nationalism.[118] As the principal advisors to the Jazz at Lincoln Center programs directed by the trumpeter Wynton Marsalis, Crouch and Murray have exerted a sizeable influence over American musical education through their "neoclassical" canon formation, organized primarily around Ellington, Armstrong, and a limited interpretation of their musical legacy.[119]

Though Crouch is in no sense Ellison reincarnate, his writings manifest the continuation and reinvention of particular traditions of American ideology and self-perception—of freedom (and blues) under siege—which Ellison's postwar literary career had helped to shape. A sharp-tongued critic of identity politics and academic cynicism, Crouch champions a "sense of heroic optimism" against the "sink holes of self-pity" and defeatist finger-pointing at "the system."[120] It seems fitting, then, to close with the verdict Crouch offered in 1995 on the impact of black Americans and their music on the course of the Cold War:

> Those given to no more than carping are unprepared to address the tragic optimism at the center of the metaphor that is the Constitution. They know nothing of heroic engagement, the engagement that would not allow one to misunderstand the singing of "We Shall Overcome" in the town square of Prague as Dubček stood on the balcony looking into the faces he had been exiled from seeing in the flesh by the Communist party. It is an engagement that would not allow one to miss the meaning of the Red Chinese troops having to destroy a crudely built Statue of Liberty with even cruder means when the night was filled with the familiar violence of totalitarianism in Tiananmen Square. That engagement would recognize that the very success of our struggle to extend democracy has inspired the world, and much of that extending has been the result of the efforts of people at war with the social limitations that were so severely imposed upon Negro Americans.[121]

Notes

1. Westad, "The New International History of the Cold War: Three (Possible) Paradigms," *Diplomatic History*, 24 (2000), pp. 551–565, quotations at p. 552; Stephanson, "Liberty or Death: The Cold War as US Ideology" in *Reviewing the Cold War: Approaches, Interpretations, Theory*, ed. Odd Arne Westad (London, 2000), pp. 81–100. For these two scholars' differing conceptions of "the Cold War," see also Chapters 1 and 2 of this volume.
2. Bell, *The End of Ideology: On the Exhaustion of Political Ideas in the Fifties* (Glencoe, I.L, 1960).
3. Westad, "New International History of the Cold War," 554 (emphasis in original). See Westad, *The Global Cold War: Third World Interventions and the Making of Our Times*

(Cambridge, 2005). On the role of ideology in Cold War high diplomacy, see also Melvyn Leffler, *For the Soul of Mankind: The United States, the Soviet Union, and the Cold War* (New York, 2007).

4. See Chapter 11 of this volume. See also David Engerman, "Social Science in the Cold War," *Isis* 101 (2010), pp. 393–400; Joel Isaac, "The Human Sciences in Cold War America: A Historiographical Review," *Historical Journal*, 50 (2007), pp. 725–746; Isaac, *Working Knowledge: Making the Human Sciences from Parsons to Kuhn* (Cambridge, MA, 2012). Among the boldest formulations of the Cold War's impact on American culture and intellectual life are Ellen Schrecker, *No Ivory Tower: McCarthyism and the Universities* (New York, 1986); Jessica Wang, *American Science in an Age of Anxiety: Scientists, Anticommunism, and the Cold War* (Chapel Hill, 1999).
5. Stephanson, "Liberty or Death."
6. See Chapter 4 of this volume; quotation at p. 77.
7. Stephanson, "Liberty or Death," p. 95.
8. Ibid. pp. 84–86. The role of enmity in American identity and foreign policy is also examined in David Campbell, *Writing Security: United States Foreign Policy and the Politics of Identity* (Minneapolis, 1998).
9. Westad, "New International History of the Cold War," p. 563.
10. Baraka, *The Autobiography of LeRoi Jones* (Chicago, 1997), p. 376.
11. Du Bois, *The Souls of Black Folk: Essays and Sketches* (1903; London, 1905), p. 3; Du Bois, "Criteria of Negro Art," *Crisis* 32 (1926), p. 296.
12. Ellison, "Haverford Statement" (1969), in *The Collected Essays of Ralph Ellison*, ed. John F. Callahan (New York, 1995), p. 429.
13. Jones (Amiri Baraka), *Blues People: Negro Music in White America* (1963; New York, 2002), p. 236 (emphasis added).
14. Quoted from the preface included in early editions of the book. See LeRoi Jones, *Blues People: Negro Music in White America* (New York, 1963), p. x. All subsequent references will be to the 2002 edition.
15. Dudziak, *Cold War Civil Rights: Race and the Image of American Democracy* (Princeton, 2000); Borstelmann, *The Cold War and the Color Line: American Race Relations in the Global Arena* (Cambridge, MA, 2003). On civil rights and diplomacy in the Cold War era, see also Carol Anderson, *Eyes Off the Prize: The United Nations and the African-American Struggle for Human Rights, 1944–1955* (New York, 2003); Penny Von Eschen, *Race Against Empire: Black Americans and Anticolonialism, 1937–1957* (Ithaca, 1997); Thomas Noer, *Cold War and Black Liberation: The United States and White Rule in Africa, 1948–1968* (Columbia, 1985); Brenda Plummer (ed.), *Window on Freedom: Race, Civil Rights, and Foreign Affairs, 1945–1988* (Chapel Hill, 2003).
16. Gaines, *African Americans in Ghana: Black Expatriates and the Civil Rights Era* (Chapel Hill, 2008); Joseph, *Waiting 'Til the Midnight Hour: A Narrative History of Black Power in America* (New York, 2006); Tyson, *Radio Free Dixie: Robert F. Williams and the Roots of Black Power* (Chapel Hill, 1999); Kelley and Esch, "Black Like Mao: Red China and Black Revolution," *Souls*, 1 (1999), pp. 6–41.
17. Du Bois, *Souls of Black Folk*, p. 3. For more on Du Bois's life and thought, see David Lewis, *W. E. B. Du Bois: The Fight for Equality and the American Century, 1919–1963* (New York, 2000); Adolph Reed, *W. E. B. Du Bois and American Political Thought: Fabianism and the Color Line* (New York, 1997); Shamoon Zamir, *Dark Voices: W. E. B. Du Bois and American Thought, 1888–1903* (Chicago, 1995).
18. Ellison, "Blues People" (1964), in *Collected Essays of Ralph Ellison*, p. 283.
19. Murray, *The Omni-Americans: New Perspectives on Black Experience and American Culture* (New York, 1970), p. 22.
20. Baraka [untitled address, September 1970], in *African Congress: A Documentary of the First Modern Pan-African Congress*, ed. Imamu Amiri Baraka (LeRoi Jones) (New York, 1972), p. 101.

21. Philip Rieff, *The Triumph of the Therapeutic: Uses of Faith After Freud* (New York, 1966); Ellen Herman, *The Romance of American Psychology: Political Culture in the Age of Experts* (Berkeley, 1995).
22. Baraka's therapeutic theorization of black power is discussed in Chapter 2 of Daniel Matlin, *On the Corner: Black Intellectuals and the Urban Crisis* (Cambridge, MA, forthcoming).
23. Reputed authors of this aphorism include Laurie Anderson, Frank Zappa, and Thelonius Monk. See Stephen Travis Pope, "Editor's Notes: Dancing About Architecture?" *Computer Music Journal*, 17 (1993), p. 4.
24. Murray, *Omni-Americans*, p. 59.
25. Ted Gioia, *The History of Jazz* (New York, 1997), pp. 29–53, esp. pp. 31–32.
26. Gioia, *The History of Jazz*, pp. 155–157; Alyn Shipton, *A New History of Jazz* (London, 2001), pp. 356–357.
27. "Bunk Johnson Rides Again," *Time*, May 24, 1943, http://www.time.com/time/magazine/article/0,9171,933016,00.html (accessed June 16, 2011); Shipton, *New History of Jazz*, p. 620.
28. For a masterly account, see Scott DeVeaux, *The Birth of Bebop: A Social and Musical History* (Berkeley, 1997).
29. Ralph Ellison, "The Golden Age, Time Past" (1959), in *Collected Essays of Ralph Ellison*, p. 240.
30. Henry Louis Gates, "King of Cats," *Thirteen Ways of Looking at a Black Man* (New York: Vintage, 1998), p. 31; Ralph Ellison, *Invisible Man* (1952; London, 2001).
31. Gates, "Introduction: Ways of Looking," *Thirteen Ways of Looking at a Black Man*, p. xxiii.
32. Ellison's claim to have been born in 1914 is convincingly refuted in Lawrence Jackson, "Ralph Ellison's Invented Life: A Meeting with the Ancestors" in *The Cambridge Companion to Ralph Ellison*, ed. Ross Posnock (Cambridge, 2005), p. 18.
33. On Ellison's trumpet playing, see Ralph Ellison, "Living with Music" (1955), in *Collected Essays of Ralph Ellison*, pp. 230–232.
34. See Ellison, "Homage to Duke Ellington on His Birthday" (1969), in *Collected Essays of Ralph Ellison*, pp. 678–681.
35. Scott DeVeaux, "Constructing the Jazz Tradition" (1991), in *The Jazz Cadence of American Culture*, ed. Robert O'Meally (New York, 1998), p. 493.
36. "Be-Bop Be-Bopped," *Time*, March 25, 1946, http://www.time.com/time/magazine/article/0,9171,888157,00.html (accessed June 16, 2011).
37. Ingrid Monson, "The Problem with White Hipness: Race, Gender, and Cultural Conceptions in Jazz Historical Discourse," *Journal of the American Musicological Society*, 48 (1995), p. 411.
38. Lewis Erenberg, "Things to Come: Swing Bands, Bebop, and the Rise of the Postwar Jazz Scene" in Lary May (ed.), *Recasting America: Culture and Politics in the Age of Cold War* (Chicago, 1989), p. 237.
39. Jones, *Blues People*, pp. 181–182 (emphasis in original).
40. Felix Belair, "United States Has Secret Sonic Weapon—Jazz," *The New York Times*, November 6, 1955, p. 1.
41. On jazz's recognition as "art music," see Paul Lopes, *The Rise of a Jazz Art World* (Cambridge, 2002).
42. The *Time* covermay beviewed athttp://www.time.com/time/covers/0,16641,19541108,00.html (accessed June 16, 2011). The accompanying article is "The Man on Cloud Nine," *Time*, November 8, 1954, http://www.time.com/time/magazine/article/0,9171,857657,00.html (accessed June 16, 2011).
43. Von Eschen, *Satchmo Blows Up the World: Jazz Ambassadors Play the Cold War* (Cambridge, MA, 2004), p. 16.
44. On Gillespie's 1956 tour, see Von Eschen, *Satchmo Blows Up the World*, pp. 31–39.
45. Von Eschen, *Satchmo Blows Up the World*, p. 18.

46. See Alyn Shipton, *Groovin' High: The Life of Dizzy Gillespie* (New York, 2001), pp. 320–334.
47. Von Eschen, *Satchmo Blows Up the World*, pp. 71, 63.
48. Quoted in Scott Saul, *Freedom Is, Freedom Ain't: Jazz and the Making of the Sixties* (Cambridge, MA, 2003), p. 15 (emphasis in Thompson's original writing).
49. On Mingus's intolerance of diminished chords and his violent reprisals against band members, see Saul, *Freedom Is, Freedom Ain't*, pp. 149, 158–159.
50. Saul, *Freedom Is, Freedom Ain't*, p. 19.
51. See Ralph Ellison, "On Bird, Bird-Watching and Jazz" (1962), in *Collected Essays of Ralph Ellison*, pp. 256–265.
52. The published correspondence appears as *Trading Twelves: The Selected Letters of Ralph Ellison and Albert Murray*, ed. John Callahan (New York, 2000). On Ellison's spell at Bard College, see Arnold Rampersad, *Ralph Ellison: A Biography* (New York, 2007), pp. 359–380.
53. Ellison to Murray, [July?] 1959, [second folder of Ellison correspondence,] box 1, Albert Murray Papers, Houghton Library, Harvard University, Cambridge, M.A.
54. James Patterson, *Grand Expectations: The United States, 1945–1974* (New York, 1996), p. 436.
55. Ellison, "On Bird, Bird-Watching and Jazz," p. 246.
56. On the enduring "grammar of manhood" in American discussions of citizenship, see Mark Kann, *A Republic of Men: The American Founders, Gendered Language and Patriarchal Politics* (New York, 1998). On the significance of "manhood" within African-American politics and culture, see Phillip Brian Harper, *Are We Not Men? Masculine Anxiety and the Problem of African-American Identity* (New York, 1996). On the blues and sexuality, see Marybeth Hamilton, "Sexuality, Authenticity and the Making of the Blues Tradition," *Past and Present*, 169 (2000), pp. 132–160.
57. Kevin Gaines, *Uplifting the Race: Black Leadership, Politics, and Culture in the Twentieth Century* (Chapel Hill, 1996).
58. Ellison, *Invisible Man*. On Ellison's Communist period, see Rampersad, *Ralph Ellison*, pp. 81–169.
59. For details of Murray's military career, see Gates, "King of Cats," p. 32.
60. Ellison, *Shadow and Act* (New York: Random House, 1964) (reproduced within *Collected Essays of Ralph Ellison*); Murray, *Omni-Americans*; Murray, *The Hero and the Blues* (New York, 1973); Albert Murray, *Stomping the Blues* (1976; London, 1978).
61. Ellison, "If the Twain Shall Meet" (1964), in *Collected Essays of Ralph Ellison*, p. 575.
62. Murray, *Omni-Americans*, pp. 16–17; Ellison, "Blues People," p. 287; Rourke, *American Humor: A Study of the National Character* (New York, 1931).
63. Ellison, "Address at the Whiting Foundation" (1992), in *Collected Essays of Ralph Ellison*, p. 851.
64. "'A Completion of Personality': A Talk with Ralph Ellison" (1974), in *Collected Essays of Ralph Ellison*, 788; "The Art of Fiction: An Interview" (1955), in ibid., p. 224.
65. Ellison, "The Art of Romare Bearden" (1968), in *Collected Essays of Ralph Ellison*, p. 688.
66. Ellison, "Remembering Jimmy" (1958), in *Collected Essays of Ralph Ellison*, pp. 273–275.
67. Ellison, "Homage to Duke Ellington on His Birthday," pp. 677–679.
68. Murray, *Hero and the Blues*, p. 39.
69. Ellison, "Remembering Jimmy," p. 277.
70. Ellison to Murray, [July?] 1959.
71. Ellison, "The World and the Jug" (1963/1964) in *Collected Essays of Ralph Ellison*, ed. Callahan, pp. 155–156, 159.
72. Ellison, "*An American Dilemma*: A Review," in *Collected Essays of Ralph Ellison*, p. 339. Though written in 1944, Ellison's review was first published in 1964, in *Shadow and Act*. See also Gunnar Myrdal with the assistance of Richard Sterner and Arnold Rose, *An American Dilemma: The Negro Problem and Modern Democracy*, 2 vols. (New York, 1944); Walter Jackson, *Gunnar Myrdal and America's Conscience: Social Engineering and Racial Liberalism, 1938–1987* (Chapel Hill, 1990).

73. King, *Race, Culture, and the Intellectuals, 1940–1970* (Washington, DC, 2004), p. 296. King offers a valuable discussion of Ellison's and Murray's perspective on black culture and American life in ibid., pp. 290–303.
74. Robert Penn Warren, *Who Speaks for the Negro?* (New York, 1965), p. 340. See also Kenneth B. Clark, *Dark Ghetto: Dilemmas of Social Power* (London, 1965).
75. Murray, "The Function of the Heroic Image" (1985), in *Jazz Cadence of American Culture*, p. 571.
76. Murray, *Omni-Americans*, pp. 47, 97–103, 143–168.
77. Ibid., p. 33.
78. Ibid., pp. 149, 76–77. On the often vexed relationship between black and Jewish writers in America, see Eric Sundquist, *Strangers in the Land: Blacks, Jews, Post-Holocaust America* (Cambridge, MA, 2005).
79. Albert Murray interviewed by Robert O'Meally for the Smithsonian Institution Jazz Oral History Program, session 1, New York City, June 30, 1994, transcript, box 1, Murray Papers.
80. On the social sciences, see Terence Ball, "The Politics of Social Science in Postwar America," in May (ed.), *Recasting America*, pp. 76–92; Ellen Herman, "The Career of Cold War Psychology," *Radical History Review*, 63 (1995), pp. 53–85.
81. Posnock, "Ralph Ellison, Hannah Arendt and the Meaning of Politics," in Posnock (ed.), *Cambridge Companion to Ralph Ellison*, p. 204. Posnock cites, as an example of this scholarly tendency, Thomas Schaub, *American Fiction in the Cold War* (Madison, 1991), to which might be added Rampersad, *Ralph Ellison*; and Jerry Gafio Watts, *Heroism and the Black Intellectual: Ralph Ellison, Politics, and Afro-American Intellectual Life* (Chapel Hill, 1994). Watts writes of Ellison's "perception of the ideal writer as politically disengaged." His study characterizes Ellison's response to the "social marginality" of African-American intellectuals as a "call for heroic individualism" in the form of "fine artistic transcendence," but does not consider how Ellison's notion of heroism appropriated the republican language of citizenship and freedom. Ibid., 48, 22.
82. Posnock, "Ralph Ellison, Hannah Arendt and the Meaning of Politics," p. 203; Ellison, *Invisible Man*, p. 13; Hannah Arendt, *The Human Condition* (New York, 1958; 1998).
83. Ellison, "Art of Fiction," p. 224.
84. Ellison, "Presentation to Bernard Malamud on the Gold Medal for Fiction" (1983), in *Collected Essays of Ralph Ellison*, p. 466.
85. For Ellison's characterization of the civil rights movement as "heroic," see Warren, *Who Speaks for the Negro?* p. 204.
86. Posnock, "Ralph Ellison, Hannah Arendt and the Meaning of Politics," pp. 204, 212.
87. Stephanson, "Liberty or Death," pp. 85–86. On the American republican Jeremiad, see also Vibeke Schou Tjalve, *Realist Strategies of Republican Peace: Niebuhr, Morgenthau, and the Politics of Patriotic Dissent* (Basingstoke, 2008).
88. Ellison, "Commencement Address at the College of William and Mary" (1972), in *Collected Essays of Ralph Ellison*, ed. Callahan, pp. 407–409; "Art of Fiction," p. 223.
89. Posnock, "Ralph Ellison, Hannah Arendt and the Meaning of Politics," 203. On the salience of Arendt's political thought to the civil rights movement, see Richard King, *Civil Rights and the Idea of Freedom* (New York, 1992).
90. Ellison, "Commencement Address at the College of William and Mary," p. 408.
91. King Jr., "I Have a Dream" (1963), in *A Call to Conscience: The Landmark Speeches of Dr. Martin Luther King, Jr.*, ed. Clayborne Carson and Kris Shepard (London, 2001), pp. 85, 82.
92. Daniel Matlin, "'Lift Up Yr Self!' Reinterpreting Amiri Baraka (LeRoi Jones), Black Power, and the Uplift Tradition," *Journal of American History*, 93 (2006), pp. 91–116; Kelley and Esch, "Black Like Mao."
93. Kevin K. Gaines, "The Cold War and the African American Expatriate Community in Nkrumah's Ghana" in Christopher Simpson (ed.), *Universities and Empire: Money and*

Politics in the Social Sciences During the Cold War (New York, 1998), pp. 135–158; Du Bois, *Souls of Black Folk*, p. 3.

94. Jeanne Siegel, "Why Spiral?" *ARTnews* (September 1966), p. 49. Bearden's complex intellectual relationships with Ellison and Murray are examined in Matlin, "Black Intellectuals and Black Urban Life in the United States."
95. David Garrow, *Bearing the Cross: Martin Luther King Jr. and the Southern Christian Leadership Conference* (London, 1993), p. 622.
96. Shepp, "An Artist Speaks Bluntly," *Down Beat* (December 16, 1965), p. 11.
97. LeRoi Jones (Imamu Amiri Baraka), "New Black Music" (1965), *Black Music* (1968; New York: Da Capo Press, 1998), p. 174; LeRoi Jones (Imamu Amiri Baraka), "New Tenor Archie Shepp Talking" (1965), ibid., p. 153.
98. Jones, *Blues People*.
99. Ellison, "Blues People," pp. 279, 282.
100. Ibid., pp. 285, 283.
101. Jones, *Blues People*, p. 236.
102. LeRoi Jones, "The Last Days of the American Empire (Including Some Instructions for Black People)" (1964), *Home: Social Essays* (1966; Hopewell, NJ, 1998), pp. 193, 197–198, 204 (emphasis in original).
103. LeRoi Jones, "The Last Days of the American Empire," pp. 190, 199–201.
104. Ellison, "The Myth of the Flawed White Southerner" (1968), in *Collected Essays of Ralph Ellison*, p. 561.
105. Ibid., p. 557.
106. Rampersad, *Ralph Ellison*, pp. 438–439.
107. Ibid., p. 439.
108. Ellison, "Myth of the Flawed White Southerner," pp. 556, 552.
109. Ellison, "Art of Fiction," pp. 223–224.
110. Ellison, "Harlem's America," *New Leader* (September 26, 1966), p. 27.
111. Ellison, "Art of Romare Bearden," p. 688.
112. Murray, *Hero and the Blues*, pp. 83–84.
113. Murray, *Omni-Americans*, p. 21.
114. Murray interviewed by O'Meally, session 4.
115. Murray, *Omni-Americans*, p. 18 (emphasis in original).
116. Ralph Ellison, "Some Questions and Some Answers" (1958), in *Collected Essays of Ralph Ellison*, p. 299; Ellison, "Blues People," p. 285.
117. Joseph Epstein, "Artist as Hero: Ralph Ellison, Indivisible Man," review of *Ralph Ellison*, by Rampersad, *Weekly Standard*, June 18, 2007, http://www.theweeklystandard.com/Content/Public/Articles/000/000/013/740rjpkv.asp (accessed June 16, 2011).
118. Crouch, *Notes of a Hanging Judge: Essays and Reviews, 1979–1989* (New York, 1990), pp. xi, xiv.
119. John Gennari, *Blowin' Hot and Cool: Jazz and Its Critics* (Chicago, 2006), pp. 339–371.
120. Crouch, *Notes of a Hanging Judge*, p. 6.
121. Crouch, "Blues to Be Constitutional: A Long Look at the Wild Wherefores of Our Democratic Lives as Symbolized in the Making of Rhythm and Tune" (1995), in O'Meally (ed.), *Jazz Cadence of American Culture*, pp. 157–158.

10

Cold War Culture and the Lingering Myth of Sacco and Vanzetti

MOSHIK TEMKIN

Nicola Sacco and Bartolomeo Vanzetti probably should never have become the stuff of angry, politically charged conflict in the late 1950s and early 1960s; they were protagonists of an earlier, entirely different era, the turbulent years that followed World War I. In May 1920, at the height of the postwar Red Scare, Sacco and Vanzetti, Italian immigrants and revolutionary anarchists who had been living and working in the United States for twelve years, the former as a skilled heel trimmer and the latter as an unskilled laborer, were arrested for taking part in the robbery and murder of a shoe factory paymaster and his guard in South Braintree, Massachusetts, an industrial suburb of Boston. Their 1921 trial did not make national headlines at first. The criminal evidence against the two men—who pleaded not guilty—was mostly circumstantial. The prosecution based much of its case against the two men on a so-called consciousness of guilt: the defendants had made false statements to the police and, supposedly, behaved "suspiciously" before they were arrested. To no one's great surprise, Sacco and Vanzetti were convicted in July 1921. As expected under Massachusetts law, they were later sentenced to death by electrocution. They were not executed, however, until August 23, 1927, by which time their previously obscure case had become a national and worldwide cause célèbre, fueled by the notion that they were innocent men punished by the authorities for their radical political beliefs, ethnic background, and social position, and resulting in a period of unprecedented global protest and domestic wrangling that involved public intellectuals, political leaders, religious figures, legal experts, social activists, business elites, artists, diplomats, and countless ordinary people.

There have been numerous volumes published on this famous case since the 1920s, most of which have focused primarily on one of two things—trying to show either that Sacco and Vanzetti were innocent or that they were guilty. Often confusing amateur sleuthing with historical scholarship, many of the chroniclers of the case have largely neglected its broader public receptions and repercussions in the United States and abroad—especially its long afterlife, the history of what happened *after* what happened.[1] This chapter will focus on one aspect of Sacco and Vanzetti's significance over space and time—the unexpected return of their case to the public sphere in the Cold War-era United States.

It may be counterintuitive to think of Sacco and Vanzetti as headliners for the atomic age. They had been anarchists, not communists; they were Italian immigrants, a group that had since been assimilated into the mainstream of American society; they were merely two men, as compared to the many millions massacred in the 1930s and 1940s in the name of total ideologies. By the late 1950s the issue of Sacco and Vanzetti had settled in the United States into a largely unchallenged narrative that depicted the case as the product of the Red Scare and of the insistence of the legal and political authorities to prefer the status quo over justice. As the prominent journalist Murray Kempton put it in 1955, "very few of Sacco and Vanzetti's enemies feel in a position any longer to dispute the major cantos of their epic—poverty, false witness, testament, and crucifixion."[2]

In an intellectual context, liberal scholars of the 1950s, including Richard Hofstadter, Frederick Hoffman, Arthur Schlesinger Jr., and Robert K. Murray, were influential in portraying the Red Scare as the product of nativist hysteria and Sacco and Vanzetti as perhaps its two most celebrated victims. The so-called consensus historians of the 1950s, as well as journalists and memoirists such as Kempton, also did much to promote the idea that the Sacco-Vanzetti affair was a critical impetus for the transition of a generation of young American intellectuals from the supposedly escapist, apolitical alienation of the 1920s to the political engagement (and leftist radicalism) of the 1930s.[3] To be sure, these ideas were not new to the 1950s. They had already been promoted during the New Deal era by such prominent policymakers and public figures as Harold Ickes, Malcolm Cowley, and Paul Kellogg, all of whom helped crystallize a point of view that turned into a commonplace over time: since the trial and execution of Sacco and Vanzetti had been unjust and irrational, by extension the ensuing radicalization could be seen as justified and logical. Liberal historians of the 1950s also implied that American political culture had come far since the 1920s, but dangerous long-term trends, such as anti-intellectualism and the hatred of foreigners and nonconformists—or the lingering power of what Richard Hofstadter, thinking primarily of the McCarthy episode, memorably termed "cranky pseudo-conservatism"—were endangering that progress.[4]

But despite the apparent accord that had developed over the Sacco-Vanzetti case since their executions, the other side of the debate had never really disappeared, and the dispute over the entire affair erupted again in an entirely different political, intellectual, and cultural context. This renewed furor had as much—if not more—to do with the American political and cultural battles of the 1950s and the early 1960s as with the Sacco-Vanzetti story itself. The reawakening of interest in the affair in the United States in this later period is illuminating to scholars not only because of the different ways in which Sacco and Vanzetti themselves were remembered one generation after their executions, but because of how their case (and cause) was adopted or co-opted, used or appropriated, championed or vilified, in order to promote competing and sometimes bitterly conflicting political visions—and more broadly, because it shows how contradictory political myths built on pre–World War II realities served post–World War II purposes.

After describing the conventional portraiture of Sacco and Vanzetti in the United States in the mid-1950s—one that was based on a sympathetic view of the men and a harsh view of Massachusetts political culture in the 1920s—this chapter will then discuss the cracks in the consensus that began to emerge because of a sudden and striking rise in Sacco and Vanzetti's public profile, in the arts, the media, television, politics, and letters, beginning in the late 1950s, and the conservative backlash that ensued, led by such rightwing writers and theorists as William F. Buckley Jr. and John Dos Passos, the former Sacco-Vanzetti literary champion turned anticommunist activist. Liberals and other leftists, even those who shared Buckley's and Dos Passos's loathing of communists, refused to take in their stride the shots aimed at the reputation of the Sacco-Vanzetti cause and returned verbal fire. But regardless of which side of the issue's divide they stood on, Sacco-Vanzetti supporters and opponents alike connected the story of the dead anarchists to what they saw as the main issue of the period: McCarthyism, its stunning rise and ignominious end. For Buckley, the fall of McCarthy, as he saw it, could only be explained by a powerful pattern of "liberal" mythmaking that began with the Sacco-Vanzetti affair. For Dos Passos, the Sacco-Vanzetti case was the start of his disillusionment with the left, turning him eventually into a radical anticommunist. For many of these two men's intellectual enemies, there was a direct line running from the railroading, as they saw it, of Sacco and Vanzetti in the 1920s and the excesses of McCarthyism in the 1950s. Thus the idea of the Cold War—or at least, the perception of that struggle's effects on American society—was at the heart of the latter-day Sacco-Vanzetti controversy and therefore helps us understand its peculiar volume, vitriol, and vividness.

In the chapter I adopt a fairly eclectic historical approach to both the concept of the Cold War itself and to "Cold War Culture" in particular. Whether or not the various figures who spent time and energy debating Sacco and Vanzetti in these years were actually participants in a geopolitical struggle taking place between the United States and the Soviet Union, or really unaware pawns in an ideological construct of homegrown American making—in other words, whether the Cold War was a real war or not—is an intriguing question that, in the case of the latter-day Sacco-Vanzetti warriors, is somewhat beside the point. Since the debates I describe and analyze here were internally American, scholars may reasonably conclude that they bolster the vision of the Cold War as representing a purely American political phenomenon. The Soviet Union, in this sense, had nothing to do with it except in the rhetoric used by American figures. On the other hand, the entire controversy would never have erupted had the people involved not perceived the Cold War as a real thing indeed. Hence in trying to understand this episode it is more useful to use the term "Cold War Culture" than merely "Cold War" in defining the context of the dispute. Put differently, the people and groups I examine tended to view the issue of Sacco and Vanzetti through the lens of the moment—the so-called Cold War, with both domestic and global dimensions—in which they considered themselves to be living. Thus, I tend to use the term "Cold War" in a modern, rather than postmodern, fashion, without interrogating the very viability of its explanatory framework—an exercise that is beyond the narrow scope of this case study. If the Cold War itself can be defined as "a kind of vague and undefined conflict that flared up into actual, real wars, but was mostly a standoff that produced a whole range of behaviors on both sides that under other circumstances would have seemed unusual"—a loose yet useful formulation with which I tend to agree—the reemergence of Sacco and Vanzetti in the political arena was, I argue, a product, or symptom, of Cold War culture in the United States. Even if it did not provoke the outbreak of an "actual, real" war, it certainly elicited a "whole range of unusual behavior" that can only be explained by the intellectual context and cultural circumstances of the years in question.[5]

The Return of Sacco and Vanzetti

The stage for renewed confrontation over the Sacco-Vanzetti case was set in the late 1950s, as the dust of McCarthyism began to settle. In 1958, after three decades of nonstop activism on the part of veteran Sacco-Vanzetti defenders, the first significant attempt was made by Massachusetts politicians to persuade the state's executive officer to pardon Sacco and Vanzetti (an effort that would eventually result in Governor Michael Dukakis's 1977 decision to grant the two anarchists what amounted to a posthumous pardon of sorts, by officially declaring that their 1921 trial had been unfair).[6] Also in 1958, CBS devoted an episode of its flagship television serial, *Camera Three*, to a sympathetic portrayal of Sacco and Vanzetti.[7] Two years later, in June 1960, as television sets were becoming even more widespread throughout the country, NBC aired a two-part program, *The Sacco-Vanzetti Story*, written by the left-wing screenwriter Reginald Rose.

The once-radical idea that Sacco and Vanzetti were innocent men who had fallen victim to the class warfare, ethnic intolerance, and political repression of the first Red Scare era was now showcased on a medium that, in the wake of the second Red Scare era, had captured the national imagination, and, more than any work of historical scholarship could ever do, sparked renewed public interest in the case.[8] Perhaps not surprisingly, right-wing pundits did not like these programs one bit. By broadcasting shows sympathetic to the executed anarchists, the indignant syndicated columnist Westbrook Pegler wrote, "CBS and NBC . . . give moral aid and comfort to the enemy and . . . exalt murderers as pathetic victims of persecution."[9] Pegler and others like him had good reason to be disturbed: Sacco and Vanzetti, it seemed, had never enjoyed such broad public respectability. The director of the NBC special, Sidney Lumet, was one of the most promising young filmmakers in the country; Sacco and Vanzetti were portrayed, respectively, by two talented young actors, Martin Balsam (who that year also appeared in Alfred Hitchcock's horror classic *Psycho*) and Steven Hill (cast a few years later in the lead role on the smash television hit *Mission Impossible*). The program was made with the help of former members of the late-1920s Sacco-Vanzetti defense committee, including the openly revolutionary anarchist Aldo Felicani, who had been Vanzetti's closest friend.[10]

In 1963 an even bigger artistic monument to the Sacco-Vanzetti legend was in the works: a high-budget transatlantic film with the Italian Dino De Laurentiis as producer and the American Richard Fleischer as director. But because of financial disputes, the project was dropped (in favor of *Fantastic Voyage*, a distinctly apolitical science fiction adventure starring the less controversial and more crowd-pleasing Raquel Welch).[11] These plans, though abandoned, were a clear sign of the growing public interest in the case; neither De Laurentiis nor Fleischer were ones to consider film projects without considerable commercial appeal. (A less expensive but commercially successful Italian film, Giuliano Montaldo's *Sacco e Vanzetti*, was eventually released in 1971, featuring music by composer Ennio Morricone and Joan Baez's hit "Here's to You, Nicola and Bart").[12]

In Europe in the 1950s and 1960s the controversy over Sacco and Vanzetti did not reach nearly the level of rancor that it would in the United States. The cataclysmic experiences of the 1930s, World War II, and its gloomy aftermath, had changed the culture, psychology, and nomenclature of European political life to such an extent that the memory of Sacco and Vanzetti, who had stirred so much emotion in Europe in the 1920s, had somewhat (but not completely) dimmed over time. As early as 1947, Albert Einstein, who had lived in Europe during the Sacco-Vanzetti episode, put it this way: "at that time [of the Sacco-Vanzetti case] the desire for justice was as yet more powerful than it is today, although it did not triumph. Too many horrors have since dulled the human conscience."[13]

In the United States the picture was quite different, and the more vivid public and artistic interest in the Sacco-Vanzetti case in the late 1950s and early 1960s was expressed in a variety of forms. One primary venue was the theater: in addition to *The Shoemaker and the Fishpeddler*, a stage success in New York, there were a number of plays produced in this period about Sacco and Vanzetti, including *The Advocate*, written by Robert Noah and first staged by the Bucks County Playhouse in Pennsylvania. In October 1963, the opening of this play on Broadway in New York was broadcast live on national television; it focused on a character named Warren Curtis, based on William Thompson, the upper-crust Boston defense attorney for Sacco and Vanzetti who had been shaken by the treatment of his clients, and, like almost all other artistic representations of the case in this period, it was quite sympathetic to Sacco, Vanzetti, and their supporters. It was also popular: this was the first time that a Broadway play was screened on television, live and free of charge, while it was still running on the stage. The play itself was an immediate hit: the Broadway debut drew a capacity audience of 1,177 to the ANTA theater. The Westinghouse Company, which had financed the television broadcast, estimated that the number of viewers of the show at any given moment reached about two million; according to *The New York Times*, "there was general agreement among viewers that the play was a welcome relief from domestic comedies, cowboys, and hospital corridors."[14] The outpouring of artistic and media product on Sacco and Vanzetti would become so prodigious that the critic Alfred Kazin eventually remarked that he was waiting for "the inevitable musical to be made out of the [Sacco-Vanzetti case]." Kazin was being facetious, but there already *had* been more than one musical staged about Sacco and Vanzetti.[15] In the words of one veteran Sacco-Vanzetti supporter, by this time "public opinion had become pretty well convinced that Massachusetts executed two innocent men."[16]

But in order to understand the ensuing backlash against Sacco and Vanzetti and their cause, it is important to take into account not only the frequency and sympathy with which their story was presented at the end of the 1950s and the start of the 1960s, but also the historical weight that accompanied that story. One important aspect of the affair was the inevitable link to communism, a topic that was made touchier than ever in these years. Kempton and many other Sacco-Vanzetti sympathizers had observed that the most immediate intellectual beneficiary of the Sacco-Vanzetti case had been the American Communist Party (CPUSA). Indeed, the lesson of the Sacco-Vanzetti affair for many young American intellectuals on the left was that liberals had badly misunderstood the significance of the case, specifically the determination of the establishment to execute Sacco and Vanzetti, and that the radicals' diagnosis of the case had been essentially correct. As a result, these intellectuals moved further to the left, ending up in or near the growing communist movement in the 1930s. As

Kempton put it, "after the final defeat [of Sacco and Vanzetti], it was very hard for some of these violated innocents not to believe that the communists had been right in one thing . . . liberalism had been blind in proclaiming that they could hope for justice from peaceful appeal to the conscience of established society." Kempton also made the observation (echoing Malcolm Cowley) that for a lot of these young people, "the myth of the thirties began . . . with Sacco-Vanzetti," and not, as is more commonly understood, with the collapse of the stock market in 1929 or even with the election of Franklin Roosevelt to the presidency in 1932.[17]

Yet even if we agree with Kempton on the lasting centrality of the Sacco-Vanzetti case, scholars still face the difficult question of how and why the issue survived over decades in the United States, during which Americans experienced grave economic depression, enormous social upheaval, total war, nuclear anxiety, and the assassination of a popular president. The Harvard historian Arthur Schlesinger, Sr., in his 1963 memoir *In Retrospect*, recognized the importance of this question: "by [our] time so many horrors [have] afflicted the world that it seems as though the lot of two insignificant individuals in Massachusetts back in the 1920s could no longer prick the public conscience." He went on to suggest an answer that can be described as self-congratulatory and even self-serving, but not necessarily wrong: "this did not prove to be the fact, probably because, whatever the malpractices of totalitarian regimes, Americans could not escape a sense of responsibility for what they themselves had permitted to happen."[18]

Schlesinger, Sr.'s view had essentially not changed since 1929, when as a former activist in the Sacco-Vanzetti campaign he had written that "history never lets bygones be bygones . . . as the Sacco-Vanzetti case recedes into the past and the miasma of hate and prejudice lifts, the failure of the commonwealth and its legal system to render justice without fear or favor becomes increasingly plain. History already sees Sacco-Vanzetti as the victims of a faulty judicial system administered by men blinded by postwar hysteria and passion."[19] This, in a nutshell, was the classic late 1920s liberal narrative of the case that continued to dominate public conversation on the topic from the 1930s through the 1950s. The complementary aspect of this postwar Sacco-Vanzetti memory in the United States was the emphasis on "better morality in public affairs," as Einstein put it in 1947: "everything should be done to keep alive the tragic affair of Sacco and Vanzetti in the conscience of mankind. They remind us of the fact that even the most perfectly planned democratic institutions are no better than the people whose instruments they are."[20] By the end of the 1950s, these were the most commonly accepted interpretations of the case, especially among liberals. For these reasons, it becomes clearer why, decades after their deaths, Sacco and Vanzetti became such prime symbolic targets for attack.

The Sacco-Vanzetti "Myth"

In 1960, William F. Buckley, rising young star of the American Catholic right and founder of the *National Review,* was still shaken from the defeat of his hero, Senator Joseph McCarthy, by what Buckley saw as an array of godless forces tolerant, if not supportive, of communism. Following *God and Man at Yale,* his brash 1951 attack on his alma mater—and the book that first made his name—Buckley wrote *McCarthy and His Enemies* in 1954 with another young Catholic conservative, his brother-in-law L. Brent Bozell. Buckley and Bozell portrayed the disgraced Wisconsin politician as having been right about the state of American politics and unfairly maligned by his nefarious left-wing enemies; McCarthy had not, in their view, created a "reign of terror," as the Tydings Committee of the US Senate had concluded after studying his allegations, and even if he had, it would have been justified under the circumstances. Most importantly, McCarthy had been an indispensable leader in the fight against communism, and Buckley and Bozell still insisted that "on McCarthyism hang the hopes of America for effective resistance to communist infiltration."[21]

The historian George Nash pointed out in his sympathetic 1977 study of the conservative intellectual movement that "the McCarthy episode had a traumatic importance for the American intellectual Right."[22] Buckley was the perfect example. He was not particularly impressed by the drubbing that the quintessential liberal Adlai Stevenson suffered at the hands of Dwight Eisenhower and the Republican Party in the presidential elections of both 1952 and 1956. Rather, in 1960, Buckley was still deeply disturbed by the downfall of McCarthy, which he attributed to the eternal dominance of liberalism in American political life, and that year he helped found Young Americans for Freedom, the national right-wing student movement.[23] He also found ideological ammunition for his cause in a book published by a seventy-one-year-old Boston lawyer, Robert Montgomery. The first new nonfiction book on the Sacco-Vanzetti case to appear since the 1940s, it argued that the two men were guilty, their trial had been fair, and that the campaign on their behalf had been little more than a disingenuous left-wing anti-American conspiracy.[24]

Soon after reading this book, Buckley caused something of a stir when he published his own article on the Sacco-Vanzetti affair—not in his own journal *National Review,* but in the more broadly disseminated *American Legion Magazine.* Nakedly borrowing from Montgomery's book, Buckley aimed his fire at what he called the Sacco-Vanzetti Myth. He picked up on Montgomery's central theme—that all forms of Sacco-Vanzetti protest were connected, starting in 1920 and ending in the present, and that the support for their cause was never about Sacco and Vanzetti themselves or even about justice, but rather about the legitimacy (or lack thereof) of American institutions. In other words, to defend Sacco and Vanzetti was to have been in cahoots with communist revolutionaries. To Buckley, the supposed lie that Sacco and Vanzetti had been innocently sent to their deaths—in other words, the Sacco-Vanzetti Myth—was an important foundation of the contemporary liberal American left. Buckley argued that the case began to attain its lasting meaning when early Sacco-Vanzetti activists

> encouraged international expressions of resentment over the verdict, and there followed . . . demonstrations and parades and strikes and explosive editorials all over the world. In the excitement all touch with reality was lost . . . for one thing, the communist party moved in . . . The communists and the ideologues never took over the Sacco-Vanzetti case in the sense that it can be said they took over the Scottsboro case a few years later; but they did, by their rabid distortions, create a hysteria and recklessness which caught on in saner circles, which continues . . . to characterize most of the rhetoric on Sacco-Vanzetti.[25]

Attempting to then connect the case to his more immediate concerns, Buckley added: "it became about as difficult to maintain the guilt of Sacco-Vanzetti in fashionable quarters—or the innocence of the executors of justice in Massachusetts—as, much later, it became to suggest that Senator McCarthy had something important to say about security standards in government."

Buckley's main concern, quite obviously, was with the events and legacy of the 1950s—specifically, his wish to salvage conservatism from the collapse of McCarthyism, or, more precisely, to rehabilitate McCarthyism in the aftermath of McCarthy's downfall. In the rise of intellectual postwar conservatism, much depended on the destruction of so-called liberal ideals, and the Sacco-Vanzetti case was supposedly one of the most cherished of these.[26] In tying Sacco and Vanzetti's history to what he saw as the circumstances of the Cold War years, Buckley's article can be seen, in a sense, as the flip side to the views of the liberal or consensus historians, who also wrote about the Sacco-Vanzetti case from the vantage point of their 1950s political sensibilities.

Buckley's main axe to grind was with the influential Schlesinger Jr., perhaps the most prominent of all the liberal historians. Following Montgomery's lead, Buckley catalogued a number of errors of fact made by Schlesinger in his work *The Crisis of the Old Order* (while making just as many, if not more, of his own) and compared the accusations of framing in the Sacco-Vanzetti case to one of the more sordid episodes in the McCarthy period: "[it is] the kind of madness," he charged, "which at a later time seized some otherwise responsible Americans who have gone about charging that the Justice Department and the FBI joined hands in a project to forge a typewriter with which to frame Alger Hiss."[27]

Toward the end, Buckley got to his most pressing point. The controversy over the Sacco-Vanzetti case, he argued, was but one manifestation of a long and unfortunate American tradition that reached its apex with the left's struggle against McCarthyism:

> why the continuing fever? Beyond the personal appeal of the poor and illiterate fish peddler and his friend the shoemaker, there was everywhere the virulence of men who despised this country and its institutions. Here was a human vehicle through which to indict the existing order, condemn our institutions, dramatize the cause of proletarian socialism, scrape away at the Puritan ethic, tear and wrench the nation and cause it to bleed across the pages of history. Their success has been considerable, and they do not give up, just as they will never give up on Alger Hiss. But they face the formidable opposition of common sense, and the toughminded honesty of Anglo-Saxon jurisprudence.

To Buckley, in sum, Sacco-Vanzetti was a myth that must be debunked so that future generations of Americans would not have to live under its shadow. To this purpose, he ridiculed even the two defendants' most hallowed moments, the speeches they made in court, and the letters they wrote to their friends and supporters: "the functional pidgin English of Vanzetti was transmuted in some of his letters into a dirge on our time of almost overpowering eloquence." Of Sacco's famous last letter to his young son Dante, in which he asked him to remember to "help the weak ones that cry for help, help the persecuted and the victim, because they are your better friends," Buckley had this to say: "this is a lesson for all of us, surely, murderers and non-murderers alike."

Montgomery's book and Buckley's article were the first shots in what would soon become a wider long-term right-wing crusade to explode the so-called Sacco-Vanzetti myth in American political culture. In doing so, the conservatives would create a lasting Sacco-Vanzetti myth of their own. One important facet of this revisionist mythmaking was the role of pre–World War II leftists, some of them former supporters of the Sacco-Vanzetti cause, now postwar right-wingers eager to use their past experience in the service of anticommunism. One such clichéd figure was the erstwhile Trotskyist founder and editor of *The Masses*, Max Eastman, who was anxious to reenter the fray because he wished to share information that, he hoped, would shatter the "myth of Sacco-Vanzetti" for good: a brief, interrupted conversation that he had, in 1941, with the former anarchist leader Carlo Tresca, in which the latter supposedly "confided" to Eastman that Sacco had been guilty.[28]

Encouraged by Buckley, Eastman wrote an article on the subject, but it was turned down, he claimed, by *Reader's Digest*, the *Saturday Evening Post*, *Time*, the

New Leader, and *Esquire*. In March 1961, still unable to find a publisher, he wrote to a friend, "I think [William] Buckley would have published it, but I was loth [*sic*] to have it look like a conservative argument . . . I must say the facts are, as I see them, a conservative argument, or a pretty severe indictment of the 'Reds' and myself among them."[29] Eventually, Buckley published Eastman's piece in the *National Review* and wrote in a preface that Eastman tried to get the article published "in a half dozen more leftward papers, because I thought it would be more effective if published there; but they all shied away from it." His explanation for that was simple: "American liberals grew up on the myth of Sacco-Vanzetti, and do not want to ruffle it—the ensuing emotional and intellectual readjustment would be too painful."[30]

In his article, "Is This the Truth About Sacco and Vanzetti?" (the answer, of course, was an emphatic yes), Eastman, too, focused on the "myth" of the executed men's innocence, concluding—based on his aborted reported conversation with Tresca—that Sacco had been guilty and Vanzetti went to his death covering for his comrade. More broadly, Eastman sought to delegitimize the Sacco-Vanzetti cause and link it to the antipatriotic pathologies already outlined by Buckley. Echoing Cowley, as well as the 1950s liberal historians—but from a right-wing standpoint—Eastman described the Sacco-Vanzetti case as "a principal cause of the stampede of the American intelligentsia to the cause of 'proletarian revolution' in the 1930 . . . it also gave its first impetus to that anti-American sentiment which, nourished by . . . the communists, is to be found today in many parts of the world." As for his own involvement in the Sacco-Vanzetti cause, Eastman remembered it as part of his "youthful Marxist idiocy" (it should be noted that he was a ripe forty years old when Sacco and Vanzetti were executed). He had just completed his "pilgrimage" to Russia, as he recalled, and on his return to the United States (in 1923), "I made no study of the case myself, but was swept along by a mixture of revolutionary dogma and pure emotion into the general outcry against their 'martyrdom' and against class rule in America."[31]

To Eastman, the Sacco-Vanzetti affair was one more example of how the entire American left, of which he had once been a part, was misguided and dangerous. By mixing the Sacco-Vanzetti cause with his own former "revolutionary dogma," he meant to show that protesting the conviction and execution of the two Italian anarchists had been thoughtless, reflexive, and unpatriotic. The fact that Eastman himself had supposedly supported the cause (albeit never in any central or visible role) could be seen as a boon for the revisionist, right-wing agenda and was particularly galling to those who continued, even in a conservative age, to uphold the principle of Sacco and Vanzetti's innocence.

While these conservative writings are riddled with factual errors and questionable assumptions, they did make some general points that have both endured as integral parts of the ongoing debates over the case and in an indirect way pushed scholars to develop a fuller picture of Sacco and Vanzetti the men and the political actors, rather than Sacco and Vanzetti the legends. They contributed to our understanding, for example, that the latter-day liberal reinvention of Sacco and Vanzetti as benign utopian dreamers was largely false, and that in fact the two were committed (and not just theoretical) anarchists, devoted to the violent overthrow of western bourgeois governments—which from the point of view of the radical left was not necessarily a bad thing.[32] But while these new debates led eventually to a partial and belated reexamination of Sacco's and Vanzetti's biographies, and specifically their insufficiently recognized radical background in an Italian anarchist milieu, they also helped give rise to the single most unfruitful aspect of the Sacco-Vanzetti scholarship (and public discussion) of the past forty years: the obsession with the question of one or both men's guilt or innocence of the 1920 robbery and murder, at the expense of the social, political, intellectual, and global context and ramifications of their case.

Perhaps one of the most intriguing witnesses to the entire course of the Sacco-Vanzetti affair was the author John Dos Passos, whose 1927 tract *Facing the Chair* was one of the earliest and most important literary condemnations of the Sacco-Vanzetti trial, and whose 1936 trilogy *USA* showed the traumatic effect of the executions on the Depression-era American left—most memorably in his stark vision of an America divided into "two nations," one the innocent "haters of oppression," the other, "strangers who have turned our language inside out, who have taken the clean words our fathers spoke and made them slimy and foul."[33] Like many other idealistic left-wing intellectuals of the interwar period, Dos Passos became disillusioned with Marxism as a result of his experience fighting for the Republican side in the Spanish Civil War, and he fell out with the communist movement in the late 1930s—precisely at the moment when its popularity peaked in the United States and the rest of the Western world.[34] In the 1940s and 1950s, driven obsessively by his hatred of the Soviet Union, Dos Passos drifted further to the right.[35] By the Cold War era, his literary prestige was not nearly what it had been twenty or thirty years earlier, but his ideological trajectory, similar to Eastman's and that of many other radicals of his generation, makes his retrospective views on Sacco and Vanzetti valuable in understanding the shifting meanings of their case.

Despite his move from radical left to radical right, Dos Passos, perhaps because he knew the details of the case much more intimately than Eastman, was not so easily willing to throw his belief in Sacco and Vanzetti's innocence out with the rest of his former radical convictions. At the same time, his letters from the early 1960s are startling in the total lack of the pathos that had once characterized his writing on the case. "I realize that the possibilities of error are endless," he wrote, for example, in 1960. "At the time I was naturally friendly disposed toward Sacco-Vanzetti because they were anarchists . . . I talked to both men, and, although I could imagine their nerving themselves up to such an attempt for political purposes . . . I just didn't think they were the men to do it."[36]

As Dos Passos remembered it, perhaps selectively, the Sacco-Vanzetti affair predated even the war in Spain in the beginning of his break with the radical left. While he remained skeptical about Eastman's assertions of Sacco's guilt, since this was for him a matter above politics (or so he now claimed), he had no problem attacking the mobilization around the Sacco-Vanzetti cause: "the propaganda use of the story is quite another business. It was the last gasp of the international anarchist movement. The way the communists gradually took it over was a preview of what was to happen in Spain a decade later."[37]

The case, which to Dos Passos once signified an irreparable and infuriating breach within American society, a casus belli between "two nations," now boiled down to the question of whether Sacco and Vanzetti's trial had been technically fair, and whether one of the men had pulled the trigger.[38] In this regard Dos Passos remained fundamentally conflicted. The revisionist historian of the case, Francis Russell, had shared with him the results of his ballistics investigations, which implicated Sacco as a perpetrator of the crime. Dos Passos was now willing to concede that perhaps Sacco's innocence was not a sure thing after all. Writing in 1962, he called Eastman's *National Review* article "excellent"; the new information on the evidence Dos Passos found "fascinating." "It makes me feel," he added, "how remiss I was not to look into the whole story more carefully."[39]

To the contradiction between his Cold War right-wing views and his lingering doubts about the Sacco-Vanzetti case, Dos Passos found a solution, or solace, in a strange and ultimately unconvincing balance between extremists on both sides. In this way he could explain away the entire Sacco-Vanzetti episode as the result of radicalism gone awry, a favorite theme in the Cold War period (among liberals *and* conservatives, who considered themselves opponents of "extremists" on the other side). The entire country, he now explained, primarily to himself, had been suffering in the aftermath of World War I from collective insanity, and both the radicals and government were equally responsible. As he wrote to an interviewer, trying to describe the political atmosphere in America in 1920, "take the 'liberal' hysteria against Senator McCarthy, turn it upside down, and multiply it by ten and you'll have [an idea] of the state of mind of 'good citizens.'"[40]

To Dos Passos, the Soviets were the star of every political show, and his disillusionment with the left began and ended with the communists' cynical, opportunistic, Soviet-directed takeover of "good causes," such as the Spanish Civil War or prior to that, the Sacco-Vanzetti case. Thus, the evils of such histories could be distilled to the intrusion of the communist movement into the arena of protest, not necessarily the conditions against which the protest was directed in the first place. He expressed this view in a 1963 West German television program on

Sacco and Vanzetti by contrasting American justice with its Soviet counterpart. "At a time when the Anglo-Saxon ideas of justice are in great jeopardy," he rationalized, "you could look back on the agitation of the Sacco-Vanzetti case with a certain satisfaction because [at least] there was justice to appeal to."[41]

In 1968, speaking to college students at the height of New Left activism and the popularity of Students for a Democratic Society (SDS), Dos Passos refused to make a link between the protest against the Vietnam War—*the* left-wing cause of the late 1960s—and the agitation over Sacco and Vanzetti in the 1920s. With age, he explained at a talk at Union College, he had understood "the way the human race works: in simple terms, top dog always gets to the top, no matter what the system is . . . no change in ideology changes that basic fact."[42] Thus, for the Cold War-era Dos Passos—i.e., a Dos Passos whose great world-historical struggle was directed against communism rather than capitalism—the Sacco-Vanzetti case no longer represented the destruction of the American Dream, as it did in the 1930s, but was an example of its enduring strength. He too had created a new, right-wing Sacco-Vanzetti myth for the Cold War years.

Aftermath of the Aftermath

Distraught by the wave of historical revisionism about the Sacco-Vanzetti case, members of the Sacco-Vanzetti "community"—mostly former leaders of their defense campaign—reacted by launching what one of them called a "counter-offensive against the defamers of Sacco and Vanzetti's memory" and another called "Operation Ambush." Ultimately, the so-called community did not succeed in totally discrediting the revisionists, but they did regain ground in the struggle over the memory of Sacco and Vanzetti, and the result of this struggle—at least on the eternal question of guilt versus innocence—should be seen as a stalemate. In many ways, the battle lines over Sacco and Vanzetti that were drawn in the early 1960s have remained in place to this day, and the two men continue to occupy diametrically opposed roles in the political imagination. For many, they were the innocent victims of a terrible injustice rooted in the American fear of immigrants, persecution of radicals, and oppression of the working class, all in high tide in the United States after World War I. For others, they were simply criminals and terrorists who benefited from a worldwide propaganda campaign led by people who despised "America" and its institutions.

It is thus difficult to determine who, if anyone, emerged triumphant from the Sacco-Vanzetti controversies of the Cold War years. Any attempt to answer this question in its shorter-term context demands a clear set of criteria and foci. In the arenas of the media, the arts, schools and universities, the belief in Sacco and Vanzetti's unfair treatment remained dominant; in the narrower world of American letters, the 1950s consensus view on Sacco-Vanzetti had been somewhat fragmented by the wave of revisionist writing on the case. And yet there is evidence that even toward the end of the 1960s, the notion that the Sacco-Vanzetti case was unjust had been accepted by much of the political and legal establishment. One example of this is a 1969 statement by Erwin M. Griswold, the United States solicitor general under President Richard Nixon (and former dean of the Harvard Law School): "there were times, long ago, when I occasionally had some doubts, but these have long since gone . . . the thought that [Sacco and Vanzetti] could have been the guilty ones is so implausible . . . [their] case is a sad chapter in [our] legal history."[43]

On the political level, advocating posthumously for the two executed anarchists—a process that moved in piecemeal fashion in the 1950s and 1960s—became not only safe, but also successful: Massachusetts Governor Dukakis's 1977 declaration that Sacco and Vanzetti's trial had been unfair proved that the once-subversive idea had become almost a commonplace, even if it did not by any means go unchallenged.[44] Indeed, the year 1977, the fiftieth anniversary of the executions, saw the return of Sacco and Vanzetti to the international agenda, though on a far more modest scale than in 1927. In an echo of fifty years past, Dukakis's proclamation in Sacco and Vanzetti's favor was preceded by requests to the White House from influential figures on the European left. François Mitterrand and Enrico Berlinguer—leaders of the French Socialist Party and the Italian Communist Party, respectively, and two men whose political career in the Cold War period was characterized by a critical stance toward both the United States *and* the Soviet Union—jointly asked recently elected US President Jimmy Carter (soon after Carter had begun his international campaign for human rights) to offer a posthumous pardon to the long-dead anarchists. Their request was forwarded to the Massachusetts governor's office.[45]

In any case, however, there are probably more pressing and interesting questions facing scholars than "who won the debate"—a question that could prove as intellectually limiting when it comes to Sacco and Vanzetti as "did they do it?" What was the controversy about? What was at stake? How did the return of the affair influence the way people thought about Sacco and Vanzetti? And what does the episode tell us more generally about Cold War America and Cold War culture? Liberal historians, leftists-turned-conservatives, Catholic pundits, the Sacco-Vanzetti community, all of these groups and others had compelling personal and political reasons for their stance and for investing considerable energy in the Sacco-Vanzetti case long after the two men had been put to death. To take just two telling examples—Schlesinger Jr., on the one hand, and Buckley on the other—their involvement had much to do with the entire McCarthy episode and the lessons that each drew from it. At the center of this renewed struggle was the history that had led from the Sacco-Vanzetti affair up to that point. How to interpret that history? For Buckley, the legacy of Sacco-Vanzetti represented an obstacle to the advancement of his ideals, since the twin beliefs in Sacco and Vanzetti's innocence and the unfairness of their trial served as foundational myths, as he saw it, for his enemies; thus, the defeat of McCarthyism, for him, was rooted in the original 1920s defense of Sacco and Vanzetti. To Schlesinger Jr., Sacco and Vanzetti's own politics were irrelevant (and distasteful); as far as he was concerned, they were destroyed by a nativist, intolerant, reactionary "old order" that he despised and whose political heirs were responsible for the political aberrations of the Cold War 1950s.

Liberal historians have often seen the early 1960s, particularly after the inauguration of John F. Kennedy as US president, as a period of renewed energy, innocence, and hope, especially among the newly confident liberals, in American political life.[46] In this sense, an episode like the Sacco-Vanzetti case became important once again for a new generation eager to exorcise the demons of the older generation, whether one looked at the case from the left or the right.

For Schlesinger Jr., Buckley, Dos Passos, and Eastman, as well as for the scores of playwrights, students, television producers, journalists, activists, and others who revisited or even discovered the case beginning in the late 1950s and early 1960s, Sacco and Vanzetti were symbols used in a broader Cold War-era struggle over American culture, politics, and memory. Even the European sources from this period show that the Sacco-Vanzetti affair held interest primarily as a precursor to more recent Cold War events that sharpened the animosities toward American justice, such as the Rosenbergs' execution of 1953, which some European observers on the left found disturbingly reminiscent of the Sacco-Vanzetti executions. By contrast, it is worth noting that the Rosenberg case was conspicuously missing from the Sacco-Vanzetti debates in the United States in the 1950s and 1960s—a sign that there was little correlation between American support or condemnation of Sacco and Vanzetti and support or condemnation of the Rosenbergs. In the tantalizingly brief words of noted sociologists David Riesman and Nathan Glazer, writing in 1955, "the Sacco-Vanzetti case united the liberals, the Rosenberg case divided them."[47] Intuitively, it is tempting to link the two cases (and that of Alger Hiss) as major left-wing causes célèbres with vibrant afterlives. Both cases emerged out of "Red Scares," and both ended in executions. In both cases, the accused were members of minority groups. Both cases aroused much European anger. Both cases were highly controversial from legal standpoints. Both cases have been the subject of much scholarship concerned with the question of guilt or innocence. Both cases have come to symbolize, for many, the persecution of political nonconformism in the United States in times of a perceived external menace. And the two cases had in common the involvement of J. Edgar Hoover and the FBI.

But these specific similarities are somewhat outweighed by the differences. The Sacco-Vanzetti affair began as a provincial trial for banditry and murder; the Rosenbergs were tried by the federal government for espionage, a political crime. Sacco and Vanzetti were anarchists and profoundly opposed to communism; the Rosenbergs were Stalinists and would have been deeply opposed to anarchism had it still been politically relevant in their day. Sacco and Vanzetti were immigrants and aliens in the United States; the Rosenbergs were citizens. Once convicted, Sacco and Vanzetti were charismatic prisoners, open and outspoken about their political affiliation and beliefs; the Rosenbergs hid theirs and evoked much less public sympathy. More crucially, Sacco and Vanzetti were supported by an eclectic public, including liberals and other groups well outside the anarchist movement, and became a truly divisive issue in the American mainstream and around the world; the Rosenbergs were championed by few, abandoned by most liberals, and were a cause principally of and for the communist movement at home and abroad (and they spent less time in prison between their convictions and executions). In the 1950s and 1960s, even as people on the right and the left were fighting over the Sacco-Vanzetti case and what it meant for contemporary politics, the link between the two cases was probably more evident for European observers than for Americans, and, in the United States, more suggestive for the conservative right than for the liberal left. In any case, Sacco and Vanzetti's most prominent American supporters were not to be found in the Rosenbergs' camp once the couple faced execution. Surprisingly (or not), the Rosenbergs barely appear in the American sources discussed in this chapter.

By contrast, for some of Sacco and Vanzetti's veteran supporters the two anarchists were not at all abstract symbols, just two people with no particular political significance. One veteran Sacco-Vanzetti defender, Michael Musmanno, wrote a letter to NBC executive producer Robert Alan Aurthur (after reading the script for the 1960 television special) that is telling. Musmanno was thrilled that NBC was to highlight the injustices of the trial and bring the Sacco-Vanzetti case to the attention of a new and younger public. But he feared that NBC was turning the program into an "ideological sermon." He did not agree with the show's message that Sacco and Vanzetti were killed because of a fear of anarchism and class war. He wanted the program to convince Americans *not* that the upper class had targeted two members of the working class, but that Sacco and Vanzetti were the victims of individual stupidity, greed, and ignorance.

This was, in a sense, a repetition of the late 1920s debate about Sacco and Vanzetti, both in the United States and abroad, between those who believed that the case represented something fundamentally rotten in the American body politic and those who felt that it was an aberration within a generally workable system, a crime or conspiracy perpetrated by region-specific, isolated individuals and not by an entire system or a society. It was also an approach typical of the politics of this period: men like Musmanno were loath to make any sort of connection between Sacco and Vanzetti and the communist victims of the 1950s, for whom they had no sympathy.[48]

In other words, the latter-day controversy over Sacco and Vanzetti can be seen as a struggle between those for whom the two men were real people, to be exonerated and vindicated long after their deaths, and those for whom the two men were part of a collective memory—political symbols. What the symbols stood for depended on what particular political beliefs one held; but it is evident that the Sacco-Vanzetti affair did not simply end in the 1920s, or even in the 1930s, and was alive and well a generation or two later. A much more crucial question than whether or not the two men were guilty or innocent—and one that should prove more fruitful as we strive to understand the workings of symbol-making and symbol-contesting over space and time, and particularly in the Cold War era—is to what degree their case represented a distinctly *political* phenomenon in American history. If Sacco and Vanzetti were merely the victims of a few individuals' irresponsibility, their deaths actually held little importance for American society in any meaningful sense. If, on the other hand, their case had broader social, political, and cultural roots and implications, it transcended the actions of a few individuals and can only be explained in broader national and international, and long-term, context. Judging only from the passion and volume of the reemergence of the affair during the cold war years, the latter seems far more likely. But all this was not incidental to the particular timing of this reemergence. What appears even clearer is that while the debates over Sacco and Vanzetti may not have died down regardless of political developments that took place decades after their deaths, the prominence and passion of the controversy in the late 1950s and early 1960s, which drew in new participants as well as veterans of the political struggles of the 1920s and 1930s, can only really be explained by its contemporary political context. In other words, without McCarthy and his enemies, and the perception, unwitting or not, that Americans were living through a Cold War, Sacco and Vanzetti's return to the public sphere—the lingering of their myth—would surely have been far less dramatic.

Notes

1. This essay draws on material included in Moshik Temkin, *The Sacco-Vanzetti Affair: America on Trial* (New Haven, 2009), which is a study of the impact of the case on broader publics and politics in the United States and abroad, and from the 1920s to the present. The previous literature on the Sacco-Vanzetti case—much of it on its criminal or legal aspects—is vast. For a few examples, see, e.g., Felix Frankfurter, *The Case of Sacco and Vanzetti: A Critical Analysis for Lawyers and Laymen* (Boston, 1927); G. Louis Joughin and Edmund M. Morgan, *The Legacy of Sacco and Vanzetti* (New York, 1948); Herbert E. Ehrmann, *The Case*

That Will Not Die: Commonwealth vs. Sacco and Vanzetti (Boston, 1969); David Kaiser and William Young, *Postmortem: New Evidence in the Case of Sacco and Vanzetti* (Amherst, 1985); Francis Russell, *Tragedy in Dedham: The Story of the Sacco-Vanzetti Case* (New York, 1962); Bruce Watson, *Sacco and Vanzetti: The Men, the Murders, and the Judgment of Mankind* (New York, 2007). For working class and ethnic Italian solidarities with Sacco and Vanzetti in parts of Europe and Latin America, see Lisa McGirr, "The Passion of Sacco and Vanzetti: A Global History," *Journal of American History*, 93/4 (2007), pp. 1085–1115. For the role of Parisian urban politics in the Sacco-Vanzetti affair, see Brooke Blower, *Becoming Americans in Paris: Transatlantic Politics and Culture Between the World Wars* (Oxford, 2011), ch. 3 ("The Sacco-Vanzetti Riots")

2. Kempton, *Part of Our Time: Some Ruins and Monuments of the Thirties* (New York, 1955), p. 56.
3. 1950s liberal historiography on interwar America includes Arthur Schlesinger Jr., *The Age of Roosevelt, Vol. 1: The Crisis of the Old Order* (Boston, 1957); Richard Hofstadter, *The Age of Reform: From Bryan to FDR* (New York, 1955); Robert Murray, *The Red Scare: A Study in National Hysteria, 1919–1920* (Minneapolis, 1955); and Frederick Hoffman, *The Twenties: American Writing in the Postwar Decade* (New York, 1955). For the role of literary figures, see Daniel Aaron, *Writers on the Left: Episodes in Literary American Communism* (New York, 1961); and James Gilbert, *Writers and Partisans: A History of Literary Radicalism in America* (New York, 1968).
4. Hofstadter, *Age of Reform*, p. 20.
5. Alan Brinkley, "A Date With History," *Newsweek*, September 9, 2002. Stephen Whitfield, *The Culture of the Cold War* (Baltimore, 1991), is a searching essay on *mentalités* that, by examining such issues as television, film, and evangelists, demonstrated the potential of viewing the Cold War more broadly to include its domestic cultural, intellectual, and religious manifestations.
6. For the 1958 hearings, see Tom O'Connor (ed.), *Record of Public Hearing Before Joint Committee on the Judiciary of the Massachusetts Legislature on the Resolution of Representative Alexander J. Cella Recommending a Posthumous Pardon for Nicola Sacco and Bartolomeo Vanzetti, Massachusetts State House, Boston, April 2, 1959* (Boston, 1959).
7. G. Louis Joughin, coauthor of *The Legacy of Sacco and Vanzetti*, was the "historical consultant" for CBS. See G. Louis Joughin papers, Rare Books Department, Boston Public Library (Joughin BPL), 16.2–17.1.
8. "The Sacco-Vanzetti Story," teleplay by Reginald Rose, in Beinecke Rare Book and Manuscript Library, Yale University. In 1972 Rose presented a play in two parts, *This Agony, This Triumph*, based on the original television show.
9. Westbrook Pegler, "Drama Rules Over Truth on Airwaves," *Boston Globe*, August 2, 1960.
10. Michael Musmanno to Aldo Felicani, June 4, 1960, Aldino Felicani Sacco-Vanzetti Collection, Boston Public Library, Rare Books Department (BPL-Felicani), MS 2030, fold. 7A.
11. Herbert B. Ehrmann Papers, Harvard Law School Library Special Collections, Cambridge, Mass. (Ehrmann Papers), Box 11, fold. 7.
12. The popular French version of the Baez/Morricone song, performed by folk singer Georges Moustaki, was "La Marche de Sacco et Vanzetti." Montaldo had been an assistant director in the production of *The Battle of Algiers*, a seminal film in left-wing European culture in the 1960s.
13. Quoted in Armand Gatti, *Chant public devant deux chaises électriques* (Paris, 1966), p. 8.
14. Milton Esterow, "'Advocate' a Hit—on TV, That Is: Viewers Praise TV's 'Advocate,'" *The New York Times*, October 16, 1963.
15. Kazin, "The World as a Novel: From Capote to Mailer," *New York Review of Books*, April 8, 1971.
16. Ehrmann papers, box 3, fold. 14.
17. Kempton, *Part of Our Time*, pp. 46, 56.
18. Schlesinger, Sr., *In Retrospect: The History of a Historian* (New York, 1963), pp. 133–134.

19. Schlesinger, Sr., "Those Two Men," *The Lantern*, August 1929, p. 8.
20. Quoted in Gatti, *Chant public devant deux chaises électriques*, p. 8.
21. Buckley and Bozell, *McCarthy and his Enemies: The Record and its Meaning* (Chicago, 1954), p. 245. See also Buckley, *God and Man at Yale: The Superstitions of Academic Freedom* (Chicago, 1951). For a sympathetic biography, see John B. Judis, *William F. Buckley, Jr., Patron Saint of the Conservatives* (New York, 1988).
22. Nash, *The Conservative Intellectual Movement in America Since 1945* (New York, 1976), p. 106; see also Jeffrey Hart, *The Making of the American Conservative Mind: The* National Review *and its Times* (Wilmington, DE, 2005); for the religious aspect of Buckley and Bozell's activism, and of the new conservatism, see Patrick Allitt, *Catholic Intellectuals and Conservative Politics in America, 1950–1985* (Ithaca, 1993). See also Michael Paul Rogin, *The Intellectuals and McCarthy: The Radical Specter* (Cambridge, MA, 1967).
23. See John Andrews, *The Other Side of the Sixties: Young Americans for Freedom and the Rise of Conservative Politics* (New Brunswick, 1997); Gregory L. Schneider, *Cadres for Conservatism: Young Americans for Freedom and the Rise of the Contemporary Right* (New York, 1999).
24. Montgomery, *Sacco-Vanzetti: The Murder and the Myth* (New York, 1960).
25. Buckley Jr., "Sacco and Vanzetti, Again," *American Legion Magazine*, October 1960, pp. 14–15, 47–50.
26. In the past decade or so there has been an explosion of scholarly interest in the history of modern American conservatism, particularly its 1960s rebirth; see, e.g., Jonathan Schoenwald, *A Time for Choosing: The Rise of Modern American Conservatism* (Oxford, 2001); Lisa McGirr, *Suburban Warriors: Grassroots Conservatism in the 1960s* (Princeton, 2001); Rick Perlstein, *Before the Storm: Barry Goldwater and the Unmaking of the American Consensus* (New York, 2001); Kevin Kruse, *White Flight: Atlanta and the Making of Modern Conservatism* (Princeton, 2005); Donald T. Critchlow, *The Conservative Ascendancy: How the GOP Right Made Political History* (Cambridge, MA, 2007); Critchlow, *Phyllis Schlafly and Grassroots Conservatism: A Woman's Crusade* (Princeton, 2005); Kim Phillips-Fein, *Invisible Hands: The Making of the Conservative Movement from the New Deal to Reagan* (New York, 2009); Patrick Allitt, *The Conservatives: Ideas and Personalities Throughout American History* (New Haven, 2009).
27. Alger Hiss was formerly the head of the Carnegie Endowment for International Peace. Accused of spying for the Soviet Union by Whittaker Chambers (an editor at *Time* and a self-proclaimed former communist sympathizer-turned-conservative), Hiss's career was destroyed after he was convicted of perjury (but not of espionage). For an unsympathetic account, see Allen Weinstein, *Perjury: The Hiss-Chambers Case* (New York, 1978). See also Susan Jacoby, *Alger Hiss and the Battle for History* (New Haven, 2009). Chambers's autobiography, *Witness* (New York, 1952), was a national best-seller, and Chambers became a mentor and father-figure to Buckley, Bozell, and other young conservatives.
28. As Eastman remembered, before Tresca got a chance to elaborate on his revelation, the two men were interrupted by other people entering the room (in the home of the socialist leader Norman Thomas). Two years later, in 1943, before Eastman was able to talk with him again about the case, Tresca was assassinated, dramatically enough, by contracted hit-men. For the limitations of Tresca's supposed revelations, see Nunzio Pernicone, "Carlo Tresca and the Sacco-Vanzetti Case," *Journal of American History* 66/3 (1979), pp. 535–547.
29. Max Eastman to F. Russell, March 1961, Francis Russell Papers, Brandeis University Archives and Special Collections Department, Waltham, Mass. (Russell Papers), fold. 1.8.
30. *National Review*, October 21, 1961, p. 261.
31. Ibid., pp. 261–264.
32. The most important study in this regard is Paul Avrich, *Sacco-Vanzetti: The Anarchist Background* (Princeton, 1991), which is not part of the revisionist scholarship. For a brief discussion of Sacco and Vanzetti in the context of the American radical tradition, see Eric

Foner, "Sacco and Vanzetti, the Men and the Symbols," *The Nation*, August 20, 1977, pp. 135–141. See also Foner's comments in "Sacco-Vanzetti Reconsiderations 1979: A Symposium," in Boston Public Library, *Sacco-Vanzetti: Developments and Reconsiderations—1979* (Boston, 1982), pp. 93–96.

33. John Dos Passos, *Facing the Chair: The Story of the Americanization of Two Foreign-Born Workmen* (Boston, 1927); Dos Passos, *USA* (New York, 1936), Part 3 (*The Big Money*), pp. 462–463: "America our nation has been beaten by strangers who have turned our language inside out who have taken the clean words our fathers spoke and made them slimy and foul . . . their hired men sit on the judge's bench they sit back with their feet on the tables under the dome of the State House they are ignorant of our beliefs they have the dollars the guns the armed forces the power plants . . . they have built the electric chair and hired the executioner to throw the switch . . . all right we are two nations."
34. Dos Passos was among many literary figures to volunteer on the Republican side in Spain in the 1930s, or at least travel there as journalists, for different political and personal reasons. These included George Orwell, Arthur Koestler, Ernest Hemingway, and André Malraux. The war served as a catalyst for many young radical intellectuals thorough disillusionment with communism, and even Marxism, as expressed for example in Orwell's *Homage to Catalonia* (London, 1938) and Koestler's *The Yogi and the Commissar* (New York, 1945).
35. See Townsend Ludington, *John Dos Passos: A Twentieth Century Odyssey* (New York, 1980); Virginia Spencer Carr, *Dos Passos: A Life* (Garden City, NY, 1984). See also John Diggins, *Up From Communism: Conservative Odysseys in American Intellectual History* (New York, 1975). For a literary analysis of Dos Passos's radicalization in the 1920s and 1930s see Alfred Kazin, "Dos Passos and the 'Lost Generation'" in Allen Belkind (ed.), *Dos Passos, the Critics, and the Writer's Intention* (Carbondale, IL, 1971).
36. Dos Passos to F. Russell, Russell papers, fold. 1.4.
37. Ibid.
38. Dos Passos to F. Russell, Russell papers, fold. 1.5.
39. Dos Passos to Russell, October 21, 1961, BPL-Felicani, MS 2030, fold. 7A.
40. Dos Passos expressed similar ideas in his *The Best Times: An Informal Memoir* (New York, 1966), pp. 208–209. He had also written the introduction to Buckley's 1959 polemic, *Up From Liberalism*.
41. The film, *Der Fall Sacco und Vanzetti*, directed by Peter von Zahn, was aired on West German television on August 23, 1963, the thirty-sixth anniversary of the executions. A transcript of Dos Passos's comments on the program is in BPL-Felicani, MS. 2030, fold. 7A.
42. See Frank Gado (ed.), "An Interview with John Dos Passos," *Idol: Literary Quarterly of Union College*, 45 (1969), pp. 22–23.
43. Erwin Griswold to Herbert Ehrmann, July 7, 1969, Ehrmann papers, box 7, fol. 18.
44. Dukakis based his decision on Commonwealth of Massachusetts, *Report to the Governor in the Matter of Sacco and Vanzetti*, July 13, 1977 (written by his chief legal counsel, Daniel A. Taylor), and on the advice of Massachusetts attorney and Harvard law professor Alan Dershowitz. The declaration was accompanied by a rancorous debate. The indefatigable Buckley wrote that "At the rate we are going, the only man left who will be universally acknowledged to have been guilty of anything is Adolf Hitler" (*Boston Globe*, August 10, 1977). The then-editor of the *National Review*, George F. Will, in "The Trial That Scarred a Generation," echoed Buckley: "Prevailing prejudices, and abuses of power, made the moment ripe for a counterattack from 'progressives.' And many 'progressives,' who in the best of times have their fair share of prejudices, used the Sacco-Vanzetti case as an excuse to fall upon Massachusetts with angry glee. In the 1920s, Massachusetts was what Arkansas was in the 1950s and Mississippi was in the 1960s. It was the state that people, especially intellectuals, loved to hate" (*Washington Post*, August 18, 1977). A Republican in the Massachusetts Senate attacked Dukakis for "using the Senate chambers for a Cecil B. De Mille

production . . . From his proclamation, you would have thought these men were victims of a lynch mob" (*Boston Globe*, August 2, 1977, 2). See also "Senate Condemns Dukakis' Sacco-Vanzetti Proclamation," *Boston Herald American*, August 9, 1977, p. 1.

45. "Sacco and Vanzetti Reconsidered," *The Economist*, July 30, 1977, p. 33. Berlinguer's appeal should be seen in its context: the Italian Communist Party (PCI) hoped to forge good relations with the Carter administration, by affirming its acceptance of NATO and of the European Community, as part of its "historic compromise" and commitment to a democratic and nonviolent road to power. But just one year later it became clear that even the PCI's most American-friendly Eurocommunism would not be enough to convince the Carter Administration to accept the PCI sharing in power in Italy. For background, see Adrian Lyttleton, "Italia Nostra," *New York Review of Books*, March 9, 2006, or Paul Ginsborg, *A History of Contemporary Italy: Society and Politics, 1943–1988* (New York, 1990), ch. 10.
46. See W. Rorabaugh, *Kennedy and the Promise of the Sixties* (Cambridge, 2002). One tangible connection to Sacco and Vanzetti was the appointment of Schlesinger Jr. (along with other liberal scholars) as an advisor to the Kennedy administration. See Arthur Schlesinger Jr., *A Thousand Days: John F. Kennedy in the White House* (Boston, 1965).
47. Riesman and Glazer, "The Intellectuals and the Discontented Classes," *Partisan Review* 22/1 (Winter 1955), p. 64. See also Terry Cooney, "Trials without End: Some Comments and Reviews on the Sacco-Vanzetti, Rosenberg, and Hiss Cases," *Michigan Law Review* 77/3 (1979), pp. 834–859, which focuses on the role and attitudes of liberals in these controversies (but does not make specific comparisons); Michael Parrish, "Cold War Justice: The Supreme Court and the Rosenbergs," *American Historical Review* 82/4 (1977), pp. 805–842; and Robert A. Ferguson, *The Trial in American Life* (Chicago, 2007), ch. 7 ("Killing the Rosenbergs").
48. Michael Musmanno to R. A. Aurthur, April 23, 1960, BPL-Felicani, MS 2030, fold. 7A.

11

Deconstructing "Cold War Anthropology"

PETER MANDLER

Something like a new orthodoxy has crystallized over the past decade or so in considering the relationship of the social sciences to the Cold War.[1] According to this orthodoxy, social science, which had been roped into the World War II effort on a fairly consensual basis, was thereafter smoothly reengineered to meet Cold War imperatives.[2] A new "behavioral science" paradigm reduced social phenomena to disaggregated and dehistoricized individuals or "primary groups" for ease of manipulation into favored Cold War postures—submissive workers and soldiers,[3] easily organized voters and efficient managers at home,[4] modernizing peasants,[5] Americanized allies,[6] and freedom-loving Russians abroad.[7] Social scientists of all disciplines and all stripes eagerly grasped not only the opportunities for funding and employment offered, but also the aspirations to manipulate and (using the precise term favored in this new historiographical orthodoxy) to control.[8] This fusion of academic and Cold War perspectives in the course of the 1940s then again proceeded seamlessly into the development and counterinsurgency fiascos of the 1960s, until exposed and shattered by the influence of the New Left, principally on the terrain of Vietnam.[9] Not all treatments of social science in the Cold War hew to the strongest versions of this orthodoxy. At one end of the spectrum, few would contend that mere acceptance of the core funding of universities by the military, government, and Cold War-oriented foundations represented the same level of complicity—as one of the most severe critics of such funding ruefully grants, such a net would catch Noam Chomsky himself.[10] It is more common to argue that social scientists avoided controversy, silencing or censoring themselves, or allowed themselves to be shunted off onto politically (and possibly intellectually) safer sidings, or at least imbibed unconsciously a "mode of knowledge production [that] was so pervasive that, for a short while, it was literally invisible," in Phil Mirowski's words. But the strongest arguments make clear that social scientists deliberately courted, initiated, and administered "behavioral science" programs in order to serve a Cold War agenda with which they were in wholehearted agreement, on professional, political, or intellectual grounds.

This chapter critiques some of the weaker as well as the stronger versions of this analysis by reintroducing three elements that I think have been selectively omitted, each of which in different ways deflects the Cold War mission to harness social science—first, the sociology of the disciplines (who enters them and why); second, generational change (at what points they enter and rise up the professional hierarchy and the different career structures they encounter at different entry-points); third, the intellectual history of the disciplines (keeping in mind historian Nils Gilman's point that "the proximate cause for most arguments is a reaction to the writing of other academics," that is, to "local intellectual contexts").[11] I take as my focus the case of anthropology, possibly a limit-case, in the sense that with its international agenda and its notorious "relativism" anthropology might be thought the least susceptible of social-science disciplines to the lures of "control," but by focusing on those elements of the profession most anxious to apply anthropology to problems of international relations I hope to make this case-study more generally applicable and to suggest ways in which its lessons could be extended to other social-science disciplines, including sociology and psychology, to which the control paradigm might otherwise seem perfectly suited. The goal is not to substitute a new paradigm for the old one, not to argue for the total inapplicability of the "behavioral science" paradigm nor for the absence of "control" in social scientists' armamentarium; rather, it is to establish a much more pluralistic scene *during* the Cold War rather than determined *by* it, in which "behavioral science" as portrayed by the orthodoxy was practiced by some but vigorously contested by others. As Anders Stephanson suggests elsewhere in this volume, the Cold War can only be understood by a process of "sedimentation of meanings." At the beginning of this process, there was scope for considerable contestation (in which the idea of the Cold War was hardly yet set and its hegemony was hardly inevitable). As that scope narrowed, disciplinary, generational, and intellectual considerations intervened to determine how conscious actors were of the changing context around them—invisibility, *pace* Mirowski, is actually in the eyes of the beholder—and how they were likely to respond. Local contexts, as several contributors to this volume observe, did matter in determining how far intellectual life *in* the Cold War was *about* the Cold War.

Wartime Recruitment

As it emerged under the tutelage of Franz Boas, the mainstream of American anthropology before World War II had a dual mission, which I would characterize as ecological and critical. In revolt against those evolutionary and diffusionist models of human development that arrayed societies and cultures on a hierarchy, Boasian anthropology was dedicated to recording and preserving the variety of human cultural patterns, particularly those most under pressure from missionaries, colonialism, and Western commerce—an ecological mission. Further, Boasian anthropology at least implicitly pursued a critical mission, using the Otherness of non-Western cultural patterns to denaturalize Western understandings of human nature and social organization. These missions—their emphasis on cultural variety and on cultural comparisons made in a relativistic and often self-critical way—gave Boasian anthropology a distinctive flavor that distinguished it not only from an older physical anthropology (emphasizing biological and often racial differences between humans) but also from the social anthropology dominant in Britain (emphasizing social and kin structures, rather closer to sociology). They also attracted to American anthropology as early as the 1920s more than its fair share of women, Jews, and sexual and political radicals. In the 1930s anthropology acquired a new electricity and attracted a younger generation of more politicized scholars, after the publication of *Patterns of Culture* by Boas's student Ruth Benedict, which further relativized culture by analogizing culture to personality: culture was increasingly seen to be almost an aesthetic choice, and relations between cultures to require the same kind of reciprocal communication as was involved in interpersonal relations.

Before World War II both the ecological and critical missions of Boasian anthropology were carried on almost exclusively at a studied distance from government. Boas himself had been badly burned by the sour political atmosphere after World War I and had systematically discouraged his students from playing any role in policymaking.[12] The principal exceptions were those anthropologists who worked with the Bureau of Indian Affairs. Boas and Benedict's most ambitious student, Margaret Mead, began to abandon this position in the mid-1930s, particularly after her marriage to her third husband, the British anthropologist Gregory Bateson. Most relevantly, Mead and Bateson felt that an understanding of culture patterns could be used to improve relations between classes and nations by teaching them to read better the intentions of others, rather than allowing unconscious reactions and counterreactions to spiral into bloody conflicts. As Bateson wrote in 1935,

> It is possible that those responsible for the policy of classes and nations might become conscious of the processes with which they are playing and cooperate in an attempt to solve the difficulties. This, however, is not very likely to occur since anthropology and social psychology lack the prestige necessary to advise; and, without such advice, governments will continue to react to each other's reactions rather than pay attention to circumstances.[13]

Furthermore, most anthropologists lacked the interest or the expertise to advise governments; thus even Mead and Bateson made a conscious decision to spend the years before the war doing fieldwork in Bali.

The outbreak of war had the potential to change all that. It represented one of a sequence of fairly sharp breaks in the 1940s and 1950s, choice points where academics could reassess their relationship with government and, to use Albert Hirschman's terminology, opt for "exit, voice or loyalty."[14] At this point, for a variety of personal, political, and patriotic reasons, most anthropologists chose not to exit. By one estimate, half of all professional anthropologists—including many of the women—signed up for fulltime government work during the war; and of course all draft-age male anthropologists in training were serving in the military.[15] But what was the impact of this war work? For the young—those who would spearhead the great postwar expansion in the profession—the experience was mostly of grinding routine at best, great personal danger at worst, with little if any connection to their interests and (where they had some) their training.[16] For those in mid-career, who had the freedom and the expertise to find more appropriate work, the experience was different—though not necessarily more satisfying. The most significant assignments were in the Office of War Information and the Office of Strategic Services, where information was gathered and proposals forged that could have an impact not only on the formulation of propaganda but also more substantively on the conduct of the war and plans for postwar reconstruction. For several reasons, academics in these offices often found their professional services useless and unwanted. As Leonard Doob, the social psychologist who ran OWI's Bureau of Overseas Intelligence, observed after the war, most of what his social scientists did was "simple fact-gathering." Decision making instead followed military and political imperatives. "The social scientist could not protest, inasmuch as his own position was too vulnerable," wrote Doob, "if he talked in terms of principles or theories, he ran the risk of being called a 'professor' and of delaying fast-moving operations."[17] Barry Katz's study of the Research & Analysis Branch of OSS came to similar conclusions.[18] Agents in the field had more freedom of action, but even greater distance from policymaking.

Only a few anthropologists retained freedom of action *and* achieved closeness to policymaking, among whom unsurprisingly the most successful was Margaret Mead. She chose her own, relatively easy job—a part-time post running the Committee on Food Habits—and used the rest of her time and considerable energy to develop a research and analysis program aimed at influencing wartime and postwar policy. Following Bateson's ideas of the 1930s, she prescribed specific forms for communication between the Allies—principally Britain and the United States—aimed at cementing their alliance and optimizing their ability to work together. Working through Ruth Benedict and Geoffrey Gorer at the OWI, she piped in suggestions for both "white" and "black" propaganda—the former to soften up for Allied invasion peoples in Axis-occupied countries, the latter to work on Axis soldiers' neuroses to weaken their resolve. Though she was relentlessly upbeat about the possibilities of this work, in practice she encountered the same obstacles faced by anthropologists in formal war work—her prescriptions were both too elaborate and too deliberate to fit with military imperatives. Benedict, whose work on Japanese culture is often cited as the most influential of all anthropological war work, had the same experience. Like most of her colleagues in OWI and OSS, for example, she opposed (unsuccessfully) the unconditional surrender demand in both Europe and Asia as likely only to solidify enemy resistance.[19] Her corresponding recommendation for the retention of the emperor in the postwar settlement was adopted, but only because MacArthur had come to this conclusion independently, and OWI's view that retention of the emperor as part of a wider psychological warfare campaign would be enough to end resistance was rejected in favor of the decision to drop the atomic bomb. As the OWI sociologist Alexander Leighton observed mordantly, "The administrator uses social science the way a drunk uses a lamppost, for support rather than for illumination."[20]

Postwar Debates

These wartime experiences are important for understanding the Cold War reception of anthropology for two reasons. First, they foreshadow the Cold War mismatch between Boasian anthropology, with its conviction of the stubborn and cohesive particularity of national cultures and the political-military establishment's preference for quick, technical fixes. But second, they contributed directly to widespread disillusionment among social scientists about the value as well as the ethics of applied anthropology. Many of the younger generation were just fed up and wanted to get back to anthropology after the trials and tribulations of war.[21] But many of the more engaged mid-career generation had the same or stronger feelings. Even Mead later granted that "of course everybody was a little tired and anxious to go home."[22] Her own husband Gregory Bateson emerged from two years working under Cora Du Bois in the Southeast Asia headquarters of OSS feeling it had all been "a total waste of time so far as any visible effect on planning and policies. . . . I brought home with me a desire to do some fieldwork in China and a profound cynicism about all policymaking folk." Worse, he bitterly regretted his role in black propaganda amongst the natives of Southeast Asia; OSS, he told Gorer, was "a dishonest outfit."[23] After the war he drifted away from Mead and turned to cybernetics and, later, the California counterculture.

Those mid-career anthropologists who remained in government service after the war did so for a variety of reasons. Some fell eagerly on the new funding opportunities offered by the military, especially the navy and the air force, which sought to fill a vacuum in the funding of basic research left by the exclusion of social science from new science funding structures.[24] Ruth Benedict insinuated herself into the Navy's Advisory Panel on Human Relations and got funding in 1947 to continue her and Mead's wartime work on "national character" in a project called "Research in Contemporary Cultures" (RCC), giving it a Cold War spin by taking up Czech, Russian, and Chinese case-studies, thus also attracting air force money through RAND. G. P. Murdock used his wartime navy service as the platform for launching the largest single anthropological enterprise of the early Cold War period, the Coordinated Investigation of Micronesian Anthropology (CIMA), as Ira Bashkow has shown, over traditionalist opposition within the profession.[25] Similarly, Julian Steward used his wartime connections with Nelson Rockefeller to get State Department funding for an Institute of Social Anthropology at the Smithsonian that would cultivate anthropological teaching and research in sensitive areas of Latin America.[26] Less eagerly, Clyde Kluckhohn agreed to direct the Russian Research Center at Harvard, possibly because he was being sexually blackmailed by the FBI, and to channel students into politically useful research, although in fact few anthropologists joined the RRC, which was principally populated by other disciplines.[27]

Some of these engagements did, of course, betoken a continuing commitment to narrowly American national interests, making the smooth transition from hot war to cold war portrayed as normal in the "behavioral science" orthodoxy. This was particularly true of those like Murdock and Steward not in the Boasian mainstream, who were more influenced by evolutionary thinking and readier to see American culture as the vanguard of a beneficently universalizing modernity, or "universal values."[28] However, it would be a mistake to view everyone who remained in public service across the hot war-cold war threshold as in thrall to this narrow construction of American national interests, still less to the promotion of a Cold War ideology of behavioral manipulation at home or abroad. Immediately after the war, some senior anthropologists remained in government service because they hoped that the postwar environment would be *more* favorable to the Boasian approach, with military considerations no longer paramount. In the State Department especially, the immediate postwar period witnessed ideological battles that for some time internationalist anthropologists still thought they could win. Even Robert Redfield, a non-Boasian but an ardent internationalist, fought these battles over the State Department's cultural programs until it became clear by the time of the Korean War that they had succumbed to an overtly propagandistic posture rather than the kind of international cultural exchanges that he favored.[29] Cora Du Bois, unusually, accepted direct decanting from OSS into the

State Department because she thought she could act as a counterweight to the permanent staff and their Indochina policy. By 1948, she later recounted,

> I saw that we were futile . . . and that we had nothing to contribute, except we did contribute a little to our policy in Indonesia. We foresaw very clearly what was going to happen in Vietnam, and tried to warn but we met this constant resistance because the policy was being formed out of reports from Paris and London, and other places, and we couldn't get into that.

She felt that while her young staff were capable of imparting valuable cultural awareness to the State Department, they were only putting this awareness to the service of a policy over which they had no control and "which we were deeply opposed to," and advised them, "Look, you've lost your judgment on this whole thing. Get the hell out of here and back to academic life. You can't stand this, it's destroying you." Finally, she came to the same conclusion herself and jumped ship in 1949.[30]

Other anthropologists who remained on the government payroll, but who were not on the frontline of American foreign policy, were able to retain their independence, or at least their illusions, for longer. They were aware that the international balance of power through the early 1950s was in flux and they were sufficiently encouraged by the general atmosphere of "do-goodism"[31] and the potential of international organizations such as UNESCO and the World Health Organization to feel that their participation might strengthen rather than weaken the integrity of non-Western cultures. There was neither an atmosphere of fear nor a conspiracy of silence—a lot of soul-searching went on in public as well as in private.[32] There was much discussion, for example, of whether Truman's Point IV program could possibly provide what it promised, strings-free and culturally appropriate technical assistance to the developing world.[33] Among Du Bois's more congenial jobs at the State Department was feeding her Boasian perspective on "understanding foreign peoples" to Edward Kennard and Ned Hall at the Foreign Service Institute, who undertook to train both foreign service officers and technical assistance workers in basic skills of cultural awareness.[34] Even more attractive than Point IV was UNESCO's technical assistance program, supposed to respond to initiatives from developing rather than from developed countries, and equipped with compulsory anthropological advisers whose explicit role was to act as a counterweight to experts and administrators, both in keeping open two-way communication and in assessing the cultural impact of development schemes. "Economists and technicians . . . become imbued with an alarming self-confidence," argued UNESCO's leading anthropologist, Alfred Metraux. Against this, anthropologists performed a service by "pointing out the danger of preaching science and industrialization with injudicious zeal." This role, he suggested, entailed both the costs and benefits of a certain detachment.

> Although anthropologists can, in a pinch, be experts on education or agriculture, there is one role they must never undertake—that of administrator. Control of a project and ethnographic research are utterly incompatible. . . . The ethnographer is obliged to show a certain humility and familiarity which are inconsistent with the authoritative attitude that must be assumed by the administrator.[35]

Metraux's formulation derives directly from two very public and very acrimonious debates that anthropologists engaged in during this early Cold War period that raised the most fundamental questions about anthropology's proper relationship to great-power politics. First was the debate over anthropology's view of "human rights," triggered by UNESCO's drafting of the Universal Declaration of Human Rights in 1947. The American Anthropological Association's contribution was a statement, drafted in a very orthodox Boasian vein by Melville Herskovits, repudiating even the lowest-common-denominator idea of "human rights" as a Western, indeed neocolonial, imposition and defending "the right of men to live in terms of their own traditions," while accepting *some* minimal degree of universalism to avoid the appearance of sanctioning "traditions" such as Nazism. This position, sometimes seen as an embarrassingly apolitical opting out by a later generation more attached to the idea of "human rights," was opposed at the time as *too* political—on the wrong side—by anthropologists like Julian Steward and Homer Barnett who wanted to stick to "scientific" principles that would give them a freer hand in their own involvement with government projects.[36]

At about the same time a second debate was carried on within the Society for Applied Anthropology about the need for an ethical code to govern anthropologists' work in policy and administration. The SAA, which originated amongst industrial anthropologists, had an in-built bias in favor of the "equilibrium state" of organizations, which took stability within the terms of the status quo as the desired goal, a position influential in the making of the new behavioral science. But a draft ethics code making this commitment explicit unleashed a torrent of criticism from anthropologists who had no difficulty discerning—and articulating—the political implications, in some cases precisely because their wartime experiences had sensitized them to the ethical and political dangers.[37] Why should anthropologists respect an "equilibrium" constructed in the interests of employers, or of either colonial or postcolonial elites in a developing country? After a lengthy debate amongst the membership and much redrafting, a new code was produced stipulating that "no applied anthropologist may undertake a commission on behalf of any interest, or segment, or section of a group . . . without a specific avowal, to those on whose behalf he undertakes the task, of his intention of taking the whole into account." As in the debate over human rights, those anthropologists most inclined to working with the American government were most hostile on "scientific" grounds to any "political" statement that might restrict their freedom to work for and with whomever they chose, but the majority agreed upon an ethics code that would make explicit the limits on what anthropologists should do in the service of administration. And, as Metraux's analysis indicates, many anthropologists went further than the terms of the ethics code to cast doubt on whether anthropologists could take any part in administration without jeopardizing their relationship to their subjects.[38]

Exit, Voice, or Loyalty

The period through the early 1950s of political contestation was hard enough on the older generation, whose wartime experience of government had equipped them either with enough idealism or with enough cynicism to fight the necessary battles with some confidence. The younger generation was necessarily more wary. Benedict and Mead found themselves constantly reassuring their younger colleagues on the RCC project that they and not their navy funders were setting the intellectual agenda. "What is the ultimate disposition of this material going to be? There is a definite vague feeling it can be transmuted into potential dynamite if *they* get hold of it," fretted one colleague in a private meeting in April 1948. Mead replied irritatedly,

> This material is *all* unclassified. . . . This research is financed by the Office of Naval Research. It was instituted in a discussion when somebody in the Navy suggested using some of the Navy's research money for peace. . . . This project is totally unrestricted; anything that comes out of this project can be published. The Navy places no restriction on any material. . . . We feel that everything we're learning in this project is as useful for peace as for war. We know more about destructive techniques than about constructive, but are not doing this order of research. Everything we're doing is potentially valuable for peace. It can also be used for war. There are no forms of research relevant only to peace. But every single point we work on in anthropology is at least as relevant for peace as for war.

More anxiously she added that the staff were free to publicize the navy's involvement, but they shouldn't make a song-and-dance about it lest they raise unnecessary suspicions.[39] RCC had at least the imprimatur of a major academic institution, Columbia University. Other anthropological work more directly for government looked even riskier to people early in their career, who wondered whether it would carry sufficient intellectual or professional prestige to lead to proper academic employment—"applied" anthropology looked both anti-intellectual and potentially dirty. While some senior social scientists (mostly not anthropologists) salivated over Point IV and the global opportunities it seemed to provide for social engineering, very much as imagined by the "behavioral science" literature—"This is the closest to experimental social science that we are likely to get. . . . It is a terrific challenge in terms of social science. If the social scientist does not move in this particular thing, the engineers will"[40]—to Mead's frustration the younger generation wouldn't touch it with a bargepole. From her point of view, the cross-cultural approach that anthropologists brought was the only available antidote to the Cold War agenda of Americanization that many of Point IV's governmental promoters had in mind. But even that good cause was not sufficient bait for career-minded youngsters. "At one point we had seven good jobs in technical assistance begging for anthropologists," Mead said bitterly many years later. "Most of them remained unfilled," as the rising generation opted for things that "paid off careerwise": "all you had to do was to write three articles on the same subject for three different journals and you could become an associate professor."[41]

CIMA fell victim to just the same pressures. The dreamchild of senior figures like G. P. Murdock who had been inspired by their wartime experiences to seek to inject anthropology into the heart of US foreign policy overseas, CIMA had gotten off the ground only after a struggle with anti-intervention traditionalists.[42] But Murdock's ultimate nemesis came not from the older generation but the younger. A fleet of young anthropologists fanned out around Micronesia in the late 1940s to undertake basic research for their PhDs. Tensions immediately arose between the navy, which wanted useful information and assistance, and the anthropologists, who wanted academic credit. Modern-day critics of "Cold War anthropology" have complained that, however much they might try to distance themselves from the navy, the anthropologists were still fatally compromised by their official connections. Many of the young anthropologists knew this at the time. They were vociferous—in public as well as in private—about the endemic racism of the naval administration and its imperviousness to the kind of anthropological knowledge of local peoples that they had to offer.[43] But neither did they see their function as primarily to provide anthropological knowledge to the navy; they had their own interests, professional and intellectual, in mind. David Schneider, probably the most scrutinized of all the CIMA anthropologists, put his cards on the table to his mentor Geoffrey Gorer even before he had spent a day in Yap, the Micronesian island to which he had been assigned:

> The real problem is this: I definitely want to get the PhD as soon as possible. If I don't I'm apt to find the market so flooded that I'd better have gotten out of the field. On the other hand, I don't want to do a cheesy piece of three months work investigating the dice games of the Navaho. This seems like a very good opportunity to get in some good field work, to get in on an area which is still untouched by American anthropological hands, to go along on an expenses-paid trip. I want the better training, the wider background, but I don't want to get hung up too long.[44]

Nor was Schneider under any illusions as to the difficulty his connection to the navy, however arm's length, might cause with his informants, and he took his informants seriously enough to try to communicate the true state of affairs to them. Sure, he granted later, much anthropology was "carried out on the back of colonial power," but the locals knew the difference between these young anthropologists and the navy, or for that matter the missionaries and traders with whom they had dealt earlier, and if they didn't he did his level best to set them straight. As for the idea promoted by Bashkow (based on a reading of Schneider's own fieldnotes) that the Yapese still saw him as their "superior," to the contrary he felt that the egalitarian Yapese were probably laughing at him for his efforts to disabuse them of illusions they would never have entertained anyway.[45] For others on the CIMA team, the encounter could be used precisely as an opportunity to reveal the difference between "in-facing" structures of authority used amongst the local peoples and the "out-facing" structures they simulated for dealing with nosy Americans (whether in uniform or not). Most of the CIMA anthropologists—as Boasians but also as budding academics rather than neocolonial administrators—felt far more interest in and sympathy with local attempts to subvert or evade naval administration than in the neocolonial enterprise to which they were supposedly attached.[46] A handful did stay and became an integral part of the administration when the navy handed over control of Micronesia to the Interior Department. But theirs was not a happy tale, either as administrators or as anthropologists. Only half of those who took on administrative roles finished their PhDs and few pursued an academic career. Those like Jack Fischer and Thomas Gladwin who were ardent defenders of their dual role at the time concluded afterward that they had failed to achieve anything in either role. Even Homer Barnett, the senior government anthropologist, had to admit that it was almost constitutionally impossible for the average anthropologist to identify with the administration to the extent that was necessary to fulfill such a role. After Barnett left in 1953, there was virtually no anthropological input into the Trust Territory administration until Peace Corps volunteers appeared in the 1960s.[47]

From Voice to Exit

The late 1940s and the early 1950s, then, saw many urgent and public debates about how far anthropologists could and should work with government and the military. John Useem and John Embree wrote critically of the navy's policy in Micronesia. Ned Hall and Thomas Gladwin traded angry charges about the complicity of anthropologists there.[48] The human rights and ethics debates aired many views and established a quasi-official consensus on the limits to anthropological collaboration with great-power efforts to "control" and "develop" subordinated peoples. This consensus resonated far beyond American circles, as is evident in the international symposium on the state of anthropology held in June 1952 at which Redfield summed up the widely held view that "a difference in value judgment between anthropologist and government administrator is likely to be real and serious, no matter how enlightened the government, because of something in the very nature of anthropology," that is, the absolute value placed on "cultural integrity."[49]

After the Korean War, however, as the Cold War deepened and the pressures on anthropologists involved in government work to conform to their masters' agenda intensified, the room for debate shrank sharply, and in response most anthropologists shifted further away from the Cold War environment, from "voice" to "exit." John Embree, with Du Bois one of the few anthropologists to persist with State Department work in Southeast Asia after the war, had quit in disgust and taken up an appointment at Yale when he died suddenly in 1950.[50] Du Bois herself had left and went to work for the World Health Organization in 1950, but quit after a year because she found WHO just as bureaucratic as the State Department and not much better at negotiating the tensions between medical aid and cultural diversity.[51] Until about 1950, George Foster at the government's Institute of Social Anthropology had, as he said, "a free hand in hiring people. It never occurred to me that I'd have to tell them, 'You have to be cleared.' After that, that's when it began being tough." Though a "token conservative" among anthropologists and (as he later admitted) relatively uncritical of the Point IV programs in which he was involved, he too decided to fold his tent and returned to academia in 1953.[52] Even the anthropologists at UNESCO found themselves sidelined. By the end of 1951 only one potential developing-world client had requested anthropological assistance—Liberia, at Embree's urging—in part because in good Boasian style too many anthropologists had positioned themselves not as interpreters but as opponents of technical assistance, taking the side of traditional elders against modernizers.[53]

Precisely how decisive the choice point of the early 1950s was can be illustrated by the choices made by Margaret Mead. As we have seen, Mead had since the mid-1930s been seeking to inject Boasian anthropology into the heart of

American foreign policy. During the war she had developed ethical rationales for her contributions: first, that she needed to embrace her Americanism fully in order to be effective both as interpreter and as reformer[54]; second, that facilitating democratic procedures was consistent with anthropological ethics in emphasizing means not ends, processes not teleologies, empowerment not manipulation.[55] Unlike most of her younger colleagues, she was determined to persist in her course after 1945, principally through the "Research in Contemporary Cultures" project for which Benedict had secured funding.[56] Mead assumed command of this program on Benedict's death in 1948, and if anything shifted it to bear more directly on American foreign and military interests, by, for example, soliciting RAND funding for a project on Russian and Soviet culture.[57]

However, once again, Mead's Boasian perspective—even when compromised by her taste for power—made impossible a meeting of minds with foreign and military policy. The crisis came again in the early 1950s, when Geoffrey Gorer's preliminary work for the project on Russian and Soviet culture unleashed bitter criticism both from the anthropological profession and from the policymakers. Gorer's argument that Russian culture was deeply imbued with psychological disposition to authority and submission pleased almost no one. The anthropologists resented the funding and attention being devoted, uncoincidentally, to one particular modern culture—as the sociologist David Riesman noted, anthropology's "cultural relativism includes among its non-relativistic assumptions the passionate belief that each power, irrespective of size or ability to threaten or be exploited, counts one: an international democracy of one culture, one vote . . . it has been an achievement of their profession to ignore merely contemporary rankings either of territories or of problem stress."[58] But neither were the policymakers happy. They disliked Gorer and Mead's emphasis on early-childhood socialization (and particularly the stress laid on the practice of "swaddling" babies), partly because of its psychiatric overtones, but mostly because it made the Russians seem too alien and unreformable. They preferred "primary group" analyses of the Soviet leadership, which portrayed the communist elite as a detachable excrescence on the healthy human body of the Russian people, such as were to be conducted subsequently mostly by sociologists under Kluckhohn at Harvard's Russian Research Centre. Furthermore, they knew that American public opinion was even more hostile to this psychocultural analysis of Russian Otherness, as witness the storm of public attacks on Gorer and Mead's "diaperology."[59]

Mead was terribly frustrated by the debacle of the so-called swaddling controversy, disgusted by the ingratitude and pusillanimity of her own profession and by the deafness and instrumentality of policymakers. Like so many of her peers, after 1951 she withdrew from government work; but for the rest of her life she kept up a tattoo of criticism of both sides. On the one hand, she did come to acknowledge the significance of the political turning point of

> the Joseph McCarthy era and the Korean War, when everybody inside the government who could have used the new material or insights that anthropologists could have produced went home or got fired. By 1952, there was no one in the government to ask for information of the sort anthropologists would have provided or to use it if it had been provided.

On the other hand, she was not about to let the anthropologists off either: "Even if the government did ask us, we were not sure we were going to tell them what we knew." They retreated into academia, "became parochial," danced around "small, specific discussions of kinship, or variations in response to Levi-Strauss," wrote those three articles and got tenure.[60] Anthropology wasn't even able any longer to perform the most elementary intercultural translation, she complained. When the Peace Corps asked for cultural training on Nigeria, all they got from the anthropologists was "nice little bits of ethnology."

> Most of them had not done any thinking about the wider scene for ten years . . . they did not care about diplomacy; they did not know anything beyond their particular point. So what did they do? They gave a course on primitive rites among the Ibo or initiation ceremonies of the Yoruba. And Nigerian students who had come over here to study international affairs picketed the course and protested.[61]

One does not have to endorse Mead's jaundiced view in order to see its significance. In the view of applied anthropology's most enthusiastic supporters, the main drift of the profession since the early 1950s had *not* been toward an embrace of the behavioral science paradigm but away from it. As even some of the "behavioral science" literature grants, a lot of steam had run out of the project already by the early 1950s.[62] The return of behavioral science in a new form, modernization theory, later in the decade owed very little to anthropological input, both because its individualism was intellectually distasteful and because its interventionism was politically distasteful to anthropologists.[63] The often-cited role of Clifford Geertz in the modernization-oriented "Modjokuto" project in Indonesia has been contested, not least by Geertz himself, who claimed to have been largely ignorant of the deeper purposes there of American foreign policy. But Geertz's involvement in Modjokuto is cited so often precisely because there are not that many instances of direct anthropological contributions to modernization programs.[64] Economists and political scientists, unencumbered by "political" objections to human-rights universalism and ethics codes, were much better partners for policymakers seeking to modernize developing countries on an American model. Even so, Robert Packenham's studies of the impact of social science on development policy found that few policymakers or officials had even heard of the key works of comparative politics supposedly so influential in piping modernization theory into policy circles.[65]

A more persuasive critique, I think, is the nearly opposite argument that Boasian anthropology contributed to "the objectification of things national."[66] But this objectification of nations did not fit well with a Cold War agenda. It came into awkward conflict with all of the various Cold War humanisms or universalisms—"human rights," modernization, Marxism—preferred by American and Soviet policy elites.[67] Mead's idea of "internationalism" in the 1950s, as in the 1930s, was the reduction of international tension by roping off nations from each other with the anthropologist acting as interpreter—but the State Department didn't want interpreters between nations, it wanted propagandists for its own brand of "one world" ideology. By 1955 it was not even interested in cultural awareness training for diplomats and decided to "clear out the anthropologists" from their last redoubt, the Foreign Service Institute, sending Ned Hall back to academia.[68] By that point, Mead herself had come to see that the new postwar nations—including the enlarged Soviet Union—were decreasingly susceptible to treatment as monolithic cultures.

Finally, we ought to consider a different critique, which is not that the social sciences necessarily conformed to or collaborated with Cold War imperatives but that they were frightened into self-censorship or irrelevance. McCarthyism did indeed truncate anthropological debate, not least by excluding some of the younger and more orthodox Marxists. Though obviously a gross violation of academic and other freedoms, in practice this truncation did not greatly shape anthropological debate, for the orthodox Marxists affected were mostly old-fashioned evolutionists (influenced by Engels), uncongenial to the Boasian mainstream, as even the FBI on occasion appreciated, and rather closer in perspective to modernization theory.[69] Marxist social scientists could be quite as scornful of anthropologists' cultural relativism as any other Cold Warriors. When the anthropologist Sol Tax raised the standard Boasian objection to technical assistance that did not respect the cultural integrity of affected peoples, the Marxist economist Paul Baran grandly swept aside such piffling scruples. "[T]he peoples living under conditions of squalor and starvation in the underdeveloped countries of the world would probably join me in assigning only low priority to this philosophical inquiry," he insisted ex cathedra, arguing that the only real consideration was how best to raise production levels as rapidly as possible—precisely the position taken up by modernization theorists, though advocating dramatic state intervention rather than capitalist markets as the best means.[70]

Boasian anthropology did not need Senator McCarthy's instructions to resist such a doctrine inimical to its own strongest intellectual traditions. Nor did it need to be hounded out of government work by a witch hunt. The mutual incompatibility of Boasian anthropology and the Cold War demands of American policy was already perfectly clear to both sides; after a period of fraught engagement in the late 1940s and early 1950s, both sides withdrew from the field, anthropologists preferring their traditional intellectual stances and their more purely academic jobs, the military especially largely giving up on "behavioral science" at least as far as anthropology was concerned. The final clearout came with the advent of the Eisenhower Administration in 1953, when businessmen and local politicians replaced experts in remaining pockets of social-scientific activity such as Point IV and the Foreign Service Institute. This mutual repulsion may not have been healthy for American foreign policy. It may have represented, as Mead thought, a failure to harness anthropological expertise for the amelioration of the Cold War,[71] or, as the New Left analysis had it, a failure to offer a head-on critique of America's role in the Cold War.[72] But it certainly does not resemble anything like the anthropological contribution to the behavioral science project in the service of the Cold War that one finds in the current historiography; to the contrary, as one lonely proponent of such service mourned in 1956, "In point of number, as well as effect, their contribution to the theory and practice of social engineering has been relatively small."[73] In periodizing the Cold War, then, this particular case study suggests that choices made by the early 1950s meant many people had already disengaged from the Cold War shortly after it began. The great anthropological scandals of the 1960s arose not because most anthropologists were already implicated but because—to pursue counterinsurgency in Southeast Asia and Latin America—government engaged in a renewed campaign to recruit them, leading to very public and very acrimonious conflicts. Today, when the tiny handful of anthropologists in military employment complain that counterinsurgency in Iraq has failed for lack of cultural understanding, they have to appeal to the wartime tradition of Benedict and Mead because (as Mead herself would surely have observed) there was hardly any "Cold War anthropology" to call upon.[74]

Notes

1. I am very grateful to Joel Isaac and Duncan Bell for their invitation to the symposium that launched this book, from which I (still a novice paddler in these waters) learned a great deal, and to the other participants in the symposium, especially Glenda Sluga and Andrew Preston. Research for this chapter was made possible by grants from the British Academy and the Arts and Humanities Research Council.
2. Michael S. Sherry, *In the Shadow of War: The United States Since the 1930s* (New Haven, 1995), pp. 35–37, 68, 88–91, 117, 164–167; Ellen Herman, *The Romance of American Psychology: Political Culture in the Age of Experts* (Berkeley, 1995).
3. Peter Buck, "Adjusting to Military Life: The Social Sciences Go to War, 1941–1950" in Merritt Roe Smith (ed.), *Military Enterprise and Technological Change: Perspectives on the American Experience* (Cambridge, MA, 1985), pp. 203–252.

4. Christopher Simpson, *Science of Coercion: Communication Research and Psychological Warfare 1945–1960* (Oxford, 1994); Ira Katznelson, "The Subtle Politics of Developing Emergency: Political Science as Liberal Guardianship" in Noam Chomsky et al., *The Cold War & The University: Toward an Intellectual History of the Postwar Years* (New York, 1997), pp. 233–258; Nils Gilman, *Mandarins of the Future: Modernization Theory in Cold War America* (Baltimore, 2003), esp. pp. 48–54.
5. Laura Nader, "The Phantom Factor: Impact of the Cold War on Anthropology" in Chomsky et al., *The Cold War & The University*, pp. 107–146, but cf. the rather different analysis in Immanuel Wallerstein, "The Unintended Consequences of Cold War Area Studies" in ibid., pp. 195–231; Michael E. Latham, "Introduction: Modernization, International History, and the Cold War World" in David C. Engerman, Nils Gilman, Mark H. Haefele and Michael E. Latham (eds.), *Staging Growth: Modernization, Development, and the Global Cold War* (Amherst, 2003), pp. 1–22; James Ferguson, "Anthropology and Its Evil Twin: 'Development' in the Constitution of a Discipline" in Frederick Cooper and Randall Packard (eds.), *International Development and the Social Sciences: Essays on the History and Politics of Knowledge* (Berkeley, 1997), pp. 150–175; Nils Gilman, "Involution and Modernization: The Case of Clifford Geertz" in Jeffrey H. Cohen and Norbert Dannhaeuser (eds.), *Economic Development: An Anthropological Approach* (Walnut Creek CA., 2002), pp. 3–22; David H. Price, "Subtle Means and Enticing Carrots: The Impact of Funding on American Cold War Anthropology," *Critique of Anthropology*, 23 (2003), pp. 373–401.
6. Gilman, *Mandarins of the Future*, esp. pp. 155–214.
7. Ron Robin, *The Making of the Cold War Enemy: Culture and Politics in the Military-Intellectual Complex* (Princeton, 2001); David Engerman, *Modernization From the Other Shore: American Intellectuals and the Romance of Russian Development* (Cambridge, MA., 2003), pp. 273–285.
8. The aspiration of social scientists to "control" is the central theme of Rebecca Lemov, *World as Laboratory: Experiments with Mice, Mazes, and Men* (New York, 2005); see also the "IC model," which prioritized the adjustment of the individual to the collective, as proposed by Andrew Abbott and James Sparrow, "Hot War, Cold War: The Structures of Sociological Action, 1940–1955," in Craig Calhoun (ed.), *Sociology in America* (Chicago, 2007), esp. pp. 301–308.
9. Terence Ball, "The Politics of Social Science in Postwar America" in Larry May (ed.), *Recasting America: Culture and Politics in the Age of Cold War* (Chicago, 1989), pp. 76–92; Robin, *Cold War Enemy*, e.g. pp. 199–200; Herman, *Romance of American Psychology*; Lemov, *World as Laboratory*; Nader, "Phantom Factor," e.g., p. 123; Michael E. Latham, *Modernization as Ideology: American Social Science and "Nation Building" in the Kennedy Era* (Chapel Hill, 2000); David Price, *Anthropological Intelligence: The Deployment and Neglect of American Anthropology in the Second World War* (Durham, 2008), pp. xiii–xvi, 264–271, 281; and surprisingly even David Engerman, "Rethinking Cold War Universities: Some Recent Histories," *Journal of Cold War Studies*, 5 (2003), pp. 87–88, after a warning against such simplifications.
10. David Price, "Cold War Anthropology: Collaborators and Victims of the National Security State," *Identities*, 4 (1997–8), pp. 391–392.
11. Gilman, *Mandarins of the Future*, p. 21.
12. Virginia Yans-McLaughlin, "Science, Democracy, and Ethics: Mobilizing Culture and Personality for World War II" in George Stocking (ed.), *Malinowski, Rivers, Benedict and Others: Essays on Culture and Personality* (History of Anthropology, Vol. 4) (Madison, 1986), pp. 185–187.
13. Bateson, "Culture Contact and Schismogenesis" (1935), in *Steps to an Ecology of Mind* (Chicago, 1972), p. 72.
14. Hirschman, *Exit, Voice, and Loyalty: Responses to Decline in Firms, Organizations, and States* (Cambridge, MA., 1970).
15. David H. Price, "Gregory Bateson and the OSS: World War II and Bateson's Assessment of Applied Anthropology," *Human Organization*, 57 (1998), p. 379.

16. Abbott and Sparrow, "Hot War, Cold War," pp. 291–293, give a very good account of this experience in the case of sociologists, which however sits uneasily with their subsequent account of the transition from "hot war" to "cold war."
17. Doob, "The Utilization of Social Scientists in the Overseas Branch of the Office of War Information," *American Political Science Review*, 41 (1947), pp. 651–653.
18. Katz, *Foreign Intelligence: Research and Analysis in the Office of Strategic Services* (Cambridge, MA., 1989).
19. Allan M. Winkler, *The Politics of Propaganda: The Office of War Information 1942–1945* (New Haven, 1978), pp. 133–134, 140–146; Katz, *Foreign Intelligence*, pp. 40–41; Doob, "Utilization of Social Scientists," p. 658.
20. John Dower, *War Without Mercy: Race and Power in the Pacific War* (New York, 1986), pp. 136–140; Dower, *Embracing Defeat: Japan in the Aftermath of World War II* (New York, 1999), pp. 220–224, 280–286, and cf. Herman, *Romance of American Psychology*, pp. 40–41; Alexander H. Leighton, *Human Relations in a Changing World: Observations on the Use of the Social Sciences* (New York, 1949), pp. 127–128.
21. William Partridge and Elizabeth Eddy, "The Development of Applied Anthropology in America" in Eddy and Partridge (eds.), *Applied Anthropology in America* (New York, 1978), p. 35.
22. Bela Maday (ed.), *Anthropology and Society* (Washington DC., 1975), p. 13.
23. Gregory Bateson to A. R. Radcliffe-Brown, August 21, 1946: Margaret Mead Papers, Library of Congress, O3; Price, "Gregory Bateson and the OSS," p. 382; David Lipset, *Gregory Bateson: The Legacy of a Scientist* (Englewood Cliffs, NJ., 1980), p. 175; Yans-McLaughlin, "Science, Democracy and Ethics," pp. 203–204.
24. Gene M. Lyons, *The Uneasy Partnership: Social Science and the Federal Government in the 20th Century* (New York, 1969), pp. 136–137.
25. Bashkow, "The Dynamics of Rapport in a Colonial Situation: David Schneider's Fieldwork on the Islands of Yap" in George Stocking (ed.), *Colonial Situations: Essays on the Contextualization of Ethnographic Knowledge* (Madison, WI, 1991), esp. pp. 179–195.
26. George M. Foster, "The Institute of Social Anthropology" in Walter Goldschmidt (ed.), *The Uses of Anthropology* (Washington, DC, 1979), pp. 205–216. It is noteworthy that in practice the young anthropologists sent out to Latin America by the ISA gravitated to the study of "primitive" peoples rather than the "modernizing" mestizos that Steward had envisioned as more important from a policy point of view.
27. Sigmund Diamond, *Compromised Campus: The Collaboration of Universities with the Intelligence Community, 1945–1955* (Oxford, 1992), pp. 58–60, 68–110, was the first to reveal the extent of Kluckhohn's connections with the FBI and, more speculatively, the CIA. Price, "Cold War Anthropology," pp. 402–407, builds on this research to make the more debatable assertion that Kluckhohn was "a strong Cold Warrior." David Engerman, *Know Your Enemy: The Rise and Fall of America's Soviet Experts* (Oxford, 2009), pp. 44–70, does not give credence to these accusations and portrays Kluckhohn's relationship to government as more equivocal.
28. See the argument in Clifford Wilcox, *Robert Redfield and the Development of American Anthropology* (Lanham, MD, 2004), pp. 109–115, that "cultural relativism" failed to survive World War II, giving way to a new evolutionary approach in anthropology more conducive to modernization theory.
29. Frank Ninkovich, *The Diplomacy of Ideas: U.S. Foreign Policy and Cultural Relations, 1938–1950* (Cambridge, 1981), esp. pp. 151–155; and cf. Wilcox, *Robert Redfield*, pp. 184–185, which thus agrees that his own subject is an exception to the appropriation of anthropology as a "policy science" by government for which Wilcox had argued earlier, pp. 109–115. Closer scrutiny of these debates is necessary to determine how many and which of the sometime "liberal internationalists" embraced the Cold War turn and how many decamped as a result of it.
30. Interview with Cora Du Bois by Lawrence C. Kelly, April 9, 1978 (2nd, corrected draft), pp. 18–19: Cora Du Bois Papers, Tozzer Library, Harvard University, Box 11; Interview with

Cora Du Bois, August 20, 1983, in Judith B. Walzer, "An Oral History of the Tenured Women in the Faculty of Arts and Sciences at Harvard University, 1981," unpublished manuscript, 1983 (Schlesinger Library, Radcliffe Institute, Harvard University).

31. Du Bois's phrase: Walzer, "Oral History."
32. E.g., in the two major surveys of world anthropology published in 1953, A. L. Kroeber (ed.), *Anthropology Today: An Encyclopedic Inventory* (Chicago, 1953), and Sol Tax, Loren C. Eiseley, Irving Rouse, Carl F. Voegelin (eds.), *An Appraisal of Anthropology Today* (Chicago, 1953), esp. ch. 11.
33. There has been a lot of casual comment but surprisingly little close attention to anthropologists' involvement in and debate over Point IV and other technical assistance programs. For a start, see Peter Mandler, "One World, Many Cultures: Margaret Mead and the Limits to Cold War Anthropology," *History Workshop Journal*, 68 (2009), pp. 149–172; and see also the interesting comment by Gilman, *Mandarins of the Future*, p. 276.
34. Edward A. Kennard and Gordon Macgregor, "Applied Anthropology in Government: United States" in Kroeber (ed.), *Anthropology Today*, pp. 838–839; Edward A. Kennard, "Understanding Foreign Peoples," n.d., and correspondence, 1946–47: Du Bois Papers, Box 31; notes and drafts of lectures to Foreign Service Institute, 1946–47 and 1951–52: Du Bois Papers, Box 67; see also criticisms voiced at sessions led by Kennard and Du Bois, March 6–7, 1952: Gordon Macgregor Papers, National Anthropological Archives, Box 3.
35. Metraux, "Applied Anthropology in Government: United Nations" in Kroeber (ed.), *Anthropology Today*, pp. 885–886, 889.
36. The original statement, with Steward's and Barnett's published objections, can be found in *American Anthropologist*, n.s., 49 (1947), pp. 539–543; 50 (1948), pp. 351–355. These thorny issues have been discussed by Alison Dundes Renteln, *International Human Rights: Universalism versus Relativism* (Newbury Park, 1990), esp. pp. 64–69, 83–87, and Karen Engle, "From Skepticism to Embrace: Human Rights and the American Anthropological Association from 1947–1999," *Human Rights Quarterly*, 23 (2001), pp. 536–559.
37. See John Embree, "Applied Anthropology and Its Relationship to Anthropology," *American Anthropologist*, new ser., 47 (1945), pp. 635–637, who pointed out the contradictions between this kind of behavioral manipulation and Boasian principles.
38. To my knowledge the only (brief) discussion of the SAA in the secondary literature is the recent account in Price, *Anthropological Intelligence*, pp. 274–277, which argues that Mead suppressed any debate and "railroaded" through a relatively conservative code: see my response in Mandler, "One World, Many Cultures." The extent of the debate can be traced in Margaret Mead Papers, E119, including the results of a poll of 75 SAA members on the draft code; the published text of the code can be found in "Report of the Committee on Ethics," *Human Organization* 8:2 (Spring 1949), pp. 20–21. See also criticism of the "equilibrium" idea in John Useem, "Applied Anthropology in Micronesia," *Applied Anthropology*, 6:4 (Fall 1947), p. 11. The professional debate spilled over into public: see the criticisms of applied anthropology as behavioral science by Nathan Glazer, "Government by Manipulation," *Commentary*, July 1946, pp. 81–86, and the response based on the SAA ethics code by Conrad Arensberg, *Commentary*, August 1946, p. 187.
39. Research in Contemporary Cultures, Minutes, 18th General Seminar, May 26, 1948: Margaret Mead Papers, G14.
40. "First Conference on Social Science Problems of Point Four," Washington, December 2, 1950: Margaret Mead Papers, E125.
41. Bela Maday (ed.), *Anthropology and Society* (Washington, 1975), p. 15. For contemporary awareness of how difficult it was to find "well-qualified and experienced people who are also available and willing to accept government employment," see Edward Kennard to Margaret Mead, September 14, 1950: Margaret Mead Papers, C22.
42. Bashkow, "Dynamics of Rapport," pp. 179–195.
43. Lt. John Useem, "Social Reconstruction in Micronesia," *Far Eastern Survey*, January 30, 1946, pp. 21–23; John F. Embree, "Micronesia: The Navy and Democracy," *Far Eastern Survey*, June

5, 1946, pp. 161–164; Embree, "American Military Government" in Meyer Fortes (ed.), *Social Structure: Studies Presented to A.R. Radcliffe-Brown* (Oxford, 1949), pp. 207–225; Useem, "Applied Anthropology in Micronesia"; Embree, "A Note on Ethnocentrism in Anthropology," *American Anthropologist*, n.s., 52 (1950), pp. 430–432, with ensuing responses from John L. Fischer and Jules Henry, ibid., 53 (1951), pp. 133–135. See further the discussion in Glenn Petersen, "Politics in Postwar Micronesia" in Robert Kiste and Mac Marshall (eds.), *American Anthropology in Micronesia: An Assessment* (Honolulu, 1999), esp. pp. 147–151.

44. David Schneider to Geoffrey Gorer, January 29, 1947: Gorer Papers, Special Collections, University of Sussex, Box 99.
45. David Schneider as told to Richard Handler, *Schneider on Schneider: The Conversion of the Jews and Other Anthropological Stories* (Durham, 1995), pp. 161–168; cf. Bashkow, "Dynamics of Rapport," pp. 188–190, 202–228. Lemov, *World as Laboratory*, pp. 181–182, repeats Bashkow's argument in simplified form and makes no reference to Schneider's retort.
46. Peterson, "Politics in Postwar Micronesia," esp. pp. 156–170; see also I. C. Campbell, "'A Chance to Build a New Social Order Well': Anthropology and American Colonial Government in Micronesia in Comparative Perspective," *Journal of Colonialism and Colonial History*, 3 (2002), n.p.
47. Robert Kiste and Suzanne Falgout, "Anthropology and Micronesia: The Context" in Kiste and Marshall (eds.), *American Anthropology in Micronesia*, esp. pp. 33–37; Suzanne Falgout, "Americans in Paradise: Anthropologists, Custom, and Democracy in Postwar Micronesia," *Ethnology*, 34 (1995), esp. pp. 104–108; J. L. Fischer, "Government Anthropologists in the Trust Territory of Micronesia" in Goldschmidt (ed.), *Uses of Anthropology*, esp. pp. 241–247. Barnett's own highly gloomy summing up of the whole episode can be found in H. G. Barnett, *Anthropology in Administration* (Evanston, 1956).
48. For Embree and Useem, see above, n. 39; for Hall and Gladwin, see Edward T. Hall Jr. "Military Government on Truk," *Human Organization*, 9/2 (Summer 1950), pp. 25–30; Thomas Gladwin, "Civil Administration on Truk: A Rejoinder," ibid., 9/4 (Winter 1950), pp. 15–23; Edward T. Hall Jr., "A Reply," ibid., p. 24.
49. Tax et al. (eds.), *Appraisal of Anthropology*, p. 182, and see in general ch. 8 and ch. 11. Further contributions to these debates include Barnett, *Anthropology in Administration*, esp. 49–85, and L. P. Mair, *Studies in Applied Anthropology* (London, 1957), esp. pp. 7–22.
50. Again, Embree was not shy about sharing in public the fruits of his State Department experiences: see, e.g., John F. Embree, "Some Problems of an American Cultural Officer in Asia," *American Anthropologist*, nest., 51 (1949), 155–158.
51. Walzer, "Oral History"; Kelly interview, p. 19.
52. George M. Foster, "An Anthropologist's Life in the Twentieth Century: Theory and Practice at UC Berkeley, the Smithsonian, in Mexico, and with the World Health Organization," an oral history conducted in 1998 and 1999 by Suzanne B. Riess (Regional Oral History Office, Bancroft Library, University of California, Berkeley), pp. 137, 160–165, 260, 280.
53. Metraux, "Applied Anthropology," pp. 888–889, 893.
54. Mead, "The Comparative Study of Culture and the Purposive Cultivation of Democratic Values" in *Science, Philosophy and Religion: Second Symposium* (New York, 1942), esp. pp. 66–69; Mead, *And Keep Your Powder Dry*, 1st ed. 1942 (Oxford, 2000), pp. 1–6.
55. Mead, "The Comparative Study of Culture and the Purposive Cultivation of Democratic Values," pp. 112–121. See also the discussion in Yans-McLaughlin, "Science, Democracy, and Ethics," esp. pp. 204–210.
56. For Mead's rethinking of her wartime rationales in a Cold War context, see Mead, "The Comparative Study of Cultures and the Purposive Cultivation of Democratic Values, 1941–1949" in Lyman Bryson, Louis Finkelstein, and R.M. MacIver (eds.), *Perspectives on a Troubled Decade: Science, Philosophy, and Religion, 1939–1949. 10th Symposium* (New York, 1950), pp. 87–108.

57. I discuss this further in Mandler, "One World, Many Cultures." While sympathetic to her general case, I cannot go all the way with Yans in arguing that Mead remained uninvolved in "military intelligence" in this period: Virginia Yans, "On the Political Anatomy of Mead-bashing; or, Re-thinking Margaret Mead" in Dolores Janiewski and Lois Banner (eds.), *Reading Benedict/Reading Mead: Feminism, Race, and Imperial Visions* (Baltimore, 2004), esp. pp. 242–243.
58. Riesman, "Comments on Dr Kluckhohn's Paper" in *Human Development Bulletin*, 6th Annual Symposium, University of Chicago (1955), pp. 39–61, 67–72.
59. Mandler, "One World, Many Cultures."
60. Maday (ed.), *Anthropology and Society*, 14–15; Mead, "Changing Styles of Anthropological Work" (1973), in Mead, *Studying Contemporary Western Society: Method and Theory*, ed. W. Beeman (Oxford, 2004), pp. 41–42. In this latter essay Mead oscillates between blaming the careerism of the 1950s and the militancy of the 1960s: cf. ibid., pp. 57–59. For a more temperate and self-critical analysis, see Mead, "Anthropological Contributions to National Policies During and Immediately After World War II" in Goldschmidt (ed.), *Uses of Anthropology*, pp. 153–154.
61. Maday (ed.), *Anthropology and Society*, p. 15.
62. Robin, *Cold War Enemy*, pp. 13–15, 44–53.
63. For a strong statement linking Boasian anthropology to modernization theory, see Latham, "Introduction," pp. 4–5; Gilman, *Mandarins of the Future*, p. 52, is properly more cautious. As argued above, Robert Redfield's biographer, while claiming Redfield as an intellectual godfather to modernization theory, grants that Redfield did not himself share the political program of the modernization theorists and was distancing himself from it at the time of his death in 1958: Wilcox, *Robert Redfield*, pp. 184–185.
64. Gilman, "Involution and Modernization," is the most extensive statement of the case; Christopher Simpson, "Universities, Empire, and the Production of Knowledge: An Introduction" in Simpson (ed.), *Universities and Empire*, p. xix, says that Geertz worked "cheek-by-jowl" with the "professional terrorists" of modernization theory; Nader, "Phantom Factor," p. 123, says that Geertz "accepted" the assumptions of modernization theory or at least offered "no critique"; Price, "Subtle Means and Enticing Carrots," pp. 388–392, says merely that Geertz's work was "consistent" with modernization theory; Ferguson, "Anthropology and Its Evil Twin," pp. 160–161, says that it is "striking" how many anthropologists signed on to modernization theory but can then only cite Geertz. For Geertz's responses, see Clifford Geertz, "Culture and Social Change: The Indonesian Case," *Man*, n.s., 19 (1984), pp. 511–532, and Richard Handler, "An Interview with Clifford Geertz," *Current Anthropology*, 32 (1991), pp. 603–613.
65. Robert A. Packenham, *Liberal America and the Third World: Political Development Ideas in Foreign Aid and Social Science* (Princeton, 1973), esp. pp. 243–253.
66. Federico Neiburg, Marcio Goldman and Peter Gow, "Anthropology and Politics in Studies of National Character," *Cultural Anthropology*, 13 (1998), pp. 56–81.
67. It is therefore not the case that Mead's idea of "national character" was simply "renamed" political culture to fit into a modernization project, as suggested by Herman, *Romance of American Psychology*, p. 170 (but cf. pp. 143–144).
68. Everett M. Rogers, William B. Hart and Yoshitaka Miike, "Edward T. Hall and the History of Intercultural Communication: The United States and Japan," *Keio Communication Review*, 24 (2002), pp. 9–10. Hall is an interesting case of someone who was highly critical of "applied anthropology" in Micronesia, then joined the State Department during the Korean War essentially for patriotic reasons, and was then driven out again by the Eisenhower Administration. It is revealing that Simpson, *Science of Coercion*, makes no mention of Hall—either his Cold War recruitment or his Cold War ouster.
69. On the impact of Marxism (and McCarthyism) on anthropology in the 1950s, see David Price, *Threatening Anthropology: McCarthyism and the FBI's Surveillance of Activist Anthropologists* (Durham, 2004), esp. pp. 38, 142, 164, 215–217, 307–310—to my mind, over-generous

as to the contribution that Marxism did make or could have made to contemporary anthropology.

70. Tax, "Selective Culture Change," *American Economic Review*, 41 (1951), pp. 315–320, with reply by Paul Baran, pp. 355–358.
71. There is even a hint of support for this position in the comment by Price, *Threatening Anthropology*, p. 353, that "The informed and questioning views of scholars like Jack Harris, John Embree, or Cora Du Bois are now rarely heard in the back rooms of the U.S. State Department or the United Nations."
72. Criticism of Mead's position is of course rife. Criticism of the New Left position—for ignoring the considerable intellectual and political continuities between the two generations—is still only evident in passing comments: see, e.g., George Stocking, "'Do Good, Young Man': Sol Tax and the World Mission of Liberal Democratic Anthropology," in Richard Handler (ed.), *Excluded Ancestors, Inventible Traditions: Essays Toward a More Inclusive History of Anthropology* (Madison, 2000), pp. 254–255; Engle, "From Skepticism to Embrace," p. 559; Peterson, "Politics in Postwar Micronesia," pp. 147–149; Peter W. Black, "Psychological Anthropology and Its Discontents: Science and Rhetoric in Postwar Micronesia" in Kiste and Marshall (eds.), *American Anthropology in Micronesia*, esp. pp. 235–237, 246; but cf. Yans, "Political Anatomy of Mead-bashing," a more extended counterattack.
73. Barnett, *Anthropology and Administration*, p. 48.
74. Montgomery McFate, "The Military Utility of Understanding Adversary Culture," *Joint Force Quarterly*, 38 (2005), esp. pp. 47–48; McFate, "Anthropology and Counterinsurgency: The Strange Story of Their Curious Relationship," *Military Review*, March–April 2005, esp. pp. 29–32; see also George Packer, "Knowing the Enemy," *The New Yorker*, December 18, 2006, p. 65.

12

Cognitive and Perceptual Training in the Cold War Man-Machine System

SHARON GHAMARI-TABRIZI

"The Cold War is not necessarily everything that happens in the Cold War," Anders Stephanson remarks in his chapter in this volume. He argues that in works calling themselves "Cold War history," one wants unmistakable perspective, in which the Cold War "is not the backdrop but the stage itself." The shuffle between foreground and background is the problem. Just how shall one impute Cold War indexicality to any datum? How shall we summon it to tell the universe of the Cold War? Catherine Gallagher and Stephen Greenblatt have described historiographical periodization as the business of crushing starchy peculiarities into an aestheticized purée. "What is the nature of . . . the 'spirit of the times'?" they ask. "What are the consequences of treating all the traces of an era, even if its boundaries could be successfully demarcated, as a single cultural formation?"[1] The binding compulsion of such work is "the presumption that one can occupy a position from which one can discover meanings that those who left traces of themselves could not have articulated."[2] It is a threadbare kind of ingenuity: the scholar alights on a gewgaw and just there reconstructs the plausible meaning of the whole. Gallagher and Greenblatt dismiss History's ambitions to drape a place and time with the winding cloths of zeitgeist as being exalted and bland. Instead of making essences of margins and centers, they poke through archival gleanings with the hopes that interesting morsels will be jostled into view as "the ones most worth pursuing." In place of epic scale and ruling principle, they offer "luminous detail . . . whereby we attempt to isolate significant or 'interpreting detail' from the mass of traces that have survived."[3] In this chapter, I will creep away from Stephanson and Westad's quarrel about the Big Picture and follow Gallagher and Greenblatt's permissive ramble into antizeitgeist historical reconstruction.

I invite you to stop a moment and consider with me the experience of monotony and occasional frenzy that arose when reading a radar screen in the early 1950s.

Jonathan Crary argues that technologies are training devices that induce in their users historically distinct, alterable modes of attention. "The management of attention depends on the capacity of an observer to adjust to continual repatternings of the ways in which a sensory world can be consumed."[4] In the *longue durée* of consumer capitalism, the neurophysiological, cognitive, and affective work of perception demanded ceaseless refocus and reformation. "Mobility, novelty and distraction became identified as constituent elements of perceptual experience." Perception itself required "subjective adaptation to new . . . speeds and sensory overload."[5] The material cultures of literacy elicit their own historically marked forms of attention. The information medium itself contributes to the meaning of any text. Historians have broadened what counts as expressive documents to include comic strips, photographs, ephemeral and educational films, radio programs, textbooks, technical manuals, lab notebooks, blueprints and diagrams, audiovisual aids, and the readouts of scientific instruments. I propose adding wargames and defense simulations to the catalogue of literate technologies that can be used to examine particular moments of reading, decision making, labor, and embodiment. From the charnel house of cold war swabs and chits I would like to retrieve a series of man-machine system experiments that System Research Laboratory (SRL) psychologists in the air force-funded RAND Corporation performed between 1952 and 1954.

These experiments pinpoint a cold war way-station in the history of literacy. The act of reading air defense radar consoles in the early 1950s necessitated alterations in the operator's mode of disciplined attention from that which had been acquired during World War II. Because console operators scanned the skies during peacetime for a surprise attack, they developed a Cold War variant of sedentary embodiment. Because combat would take place in the air over American soil, the tempo in operations would be as fast as the fastest bombers. Because of the need for speed in alerting and interception, a stepped-up awareness of time and a need for a faster method of sorting between noise and information was necessary. The pressure for speed in information processing during combat operations was continuous between the war years and the early Cold War. That's not where the difference lies. Rather, with changes in the strategic threat, as well as advances in the material instrumentation of aircraft, radio, radar and air defense, the actual labor of radar literacy changed accordingly. Slightly altered perceptual and cognitive aptitudes arose in the early years of the Cold War. The legacy of Cold War habits of console-reading come down to us more than a half-century later in surviving forms of responses to pressure for speed in separating information from noise in computer displays. We anxiously recognize these as shortcuts in literacy even now.

But why is this specifically a *Cold War* mode of literacy? Atomic and hydrogen bombs are often invoked as synecdoches for the scores of technical inventions that facilitated the Cold War. If we add flesh and metal to the spare idea of the A-bomb by recognizing the reorganization of military operations, installations, cultures, research, and activities it engendered, we unfailingly stumble across one of the most significant mutations that occurred in America during this period, something that involved no less than an alteration of contemporary notions of what counts as real. With President Truman's embrace of the bomb, space opened up between the antinomies of empirical reality and abstract ideas. Necessitated by political, economic, and military exigencies, this intermediate space—the space of defense simulations of World War III—sprang into being in the early years of the Cold War.

Thoughtful observers had recognized that the existential fact of the bomb altered time significantly and permanently. But for the people invested in its operational readiness, the present, future, and conditional worlds ran together. The significance of blurring the actual present with a conditional present for a specifically Cold War emotional and perceptual habit of mind cannot be overemphasized. For the people involved in strategic defense in these years, being prepared to fight an atomic war meant daily experiencing future possibility. Surprise attack could happen anytime, anyplace, at any point in the continuum of now. The conditional possibility became the lived experience of the air defense radar operators who I consider in this chapter.

Here I am anchoring Cold War perceptual habits to a historically inflected form of literacy: a surprise Soviet attack on North America was detected, perceived, evaluated, that is to say, fought by deciding what was noise and what was information in an ambiguous display of symbols under conditions of maximum stress and uncertainty. Whether or not the Soviet Union could actually mobilize bomber forces to execute sneak raids into North American airspace doesn't matter for this microhistory. What counts as a Cold War habit of mind, Cold War embodiment, and Cold War perceptual and cognitive aptitudes has to do with the significance that the historical actors attached to just these acts of reading, deciding, and message-handling. Only by recognizing that everyone involved in the mise-en-scene in Santa Monica believed in a persistent Soviet threat—anytime, anyplace—can the states of mind, emotions, and body underlying these acts of reading, be understood.

I take a pragmatic view on the question of whether the epochal descriptive "Cold War" is helpful in characterizing what took place in the chambers of the System Research Laboratory in the early 1950s. In order to get at the idea that man-machine systems engendered a mode of thinking, feeling, reading, and deciding, let us accept that the actors believed that the threat was real, and that such a belief excited the urgent lived experience of the simulationists.

Air Defense in the Atomic Age

Variations of the idea that "Men are already living the strange, lonely war of tomorrow" were commonplace in atom-age journalism of the late 1940s and early 1950s. "In that war, small bands of highly skilled men, armed with complex machines, will be scattered many miles from civilization," wrote a reporter describing the first generation of the information processors of the atomic age. "Their work will be vitally important—and deadly monotonous."[6]

While reporters enjoy the social warrant to amplify any contour in the cultural landscape with the blare of novelty, very little in cold war American cognitive and perceptual habits was discontinuous with World War II-era literacy and labor. It is a challenge to sift through the practices persisting from the immediate past in order to alight on a slight alteration, something barely new arising in the world. An antizeitgeist historical reconstruction can begin by pitching three medallions into the circle of our attention and creating a social force field between these orienting markers and the standpoints of the radar crews and social scientists in the SRL experiments. The specificities of the simulations can be connected to the specificities of these outlying landmarks: the radar operator, the other-directed American consumer, and the wargamer. The three cameos reporting an event, an aperçu, and an insight, as well as the story of the SRL simulations, demonstrate the felt urgency of the reader's anxious interaction with communication technologies. Together they encompass the behaviors that arose in these experiments and suggest the texture of information processing in the Cold War.

The first medallion is a report about the everyday labor of a radar console operator:

> In a small isolated Air Force camp called "Mother Goose," an enlisted man sat staring at the poker face of a radar set, almost hypnotized by the arm of light that circled endlessly around the screen. It was dark in the windowless, double-doored building, and the air he breathed had been sterilized and air-conditioned. Round and round the arm went, hitting the same landmarks he had seen last night, the week before, the month before. Then suddenly a blip appeared, a strange speech of light. The arm hit it again and again. It was a plane, headed straight for Los Alamos. The watcher reported his blip. Mother Goose had just one minute to identify it. A man behind him checked copies of all flight plans through the area.

> This plane was not on them. The unknown's position and course were marked in colored chalk on a radar map at the front of the room for everyone to see. Another man, at a second radar set, double-checked the blip. Word was flashed to division headquarters Carrot; at the same time a message went to Continental Air Defense Command Headquarters at Colorado Springs. There, information from all over North America is immediately plotted on a three-story-high map so that the pattern of an attack can be spotted instantly.
>
> Back at division headquarters, other airmen had one more minute to identify the plane. They checked their information, checked other radar sites and spotters. No identification. At the end of the second minute a button was pushed. At a nearby airfield, pilots, sitting ready in flying suits, raced to rocket-armed jets and blasted down the runway. Within another two minutes the interceptors were in the air, getting their instructions by radio. Five minutes later they found the plane. It bore the markings of an American airliner.
>
> Flying off its wingtips, the interceptors radioed back the serial numbers, the plane was identified and the pilot was headed back on his proper course. The jets peeled off and returned to their base. The now-identified plane was wiped off the maps at headquarters, at Carrot, at Mother Goose. And the enlisted man at the radar screen went on with his dreary task.[7]

The next cameo portrays the media-saturated, lonely adult of the early cold war years. Whereas it would be too much for me to claim that Americans thought of themselves in 1950 as being like radar operators, somebody did. In a quirk of fate in which a sociology volume became a bestseller, David Riesman described a society of conformists who compulsively scanned the world for messages in response to which they instantly adjusted their attitudes and behaviors. Americans rushed to bookstores to see what else he had to say. The radar operator had become Everyman.[8]

> The other-directed person learns to respond to signals from a far wider . . . social environment to which he early becomes attentive. . . . The other-directed person must be able to receive signals from far and near; the sources are many, the changes rapid. What can be internalized, then, is not a code of behavior but the elaborate equipment needed to attend to such messages and occasionally to participate in their circulation. . . . One prime psychological lever of the other-directed person is a diffuse *anxiety*. This control equipment, instead of being like a gyroscope, is like a radar.[9]

The final passage comes from a military strategist writing about the pitfalls of believing too much in one's experience of fighting World War III in a military wargame. In the age of atomic warfare, the distinction between simulation and actual combat had collapsed. Real war was fought with electronic media.

> Very often it is not . . . remembered that the full blazing glory of reality itself is rarely experienced, even when one has extremely vivid impressions of reality. Consider, then, the additional filtering that comes between reality and its common representations during military combat. The enemy bomber, no longer even a dot in the sky, becomes a blip on a radar scope, a counter on a plotting board, or even a number on a vertical screen. The 'fog of battle' becomes a blur of numbers on a tote board or a battery of blinking lights at the computer console. *Thus much of our relatively direct experiencing of reality is flooded with abstraction.* Much of the simulation in war gaming and computer simulation is admirably suited to the production of the standard abstractions. The colored pins in the maps of the game room are hardly distinguishable from those of the command post. The computer output of the simulation can certainly emulate the clickety-clack of the teletype or even the cathode-ray tube of the radar. These results surely look real.[10]

So let us take a look at perception and cognition right here at the tedious, angst-ridden human-machine interfaces of the early 1950s. People working with avant-garde defense technologies such as radars and analogue and digital computers experienced a new sort of mediation of what counted as real objects in the world. These medallions refract the SRL story meaningfully. The first is the most literal echo of the air defense experiment, except that this is a journalist's report of a real simulation in the operational world of the Air Defense Command (ADC), not a laboratory simulation. Another has to do with a defense analyst's momentary confusion between the electronic signals of a real combat information center and a simulated one. The words come from a military strategist; they are not the speculations of an experimental psychologist or philosopher. The third angle of refraction on the SRL experiments is a portrait of Americans receiving the expert advice broadcast by columnists, dramatists, and advertisers about how to be socially adjusted, sexually fulfilled, happy adults and successful parents as though they were friendly, hostile, or unknown stimulus inputs. Here are three pinpoints for noticing how people experienced an alteration in their cognitive, perceptual, and affective notions of what counts as real objects and real experiences. Here we have the boredom and terror of the radar operator routinely exercised by readiness tests, the blurring of simulated and real blips of enemy movement within the defense electronic media environment, and the counterpart to the professional wargamer, the jittery American who experiences daily life through the pressured relay of mass communication technologies. These medallions suggest a historically distinct pattern. If the air defense simulations tell us about how the cold war inflected dimensions of reading, decision making, labor, and embodiment in these years, they join the specificities of this constellation as well.

In November 1945 the commander in chief of the US Army Air Force, General Henry Arnold, declared that from now, the shift from peace to war would have to be instantaneous. "Although we were woefully unprepared as a nation" in the last war, he wrote, "we still had the time . . . to build a military force. . . . That precious time . . . will not be given us again." V-2 rockets and the atom bomb had made it clear that the next war would be radically different.

In his report, Arnold articulated the new assumptions of atom-age combat:

- Combat operations would not take place on battlefields but in the airspace over cities: "With present equipment, an enemy Air Power can, without warning, pass over all formerly visualized barriers or 'lines of defense' and can deliver devastating blows at our population centers and our industrial, economic or governmental heart even before surface forces can be deployed."
- A rocket war would be fought without an army or navy: "In any future war the Air Force . . . will undoubtedly be the first to engage the enemy. . . . It is entirely possible that the progressive development of the air arm, especially with the concurrent development of the atomic explosive, guided missiles and other modern devices, will reduce the requirement for or employment of mass armies and navies."
- War would begin without warning: "War may descend upon us by thousands of robots passing unannounced across our shorelines—unless we act now to prevent them."
- The enemy would attack America's major cities and industrial heartland: "The first target of a potential aggressor might well be our industrial system or our major centers of population."[11]

That week, *Life* magazine compressed these ideas into a three-page graphic illustration called, "The 36-Hour War." Its panels depicted masses of atomic-tipped rockets striking American cities out of the blue. "The enemy's purpose is . . . to paralyze the US by destroying its people," read the caption beneath a cartoon showing rockets devastating Washington, DC, and New York City. "Even 30 minutes is too little time for men to control the weapons of an atomic war."[12]

By 1947, Americans seemed to be gripped by "forebodings of evil which, though horribly real, are yet intangible and elusive," observed an author in *Harper's Magazine*. "In place of the sharp prick of fear—the healthy, useful response to actual danger—there is the dull, insidious gnawing of anxiety." In an article that filled in the particulars of its title query, "What are we afraid of?" Joseph Spigelman noted that every remedy offered to ameliorate definite problems could not soothe American dread. "The truth is," he wrote, "that nothing we might do, nothing that might happen to any of the things that particularly worry us would lessen our anxiety or the reasons for it. . . . Our peril and our anxiety outlast not only whatever we might do about them, but *all the specific forms they may assume.*" Free-floating anxiety was occasioned not only by the existential fact of the bomb, but also by the fact that the bomb had stolen the time needed for "the healthy useful response to actual danger." Spigelman remarked, "Its very nearly absolute destructiveness; the almost certain inadequacy of any possible defense against it; . . . the likelihood that the atom bomb in hostile hands would deprive us of the 'cushion of time' that we have always hitherto enjoyed, . . . what better explanation could we find for the terror that pervades our lives?"[13] It was the Bomb delivered by surprise attack that excited anxious vigilance.

The beginning of war in Korea in June 1950 touched off panic. Many believed that combat operations in Asia were a gambit to tie down American forces in the East in order to smooth the path for a Soviet invasion of Western Europe. During the first six months of the war, people regarded their present moment as the prologue to World War III. 1950 and 1951 saw the production of lurid civil defense films, as well as persistent efforts from commentators to describe the threat to the continental United States. "It soon becomes clear that the Russians would try to hit military and industrial targets simultaneously," summarized one observer in November 1950. "His deadliest weapon is not the bomb alone, but the bomb coupled with the element of surprise—and surprise is a weapon that he could use but once. . . . He would 'go for broke' . . . in one tremendous effort to knock out our industrial potential [and] destroy our capacity to strike back."[14] Most people framing attack scenarios agreed with the author, Harold Martin, that one should anticipate a concentrated and simultaneous strike of massed Soviet bombers on American cities.

"How much warning would we have?" Martin asked. "And what could we do to stop them?" What was the state of America's air defense five months into the Korean War? From the end of World War II right up to September 23, 1949—the day that President Truman announced that the Soviets had broken America's atomic bomb monopoly with a successful test explosion on August 29, 1949—America's air defense equipment, crews, and vigilance were negligible. (As soon as they learned about the Soviet test, the air force immediately ordered a comprehensive air defense system to be fully operational by 1952.) Martin, writing at the height of the World War III scare in November 1950, sketched out the current state of the continent's air defense capability. The northern approaches to the American frontier, from Maine to Lake Superior and across the Pacific Northwest, had the most continuous surveillance network. But they were badly situated.

They were located on rent-free government property rather than positioned strategically, which meant that there were significant gaps even in important areas in the country. The Air Defense Command's stations used World War II-era equipment, had a few mothballed anti-aircraft guns, and were staffed by poorly trained men during daylight hours only. These radar crews were complemented by a handful of ground-based anti-aircraft squadrons located close to strategically vital cities, as well as a few fighter-aircraft squadrons and ground-controlled interception stations scattered around the country. It was, in Martin's words, "only feebly effective."

In 1950 there were many problems with America's air defense network. "Even if all the radars . . . were functioning around the clock, the control centers were manned 24 hours a day and fighter planes were constantly on strip alert, ready to scramble aloft to battle, we still might have too little warning of the approach of hostile planes."[15] The problem was the radar's line of sight. It could not see below the horizon; its range was limited to 150 miles. At the start of the Korean War, there were no radar picket ships 150 miles north in Canadian seas, no early warning radar network in Canada, Alaska, or the Arctic. Planes entering American airspace from Canada were not even required to file their flight plans with the Civil Aeronautics Administration (CAA) as other aircraft did when approaching the American frontier from the oceans. To make matters worse, even if the radar stations could reliably identify a hostile flight crossing the border in time for planes to intercept it, air defense combat could only take place in perfect weather. The fighter aircraft designated for interception could not find their targets at night or in fog. Martin threw up his hands. The bomber would always get through. "There is no defense known which can infallibly stop bombing planes, whether they come in great numbers, fiercely pressing home their assault upon a single target, or sneak in by scattered twos and threes, approaching many targets from many directions all at once. No matter how many millions we might spend on defensive measures, some planes would get through, some cities would be destroyed, some people would be killed."[16]

This was why senior officers dismissed arguments justifying a robust air defense system for North America. General Hoyt Vandenberg, the chief of staff of the air force, openly scoffed at the strategic value of air defense. "There is a dangerous delusion that radar screens and complicated electronic devices will give us an airtight defense against bombing," he remarked in February 1951. "We could place an unbroken line of radar screens, ring our cities with automatic antiaircraft guns and perfect a foolproof warning system for distinguishing between friendly and hostile aircraft approaching our boundaries around the clock. We could put an umbrella of interceptor planes over the entire country—and we could not keep out a determined enemy attack in strength."[17] Even with a continental network and the provision of all-weather interceptor aircraft, he predicted "we can be expected to destroy no more than 30 percent of the planes massing an attack in strength on the United States."[18] There was simply no point in pouring money into air defense. It was better invested in overwhelming offensive capability and in civil defense. The first was deterrence, the second, insurance. But air defense was neither one nor the other.

While the senior generals in the air force would always downplay the defense mission in favor of acquiring the strongest possible strategic force, the air force did have an air defense capability and it grew exponentially in the decade following the establishment of a separate air defense command in 1951. Its radar and interceptor squadrons multiplied and it acquired airborne early warning aircraft, offshore radar picket ships, offshore radar stations, and several lines of early warning radar in successively more northern latitudes in Canada: the Pinetree Line, the Mid-Canada Line, and The Distant Early Warning Line. By 1958, the radically new computer-based Semi-Automated Ground Environment (SAGE) system became operational.

The Man-machine System: Air Defense as Information Processing

By the end of World War II, many people in the navy and the army air force had begun to think that all complex combat operations required the establishment of an "information processing center"—the navy's word—for anti-aircraft fire control. "Fire control systems," explained David Mindell, "sought to solve the basic task of aiming a gun by breaking it into three acts: perception (looking through the sight), integration (leading the target, estimating the trajectory), and articulation (pulling the trigger)."[19] During the war, the navy and the army air force had established combat operations centers where information regarding enemy planes or ships could be transmitted and integrated in central plotting media. They were called the shipboard Combat Information Center (CIC) and the Air Defense Direction Center (ADDC). In these command-control centers, crews worked out "fire control solutions," which meant "tracking a target, predicting its future position, and calculating the 'lead' so that the guns could aim at the aircraft's future position."[20]

Where does combat take place in the information-processing center? Whereas one might regard the man who pulls the trigger as a combat soldier, the armed services had come to understand that *everyone* who operated a component of fire control—those surveying the skies and seas or estimating the trajectory of the target as well as those shooting the guns—were engaging in combat. Fighting meant more than the work of the man nearest the enemy. While psychologists and communications experts famously scrutinized the vulnerabilities, attitudes, and morale of the infantryman, by the war's end, the senior command recognized that the next war would be fought with weapon *systems*, not troops. Given the rapidity of a concentrated attack by bomber and missile, it was widely understood that the arsenal of the future battlefield included electronic pulses and relays.

The new term was *information processing*. Just what operations did crews perform in combat? "Men plotting information on a visual display board, men transmitting over a communications network, men reading off ranges and bearings from a radar presentation, men operating as trackers in a gun-control system—all are essentially processors of information," noted a prominent operations researcher.[21] Atomic-age warfare had next to nothing to do with GI Joe. Rather, crews at machine interfaces would make critical discriminations quickly and accurately as they passed data along its course through the system.

Surveillance operators in an Air Defense Direction Center (ADDC) sat before plan position indicator (PPI) cathode-ray tube consoles, whose round faces displayed radar signals in their sector. They graphed the movement of an aircraft passing through successive radar beams by daubing the surface of their scopes with a grease pencil. They regularly telephoned the position, direction, and speed of these flights to plotters in the ADDC who traced them on a large sectoral map. The chief difficulty was sorting out significant tracks from noise such as "ground clutter, storm centers, ships at sea . . . weather phenomena (inversions), and relative reflexivity of various aircraft."[22] Other crew were tasked with identifying air traffic as friendly, unknown, or hostile. The Civil Aeronautics Authority routinely provided the air force with copies of flight plans filed by all commercial and military craft crossing through each sector. Track identifiers would check this list in order to determine the status of any unknown. Planes that did not match available flight plans had to be identified by aircraft type and serial number. An officer would decide whether or not to order an interceptor to scramble nearby for visual inspection. A third set of operators, called "interceptor controllers," also sitting before PPI consoles, guided the pilot to the target by radio command. Should the unknown appear hostile, the senior officer had the authority to order the interceptor to fire. He would also put his sector on alert and notify his commanding officer, who, in turn, would alert all of the continent's ADDCs as well as the national civil defense agency. Day-to-day air defense operations are "so difficult and so tedious," reflected two analysts, "that the men are rotated every hour to keep from 'going ape.'"[23]

One might suppose that the number of unknown tracks would have been scarce to nonexistent. But in the remoter parts of the United States there were many unidentified aircraft in the skies in these years. "We are averaging 35 unknowns a day, but we scramble around 140 a day," remarked the commander in chief of the North American Air Defense Command in 1957. "This figure will go down, depending on the season of the year. . . . We have a lot of unknowns in the system when the fishing season starts up in Minnesota, because those small planes come up and appear on the radar. . . . It's the same in Maine and other places."[24]

"The continental air defense system is a good example of what's been happening" exclaimed RAND Corporation psychologists Robert Chapman and John L. Kennedy. "Just a few years ago, an aircraft-warning net that surrounded the entire country would have been little more than a wild dream—a communication network of thousands of men and machines that linked together fighter bases, radar sites, interceptors, civilian-defense groups, the Civil Aeronautics Authority, and other organizations that had to work together on split-second schedules was patently out of the question. But this . . . tremendously complicated system is in operation today."[25] For Chapman and Kennedy, the best way to regard the air defense system was not as a spectacular technical array, but as "*man*-machine systems, deliberately considering men as integral parts of the system." Air defense was ideal for thinking about human performance. Given the fact that the sector was a closed system—they assumed the crews had "all the information available about the air traffic in its area and control[ed] weapons for stopping enemy air attacks,"—whether or not an ADDC did well "depended . . . on each crew's skill in using the resources it already had."[26] The unknown factor was human decision making. "It's necessary to understand the behavior of the men who operate these systems. . . . Today's problems have become those of group coordination and integration, of team performance and team learning, problems that are . . . critical [to] . . . understanding and operating man-machine systems."[27] Remember General Vandenberg's assertion that even if one could blanket the nation with the best possible radar and interception network, air defense could intercept only 30 percent of an attacking fleet of bombers.

Was there anything to this? The memory of the kamikaze attacks against the navy in the spring of 1945 was still appallingly fresh. Okinawa was the last of the island chains in the Pacific from which the Allied forces planned to stage the invasion of the Japanese mainland. While the Japanese Air Force had used kamikaze tactics in the Battle of Leyte Gulf, the campaign for Okinawa was the first time that hundreds of suicide bombers strafed the navy. At the end of the 82-day struggle, 1,465 kamikaze flights had smashed into American ships.

The radar picket ships circling the fleet's perimeter became the special focus for fighter assault. Their mission was to alert the Combat Air Patrols (CAPs) policing the airspace above the main battle group. Kamikaze were massed in such strength that at least half of them breached the CAP's defensive ring. Once through, they slammed into the nearest targets, which were the picket ships. Over time, the Japanese shifted their objective from pressing through CAP lines in order to try to reach the center of the fleet to aiming directly for the radar ships. By the last month, the picket ships were "the prime kamikaze targets."[28]

The recent memory of an overwhelming assault against radar units would be reason enough to think American air defenses could not intercept more than a fraction of a concentrated Soviet formation. But more importantly for studies of man-machine systems, the navy determined that "improper use of support gunboats, failure to establish land-based radar at the earliest possible time, the assignment of ships ill-equipped for picket duty, and, as time went on, crew fatigue" were significant factors contributing to the dreadful losses from kamikaze assault.[29]

In 1950, as America was fighting a communist army, coupling unstoppable masses of suicidal fighters with atomic weapons was an intolerable thought. Everyone in the air defense business was intensely motivated to try to teach radar operators to do their job *perfectly*: accurately, quickly, unhesitatingly, tirelessly. It was that last element in the navy's analysis—crew fatigue—that Chapman and Kennedy thought they could do something about.

In the summer of 1950, just weeks into the Korean War, psychologists at the air force sponsored nonprofit RAND Corporation convened a conference on human factors in man-machine systems. Among the attendees was John L. Kennedy, who had been running a series of experiments for the navy concerned with improving the design of radar equipment as well as crew message-handling procedures.[30] At the close of the meeting, he was enthusiastically invited to study these problems at RAND. In turn, Kennedy recruited two colleagues who were also working on team training and performance. These men, Robert Chapman and William Biel, along with Kennedy and a RAND logistician, Allen Newell, formed the nucleus of what they would call the Systems Research Laboratory (SRL).

The Systems Research Laboratory

Once assembled at RAND in early 1951, Chapman, Kennedy, Biel, and Newell built a replica of the Tacoma, Washington, ADDC as well as several early warning (EW) stations in a large back room of a Santa Monica billiard hall. All of the hardware the crew required for information processing—"information-gathering equipment (radar sets), the communications net (radios and telephones), information storage aids (central displays and written records), and its response equipment (interceptor aircraft and their weapons)"—were on hand.[31] From 1952 to 1954, SRL psychologists conducted four large experiments, employed 140 men as experimental subjects, and spent a million dollars. They simulated the first eight hours of World War III.

Chapman and his SRL colleagues planned to document information processing behavior, try out methods for man-machine system experimentation, and capture "organizational learning" as it occurred. Instead of casting crew tasks in terms of the air defense mission, they pinned their hopes on a model of information processing. This was not the same thing as thinking but a description of *doing*. In their earliest paper, they described the simulation as an Information Processing Center (IPC) within which information was "gather[ed], integrat[ed] and disseminat[ed]" in a continuous flow of inputs and outputs.[32] In order to measure the rate and accuracy of the crew's data handling, they broke down the human operator tasks: "*Translation*: information is transferred from graphic to verbal form . . .; *Transmission*: information is simply passed on . . .; *Dissemination*: items are selected . . . and sent to several of many possible addresses; *Verification*: information is . . . checked against another source."[33] They would try to measure each of these operations for all of the crew members.

The sticking point of air defense was how much traffic the radar operators could handle without error. What was the threshold beyond which they became overwhelmed? What conditions would stimulate crews to perform better? The SRL team wondered, "Could men *learn* to improve system performance? 'What' did they learn? and 'Why' did they learn?"[34] Organizational theorists hypothesized about group behavior, but the men at RAND wanted to evoke desired behavior in controlled circumstances. Would the group accept the simulacrum well enough to perform as they would in real life? Chapman and Kennedy were painfully aware of the difficulty of translating their theories into rigorous experimental form.

The problem broke down into several parts: could one reliably control social, cultural, technical, and environmental conditions, introduce varying information inputs, and watch the organization react and adapt? In other words, could one confidently control the stimulus well enough so that important variables in information processing could truly be isolated? Second, assuming the validity of the inputs, could one get the experimental subjects to behave coherently as a group in response to them? How could one be sure that alterations in group behavior were a direct response to one's chosen stimulus? Could real learning be induced? And if so, could the factors that triggered a crew's successful adaptation be identified and reproduced?[35]

The initial challenge was to manage the subjects' experience of the simulation so that they would throw themselves wholeheartedly into the experiment. From a motley assembly, the SRL psychologists had to engender a real organization whose members were committed to the tasks they would perform in the lab. They speculated that people were willing to learn only when they thoroughly understood how their task contributed to the system's objective. The manager of a complex man-machine system would have to "sell the team's purpose to them."[36] They proposed to excite crew morale by identifying their activity with the "stated system purpose" as much as possible.[37] One way they did this was by conducting a formal review at the close of each day's session. Immediate feedback reinforced the idea that behavior was evaluated en masse. Everyone felt crushed when they were presented with a detailed report of their errors.

So far, information processing seems removed from the terrifying information overload of the Okinawan kamikaze attacks. Let us recall the actual scene for information processing—an air defense direction center. The SRL psychologists attempted to "tap intense motivation" by stressing the importance of "defending our country from enemy bombs . . . with as much dramatic impact as we could muster."[38] It worked. They succeeded in "getting organizational behavior" to appear in the laboratory.

> Each of the four crews gradually came to behave as if it were in a real-life situation. . . . During enemy attacks, the noise level in the station rose, men came to their feet, and the excitement was obvious. Crew members reported restless nights and bad dreams—attackers boring in without an interceptor available. On one occasion, an officer slipped while stepping off a dais and broke his leg. We were not aware of this event for some ten minutes because there was no perturbation in the crew's activity during the attack in progress. He was back the next day, cast and all, because, as he said, they couldn't get along without him.[39]

Let's consider this description. Not only did the crews accept the simulacrum and adopt the organization's purpose as their own, but "the excitement was obvious." What was happening here? The SRL team pushed to near-breaking point the intensity of the crew's motivation to defend the United States. The historian of man-machine systems Henry Parsons called this "a pioneering attempt to structure 'stress' in motivational terms rather than as something which degrades performance or physiological functioning."[40] Failing to intercept Soviet bombers forced the group to look for ways to ease the sharp margin of error. Chapman and his colleagues believed that "group learning must include . . . discomfort and failure that act as pressures to learn."[41] The experiment's crowded airspace induced two kinds of pain: "failure stress" and "discomfort stress": "The first of these arises from the disparity between aspiration and performance; the second from the difference between the effort demanded by the task and that which can be comfortably afforded."[42]

Once these stressors were introduced into the simulation, the crews became petulant: "They questioned the organization's goal ('the best defense is a good offense'), the adequacy of their equipment ('these grease pencils are no damn good'), the competence of their own members ('Lt. Blank doesn't know what he's doing'), and registered many signs of bad morale."[43] But scowls seemed always to be followed by faster times. "The discomfort stress forces discriminations and short cuts in response; the failure stress guides the gradual acquisition of short cuts that do not degrade effectiveness."[44]

Organizational effectiveness depends on group learning, group learning depends on stress, stress forces the organization to adapt. This chain of reasoning had direct consequences for the SRL's training program for the North American Air Defense Command (NORAD) and Strategic Air Command (SAC) later in the decade. Only when the man-machine system was forced to operate at its limit could human factors specialists understand the best way to train crews to exert supreme effort. The SRL team concluded, "The adaptive capabilities of the operators is implicit in the design of most of these systems, but unfortunately developing these capabilities so that the system will perform . . . in an emergency requires experience under critical stresses equivalent to those of an emergency. These experiments have shown that system training, which can impose such stresses, . . . is one way of making the full potential of a system available before an emergency occurs."[45] In short, air defense might not work when needed unless its crews practiced the transition to a war emergency in perpetual rehearsal.

Learning how to read the air defense messages meant learning how to ignore most data streams. It entailed a split cognition: operators had to learn what to ignore, what merited close attention, and how to refocus their attention. The simulation scenario was a surprise attack of Soviet bombers against a background of peacetime commercial air traffic. The signal loads varied in kind and in tempo. The information processing tasks were sorting through the increasing pace of radar traffic, identifying friendly flights, identifying unknowns both from their direction and mass, isolating hostiles, and accurately guiding pilots to intercept them.[46]

The air defense "task environment" was driven by two variables: "one determined the kind of unknown and hostile aircraft the crew had to intercept, the other determined the characteristics of the friendly traffic from which these critical flights had to be distinguished."[47] Over the course of the experiment, the number and types of hostile aircraft grew: "massed raids of 5 to 20 bombers each; massed attacks with diversionary aircraft, 10 to 25 in number; low altitude raids averaging 2 aircraft each; and submarine-launched missiles. The two types of massed raids totaled 30 in the first set of sessions, 48 in the second, 70 in the third, and 90 in the last." The enemy attacked in different patterns: "sneaks, split sneaks, massed attacks, massed attacks with diversions, low altitude attacks, submarine-launched attacks, and 'friendlies' without flight plan." There was also a "distraction" attack, i.e., "the simultaneous appearance . . . of a friendly flight without a flight plan in the vicinity of an attack."[48]

In the beginning, the crews attempted to identify everything visible on their scopes, but they eventually drifted into a settled pattern of information processing. The psychologists measured their expenditure of effort by the number of items the crew handled. Unpredictably, these remained the same from the opening session to the last hour of the last day. By the end of the experiment, the rate of incoming data had tripled but "the crew used just about the same amount of information it did during the first hour."[49] The men had adjusted their data handling procedures by filtering the information according to the following decision analysis:

> A. Is it an established track? If yes, then report it. If no, then go to (b).
> B: Is it potentially critical? If no, then forget it. If yes, then go to (c).
> C: Are we already carrying our limit? If no, then report it. If yes, then go to (d).
> D: Can we drop something less important? If no, then delay action. If yes, then go to (e).
> E: Drop old track and report new.[50]

Faster, faster, faster, the crews pared information processing to the bone. "Load increases finally caused a pruning of almost all behavior not critical to defending the area. . . . The crews also . . . tended to carry tracks for shorter and shorter times . . . with fewer and fewer reports."[51]

Learning to Read the Information Stream

Beginning on February 4, 1952, for four hours every Tuesday, Thursday, and Saturday until June 8, twenty-eight college students became an ADDC crew in "Casey," the SRL's first experiment. While the track load included enemy sneak attacks, the crews did not face an increased tempo or density of targets. The SRL team was astonished by the students' proficiency. They intercepted all of the twenty-one enemy raids, and sixty-seven of seventy unknown flights.[52] The psychologists had pitched the task too low when they replicated the background peacetime air traffic over Tacoma, Washington. They marveled, "The organization learned its way right out of the experiment. Within a couple of days the college students were maintaining highly effective defense of their area while playing word games and doing homework on the side."[53]

Before releasing the students from the project, they added two additional sessions with a doubled task load. Whereas in Casey, between four and ten tracks penetrated the sector from dangerous directions, in the first of the additional sessions, "99 tracks penetrated from dangerous directions, 12 were unknown and 3 of these sneak raids." This meant there were between twenty to eighty planes in the air. The students intercepted all of the sneak attacks. In the second session, the task load was increased yet again. Whereas the number of tracks the crew followed at any one time remained the same from the first extra session—twenty to eighty—to the second—twenty to ninety—this time 159 aircraft penetrated the sector. The students performed fairly well for most of the seven-hour period, but in the last ninety minutes, there was a "progressive deterioration of the organization": an enemy bomber attacked Seattle, another "hostile" was misidentified as friendly, and six nonhostile unknowns were either misidentified or overlooked.[54] Right here, then, was the condition for breakdown. They did, finally, push the crew too hard.

The extra sessions surprised the air force. The SRL team trooped over to Ent Air Force Base to brief the senior officers of the Air Defense Command (ADC) on the results of their study. The very fact that the crew collapsed showed that one could pinpoint the range and circumstances of information overload. The commander was impressed. A bunch of college kids had stood up to exceptionally heavy track loads. Just imagine how much better real air force personnel would do in the simulation! ADC offered them funds to conduct a follow-on experiment and this time use its officers and enlisted men as subjects.

In the next experiment, called "Cowboy," the psychologists redesigned the way in which the stimulus variables were introduced into the task environment. "We realized that task difficulty was not the *number* of aircraft in the area but . . . the number of aircraft and the crew's load carrying capacity *of the moment*: the traffic load that was difficult to handle today might prove quite easy a week from now." They decided to augment the task load by stages in order to give the crews time to accommodate to each change. "We had to estimate how fast the crew would learn in order to increase task difficulty fast enough to continue to challenge it but not so fast that the task would be too difficult."[55] The pace of the experiment itself was also compressed. Whereas Casey ran for four months and consisted of fifty-four four-hour sessions, Cowboy began and ended in January 1953. It comprised six practice and sixteen experimental sessions at night. These were eight hours long, a typical air defense shift. Much to the air force's satisfaction, the crew intercepted 206 of 238 Soviet bombers in massed formation.[56] What seemed most significant was the fact that the crew's progress in accommodating the heavier loads showed strict conformity to the stepped-up increase of radar inputs. What had been a heavy load earlier in the experiment could be easily managed later on.[57]

After the Cowboy series were complete, the SRL team delivered their raw data to a Joint ADC-RAND air defense study group that met from March to May 1953. In a summary letter to the secretary of the air force, ADC Chief of Staff Major Jarred Crabb endorsed SRL's philosophy of stress-based training. He recommended that the Cowboy protocol be translated into a training exercise. Such an "Air Defense System Training Program," he wrote, "offers the most outstanding improvement of all items being considered" in the RAND study.[58] SRL hastily hired eight more psychologists to help convert their experimental design into a program for crew indoctrination. The additional labor was dedicated to improving the realism of the stimulus inputs and refining the lab's data collection system. These were extraordinarily complex affairs. Chapman remarked, "Getting one of these experiments started . . . looks as involved as the takeoff of a superbomber. . . . The extensive pre-run check lists, ringing of bells and flashing of lights, and down-to-the-second timing are all part of getting 9 input mechanisms, 7 timing devices, 16 clocks, 22 recorders, and 65 people off and running at the same time. No mean trick."[59]

"Cobra," which took place in February 1954, was nearly identical to Cowboy. It employed forty ADC officers and airmen and was made up of twenty-two eight-hour sessions. Its crew performed as well as Cowboy's. This was followed by one last, short experiment, "Cogwheel," in June 1954, which consisted of only fourteen four-hour sessions. By now, the rudiments of the system training program had been well established. If Cobra had been a check on Cowboy, Cogwheel was a confirmation of the notion that a training system comprised of stepped-up task loads that pushed crews to breaking point was an effective way to drill the men patrolling America's airspace.

In August 1953 ADC gave RAND a contract to develop a prototype indoctrination system at the ADDC in Boron, California. SRL was given a year to build and install it. A year later, in August 1954, the SRL team launched their new System Training Program (STP).[60] In the meantime, they had undertaken the Cobra and Cogwheel laboratory simulations in Santa Monica and felt confident in the application of their experimental technique to professional training. The field test was not a success. There was nothing to show that crew performances had been "significantly affected."[61] Nevertheless, the air force had pledged itself to the man-machine system training philosophy. In October 1954 it awarded RAND a contract to install the STP in all 150 ADDCs in the United States. In March 1955 the group moved out of the Santa Monica Billiard Hall into several floors of a large rented building. By September 1955 SRL had grown to three hundred people; by December, it employed four hundred and fifty. By 1956 there were more than a thousand. Not only were teams of psychologists needed to train ADDC crews around the country, engineers and programmers were now working in the System Development Division in Lexington, Massachusetts, on a breakthrough technology, the SAGE system, which would become the nation's first computerized air defense network. SRL had grown bigger than the rest of RAND's divisions put together. In October 1956 the air force and the RAND Board of Trustees decided to split it off and make it an independent nonprofit corporation, which was henceforth called The System Development Corporation (SDC).[62]

During the second half of the 1950s, SDC developed training systems for the nation's air defense and SAGE network. It became the sole source contractor for indoctrination as well as readiness exercises for the North American Air Defense Command (NORAD) in the United States and Canada. Between July 1957 and July 1960, SDC delivered nine hundred separate STP "exercise packages" to its sponsors.[63] By the end of the decade, it had grown into the largest employer of social scientists in the United States other than the government.

The senior officer corps in the armed services were enamored with its system training philosophy. In March 1958 the commander of the Strategic Air Command (SAC), General Curtis LeMay, authorized development of a worldwide SAC Command-Control System (SACCS). He gave SDC the contract to train his staff in the new system.[64] In 1960 the air force awarded SDC a contract to design the system for the new NORAD Combat Operation Center (COC), which would act as the nation's supreme ADDC. The COC received radar inputs from all of the ADDCs in North America including the SAGE system, SACCS (which became operational in 1961), and the Canadian radar networks—the Pinetree Line, the mid-Canada line, the Distant Early Warning Line, and the Ballistic Missile Early Warning System. NORAD gave a second contract to SDC in 1960 to develop a surveillance system to track and identify space objects (such as satellites, rockets, and meteors) and integrate it into the COC system.[65]

In 1960 the joint chiefs of staff awarded a contract to SDC to develop the Defense National Communications Control Center. Later that same year, the Defense Atomic Support Agency engaged SDC to contribute to a command-control system assessing damage and fallout from a nuclear war. Then, in April 1961, the Naval Weapons Laboratory awarded it a contract to help develop a tracking system for the Naval Space Surveillance System.[66]

Cognitive Paralysis in the SRL

The SRL psychologists came up with reasonable ideas: they instrumented the simulation environment, recorded subject behavior during the experiment, and conducted a daily free-for-all After Action Review. Mistakes and successful innovations were documented, analyzed, and presented to the crews for discussion. Establishing morale by identifying errors and praising improvements, compelling procedural flexibility by introducing heavy task stressors—all of these became hallmarks of the SDC philosophy and, indeed, of the American armed forces' approach to training.

While the air force's embrace of the SRL's experiments seems hurried and overextended, it appeared to most observers as though the research program was a triumph. Yet the information stream of the Cold War man-machine system was too much of a good thing. Suddenly it was possible to gather too much data. Just as the operators of the new systems had to learn how to read its inputs accurately, they also had to learn how to ignore them. Filtering information required persistent efforts to pay close attention. The same energies inevitably gave rise to their own peculiar pathology, *cognitive paralysis.*

The SRL scientists were not as nimble as their subjects. The task load was too difficult: they could not distinguish between what was important and what was not. They had begun with high hopes, writing in 1952 that the Takoma air defense station "processes only one commodity, information; a good deal of it will flow in verbal form. The Systems Research Laboratory is well set up to record this verbal behavior, both that which goes into the communication net and that which does not."[67] When they designed the physical space of the SRL, they built a balcony in the upper reaches of the back of the room where the experimenters could listen to and observe everything. They placed microphones at every console station and by each display map so that they could overhear every conversation. "Give a man a phone and he'll talk," they wrote in 1959. "This characterizes a good deal of an air-defense crew's behavior—it's verbal. Information about the air traffic is passed from man to man by telephone and in face-to-face conversations."[68] They bugged the phones and radio headsets of every crew member's station. In addition to capturing audible speech, in the first experiment, they coded crew behavior with IBM punch cards every thirty seconds, photographed the display maps every twenty minutes, recorded the crews' chitchat before and after the experiment, and drew sociometric diagrams showing spatial distances among crew members each day. They audiotaped after-action reviews. They collected surveillance logs and position reports. They compiled individual and group performance records, including "critical track" histories.[69] Before the experiment, they administered psychological tests to their subjects; after it had concluded they revisited the men several months later for additional tests and interviews.[70]

One of the chief aims of the experiments was to locate the threshold for information processing collapse. The SRL psychologists were keen to find the crew's breaking point, but they weren't sensitive to their own research as labor. They could not see how their own stepped-up task loads mirrored that of their subjects. They faltered under too many tracks, too many points to follow. For the second experiment, to their data collection effort they added "logs of embedding organizations [such as early warning stations, the civil aviation authority]; semi-structured observations of crew activities, including some by experimental personnel with backgrounds in group dynamics and sociological experimentation."[71]

The third experiment was the make-or-break test of the philosophy of stress-induced adaptation. SRL hired more psychologists to collect even more types of data. "The staff watched . . . the crew for indications of involvement, reactions to the experimental conditions, and instances of problem solving. . . . Expressions of attitudes . . . were noted by coding 'attitude' cards." After the experiment, the crew were bombarded with sociometric, attitude, and procedural questionnaires. They were also coaxed into participating in "psychodrama sessions."[72]

Anxious that they might miss something, the SRL researchers succumbed to the temptation to achieve what their colleagues in RAND's logistics simulation laboratory called "total event recording."[73] "Instead of presenting just the bare facts," they wrote in 1959, "we should like to describe the air defense experiments as a *search* for understanding organizational behavior."[74] They sketched out a theory of organizational behavior as a dynamic of the social organism as a whole rather than by "examining variables separately and postponing their integration."[75] While this might have been an inspiring idea, in practical terms it resulted in indiscriminate hoarding. They coded one hundred thousand IBM punch cards for each of the four experiments, and accumulated sixty file drawers of notes and twelve thousand hours of voice recordings.[76] "In sheer volume," Chapman wrote soon after the last experiment had ended, "the data was overwhelming. We hadn't gone far before the question of how to code the data gave us as much concern as how to collect it."[77] Several years later, the group reflected, "For observers to penetrate with the naked eye the devious machinations of a growing organization, to translate behavior into meaningful codes, and to maintain a standard set over the entire experiment is a data collection problem that can only be described as horrid."[78]

In the end, the SRL psychologists were dumbstruck by masses of records. One could engineer a system to collect heaps of data, but no one could figure out what to do with it. They managed to analyze only a fraction of their harvest. But in their memoranda and reports, they repeatedly entertained hopes that as soon as they arrived at a satisfactory theory of organizational behavior, they would return at once to this collection, promising that the indigestible material stuffed in their file cabinets "should prove of more general value once we know the appropriate questions to ask of it."[79] As it happened, they stopped asking. The System Research Laboratory mushroomed into the System Development Corporation. They were a success. It no longer mattered what the data meant. They incinerated all of their records and stopped talking about the disproportion between titanic machine capacity and modest human powers.[80]

Trance and Boredom

Man-machine interaction was a reading and labor experience rather than an engineering problem to be solved. Whereas the simulation subjects figured out shortcuts as technical solutions to the emergency of overwhelming attack, the SRL scientists drowned in the horrors of reading in the man-machine world. Given the torrent of data collection, one can only imagine the thoughts and feelings of the moment-by-moment experience of reading the consoles, the operators' focused speedy attention, the scientists' finicky procedural observations, their enthusiasm when designing the experiment, their creeping fatigue when executing the experiment, their barely suppressed revulsion when sifting through impenetrable heaps of records. Their eventual disgust. Closing the file.

This was not only a matter of thinking—concentrated attention leads to bodily self-forgetting. Staring up at the sector map at the front of the room, a crew member stepped off the platform on which his console was mounted and broke his leg. Crary described absorptive "auto-hypnosis" as "an intense refocusing and narrowing of attention, accompanied by . . . a relative suspension of peripheral awareness."[81] Surely this describes the airman's fall. For Crary, attention and distraction are the twin effects of just this kind of engrossment with spectacular display. Paying attention is a double movement: one fixes one's mind on an isolated object while suppressing other immediate stimuli. Eventually thought wanders into fantasy or relaxes into blankness, and one is propelled into motion: fidgeting, staring, humming, doodling. Concentration has physiological limits. Daydreaming is as much a consequence of concentrated attention as is alertness; they are the alternating effects of the same expenditure of psychic energy.

Overstimulated trance, information overload, and boredom are all pathologies of the attention regime. The Casey crew's loss of control that resulted in the simulated obliteration of Seattle, the airman's fractured leg, the hopeless cognitive paralysis the SRL psychologists felt when beholding a row of file cabinets brimming with records—all of these depict moments of engulfment in which it was no longer possible to make distinctions within the information stream. "In any number of ways, attention inevitably reaches a threshold at which it breaks down," Crary observes.[82] Engagement with man-machine systems not only provoked discomfort, excitement, concentration, and trance states in its operators; it was labor. For people who were not integral nodes in the air defense network, for those before whose eyes a great deal of irrelevance and very little of importance passed, for those who were not in a position to attain mastery of the information stream, information processing could induce unspeakable boredom. "A minute asleep could mean a city destroyed," wrote a visitor to an ADDC in 1955. "The Air Force needs men of high intelligence, training and maturity to do these jobs, yet . . . they are jobs of dreary monotony."[83]

The danger of inattention "involves possibilities of human error on a far more disastrous scale than at Pearl Harbor," noted the physicist Ralph Lapp and columnist Stewart Alsop in 1953. "Someone—a bored corporal, perhaps, who has been straining his eyes at nothing for months—must see the blip, no bigger than the wart on a man's nose on a television screen. He must recognize the blip for what it is."[84] Perhaps one reason why the metaphor of the modern American as other-directed radar operator struck home was that people instinctively understood the oppressive languor of such a job. Just how could one teach someone "to sit in a dark room hour after hour, day after day, week after week, staring at a radar screen, waiting for that one blip that means a decision to be made"?[85] How can one train a man *not* to grow careless, *not* to make mistakes? "It simply is hard as hell to stay awake," another observer wrote wonderingly. "Instead of scanning an ever-changing countryside or shoreline, the man at a radar site must focus his eyes on one small, seldom-changing radar screen, on which nothing moves but the hypnotically circling line."[86]

"Monotony is something about which nothing can be done," observed a journalist visiting the crew living aboard a radar station 110 miles off Cape Cod.[87] To every man stupefied with tedium by his work, the texture of daily life must have felt timeless. But the fixation of attention in all of its variations—vigilance, trance, cognitive paralysis, automatic behavior and boredom—has a deeply historical character. The tempo of the information stream the Casey, Cowboy, Cobra, and Cogwheel crews confronted between 1952 to 1954 accelerated over the course of the decade as jets and then missiles entered the US arsenal. The man-machine interface migrated in the late 1950s to civilian domains of work such as the SABRE airline reservation system and space exploration. As the manufacturers of digital computers in the 1950s and 1960s invented ever-new functions and efficiencies for their device in their search for new markets, information processing mutated as it absorbed an endless proliferation of additions to its cognitive and affective repertoire. If one really wanted to pursue the mosaic historical reconstruction of man-machine literacy from the Cold War to the present, one would find other way-stations—say the airline consoles—and other medallions—say the speculation about digital computers as "information appliances" of the early 1960s—in order to follow the chain of cognitive and affective training step by step. At each mise-en-scène, one would have to consider how the experience of reading felt: as the realization of embodiment, as labor, as social communication, as team-work, as a relay in a complex system network. And at each point, one would have to examine how the interaction reflected the precise social function of just that niche, whether that is programmed education, medical record keeping, currency transactions, traffic engineering, and so on.

The formulation of a standing repertoire of literacy in instrument reading should be folded into the uncontroversial literatures of machine representation in the histories of communication and transportation technologies, engineering, experimental science, medicine, warfare, and industrial labor, especially machine tending and skilled shop work. There isn't very much in the SRL simulation experiments that could be said to be an irruption of something that hadn't appeared on the scene before. But what *was* new was the way in which the generalized expectation of a surprise attack of Soviet bombers penetrating North American airspace governed the organization, engineering, and practical decisions underlying the instrumentation and human factors of the air defense man-machine system. Vigilance against surprise attack resulted in the repertoire of behaviors inflected with the preoccupations of the Cold War. It changed habits of time: the present, future, and conditional worlds blurred and dissolved. It demanded the evolution of perceptual and cognitive skills. And it elicited new kinds of boredom, distraction, trance states, and monumental error.

Notes

1. Gallagher and Greenblatt, *Practicing New Historicism* (Chicago, 2000), pp. 7, 8.
2. Ibid., p. 8.
3. Gallagher and Greenblatt, *Practicing New Historicism*, p. 15.
4. Crary, *Suspensions of Perception: Attention, Spectacle, and Modern Culture* (Cambridge, MA, 1999), p. 33.
5. Ibid., p. 30.
6. Don Murray, "They Guard the Ramparts," *The Saturday Evening Post*, June 11, 1955, p. 28.
7. Murray, "They Guard the Ramparts," p. 28.
8. Todd Gitlin, "Introduction" in David Riesman, Nathan Glazer, Ruel Denney, Todd Gitlin, *The Lonely Crowd* (New Haven, 2001), p. xii.
9. Riesman, Glazer, Denney, Gitlin, *The Lonely Crowd*, p. 25.
10. Clayton Thomas, "Military Gaming" in Russell Ackoff (ed.), *Progress in Operations Research Vol. I* (London, 1961), p. 460.
11. General Henry Arnold, "Text of Final Section of Arnold's Report Blueprinting Needs for Maintaining Air Power," *The New York Times*, 11/122 (1945), p. 14.
12. "The 36 Hour War," *Life*, 11/19 (1945), pp. 27–34.
13. Spigelman, "What Are We Afraid Of?" *Harper's Magazine*, 195/1167 (August 1947), p. 124.
14. Martin, "Could We Beat Back an Air Attack on the U.S.?," *The Saturday Evening Post*, 11/4 (1950), p. 146.
15. Ibid., p. 148.
16. Ibid., p. 150.
17. General Hoyt S. Vandenberg, Stanley Frank, "The Truth about Our Air Power," *The Saturday Evening Post*, February 17, 1951, p. 101. But also see Dr. Ralph E. Lapp, Stewart Alsop, "We Can Smash the Red A-Bombers," *The Saturday Evening Post*, March 21, 1953.
18. Vandenberg, Frank, "The Truth about Our Air Power," p. 20.
19. Mindell, *Between Human and Machine: Feedback, Control, and Computing before Cybernetics* (Baltimore, 2002), p. 22.
20. Ibid., p. 9.
21. Gilbert Krulee, "Information Theory and Man-machine Systems," *Journal of Operations Research Society*, 2(3), August 1954, p. 320.
22. Anders Sweetland and William W. Haythorn, "An Analysis of the Decision-making Functions of a Simulated Air Defense Direction Center," *Behavioral Science*, 6(2), April 1961, p. 105.
23. Sweetland and Haythorn, "An Analysis of the Decision-making Functions of a Simulated Air Defense Direction Center," p. 105.
24. "Interview with General Earle Partridge, Commander in Chief, North American Air Defense Command," *U. S. News & World Report*, 43, 9/6 (1957), p. 85.
25. Chapman and Kennedy, *The Background and Implications of the Systems Research Laboratory Studies*, P-740, The RAND Corporation, Santa Monica, California, 9/2, 1955, p. 2.
26. Ibid., p. 3.
27. Ibid., pp. 1, 2.
28. Promotional text for Robin Rielly, *Kamikazes, Corsairs, & Picket Ships: Okinawa, 1945* (Havertown, PA, 2008).
29. Ibid.

30. See Parsons, *Man-machine System Experiments* (Baltimore, 1972), pp. 105, 106, 112, 128, 162.
31. Robert L. Chapman, John L. Kennedy, A. Newell, and William C. Biel, "The Systems Research Laboratory's Air Defense Experiments," *Management Science*, 5/3 (1959), p. 254.
32. R. L. Chapman, W. Biel, J. Kennedy, A. Newell, *The Systems Research Laboratory and its Program*, RM-890, The RAND Corporation, Santa Monica,1/7, 1952, p. 3.
33. Ibid., p. 21.
34. Robert L. Chapman, *Simulation in RAND's System Research Laboratory*, P-1074, 4/30 (Santa Monica: The RAND Corporation, 1957), p. 1.
35. Chapman and Kennedy, *The Background*, p. 7.
36. Chapman, Biel, Kennedy, Newell, *The Systems Research Laboratory and its Program*, p. 18.
37. Ibid., pp. 11–12.
38. Chapman, Kennedy, Newell, Biel, "The Systems Research Laboratory's Air Defense Experiments," p. 259.
39. Ibid., pp. 263–264.
40. Parsons, *Man-machine System Experiments*, p. 184.
41. Chapman and Kennedy, *The Background*, p. 10.
42. Chapman, Kennedy, Newell, Biel, "The Systems Research Laboratory's Air Defense Experiments," p. 266.
43. Ibid., p. 264.
44. Ibid., p. 266.
45. Chapman and Kennedy, *The Background*, p. 14.
46. Parsons, *Man-machine System Experiments*, p. 175.
47. Allan Newell, 1955, *Description of the Air-Defense Experiments II. The Task Environment*, P-659, October, p. 2.
48. Parsons, *Man-machine System Experiments*, p. 175.
49. Chapman and Kennedy, *The Background*, p. 8.
50. Sweetland and Haythorn, "An Analysis of the Decision-making Functions of a Simulated Air Defense Direction Center," p. 115.
51. Ibid., p. 109.
52. Parsons, *Man-machine System Experiments*, p. 174.
53. Chapman, Kennedy, Newell, Biel, "The Systems Research Laboratory's Air Defense Experiments," p. 260.
54. Parsons, *Man-machine System Experiments*, p. 174.
55. Chapman, Kennedy, Newell, Biel, "The Systems Research Laboratory's Air Defense Experiments," p. 260.
56. Parsons, *Man-machine System Experiments*, p. 177.
57. "Group learning is most clearly indicated by the marked improvement with which the crew deals with the same penetrating load in successive sets: 19 percentage points improvement for load 3 between the second and third sets, and 36 points difference for load 4 between the third and fourth sets." Staff, Systems Research Laboratory, 1953, revised 1954, *Crew Learning in an Experimental Air Defense Organization*, Report RM-1024-1, RAND Corporation, cited in Parsons, *Man-machine System Experiments*, p. 177 with no page citation.
58. Claude Baum, *The System Builders: The Story of SDC* (Santa Monica, 1981), p. 17.
59. Robert L. Chapman, *Description of the Air-defense Experiments III. Data Collection and Processing*, P-658 (Santa Monica, 1955), p. 4.
60. Baum, *The System Builders*, pp. 17–19.
61. See Parsons, *Man-machine System Experiments*, pp. 181–182. He offers no details to support this observation.
62. Baum, *The System Builders*, p. 27.
63. Ibid., p. 46.
64. Ibid., pp. 46–47, 54–57.
65. Ibid., pp. 71–72.

66. Ibid., pp. 73–75.
67. Chapman, Biel, Kennedy, Newell, *The Systems Research Laboratory and Its Program*, p. 22.
68. Chapman, Kennedy, Newell, Biel, "The Systems Research Laboratory's Air Defense Experiments," p. 262.
69. Parsons, *Man-machine System Experiments*, pp. 168–169.
70. Ibid., p. 170.
71. Ibid., p. 169.
72. Ibid., p. 169.
73. "It was decided to risk the inclusion of a certain amount of useless, redundant, or superficial data related to sensitive resources, in the expectation that many data would turn out to be valuable that would not have been collected otherwise." William W. Haythorn, 1957, *Simulation in RAND's Logistics Systems Laboratory*, P-1075, 4/30 (Santa Monica, 1957), pp. 9–10.
74. Chapman, Kennedy, Newell, Biel, "The Systems Research Laboratory's Air Defense Experiments," 252.
75. Ibid., 251.
76. Chapman and Kennedy, *The Background*, p. 11.
77. Chapman, *Simulation in RAND's System Research Laboratory*, pp. 2, 3.
78. Chapman, Kennedy, Newell, Biel, "The Systems Research Laboratory's Air Defense Experiments," p. 262.
79. Ibid., p. 263.
80. Parsons, *Man-machine System Experiments*, p. 170.
81. Crary, *Suspensions of Perception*, p. 66.
82. Ibid., p. 47.
83. Murray, "They Guard the Ramparts," p. 28.
84. Lapp and Alsop, "We Can Smash the Red A-Bombers," p. 82.
85. Murray, "They Guard the Ramparts," p. 28.
86. Ibid. p. 116.
87. Craig Thompson, "America's Strangest Island," *The Saturday Evening Post*, 7/7 (1956), p. 85.

INDEX